Thomas Hardy

A Textual Study of the Short Stories

To my parents

Leonard and Sheila Ray

in commemoration of their
Golden Wedding Anniversary

Thomas Hardy

A Textual Study of the Short Stories

MARTIN RAY

Published by
Ashgate Publishing Limited
Gower House
Croft Road
Aldershot
Hants
GU11 3HR
England

Ashgate Publishing Company
Old Post Road
Brookfield
Vermont 05036–9704
USA

The author has asserted their moral right under the Copyright, Designs and Patents Act, 1988, to be identified as the author of this work.

British Library Cataloguing in Publication Data
Ray, Martin
    Thomas Hardy: A Textual Study of the Short Stories.
    (Nineteenth Century series)
    1. Hardy, Thomas, 1840–1928—Criticism and interpretation.
    2. Short stories, English—History and criticism.
    I. Title.
    823.8

    ISBN 1–85928–202–4

Library of Congress Cataloging-in-Publication Data
    Thomas Hardy: a textual study of the short stories/Martin Ray.
        p.   cm.
    Includes bibliographical references and index.
    ISBN 1–85928–202–4 (hb: acid-free paper)
    1. Hardy, Thomas, 1840–1928—Criticism, textual. 2. Hardy,
    Thomas, 1840–1928—Fictional works. 3. Short story. I. Title.
    II. Series: Nineteenth Century (Aldershot, England).
    PR4755.R39   1997
    823'.8—dc21
                                                            97–15585
                                                              CIP
ISBN 1 85928 202 4

This book is printed on acid free paper

Printed in Great Britain by The Ipswich Book Company, Suffolk.

Contents

The Nineteenth Century
General Editors' Preface

The aim of this series is to reflect, develop and extend the great burgeoning of interest in the nineteenth century that has been an inevitable feature of recent decades, as that former epoch has come more sharply into focus as a locus for our understanding not only of the past but of the contours of our modernity. Though it is dedicated principally to the publication of original monographs and symposia in literature, history, cultural analysis, and associated fields, there will be a salient role for reprints of significant texts from, or about, the period. Our overarching policy is to address the spectrum of nineteenth-century studies without exception, achieving the widest scope in chronology, approach and range of concern. This, we believe, distinguishes our project from comparable ones, and means, for example, that in the relevant areas of scholarship we both recognize and cut innovatively across such parameters as those suggested by the designations 'Romantic' and 'Victorian'. We welcome new ideas, while valuing tradition. It is hoped that the world which predates yet so forcibly predicts and engages our own will emerge in parts, as a whole, and in the lively currents of debate and change that are so manifest an aspect of its intellectual, artistic and social landscape.

Vincent Newey
Joanne Shattock

University of Leicester

Acknowledgements

I would like to record my deep gratitude to the following friends and colleagues for their many acts of kindness and assistance during the past four years. They will always be memorably associated for me with the writing of this book: Mrs Krassimira Abadjieva, Mr and Mrs Dennis Burden, Mr and Mrs Frank Bush, Dr Robert Carver, Mrs Saloua Chérif, Dr Simon Curtis, Dr Julian D'Arcy, Helena Davidson, Professor R.P. Draper, Dr David Fairer, Dr and Mrs Robin Gilmour, Barclay Green, Rupa Gupta, Eva-Lynn Alicia Jagoe, Parmita Kapadia, Mrs Elzbieta Leskier, Colin Maclaren, Professor Hans van Marle, Mrs Elizabeth Mavor, Dr Isobel Murray, Dr Jenny Newman, Professor and Mrs David Paroissien, Dr Seamus Perry, Dr Joan H. Pittock Wesson, Fiona Rankine, Patricia Rennie, Professor Christopher Ricks, Dr Fiona Robertson, the Revd David Scott, Rhoda Nadine Switzer, Professor and Mrs George Watson, Professor J.R. Watson.

The University of Aberdeen has been very generous in its provision of study leave and grants which have allowed me to concentrate on this work, and I would especially like to acknowledge the support and encouragement of Dr Graeme Roberts, Dean of the Faculty of Arts and Divinity, whose highly considerate efficiency has done a great deal to facilitate this book. My friends and colleagues at the University of Massachusetts have provided the most congenial and stimulating company, and I would like to thank UMASS and the President and Fellows of Trinity College, Oxford, for enabling me to spend the last ten summers living in the beautiful setting of the Garden Quad, where much of the writing of this book was done.

It would have been impossible to complete this work without the invaluable co-operation of many people. Any writer on Hardy owes a principal debt to Mr Richard de Peyer, Curator of the Dorset County Museum and its Thomas Hardy Memorial Collection: he and his staff have given most generously of their time and knowledge. The Trustees of the Hardy Estate have kindly permitted me to gain access to manuscripts throughout Europe and North America. The librarians and staff of the following institutions have enabled me to consult manuscripts and other material: the British Library; the Bodleian Library, Oxford; Trinity College Library, Oxford; Manchester University Library; Manchester Central Public Library; the National Library of Scotland; Aberdeen University Library; the Fondation Martin Bodmer in Geneva; the Berg Collection of the New York Public Library; the Pierpont Morgan Library in New York; the Humanities Research Center at the University of Texas in Austin; Yale University; the Huntington Library in San Marino; Iowa State Historical Library.

Caroline Cornish of Ashgate has been a dedicated and meticulous editor at every stage of composition.

A Chronology of
Hardy's Collected Short Stories

Titles of stories as they are best known are used throughout.
Some dates of composition are approximate.

		Short Stories	Hardy's Life and Other Writings
1878	Jan		*The Return of the Native* begins in serial
	Mar		Moves to Wandsworth Common
	Apr	'The Duchess of Hamptonshire' (as 'The Impulsive Lady of Croome Castle') pub.	
1879	Apr	'The Distracted Preacher' pub.	
1880	Jan		*The Trumpet-Major* begins in serial
	Apr	'Fellow-Townsmen' pub.	
	Oct		Hardy seriously ill for next six months
	Dec		*A Laodicean* begins in serial
1881	June		Moves to Wimborne
	Dec	'What the Shepherd Saw' pub. 'The Honourable Laura' pub.	
1882	May		*Two on a Tower* begins in serial
	July	'A Tradition of Eighteen Hundred and Four' sent off	
	Nov	'A Tradition of Eighteen Hundred and Four' pub.	
1883	Feb	'The Romantic Adventures of a Milkmaid' sent off	

		Short Stories	**Hardy's Life and Other Writings**
1883	June	'The Romantic Adventures of a Milkmaid' pub.	Moves to Dorchester
1884			Working on *The Mayor of Casterbridge* this year
	Feb	'The Duchess of Hamptonshire' (as 'Emmeline; or, Passion versus Principle') pub.	
1885	Feb	'A Tryst at an Ancient Earthwork' written	
	Mar	'A Tryst at an Ancient Earthwork' pub. in USA	
	Apr		*The Mayor of Casterbridge* finished
	June		Moves into Max Gate
	Oct	'A Mere Interlude' pub.	
1886	Jan		*The Mayor of Casterbridge* begins in serial
	May		*The Woodlanders* begins in serial
1887	Feb		Finished writing *The Woodlanders*
	Mar		Visits Italy
	Aug	'Alicia's Diary' written	
	Sept	'The Withered Arm' written	
	Oct	'Alicia's Diary' pub.	
	Dec	'The Waiting Supper' pub.	
1888	Jan	'The Withered Arm' pub.	
	May	*Wessex Tales* pub. by Macmillan	
	Aug	'A Tragedy of Two Ambitions' written	
	Sept	'The First Countess of Wessex' written	
	Dec	'A Tragedy of Two Ambitions' pub.	
1889	Sept		About half of *Tess* sent off
	Dec	'The First Countess of Wessex' pub.	
1890	Jan	'The Lady Penelope' pub.	

		Short Stories	**Hardy's Life and Other Writings**
1890	May	'A Group of Noble Dames' sent off	
	July	Revised 'A Group of Noble Dames' sent off	
	2nd half	Most of stories in *Life's Little Ironies* written	
	Nov–Dec	'A Group of Noble Dames' pub. (i.e. 'Anna, Lady Baxby', 'Barbara of the House of Grebe', 'The Lady Icenway', 'Lady Mottisfont', 'The Marchioness of Stonehenge', 'Squire Petrick's Lady'	
1891	Mar	'For Conscience' Sake' pub.	
	Mar–June	'A Few Crusted Characters' pub.	
	Apr	'The Son's Veto' written	
	May	*A Group of Noble Dames* pub. by Osgood, McIlvaine	
	June	'To Please His Wife' pub.	
	July		*Tess* begins in serial
	Nov	'On the Western Circuit' pub.	
	Dec	'The Son's Veto' pub.	
1892	July		Death of Hardy's father
	Oct		*The Well-Beloved* begins in serial
1893	Jan	'The Fiddler of the Reels' sent off	
	Mar	'Master John Horseleigh, Knight' sent off	
	May	'The Fiddler of the Reels' pub.	Meets Florence Henniker
	June	'Master John Horseleigh, Knight' pub.	
	Sept	'An Imaginative Woman' finished 'A Tryst at an Ancient Earthwork' revised	
	Oct	*Life's Little Ironies*	

		Short Stories	**Hardy's Life and Other Writings**
		assembled	
	Dec	'A Tryst at an Ancient Earthwork' pub. in UK	Working on *Jude*
1894	Feb	*Life's Little Ironies* pub. by Osgood, McIlvaine	
	Apr	'An Imaginative Woman' pub.	
	Dec		*Jude* begins in serial
1895	Mar		Finishes writing *Jude*
	Nov		*Jude* pub. in book form
1896	Aug	'A Committee-Man of "The Terror"' sent off	
	Nov	'A Committee-Man of "The Terror"' pub.	
	Dec	'The Duke's Reappearance' pub.	
1897	Mar		*The Well-Beloved* pub. in book form
	July	'The Grave by the Handpost' finished	
	Nov	'The Grave by the Handpost' pub.	
1898	Dec		*Wessex Poems* pub.
1899			
1900	Jan	'A Changed Man' written	
	Apr	'A Changed Man' pub.	
	Dec	'Enter a Dragoon' pub.	
1912		*Life's Little Ironies* pub. (Wessex edition; Preface dated May 1912) *Wessex Tales* pub. (Wessex edition; Preface dated May 1912) *A Group of Noble Dames* pub. (Wessex edition)	
	Nov		Death of Emma Hardy
1913	Oct	*A Changed Man and Other Tales* pub. by Macmillan	
1914		*A Changed Man and Other Tales* pub. (Wessex edition)	

Preface

This work is a textual study of Hardy's four volumes of short stories: *Wessex Tales* (1888), *A Group of Noble Dames* (1891), *Life's Little Ironies* (1894) and *A Changed Man and Other Tales* (1913). I examine, where possible, the history of the stories' composition and revision from manuscripts through serial publications, galleys, revises and collected publications, all stages of which show significant alterations. I have omitted discussion of Hardy's seven uncollected stories, precisely because they do not have a textual history of the kind which the other 37 possess.

There has been little previous research into Hardy's short stories, and there are only three critics who have concentrated on the textual evolution of some of the tales. Kathryn King's excellent 1988 thesis and her edition of *Wessex Tales* are perhaps the most substantial contribution to our knowledge of Hardy's shorter fiction: I decided not to consult her thesis until I had completed my own study of *Wessex Tales*, so that I could acknowledge the specific points for which I am indebted to her work. Alan Manford has published a very detailed and thorough analysis of the manuscripts of three stories from *Life's Little Ironies*, and I regret that his invaluable edition of that volume appeared too late for me to make more than brief references to it. Finally, Simon Gatrell has done some outstanding research into a variety of Hardy's tales, especially 'A Few Crusted Characters' and some of the Noble Dames.

I have concentrated in this book on the publication of the stories up to and including the 'definitive' Wessex edition, and I have not described later editions except where Hardy was already known to have introduced revisions. I do not claim that all conceivably relevant forms of the texts have been examined, but the findings of this study arise from a careful collation of all the forms likely to have played a role in the development of the stories. The surviving manuscripts, which are widely dispersed, have been studied in photographic reproduction only (with the exception of 'An Imaginative Woman'), and therefore I have not been able to take into account, for instance, the possible use of different colours of ink which might indicate distinct patterns or layers of revision.

I have occasionally repeated some information, in the expectation that most readers will be consulting only individual chapters rather than working their way through the entire volume. Such repetition is kept to an absolute minimum.

In quotations from manuscripts, autograph insertions are given within vertical lines, while double vertical lines indicate insertions within insertions.

Abbreviations

Brady   Brady, Kristin (1982), *The Short Stories of Thomas Hardy: Tales of Past and Present*, Macmillan, London.

Gatrell   Gatrell, Simon (1988), *Hardy the Creator: A Textual Biography*, Clarendon Press, Oxford.

Hutchins   Hutchins, John (1861–73), *The History and Antiquities of the County of Dorset*, 3rd ed., 4 vols., J.B. Nichols, London.

Letters   Purdy, R.L., and Millgate, Michael, eds. (1978–88), *The Collected Letters of Thomas Hardy*, 7 vols., Clarendon Press, Oxford.

Life   Millgate, Michael, ed. (1984), *The Life and Work of Thomas Hardy by Thomas Hardy*, Macmillan, London.

Millgate   Millgate, Michael (1982), *Thomas Hardy: A Biography*, Clarendon Press, Oxford.

Orel   Orel, Harold (1967), *Thomas Hardy's Personal Writings: Prefaces, Literary Opinions, Reminiscences,* Macmillan, London.

Purdy   Purdy, R.L. (1954), *Thomas Hardy: A Bibliographical Study*, Oxford University Press, London.

Taylor   Taylor, Richard H., ed. (1978), *The Personal Notebooks of Thomas Hardy*, Macmillan, London.

Weber 1939 Weber, Carl J. (1939), *Rebekah Owen and Thomas Hardy*, Colby College Library, Waterville, Maine.

Weber 1952 Weber, Carl J. (1952), *Hardy and the Lady from Madison Square*, Colby College Press, Waterville, Maine.

PART ONE

Wessex Tales

INTRODUCTION

Wessex Tales

Wessex Tales was Hardy's first collected edition of short stories when it appeared in two volumes in 1888. The five stories in this first edition were written over a period of nine years, from 'The Distracted Preacher' in the winter of 1878–9 to 'The Withered Arm' in late 1887. The periodicals in which they had appeared previously ranged from an established journal like *Blackwood's Edinburgh Magazine* ('The Withered Arm') to newly launched ones such as the *New Quarterly Magazine* ('The Distracted Young Preacher' and 'Fellow-Townsmen'), *Longman's Magazine* ('The Three Strangers') and *English Illustrated Magazine* ('Interlopers at the Knap'). *Wessex Tales* was Hardy's first use of the term 'Wessex' in any of his titles and as such it represents a declaration of his sovereign right to use the name for his fictional landscape. It was probably around this time that he wrote to Edward Marston, the publisher, with instructions to 'use the words "Wessex novels"' when advertising his work: 'I find that the name *Wessex*, wh. I was the first to use in fiction, is getting to be taken up everywhere: & it would be a pity for us to lose the right to it for want of asserting it' (*Letters*, I, 171).

Hardy wrote to Macmillan & Co. on Leap Day 1888 to suggest that they publish the stories in a collected edition:

> I send herewith some short stories of mine which have appeared in various periodicals, to ask if you would be willing to publish them as collected. Some well-known critics have often advised me to reprint them, informing me that they are as good as anything I have ever written (however good that may be).
>
> I shall be glad to know what you think of them. I would leave to you the question as to the form in which they should be issued – whether 2 library vols., 1 library vol., 1 cheap vol., or what not. (I, 174)

One of the 'well-known critics' whom Hardy mentioned was Leslie Stephen, who had advised him as long ago as November 1880 that

> you might write an exceedingly pleasant series of stories upon your special topic: I mean prose-idyls of country life – short sketches of Hodge & his ways, wh. might be made very attractive & would have a certain continuity, so as to make a volume or more at some future date. (Quoted in Brady, p. 180)

Macmillan immediately dispatched the stories to R. & R. Clark of Edinburgh, the firm's usual printers, asking them to cast off the material and determine whether there was sufficient for two volumes (Macmillan Archives, 1 March 1888). Five days later, Frederick Macmillan wrote to Hardy offering terms of one-sixth of the retail price of all copies sold, with £50 in advance and a further

£50 for a Colonial Library edition (the letter is in the Dorset County Museum). On 9 March, Hardy replied from the Savile Club and made his first recorded reference to the title of the volume: 'I shall be happy to accept the terms you offer for "Wessex Tales" [...]. I can read the proofs at any time that you send them' (*Letters*, I, 175). The following day, Macmillan instructed the printers to send page proofs to Hardy at the Savile Club. On the same day, Hardy wrote to William Blackwood for permission to reprint 'The Withered Arm', which had appeared in *Blackwood's Edinburgh Magazine* in the previous January. A note in the Macmillan Archives dated 14 March records that Hardy had not yet received the proofs, but they must have arrived soon after because Macmillan on 27 March estimated that *Wessex Tales* would be ready for publication within a month or five weeks.

Wessex Tales was published in two volumes on 4 May 1888 in an edition of 750 copies, priced 12s. Uniquely, this first collected edition had a sub-title, 'Strange, Lively, and Commonplace', and this stress on the varying tone to be found in the volume was repeated in Hardy's letter to Henry Stainsby many years later, where he described 'The Three Strangers' and 'The Distracted Preacher' as being 'of light dramatic character' while the others were 'more serious' (*Letters*, IV, 284). Purdy notes that 116 copies were left unbound, and these were later remaindered (p. 59). The first volume contained 'The Three Strangers', 'The Withered Arm' and 'Fellow-Townsmen', while the second contained 'Interlopers at the Knap' and 'The Distracted Preacher'. An American edition of *Wessex Tales* was published at the end of May 1888 by Harper & Brothers in their Franklin Square Library, which is presumably the paper-covered edition which Hardy described as 'such a flimsy one' (*Letters*, I, 184 and nn.) when sending it as a presentation copy to Mary Sheridan; it included a portrait of Hardy as frontispiece, for the first time in any of his books (Purdy, p. 60). Meanwhile, the Clark compositors had begun setting type for the Macmillan Colonial Library edition in late March or early April after the two-volume British edition had been prepared for press (Macmillan Archives). The single cash payment of £50 which Hardy received for the Colonial edition was the same payment he had accepted for such editions of *The Mayor of Casterbridge* and *The Woodlanders*.

Hardy sent a presentation copy to Robert Browning on 7 May (his seventy-sixth birthday): 'I send this little collection, in preference to a regulation novel, in the hope that the varied character of the stories may enable you to find one among them to your liking, if you should have time to look into the volumes' (*Letters*, I, 175–6). He also gave a copy to Frederic Harrison on 17 May, observing that 'It will give me much pleasure if you will accept a copy of "Wessex Tales", which I send in separate parcel. If you read them you will probably find some but indifferently good: there may however be one or two to your liking' (I, 176). Hardy's only recorded response to the volume's critical reception is a brusque letter of 17 July to R.H. Hutton, the joint editor of the *Spectator*: 'I published "The Woodlanders," & the *Spectator* objected to that story. I publish "Wessex Tales" which are unobjectionable, & the *Spectator* takes no notice of them at all' (*Letters*, I, 178). Hutton replied that Hardy was being 'a little unreasonable' and that if any novelist had been well treated in the *Spectator* it was Hardy himself. A favourable review of *Wessex Tales* appeared in that journal on 28 July.

On 13 October 1888, Hardy wrote again to Frederick Macmillan with a proposal for a one-volume cheap edition:

> It occurs to me to ask if you think it worth while to print a cheap edition
> of the "Wessex Tales" – or to make a cheap edition of the same typesetting,
> so as to produce a companion volume to the 6/– edn of The Woodlanders.
> (I, 180)

Macmillan agreed to Hardy's suggestion, and a letter from Macmillan to the printers in late December of 1888 expresses the hope that the new edition will be ready for publication in mid-January. In the event, *Wessex Tales* was reissued in late February 1889 in one volume in an edition of 1500 copies priced at 6*s*. (Purdy, p. 60), and its format was closely similar to the 1887 one-volume edition of *The Woodlanders*. Hardy introduced one change to this 1889 edition, involving five substitutions of the real name, 'Long-Ash Lane', for 'Holloway Lane' in 'Interlopers at the Knap' (see Chapter 6 on that story below).

The next significant development in the evolution of *Wessex Tales* was its publication by Osgood, McIlvaine in April 1896 as Volume XIII in their Wessex Novels edition, the first uniform and complete edition of Hardy's works. In a letter of 18 September 1894 to Frederick Macmillan, Hardy mentioned *Wessex Tales* as one of four volumes in which he proposed to introduce only 'very slight alterations' (see *Letters*, II, 63), but he eventually made substantial changes to the edition. 'An Imaginative Woman', published in 1894 and not previously collected, was introduced as the first story, and he revised all of the other five tales. He also added a Preface, dated April 1896. An etching of 'Higher Crowstairs' by Henry Macbeth-Raeburn was used as the frontispiece.

This Osgood, McIlvaine edition of *Wessex Tales* had involved Hardy in a complicated copyright dispute with Macmillans since 1893. The copyrights of those novels held by Sampson Low were about to expire in June 1894, at which time Hardy wished to publish them and all his other works in the Osgood, McIlvaine Wessex Novels edition. He therefore needed to regain his rights to *Wessex Tales* (and *The Woodlanders*) from Macmillan, and he wrote to them accordingly to declare his intention to withdraw the two works in the manner which he believed their agreement allowed. Hardy's letter has not survived, but Frederick Macmillan's reply, dated 1 June 1893, shows a firm opposition to Hardy's wishes:

> Having discussed the question carefully with my partners, I write to say that
> we do not see our way to transfer the publication of 'The Woodlanders' and
> 'Wessex Tales' to any other house. Although we should be glad to oblige
> you, we feel that it is a great honour to have your name in our catalogue,
> and we are most unwilling to take it out and to close a connection which,
> although it has been so far limited to two books, has been a pleasant one to
> us, and one we hope might continue and increase. (Quoted in Kramer, ed.,
> *The Woodlanders*, p. 12)

Macmillan closed his letter by offering to bring out a uniform edition himself, and offered an advance of £500.

Hardy replied a week later and insisted that he still wished to reprint *Wessex Tales* and *The Woodlanders* as he had announced:

> I am sorry to receive Mr F. Macmillan's letter concerning "The Woodlanders" and "Wessex Tales" – which I must confess somewhat surprises me after my explanation to him that my object is purely and simply a literary one – easily understood – in withdrawing the two books in question from your list, and that as a matter of personal feeling I much regretted doing so.
>
> Mr F. Macmillan appears to take an erroneous view of the arrangement between us, and I think it best, in order to prevent misapprehension, to say that the licence I granted you was revocable at will, of which he seems to be unaware.
>
> In the circumstances I have no alternative but to give you notice, which I hereby do, of my intention of publishing "The Woodlanders" and "Wessex Tales" as I may be advised, after Midsummer 1894. Meanwhile you are of course at liberty to provide copies to meet the demand as indicated by the present average sales. (*Letters*, II, 12)

Macmillan replied on 9 June to explain more fully their legal and financial position:

> As we understand the matter we are at liberty to continue the publication of these books during the term of copyright, so long as we pay you the stipulated royalty on the sales. We have no liking for standing on purely legal rights, but we think you will agree that we are not unreasonable in wishing to keep the books in our hands when we tell you that there is still a debt against them of nearly £200 for the liquidation of which as well as for our profit, we must look to future sales. (Quoted in Kramer, ed., *The Woodlanders*, p. 13)

Hardy replied three days later with a reassertion of his rights:

> I regret to learn from your letter of a debt against "The Woodlanders" and "Wessex Tales" of nearly £200, which I am quite unable to understand in the face of the sales as rendered, and the now well-known cost of production.
>
> I can assure you that you are mistaken in supposing me to have used in any agreement words empowering you to continue the publication of those books during the term of copyright, as I understand you to assert. So far from it I have, ever since producing my first or second novel, carefully avoided selling a copy-right from the very consideration that the present contingency of having to collect my writings might arise. (*Letters*, II, 14–15)

Macmillan's response was a conciliatory one: on 14 June he sent a statement of expenses and receipts showing a debt of £204 against the two books, and his accompanying letter suggested a compromise:

> The claim you make that in the absence of any specific agreement to the

contrary you are at liberty to withdraw the publication of your books from us at any moment is one we feel bound to resist to the utmost as it involves a principle that might affect us seriously in other quarters. Apart from that we are prepared to meet you, as we have no wish to be disobliging, and we therefore write to say that we are willing to hand over to you the stereotype plates and sheet stock of these two books for the sum of £250, but only on condition that your present claim is withdrawn; that it is distinctly understood that our right in the books is undisputed, and that we do not surrender them on compulsion. (Quoted in Kramer, ed., *The Woodlanders*, p. 13)

On the following day, Hardy replied to assure Macmillan that 'it is furthest from my wish to put you to any inconvenience or loss' (*Letters*, II, 15), and he mentioned to W.M. Colles, the literary agent, on 13 July that Macmillan would 'let me have the books in a year, or whenever I require them, on reasonable terms – the principle, or meaning of our agreement, not to be contested' (II, 22). The nature of the final agreement between Hardy and Macmillan is not clear, but a memorandum in the Macmillan Archives dated 22 May 1894 notes an agreement giving Macmillan & Co. the right to publish 14 books by Hardy in their Colonial Library in exchange for their release of the British rights to *Wessex Tales* and *The Woodlanders*. Perhaps this exchange of rights was in lieu of a financial settlement, and it is possible that Macmillan simply sold off the remaining stock of the two works and retained the plates (see Kramer, p. 14).

The Macmillan Uniform *Wessex Tales* was first published in 1903 and was reprinted three times between 1910 and 1928. It was printed from the 1896 Osgood, McIlvaine plates, which Macmillan purchased from Osgood, McIlvaine's successors, Harper & Brothers (London). Hardy's only revision was the change of a place-name in 'Interlopers at the Knap'. The same plates were used for the Macmillan Pocket edition of *Wessex Tales* in 1906: this was a thin-paper edition, priced at 2/6, which was reprinted ten times between 1910 and 1930.

Wessex Tales was published by Macmillan as Volume IX of the Wessex edition in August 1912. It was set from a marked copy of a 1906 printing of the Macmillan Uniform edition. In this edition, 'An Imaginative Woman' was transferred to *Life's Little Ironies* which, as Hardy says in the Prefatory Note, is 'more nearly its place, turning as it does upon a trick of Nature, so to speak'. At the same time, 'A Tradition of Eighteen Hundred and Four' and 'The Melancholy Hussar' were removed from that volume to *Wessex Tales*, where 'they more naturally belong'. (The Macmillan Archives show that the publishers were negotiating these changes with the printers throughout May 1912.) The result of these alterations was to make the stories in *Wessex Tales* more traditional and those in *Life's Little Ironies* more consistently contemporary.

For this edition of *Wessex Tales*, Hardy added a note to 'The Distracted Preacher' which gave the 'real' ending. All of the other stories were slightly revised. There was a frontispiece entitled 'The Hangman's Cottage at Casterbridge'. Hardy revised and extended his original Preface in May 1912, and he further extended it, with a note on 'A Tradition of Eighteen Hundred and Four', in June 1919 for the Mellstock edition, published by Macmillan in 1920.

CHAPTER 1

'The Three Strangers'

Hardy's earliest reference to 'The Three Strangers' is in a letter to Anne Procter from Wimborne, dated 17 January 1883: 'I have lately been writing a little story of a few pages which has amused me in producing it, & I hope may amuse you if you read it' (*Letters*, I, 114). Hardy apparently told Rebekah Owen that this tale of the escaped prisoner and the hangman was 'true' but 'the incidents did not all happen at one time, as in the story' (Weber, 1952, p. 238). He was 'surprised' to be told in 1896 that Owen preferred 'The Three Strangers' to 'The Son's Veto', his own favourite (see Weber, 1952, p. 114), and he showed a similar regard for the story when he wrote to Florence Henniker in 1904 that 'I think you are right in preferring "Fellow Townsmen" to "The Three Strangers": there is more human nature in it' (*Letters*, III, 151). He characterized the story in 1913 as being of a 'light dramatic character' and not one of the 'more serious stories in the volume' (IV, 284).

The versions of 'The Three Strangers' which have textual significance are as follows:

Longman's Longman's Magazine, 1 (March 1883), 569–88.

HW   *Harper's Weekly*, 3 March (pp. 134–5) and 10 March (p. 151) 1883. The division occurred after 'another knock was audible upon the door'.

1888   *Wessex Tales*, 2 vols. (London: Macmillan, 1888), I, 1–54. Published at 12*s.* in an edition of 750 copies on 4 May 1888.

1896   *Wessex Tales* (London: Osgood, McIlvaine, 1896), pp. 33–61. Volume XIII in the Wessex Novels, the first uniform and complete edition of Hardy's works.

1912   *Wessex Tales* (London: Macmillan, 1912), pp. 3–29. Volume IX of the Wessex edition.

The manuscript

A bound manuscript of 'The Three Strangers' is currently located in the Berg Collection of the New York Public Library. It is written on 33 leaves, with numerous deletions and additions, but compositors' surnames on eight of the leaves indicate that it was the printers' copy for the serial (see Purdy, p. 59). Hardy gave the MS. to Sydney Cockerell on 29 September 1911 to acknowledge his help in distributing his other MSS. among public collections (see *Letters*, IV, 178, and Taylor, p. 68).

Many of the changes within the MS. fall into one of two groups. The first contains a number of revisions which serve to make the condemned man appear a sympathetic, admirable and resourceful character. The second concerns the many alterations which seek to establish the pattern of numerous contrasts and oppositions which structure the tale and which Hardy can be seen to be gradually evolving and refining at different stages of revision: these oppositions include indoors/outdoors, natives/outsiders, rural/urban, bright/dark, comic/tragic, security/storm, present/eternity, birth/death, custom/change, young/old and private/public.

Hardy's gradual improvement of the condemned man's character can be seen in the story's only reference to his name, Timothy Sommers, which occurs in a passage which Hardy revised both in the course of writing it and subsequently. The guests at the party refer to the hangman coming to execute 'a |the| man for sheepstealing – a |the| poor clock-|c|leaner we heard of,| who used to live |away| at Anglebury |& had no work to do – | I don't know his Timothy Sommers, whose family were a starving' (fo. 20). The speaker was originally to have said that 'I don't know his' name, presumably, but Hardy immediately decided to delete this and continue by identifying the man as Timothy Sommers, giving him a particular individual identity and enabling the guests (and readers) to sympathize more readily with his plight. At a later stage, Hardy then introduced the important reference to Sommers having 'no work to do', a phrase which has a number of functions: it explains why his family are starving, it mitigates his crime of sheep-stealing by portraying him as the victim of the widespread rural poverty of the period, and, finally, it establishes a grimly ironic parallel between Sommers and the hangman, who, we learn later in the same paragraph, is coming to Casterbridge because he has 'not enough to do' in his home town.

The sympathy for the condemned man is also achieved by the increasingly satanic appearance of the hangman. When the executioner is initially introduced in the manuscript, he seems a decidedly nondescript and worldly figure: his clothes are repeatedly described as 'pepper-and-salt' and a deleted phrase refers to his 'man-of the-worldliness' (fo. 13). However, when Hardy had written three-quarters of the story, he hit upon a description of the hangman as being 'cinder-grey' (fo. 24), and he was apparently so taken with this phrase and its demonic connotations that he went back and altered eight of the 'pepper-and-salt' descriptions to 'cinder-grey', deleted two more and added a further four references to 'cinder-grey' throughout the story. Hardy seems to have wanted to reserve this sinister notion of greyness uniquely for the hangman's clothing, because he removed both of the other references to 'grey' in this story: thus, the hangman's 'grey' hair became 'slightly frosted' (fo. 13), while a 'grey' cloud was altered to a 'dripping' one (fo. 7).

Hardy on four occasions refers to the hangman as a 'gentleman' in the MS., one of which replaces a reference to him as a 'being' (fo. 24), and he gave this notion a further emphasis in revising the serial proofs, where he altered a description of the party guests moving away from 'the grim gentleman's chair in their midst' (fo. 22) so that it read in the serial 'the grim gentleman in their midst, whom some of them seemed to take for the Prince of Darkness himself'. This linking of Satan and gentility has its source in Edgar's comment in *King*

Lear that 'The Prince of Darkness is a gentleman' (III.iv.147), an allusion that does not appear to have been noted before.[1] This increasing stress on the notion of the hangman as gentleman may have prompted Hardy to introduce as an afterthought the comic idea of it being vulgar and improper for the condemned man to escape: the constable who arrests Sommers's brother, who is mistaken for the condemned man, charges him with not staying in Casterbridge jail in a 'ldecentl' (fo. 28) manner to await his execution.

One of the story's dominant contrasts, between the gaiety of indoors and the harshness of the world outside, is one which gradually emerged as Hardy cumulatively evolved and refined it at successive stages of composition. For instance, the key word 'bright' came to define the indoors by being inserted at different times of revision: in the MS., the women at the party were originally said to be wearing their 'best costumes', but this was scored out and replaced by 'bright coloured gowns' (fo. 14), and Hardy gave the word greater prominence at the serial proof stage by altering a description of their 'gowns of various purples' (fo. 4) to read 'gowns of bright hues'. This domestic cheerfulness is in opposition to the dark and harsh weather without, which Hardy emphasizes early in the story by interlined references to 'the long inimical seasons' (fo. 1) and 'the gloomy night' (fo. 6), and by the alteration of 'rain' to 'rain-storm' (fo. 2).

Shepherd Fennel's cottage, Higher Crowstairs, was called Higher Polenhill on its first appearance in the story (fo. 2), but this was altered and subsequent references to it are by its familiar name.[2] All allusions to Elijah New, the parish-clerk, and to the serpent which he plays are interlined, indicating that the rustic humour of his role was a late addition to the story. The escaped prisoner, Timothy Sommers (as he was called in early versions of the story), originally gave his occupation as a 'paper-stainer' (fo. 18), but this was deleted and 'wheelwright' substituted. This change was necessitated by the later addition on a verso which showed Fennel and the constable discussing Sommers's claim to be a wheelwright ('The wheels o' clocks & watches he meant, no doubt', fo. 30^v, stressing his ability to maintain his wit under pressure). The scene which was most heavily revised is the return of Sommers and the hangman to the cottage to have some more cake and mead after the other guests have gone out in pursuit of the third stranger: there are many interlined additions on fo. 26, and about a third of the scene is written on the verso of the previous leaf and marked for insertion, substantially increasing the prominence of this comic episode and stressing Sommers's heroic coolness. There are also seven lines thus marked for inclusion near the end of the MS., in which Sommers's real and bogus occupations are discussed.

There were some forty substantive proof alterations for the serials, which account for the different readings in the MS. Ten of these proof revisions involved the removal of dialect words which are found in the MS., so that, for example, 'yer', 'maister' and ''taint' become 'your', 'master' and 'it is not' in the serials. The topography was slightly altered: in the MS., Higher Crowstairs was said to be four miles from Casterbridge, but this becomes five miles in the serials. In the opening sentence of the story, the downs on which the cottage stands are described as 'high': this was a deleted reading in the MS. which Hardy restored for the serials, indicating that he at least began by proofreading copy against the MS. Mrs Fennel's dowry was originally said to be £100 and then 100 guineas in the MS., but the amount was halved in the serials. Timothy Sommers was described as a 'clock-|cleaner|' (fo. 20) in the MS., but this was later altered to 'clock-maker'. His behaviour with the hangman is made more swaggering in the serials, where we see him 'waving cups with the singer so heartily that his mead splashed over on the hearth', although we also learn here that he ate his cake 'with some effort' when the hangman returns to the cottage: true to the story's delayed decoding (we do not yet know that Sommers is the escaped prisoner), his unease is allowed to appear to be simply embarrassment at being caught purloining the food. The hangman in turn is demonized in the serials, where he becomes a figure 'whom some of them seemed to take for the Prince of Darkness himself'.

When the other guests realize who the hangman is, they withdraw from him and form a remote circle round him, which Hardy describes by a Latin allusion: 'circulus, cujus centrum diabolus' (fo. 22: 'a circle, whose centre is the devil'). In the MS., however, the Latin quotation begins with 'Chorœa', a word which is not deleted. 'Chorœa' would appear to be Hardy's mistaken rendering of 'chorea' ('a dance' especially 'a dance in a ring'). Since 'chorea' and 'circulus' are both nouns, they must be in apposition, so that the quotation originally read 'a ring-dance, a circle, ...'. Perhaps Hardy omitted 'chorea' from printed versions of the story because he was uncertain of the word or because he felt it was too arcane. The source of the 'quotation' has never been identified: my colleague, Dr G.P. Edwards, suggests that it does not seem to be either classical or biblical but could be from some medieval or neo-Latin source.

The serials and *1888* Macmillan

The two serial versions are effectively identical to each other. Each has a unique misprint, and *HW* adds an article and omits another, where the British version follows the manuscript reading on each occasion. *HW* also lacks the archaic spelling of UNTILL on the side of the mug, which is probably an editorial revision.

There are some 34 substantive differences between *Longman's* and *1888*. In the serials, Timothy Sommers and his brother live at Anglebury (Wareham), but in *1888* this becomes Shottsford (Blandford Forum, a town which is sixteen miles north-east of Dorchester). King suggests that 'the change may reflect Hardy's effort to associate Summers with the unrest in the 1820s and 1830s in the Vale of Blackmoor' (1991, p. 228).

There are three explicit references by the narrator to 'the hangman' in the version of the story which is familiar to readers now, and all three were introduced in *1888*, either being entirely new additions to the text ('the hangman's song', 'hob-and-nobbing with the hangman') or replacing the serials' euphemistic description of the second stranger as 'the grim songster'. Similarly, the serials' allusion to his 'terrible trade' becomes 'deadly trade' in *1888*. It is as if the narrator of the serial shares the characters' horrified inability to utter the truth about the stranger ('Oh, he's the — !'), while the later narrator is more detached from them and is free of their superstitious evasion. Another alteration for *1888* involved the removal of four instances of dialect from the serial, so that 'yerself', 'afore', 'into ye' and 'o'' became 'yourself', 'before', 'into your dwelling' and 'of' respectively.

1896 Osgood, McIlvaine

There are only thirteen substantive changes for *1896*. The escaped prisoner's surname is altered from Sommers to Summers, a revision which King conjectures was 'possibly to bring out the element of warmth implicit in his name' (1991, p. 228). Mrs Fennel was previously said to have grown up in 'the valley below', but Hardy noticed that this was now inconsistent with a change which he had made for *1888*: Mrs Fennel and Summers are said to come from the same neighbourhood, but in *1888* Summers's home was altered to Shottsford, so that now Hardy had also to move Mrs Fennel's birthplace to 'a vale at a distance'.

1896 reverses the serials' removal of non-standard speech by introducing two dialect words: Mrs Fennel now says 'so be I' instead of 'so am I', and the previous inconsistency of allowing Shepherd Fennel to use the standard and the dialect form of the same word in consecutive sentences is corrected by changing both 'seen' and 'seed' to 'zeed'. Hardy also altered the spelling of 'lynchets' (flint slopes) to 'lanchets' (William Barnes gave the word as 'linch' or 'linchet' in his glossary to *Poems of Rural Life in the Dorset Dialect*).

1912 Macmillan Wessex edition

There are only eight substantive changes for the Wessex edition, and six of these are topographical refinements. For instance, the 'high' downs on which the cottage stands become the 'long' (p. 3) downs, probably because Hardy noticed that 'high downs' looks like an oxymoron. He also distinguished for the first time between downs, coombs and ewe-leases: in earlier versions of the story, the opening sentence had said that such features of the landscape were 'indifferently called' by such names, but in *1912* we learn that they were 'called according to their kind' (p. 3). The site of Higher Crowstairs was previously on a coomb, but in *1912* this becomes a down, which, as Kathryn King precisely observes, 'calls attention to the uplands location of the cottage and helps set up the contrast which follows between dwellers on the heights and those of the lowlands. (A coomb is located on the upland downs, but the word *down* emphasizes the uplands; *coomb*, which means valley or hollow, does not)' (1988, pp. 168–9). The distance of the cottage from Casterbridge is reduced from five miles to three. One other revision sees Hardy inserting a reference to the 'straw hackles' (p. 8) over the beehives, evidence perhaps of his wish to record the custom of covering a hive with a sheaf of straw.[3]

Notes

1 I am indebted to my colleague, Dr Robin Gilmour, for identifying the allusion.
2 King suggests that the deleted name may have been 'Higher Poleshill' (1991, p. 226). In 1893, Hardy and Rebekah Owen discussed the location of Higher Crowstairs: '[Hardy] pointed out to me a high and solitary house on Came Down, which he said his friend Mrs. Eliot of Weymouth declared was Higher Crowstairs; but the house was evidently a farmstead and not more than three and a half miles from Casterbridge. I said that I had always fancied Crowstairs to the *north* of Casterbridge; Mr. Hardy partly agreed, and said, too, that the hangman would come from the north or north-east, from Sherborne or Salisbury' (Weber, 1939, p. 31).
3 For the sake of a complete record, the other revisions to *1896* for the Wessex edition which have not previously been mentioned are as follows (*1912* is quoted first, and the pagination is that of *1912*): 'grassy/grassy,' (p. 3); 'the boy/the boy,' (p. 6); 'position/position,' (p. 6); 'dwelling/dwelling,' (p. 7); 'tread/tread,' (p. 7); 'stood/stood,' (p. 8); 'enigma/enigma,' (p. 16); 'together/together,' (p. 24); 'threw/looked' (p. 27); 'the slope of the coomb/the coomb' (p. 28).

CHAPTER 2

'A Tradition of Eighteen Hundred and Four'

Hardy probably wrote 'A Legend of the Year Eighteen Hundred and Four', as it was originally entitled, in the summer of 1882 in Wimborne, while he was completing work on *Two on a Tower*. His earliest surviving reference to it is in a letter to R.R. Bowker, Harper's London representative, dated 12 July 1882: 'Tile Club MS. was sent some days ago' (*Letters*, I, 106). The story first appeared later that year in *Harper's Christmas*, an annual composed of 'Pictures & Papers done by the Tile Club & its Literary Friends'.[1] 'A Tradition' draws on Hardy's reading and research in the British Museum in 1878 and 1879 which contributed to *The Trumpet-Major* (1880), another tale set in Napoleonic times. Two specific entries in the 'Trumpet-Major Notebook' provide details for 'A Tradition': the first concerns a report from the *True Briton* of 2 November 1803 which Hardy transcribed about an elevated signal post some four miles from Deal:

> Nothing new has been observed from thence lately, except a review of troops on the French coast, which occupied the whole of Thursday & Friday last. The Officer states that both those days the horizon was so very clear, that he could distinctly see with glasses an immense body of troops. (Taylor, p. 118)

In the original serial version of the story, which was set in Sussex, Selby the narrator remembers how, 'our house being so high on the down, on fine days we could see this drilling actually going on – especially with a spy-glass'. The second entry in the Notebook describes how 'the autumn of 1804 was one of alarm at the expected invasion, equally with 1803, though perhaps not to such an intense degree' (Taylor, p. 142). This note is perhaps the basis for Selby's comment that 'of all those years of my growing up the ones that bide clearest in my mind were eighteen hundred and three, four, and five' (serial version). Another source for the story was Hardy's childhood memories, and S.M. Ellis recalled in 1928 that 'Hardy told me how as a boy he had delighted in hearing from his father and aged people, such as "Solomon Selby," stories of the war times when troops were encamped on the downs above Weymouth' (p. 398).

The versions of the story which have textual significance are as follows:

Harper's   As 'A Legend of the Year Eighteen Hundred and Four', *Harper's Christmas*, December 1882, pp. 26–7. This was a Christmas annual, described as 'Pictures & Papers done by the Tile Club & its Literary Friends', published on 25

	November. Purdy notes that the story was called 'Napoleon's Invasion' in advertisements for *Harper's Christmas*.
1894	'A Tradition of Eighteen Hundred and Four', *Life's Little Ironies* (London: Osgood, McIlvaine, 1894), pp. 205–16. Published at 6s. in an edition of 2000 copies on 22 February 1894.
1894H	'A Tradition of 1804', *Life's Little Ironies* (New York: Harper & Brothers, 1894), pp. 175–83. Published March 1894.
1896	'A Tradition of Eighteen Hundred and Four', *Life's Little Ironies* (London: Osgood, McIlvaine, 1896), pp. 205–16. Volume XIV of the Wessex Novels, the first uniform and complete edition of Hardy's works. Purdy notes that the volume was reprinted from the same plates as the first edition in 1894. The story here is identical to the first edition.
1912	'A Tradition of Eighteen Hundred and Four', *Wessex Tales* (London: Macmillan, 1912), pp. 33–41. Volume IX of the Wessex edition. Hardy's Prefatory Note to *Life's Little Ironies* in the same edition states that 'A Tradition' and 'The Melancholy Hussar of the German Legion' have been 'transferred to *Wessex Tales*, where they more naturally belong' (p. vii).

No manuscript of the story is known to have survived.

Nearly forty years after 'A Tradition' was first published, Hardy began suddenly to utter conflicting accounts of its origin and reception: as Kathryn R. King has observed, 'it was in 1919 that the story attained in Hardy's mind the status of a minor obsession'.[2] In that year, Hardy implied at different times that 'A Tradition' was an invented story which he learned later coincided with an already existing tradition of which he had known nothing, and also that it was an invention which might itself have given rise to a general belief that Napoleon had indeed landed in England. The first of Hardy's comments in 1919 was made in June, when he added the following paragraph to the Preface of the Mellstock edition of *Wessex Tales*, the only change he made to the entire volume:

> An experience of the writer in respect of the tale called "A Tradition of Eighteen Hundred and Four" is curious enough to be mentioned here. The incident of Napoleon's visit to the English coast by night, with a view to discovering a convenient spot for landing his army of invasion, was an invention of the author's on which he had some doubts because of its improbability. This was in 1882, when it was first published. Great was his surprise several years later to be told that it was a real tradition. How far this is true he is unaware.[3]

In this account, 'several years' have elapsed before Hardy hears the suggestion that his 'tradition' was true, enough time for the invented story to have circulated and been mistakenly understood as an old legend that Hardy had simply recorded. He leaves open the possibility, though, that a 'real tradition' had existed. Later in 1919, however, Hardy wrote a note about the story's reception and its puzzling context which gives a conflicting account of events:

> October 1919. A curious question arose in Hardy's mind at this date on whether a romancer was morally justified in going to extreme lengths of assurance – after the manner of De Foe – in respect of a tale he knew to be absolutely false. Thirty-seven years earlier, when much pressed to produce something of the nature of a fireside yarn, he had invented a picturesque account of a stealthy nocturnal visit to England by Napoleon in 1804, during the war, to spy out a good spot for invasion. Being struck with the extreme improbability of such a story he added a circumstantial framework describing it as an old local tradition to blind the reader to the hoax. When it was published he was much surprised at people remarking to him: "I see you have made use of that well-known tradition of Napoleon's landing." He then supposed that, strange as it seemed, such a story must have been in existence without his knowledge, and that perhaps the event had happened. So the matter rested till the time at which we have arrived, when a friend who was interested made inquiries, and was assured by historians and annalists whom he consulted, that such a visit would have been fatuous, and well-nigh impossible. Moreover, that there had never existed any such improbable tradition. (*Life*, p. 424)

According to this version, Hardy heard that it was a 'true' story immediately after publication, not 'several years' later as it had been in the Mellstock Preface, so that his story could not have been responsible for the legend. In this account in October 1919, Hardy seems to be defensive and self-justifying. His original doubts about the story's 'improbability' in the Mellstock Preface in June have now in October become doubts about its 'extreme improbability', showing that, forty years earlier, he had certainly not been so foolish as to believe a story which the 'historians and annalists' have recently declared to be 'fatuous and well-nigh impossible'. He had known very well that his story was a 'hoax', but the historians are nevertheless wrong to deny that a *tradition* existed, for Hardy was questioned about it immediately after the story's publication. So, Hardy proves himself correct on all counts: he was correct to believe that Napoleon never landed, but he was also correct (albeit accidentally) to imply that a tradition that he had done so existed. As Kathryn King shrewdly observes in her comments on this note, 'the accumulation of circumstantial detail, the quotation (including the nice bit about "that well-known tradition"), the show of authorial bemusement, all add to the whiff of the specious given off by this anecdote. It is hard to escape the conclusion that Hardy the storyteller is engaged here in an imaginative working-up of his meta-tradition, a process of lending fictitious exactitude to a fictive account'.[4]

Why was Hardy suddenly interested in 'A Tradition' in 1919? The answer is to be found in a letter to Sydney Cockerell dated 12 October 1919, which King overlooked. Hardy thanks Cockerell for investigating the tradition:

> You should not have given yourself trouble about the legend, or otherwise, of Napoleon's landing to reconnoitre. It would certainly be very strange if an invented story should turn out to have already existed. If it would amuse you to send a letter to the Literary Suppt you might do so, but I leave it for you to judge. What you may be sure of is that I never heard of any such tradition. It may be that my having, with the licence of a storyteller to tell lies, *pretended* there was such an account in being, led people to think there was. Of course I did it to give verisimilitude to *my* story.
> (*Letters*, V, 326)

The note which Purdy and Millgate append to this letter explains what had led Cockerell to inquire into the tradition: 'according to a note of Cockerell's (Adams), Herbert Trench's play *Napoleon* (London, 1919) had taken as factual the central episode of TH's story "A Tradition of Eighteen Hundred and Four" (first pub. 1882), in which Napoleon personally lands on the Dorset coast to inspect the site of his projected invasion; Cockerell wrote 9 Oct 19 (DCM) to report that he could find no historical basis for the episode'. Trench's play was reviewed in the *Times Literary Supplement* on 19 June 1919, and it would seem to be this review which prompted Cockerell to make inquiries about the legend and which also, perhaps, caused Hardy to write his new Preface for the Mellstock edition in the same month. (The review, incidentally, makes no mention of Hardy, and gives mainly a summary of the plot.)[5] It thus appears to have been Trench's use of the legend which obliged Hardy to define his own relationship to the 'tradition'. On 21 July 1919, a month after the review, Hardy asked Elliott Felkin to investigate the status of the tradition: as Felkin records, 'Hardy talked about a story he had written about Napoleon coming to investigate the English coast at night which he invented and then, after it was published, heard that it was a tradition. Was this so? Would I find out from Dr. Holland Rose?'.[6] John Holland Rose (1855–1942) was a Fellow of Christ's College, Cambridge, and Professor of Naval History, so it is possible that he was involved in the research, as well as Cockerell.

Vere H. Collins asked Hardy during a conversation on 18 August 1922 whether he had read Trench's *Napoleon*, and Hardy replied:

> That's the play where Napoleon is supposed to come to England? No. There's something strange there. I wrote a story called "A Tradition of Eighteen Hundred and Four." I had a long discussion with Colvin about the place where he might have landed. We were agreed that it could only be Lulworth Cove. I mentioned that it was a tradition in order to add credibility to the tale. There was not any tradition. I invented it.[7]

The serial and the galleys of *1894*

The distinctive features of the serial version of the story in *Harper's Christmas* are best seen by comparison with the revised version of the story in its first collected form in the 1894 edition of *Life's Little Ironies*.

The first galley proofs of *1894* have survived (they are located in the Dorset County Museum), and the sheets of 'A Tradition' bear the printers' date stamp 23 December 1893. Hardy revised the story in three distinct stages when preparing it for publication in *1894*. Most of the revisions (nearly fifty, of which all but two are substantive) were made when producing what was presumably a printers' copy from which the first galleys were set up. The next stage was Hardy's marginal emendation of these proofs (27 revisions in total, of which thirteen are substantive). These emended proofs must have been the basis of a second set of proofs, or revises, because *1894* has, on eight occasions, a reading which is different from the emended galley proofs, and which must therefore have been introduced at a later stage. (Of these eight alterations, three are substantive.)

The serial and the first galley

All of the revisions to the serial which are described in this section were printed in the galleys and thus belong to the first stage of revision.

Solomon Selby, who witnesses Napoleon's landing, was originally called Shepherd Selby in *Harper's Christmas*,[8] and he explains in the serial that he was a Sussex man, like his father, though 'I have lived here so long as almost to call this my native place'. His current place of residence is not identified, but the serial specifies that Napoleon landed in Sussex: Selby's childhood home is 'several miles' east of the downs above Brighton, where his uncle Job, the sergeant, is in camp, and his cottage is about half a mile from the shore where he sees Napoleon. (Incidentally, 'A Tradition' is thus the only one of Hardy's short stories originally conceived as having a non-Wessex setting.) In *1894*'s galleys, however, his father is said to have lived 'out by Lullstead Cove' in South Wessex, and Selby 'moved here shortly afore I wer married' (in a marginal emendation, Hardy deleted 'Lullstead' but added that the cove is 'four miles yonder' from where Selby now lives, and he later made another marginal insertion, noting that Budmouth – or 'King George's watering-place', as it now became – is several miles to the west 'yonder' from his house). The story is thus made an exclusively Dorset tale in its setting and characters. Indeed, this as yet unrevised proof is the only version of the story which contains Wessex place-names, for Hardy later removed all of them when he made marginal revisions to the proof, preferring instead to use real Dorset placenames, no doubt in the cause of giving a spurious historical veracity to his 'tradition'. For instance, the unrevised galleys describe a convenient place for Napoleon's landing as being 'most likely one of the little bays inside the Isle of Portland, between Budmouth and St. Alban's Head', but this uneasy mixture of real and fictional places is resolved by Hardy altering 'Budmouth' in the margin to read 'the Beal', one of the actual names for Portland Bill. To summarize: the serial is set in Sussex, the unrevised galleys of *1894* locate the story in Wessex, while Hardy's revision of the galleys identifies the setting as Dorset.

The Sussex setting of the serial means that Selby can see Napoleon's soldiers parading on the beach across the Channel when he is standing 'on my father's door-stone', especially if he uses a spy-glass. The change of location to Wessex in *1894* required Hardy to introduce the following revision to allow the French soldiers still to be seen over the water: 'My father drove a flock of ewes up into Sussex that year, and as he went along the drover's track over the high downs thereabout he could see this drilling actually going on'. Kathryn King rightly suggests that this sheep drive of over 100 miles is highly implausible, and shows Hardy's reluctance to abandon the historical snippet which he had found in the *True Briton* newspaper account (King, 1988, p. 140).

In the serial, the narrator, Selby and his audience are sitting in a farm-house kitchen, awaiting the farmer's return, but in *1894* they are all sitting around an inn-kitchen. The setting for Selby's story is now less intimate and the narrator appears more of an outsider, one who is not on casual visiting terms with the local farmer. Hardy's evocation of a common agricultural life in the serial no longer exists a dozen years later in *1894*. Similarly, in the serial, Selby remained a shepherd all his life, but in *1894* we learn that he was 'took away from the sheepkeeping to be bound prentice to a trade'. The continuity and traditions of a stable rural world are broken, and the childhood of which Selby speaks belongs to an age which seems more remote.

1894 introduces the story's two detailed references to smuggling: uncle Job takes a drink from 'the tub of sperrits that the smugglers kept us in for housing their liquor when they'd made a run, and for burning 'em off when there was danger'. This replaces the serial's throwaway mention of 'the tub of hollands we bought from the smuggler's wife'. Another entirely new description in *1894* concerns the Cove which, Selby says, 'I've climmed up with two tubs of brandy across my shoulders on scores o' dark nights in my younger days'. These references to smuggling not only record Wessex lore of the kind which Hardy had commemorated in 'The Distracted Preacher', but they also allow the possibility that the two uniformed officers whom Selby sees are in fact Customs men.

Moving the story to Dorset allowed Hardy to introduce a number of Wessex dialect pronunciations into his characters' speech. Thus, Selby and his uncle Job in the galleys say 'Bonaparty', 'Proossians', 'afeard', 'what be they', 'mid' (for 'may'), 'yaller' (i.e. 'yellow', replacing the serial's 'sallow'), 'crope' ('crept') and 'climmed' ('climbed'). With the exception of 'yaller', all of these Wessex dialect forms replace what had been their standard English equivalents in the serial.

The final paragraph of the serial began by saying how 'the grass has been green' for twenty years on Selby's grave, but Hardy altered this in *1894* to read 'We who listened to old Selby that night have been familiar with his simple grave-stone for these ten years past' ('simple' was a marginal insertion to the galleys). This makes Selby ten years older at the time of his death, increasing the sense of him being one of the last living links with Napoleonic times. A more immediate reason for Hardy's revision, however, may be that the first words of the final paragraph in the serial were almost identical to the opening of the final paragraph of another of his short stories, 'The Three Strangers', which mentioned how 'the grass has long been green' on the grave of another shepherd, Fennel, and his wife. While 'The Three Strangers' had originally been published serially in the year following the first appearance of 'A Tradition', it had already been collected in *Wessex Tales* in 1888, some six years before 'A Tradition' was collected in *Life's Little Ironies*. Hardy perhaps wished to avoid any repetition in the closing description of the graves of the two men.

Galley revisions

When he was revising the first galley proofs, Hardy took the opportunity to increase the size of the French army across the Channel by 10,000 to 160,000 men, and he added 15,000 horses. He also introduced a couple more non-standard English usages: 'wounds' became 'wownds', and 'those years' became 'them years' (later revised again to 'the years'). Selby's description of 'a slight mist' was altered in the margin to read 'a bit of a mist'. While this gives a more appropriate colloquial tone to Selby's narration, there may be a further stylistic reason for the change: in a short paragraph which already contains 'right', 'to-night', 'nights' and 'light', perhaps Hardy felt that 'slight' would be one 'rhyme' too many.

These emended proofs must at this stage have been sent to Harper & Brothers in New York to form the basis of *1894H*, since they are virtually identical in substantives. For the British edition, however, as has been mentioned, the proofs underwent a further revision, and the account given below of these second proofs is therefore an account of most of the differences between the British and American editions of 1894. For instance, there are three substantive occasions on which Hardy revised again the emended proof; *1894H*, however, retains the readings of the emended proof, showing that it was based on this intermediate stage of the galley.

The three substantive alterations which Hardy made to the second proofs all occur in the first two pages of the story. The longest is a clause of eight words in which the narrator explains why he went to the inn on the night he told his tale: 'and I entered for shelter from the rain'. This replaces 'awaiting the cessation of the rain'. Perhaps Hardy felt that this was rather too Latinate and polysyllabic for his narrator to say, and would separate him too much from the idiom of Selby and his audience. The two other second proof revisions remove dialect or non-standard forms of English, so that 'I wer' becomes 'I was' and 'them years' becomes 'the years'.

1894 Harper

In addition to the three substantive variants described above, there are some eighteen differences in accidentals between *1894* and *1894H* (ignoring US spelling), all of which were no doubt caused by Harper's house-styling. The American edition also ignored Hardy's marginal alteration of 'wounds' to 'wownds'.

1912 Macmillan

The only alteration to the story which Hardy made when preparing *Wessex Tales* in 1912 was to change Selby's comment that he could see a boat 'a little way out' in the Channel. This became 'a short way out' (p. 40), in order to avoid repeating 'little' at the start of the next sentence.

Notes

1 The 1882 number of *Harper's Christmas* is discussed in J. Henry Harper (1912), pp. 492–3. Harper notes that the number 'was admitted to be the most attractive Christmas paper ever issued' and contained work by, among others, Howells and Twain.

2 See King (1992), pp. 20–26. Frank G. Healey (1992) agrees with King's scepticism about a local tradition imitating Hardy's fiction.

3 Quoted in Orel, pp. 23–4. Hardy certainly seemed to believe that a tradition existed in 1901 during his interview with William Archer. Hardy told him that

> in several of my stories there is a very large element of fact, or tradition. For instance, the story of Napoleon's landing in person on the Dorsetshire coast – I don't know whether you remember it – is related as a fact.
> *W.A.* Do you yourself believe it?
> *Mr Hardy*. I cannot honestly say I do (Archer [1901], p. 309).

Similarly, in May 1909, Hardy had told Mrs Belloc Lowndes that, 'as to the story of Napoleon having landed on the shore of Dorset, he declared he had only been told of such a tradition since he had written the story, and repeated that he never heard of it before he wrote what he called "the tale"'. See Lowndes (1946), pp. 147–9.

4 King (1992), p. 22.

5 See *Times Literary Supplement*, 19 June 1919, p. 334.

6 Felkin (1962), p. 30.

7 Vere H. Collins (1928), p. 84. Hardy appears to have forgotten that the story was originally set in Sussex.

8 F.B. Pinion notes in his *Dictionary* (p. 275) that Selby's name derives from that of James Selby, a mason, of Broadmayne, Dorset, who is described in the *Life* as 'the quaint old man already mentioned, who worked forty years for Hardy's father, and had been a smuggler' (p. 170; see also p. 119).

CHAPTER 3

'The Melancholy Hussar'

'The Melancholy Hussar' was the last of the stories in *Wessex Tales* to be written. Hardy had nearly finished it in July 1888 for a new journal, the *Universal Review*, when he wrote to its editor, Harry Quilter, to suggest that he might prefer instead a more modern story, and he ended the letter by outlining details of a tale which would become 'A Tragedy of Two Ambitions':

> I am settling down to your story. It is of a picturesque kind – a tale of the camp of German Hussars on the hills near here, when Geo. III was King, & living at Weymouth. It has some foundation in truth. The scenery is of course of the period; York Hussars, a camp, downs, old stone manor-house inside a wall, sea in the distance, &c. Daughter of the house is the heroine. Then there is an escape by night, a boat, Weymouth harbour, &c.
>
> Now the question has occurred to me:– suppose you do not want a tale of that sort for your very modern review? I have in my head a story of a different character – embodying present day aspirations – i.e., concerning the ambitions of two men, their struggles for education, a position in the Church, & so on, ending tragically. If you much prefer the latter sort of thing I will abandon the first – though that is the most advanced, & could be sent in a week or ten days. The other would take a little more time, as it exists at present only in the form of half a dozen notes. (*Letters*, I, 178)

'The Melancholy Hussar' was then laid aside for more than a year until, on 25 September 1889, Tillotson's rejected *Tess* and returned the manuscript. As a sign of their continuing good will, however, Tillotson's solicited a short story for early syndication, and Hardy's response was to complete 'The Melancholy Hussar' and send it to them on 22 October.[1] He returned the corrected proofs of the story on 2 December (see *Letters*, I, 204), and it was published a month later.

Hardy knew details of the actual events on which his story is based as early as 1877, for the *Life* includes a note which he made at that time:

> "July 27. James Bushrod of Broadmayne saw the two German soldiers [of the York Hussars] shot [for desertion] on Bincombe Down in 1801. It was in the path across the down, or near it. James Selby of the same village thinks there is a mark." [The tragedy was used in "The Melancholy Hussar", the real names of the deserters being given.] (p. 119; the square brackets are Hardy's, indicating his addition of details to the original note)

In his study copy of the Wessex edition of *Wessex Tales* (now in the Dorset County Museum), Hardy wrote the following note at the end of the story: 'The execution of the two York Hussars was witnessed by James Bushrod of Broadmayne, who described the details to James Selby, a few years younger than himself. Selby in his old age told them to the writer.' James Selby was a mason, of Broadmayne, Dorset, and he is described in the *Life* as a 'quaint old man' who 'worked forty years for Hardy's father, and had been a smuggler' (p. 170; see also p. 119). Beneath this note, Hardy pasted in a newspaper cutting from *The Times* of 6 July 1801 which gives an account of the execution: this is a reprint of the *Morning Chronicle* report two days earlier, except for the omission of the final sentence (see below).

Hardy also made detailed use of the research which he undertook at the British Museum in 1878–79 for *The Trumpet-Major*, a story set in the same time and place as 'The Melancholy Hussar'. The 'Trumpet-Major Notebook' records the following report from the *Morning Chronicle* of 4 July 1801:

> On Wedny. morning │ two privates │ of the York
> │ private and corporal │
> Hussars were shot on Bincombe Down, nr. W[eymouth]. pursuant to the
> sentence of a court martial, for desertion, & cutting a boat out of the
> harbour, with intent to go to France, but by mistake they landed at
> Guernsey, & were secured. All the regts. both in camp & barracks, were
> drawn up, viz the Scotch Greys, the Rifle Corps, the Stafford, Berks, & N.
> Devon Militia. They came on the ground in a mourning coach, attended by
> 2 priests; after marching along the front of the line they returned to the
> centre, where they spent about 20 minutes in prayer, & were shot at by a
> guard of 24 men; they dropped instantly, & expired without a groan. The
> men wheeled in sections, & marched by the bodies in slow time. (Taylor,
> pp. 124–5; the vertical lines enclosing the alternative reading are Hardy's)[2]

As we shall see, Hardy did not use most of this material until he came to revise the serial version of the story for its collected edition in 1894, some fifteen years after he made the entry in the Notebook.

In his Preface to the 1896 Wessex Novels edition of *Life's Little Ironies*, in which 'The Melancholy Hussar' had appeared before being transferred to *Wessex Tales*, Hardy reflected on the sources of the story (unfortunately, the Preface was not reprinted in the 1912 Macmillan Wessex edition):

> A story-teller's interest in his own stories is usually independent of any
> merits or demerits they may show as specimens of narrative art; turning on
> something behind the scenes, something real in their history, which may
> have no attraction for a reader even if known to him – a condition by no
> means likely. In the present collection 'The Melancholy Hussar of the
> German Legion' has just such a hold upon myself for the technically
> inadmissible reasons that the old people who gave me their recollections of
> its incidents did so in circumstances that linger pathetically in the memory;
> that she who, at the age of ninety, pointed out the unmarked resting-place of
> the two soldiers of the tale, was probably the last remaining eyewitness of
> their death and interment; that the extract from the register of burials is
> literal, to be read any day in the original by the curious who recognize the
> village.

A note by Hardy about the story, dated 16 August 1907, adds a couple of new details:

> "The Melancholy Hussar" is largely founded on fact. The Bincombe Register of burials (kept at Broadway Rectory) contains the entries quoted in the story. The deserters were buried at the back of the churchyard, but there is no stone. The old people used to point out the spot.[3]

This exactly echoes some phrases in the final paragraph of the story: 'Their graves were dug at the back of the little church, near the wall. There is no memorial to mark the spot, but Phyllis pointed it out to me.' S.M. Ellis recalled a further comment by Hardy about one of his sources of information: 'the incident on which the story is based was related by an old woman to Hardy in 1855, when he was a boy of fifteen. The scene, he told me, was Bincombe.'[4] This matches the chronology of the story in its collected editions: 'Phyllis told me the story with her own lips. She was then an old lady of seventy-five, and her auditor a lad of fifteen.' She lived for twelve more years and has been dead for nearly twenty, which approximately puts the narration of the story in 1887, the year before Hardy wrote the first draft.

Hardy also confirmed the location of the story in a letter to Bertram Windle in 1896:

> *Bincombe Down* (near W[eymouth].) is the scene of the military execution in "A Melancholy Hussar" a true story, the names of the deserters from the German Legion, shot in 1801, being still to be read in the register of the parish. They were shot where the roads cross. (*Letters*, II, 131)

Rebekah Owen and her sister inspected the parish registers in November 1893:

> [They] walked to Broadway Vicarage [...] and at last saw the Bincombe church registers for 1801. The Vicar had never examined them [...] "though he told me that Mr. Hardy the novelist [...] had about three years ago examined them in order to write about them. [...] The Vicar could not tell me who 'Phyllis' was, but had understood from Mr. Hardy that she was engaged to one of the deserters, or had kept company with him." (Weber, 1952, p. 93)

Hardy must have inspected the church registers when he was completing the manuscript of the serial version in 1889, because the burial entries are quoted on the final two leaves of the story.

The versions of 'The Melancholy Hussar' which have textual significance are as follows:

Bristol Times   'The Melancholy Hussar', *Bristol Times and Mirror*, 4 January (p. 9) and 11 January (p. 9) 1890. The division occurred at the end of Section III. The story was the last of the four which Hardy had sold to Tillotson & Son for their syndicated fiction business, and Purdy notes that it was to be 'widely printed, especially in provincial newspapers' (p. 82).

TNS 'The Melancholy Hussar', *Three Notable Stories* (London: Spencer Blackett, [June] 1890), pp. 153–211. The other two stories are 'Love and Peril' by the Marquis of Lorne and 'To Be, or Not to Be' by Mrs Alexander, which were both Tillotson stories. Purdy notes that sheets of this printing of 'The Melancholy Hussar' were remaindered and plates were sold to Donohue, Henneberry & Co. (Chicago) and used repeatedly for cheap reprints (p. 82).

1894 As 'The Melancholy Hussar of the German Legion', *Life's Little Ironies* (London: Osgood, McIlvaine, 1894), pp. 149–75. Published at 6*s.* in an edition of 2000 copies on 22 February 1894.

1894H As 'The Melancholy Hussar of the German Legion', *Life's Little Ironies* (New York: Harper & Brothers, 1894), pp. 129–51. Published March 1894.

1896 As 'The Melancholy Hussar of the German Legion', *Life's Little Ironies* (London: Osgood, McIlvaine, 1896), pp. 149–75. Volume XIV of the Wessex Novels, the first uniform and complete edition of Hardy's works. Purdy notes that the volume was reprinted from the same plates as the first edition of 1894. The story here is identical to the first edition.

1912 'The Melancholy Hussar', *Wessex Tales* (London: Macmillan, 1912), pp. 45–66. Volume IX of the Wessex edition. Hardy's Prefatory Note to *Life's Little Ironies* in the same edition states that 'The Melancholy Hussar' and 'A Tradition of Eighteen Hundred and Four' have been 'transferred to *Wessex Tales*, where they more naturally belong' (p. vii).

A fragment of an early draft of the story (not noted by Purdy) is in the Charles Aldrich Autograph Collection, located in the Iowa State Historical Department, and a fair copy of the complete manuscript is now in the Huntington Library. The first galley proofs of *1894* are in the possession of Dorset County Museum.

The Iowa manuscript

This fragment consists of the first three pages of a draft MS., which Hardy sent to Charles Aldrich, founder and curator of the Iowa State Historical Department, on 31 December 1889, with an accompanying letter: 'In response to your request of last summer I send herewith 3 pages of MS. & a photograph. The story is a short one which will appear during the coming spring' (*Letters*, VII, 112). In fact, the first instalment of the story was to appear just four days later in the *Bristol Times*, suggesting that Hardy was unaware of Tillotson's arrangement for syndication.

The top of the first leaf bears the date 'Oct. 1889' in Hardy's hand, but this probably indicates when he completed the story, rather than the date at which he wrote this fragment, since it appears to be an early draft and therefore may date from the summer of 1888, when Hardy first began work on the story. There are many revisions and cancellations within the fragment, and there were numerous additions to it when the printers' MS. was prepared. The fragment contains the gist of the opening four pages of the story as it stands in the Wessex edition, ending with a description of Phyllis's pride that Humphrey Gould had chosen her for his wife 'when he might have made a more ambitious choice' (fo. 3). The title is given uniquely as 'The Melancholy Hussar / The Corporal in the German Legion'.

The first reference to Phyllis by name is simply as an abbreviated 'P.', and her name is later spelt 'Phillis' and then 'Phyllis'. Other abbreviations, whose use suggests that this manuscript is a rough draft, are 'G.' for Gould and 'G. Lodge' for Gloucester Lodge. The fragment does not have the paragraph introducing Phyllis as the old lady who told the narrator the story from her own lips, and so the first mention of her is in a reference to 'her father', again indicating the early status of this manuscript, as if Hardy were blocking out some of the major paragraphs in the story, with the intention of filling in the necessary linking passages later. Similarly, in the margin alongside the first mention of her courtship by Gould, Hardy jotted down some cancelled notes for future plot developments: '– (Her engagem^t – At this point of time .... She felt unlimited joy.)'

The Iowa manuscript lacks two passages later inserted into the Huntington printers' copy which concern Dr Grove's gardening. We learn in the Huntington MS. that he ground his sickle 'for his favourite ~~amusement~~ relaxation of trimming the box-tree borders to the plots', and that the bush by the gate was cut into '~~an~~ la quaint &l' (fo. 3) attenuated shape. In the Iowa MS., Phyllis's father had merely cut the bushes 'for tidiness', but the introduction of his topiary creates what Brady calls 'the artificiality of her pastoral surroundings' (p. 42). Originally, in the Iowa MS., Dr Grove was said to be an 'unsuccessful medical man' but this was cancelled and replaced with what appears to read 'lrespected clergymanl', before this in turn was deleted and the original wording was marked for retention by a dotted underlining. In the Huntington MS., his occupation is unspecified at this point, and we learn only that 'he had been a professional man' (fo. 3) whose 'practice' had diminished, although Hardy twice refers to him as Dr Grove near the end of the story. He had obviously not intended to create any ambiguity about his occupation, and a serial proof revision altered the phrase to read 'Dr. Grove had been a professional man'. In the Iowa MS., Grove moved to the country simply because he had been unsuccessful and could not afford to live in town, but in the later MS. we learn the reason for his failure: he had a 'taste for lonely meditation over metaphysical questions' (fo. 3) which had ruined his practice, and he now grew 'more & more irritable with the lapse of time, & the increasing perception that he had wasted his life in the pursuit of ~~chim~~[eras] illusions' (fo. 4). Phyllis's isolation, then, is not merely the result of her father's professional failure but is caused directly by his indulgence of his sentimentality.

The portrayal of Gould differs in the two manuscripts. In the earlier one, he must postpone his return to Phyllis because he could not leave his parents at Bath. In the Huntington MS., however, he has only a father, and he cannot leave him because he has no other relative near him. This change better motivates Gould's inability to return to Phyllis, and incidentally creates a contrast between Phyllis's two suitors, Gould with his lonely father and the melancholy Hussar with his lonely mother. Phyllis's social success in capturing Gould is increased in the Huntington MS., which informs us that 'he was of an old llocall family, some of whose members were held in respect in the county' (fo. 4). There is a contradiction in Gould's portrayal in the Iowa MS., where he is said to be an approximately fashionable man 'of a slow st landl quiet kind', and yet Phyllis is attracted to the 'lmethodicall energetic' (fo. 3) way in which he took his pleasure. The Huntington MS. resolves this contradiction by altering the two phrases to read respectively 'of a slow mild type' and 'methodical & dogged' (fos. 4, 6).

The Huntington manuscript

This manuscript of 'The Melancholy Hussar', as the story is called here, consists of 27 quarto leaves, and was the printers' copy for the *Bristol Times*. For instance, the first leaf has 'Now First Published' written at the top in a hand other than Hardy's, and the end of Section III has the insertion 'To be concluded', both phrases appearing in the newspaper. The many additions and deletions within the MS. concern five main areas: style, location, chronology, characterization and propriety.

The most interesting revisions are those which serve to emphasize the decorum of Phyllis's relationships with both Humphrey Gould and Matthäus, the hussar. For instance, an insertion shows that Gould is careful to make her 'lfather'sl' (fo. 4) acquaintance before he meets Phyllis. Another later addition shows Matthäus stressing to Phyllis that 'lyou will not fly alone with mel' (fo. 15) when he is explaining that his friend Christoph will accompany them on their elopement. Originally, Phyllis hesitates to accept his proposal because it was so 'unbecoming', but this suggestion of impropriety is removed by altering it to 'lventuresomel' (fo. 19).

The hussar becomes increasingly homesick in the MS. When Matthäus first meets Phyllis, he originally tells her that he is reading 'an old' letter from his mother, but this becomes 'lreperusingl' (fo. 8) a number of letters from her. Later, he is described as having a 'lonely' nature, but this was deleted and replaced by 'lmusingl' (fo. 10), perhaps because Hardy wanted to stress that his melancholy was not temperamental but was specifically caused by his isolation in England. An initial reference to his 'passionate admiration' for his country is strengthened by revising it to a 'passionate llongingl' (fo. 15) for his country *and* his mother. Such increased loneliness serves to mitigate his desertion from the army, as does the new note of desperation which Hardy adds to Matthäus's plea for Phyllis to elope with him: 'lNow is the time, as we shall soon be leaving here, & I might see you no morel' (fo. 15).

The symbolic wall which chastely separates the two lovers receives much attention in the manuscript. The initial description of Phyllis's ability to climb it as 'an easy feat' was deleted and replaced with 'la feat not so difficult as it may seeml' (fo. 7), because the walls 'lin this districtl' (another new phrase) were made of rubble and provided many footholds; the explanation of this local feature seems to be for the benefit of an urban audience. A little later, Hardy said that the wall 'prevented anything like intimacy' between the lovers, but this was altered to 'lmadel anything like intimacy ldifficultl' (fo. 10), presumably after Hardy had added the description two leaves later of Phyllis stretching down her hand to Matthäus from the top of the wall, an act which made the earlier assertion that the wall prevented any intimacy strictly inaccurate. Near the end of the story, Phyllis goes to the bottom of the garden and notices that she had 'lleft marks of garden-soil on the stepping-stones by which she had mounted to look over the ~~wall~~ lltoplll' (fo. 24); this is a late insertion and replaces the suggestion that trampled grass had presumably betrayed her trysts at the wall to her father.

The chronology undergoes a slight revision. Originally, Matthäus and Christoph were to have been executed 'the next' morning after their desertion, but Hardy must have realized that more time would have to pass for them to be apprehended, court-martialled and returned from Jersey.[5] He therefore introduced a sentence which shows Phyllis lingering in her house for 'lseveral daysl' (fo. 23) before she emerges one morning and witnesses their execution.

A couple of Hardy's stylistic changes typically show him seeking to avoid repetition. For instance, in a passage which reads '[...] one of the foreign regiments ~~before~~ labovel alluded to. Before that day [...]' (fo. 2), the first 'before' seems to have been deleted after Hardy began the next sentence with the same word. ('Mist' is changed to 'lhazel' on fo. 24 for a similar reason). Another minor alteration gives a slightly more sympathetic characterization to Dr Grove: originally, his taste for lonely meditation was said to have 'ruined him professionally', but this became the less ruinous 'diminished his practice' (fo. 3). The name of the Colonel of the Regiment who orders the dead hussars to be turned out of their coffins on to the grass was given as Colonel Long before being deleted (fo. 25); this does not seem to be a name which occurs in the 'Trumpet-Major Notebook'. Finally, Hardy appears to have had some difficulty deciding on Matthäus's nationality and place of origin. At first, he told Phyllis that his country was Prussia, but this was altered to 'lBavarial' (fo. 14), which appeared in the *Bristol Times*; Hardy corrected it to read that his country was 'by the Saar' in a marginal emendation to the *1894* proofs. His native town was initially said to be 'Saarsbruck' (fo. 9; Hardy added an umlaut in a marginal revision to the *1894* proofs), but this is rendered in the transcription of the register of burials at the end of the story as 'Sarsbruk' (fo. 26). This was how the name appeared in the *Bristol Times* version of the register entry, but Hardy altered it at the second proof stage of *1894* to 'Sarrbruk', which was retained in *1912*. The correct name of the town at the time of the story would have been Saarbrück.

The Huntington manuscript and the *Bristol Times and Mirror*

There are some 44 substantive differences between this MS. and the serial, most of which were probably introduced during proof revision. Of these 44 variants, fourteen of the serial readings are unique because they are not transmitted to the first collected edition of 1894, which instead reverts to the original MS. reading. There would seem to be two possible explanations for this. One is that Hardy did not copy these fourteen proof revisions on to a duplicate set of proofs which he consulted when preparing *1894*, but did copy the remainder. Hardy is known to have retained proofs of the story (which are not extant) because he explained to a friend in September 1892[?] when lending her a copy of the tale that 'I send you the story "The Melancholy Hussar" which I promised [...]. I am sorry I have only the old proof sheets; but a copy of the periodicals in which the tale appeared did not reach my hands' (*Letters*, I, 285). The other explanation for the unique serial readings is that the *Bristol Times* accidentally introduced them when setting up the story from a batch of Tillotson's proofs; in other words, Hardy corrected proofs for Tillotson's and retained a marked copy of them, but he did not correct proofs for any syndicated publications of the story which they subsequently generated. His ignorance of the story's first impending appearance in print, which was noted earlier, together with the nature of the unique serial variants, may make this explanation the more likely one.

All but one of the fourteen variants involve individual words. There is one misprint in the serial ('were' for 'where'). Four omissions of words which do not affect the sense of the sentence may also be compositorial errors. The serial adds two words ('now', 'and') in what could be an editorial revision. Another such apparent revision occurs in the description of Christoph going ahead of Matthäus and Phyllis and meeting them on the other side of the promontory, 'which they were to do' by crossing a bridge. This does not make sense, unlike the manuscript's 'which they were to reach' (fo. 17). A phrase of four words reads 'no longer paid him' (fo. 3) in the MS. and 'paid him no longer' in the serial, a change which could be compositorial or editorial in origin. There do not appear to be any unique readings which are authorial, so it seems unlikely that Hardy read proofs for the story's appearance in the *Bristol Times and Mirror*.

There are 31 substantive variants in the *Bristol Times* which were transmitted to the first collected edition. This is presumably because they were proof revisions which Hardy noted on the duplicate proofs which he retained. He appears to have read the proofs against the Huntington MS. because there is one occasion when he restored a reading that had been deleted in the MS.: on fo. 9, a phrase reads 'our ~~native~~ officers', where 'native' was interlined and deleted in the MS. but restored to the serial. Two apparent misprints in the serial were not noticed and have been repeated in all later editions. The first is a reference to the 'father's house' (fo. 7), as it seems to read in the manuscript, which was printed as the 'father's home'. The other is more significant because it affects the meaning of the sentence. In the manuscript, Hardy clearly wrote that 'lThere came al morning lwhichl broke in fog & mist, behind which the *down* could be discerned in greenish gray' (fo. 23, my italics); all printed versions of the story, however, read 'dawn' instead of 'down'. One can see how 'morning' and 'broke' could lead a reader to expect 'dawn', though not, perhaps, a bizarrely 'greenish gray' one. Another variant may possibly be a misprint which Hardy overlooked: Phyllis's eyes, when she first sees the scene of the execution, are clearly said in the MS. to be 'starting' out of her head (fo. 24), but all printed versions read 'staring'.

Hardy took the opportunity when revising the serial proofs to correct an error in the plot. In the MS., the hussars, 'having no compass' (fo. 26), steered unwittingly into Jersey; six leaves earlier, however, Christoph was said to have brought a compass and chart, so Hardy replaced the inconsistent phrase with 'mistaking their bearings' in the serial. The most interesting addition to the story at this stage is the suggestion that Phyllis is 'like Desdemona' in pitying Matthäus and listening to his experiences. Kathryn King has commented that this comparison hints at 'the quiet yet passionate yearnings of this isolated daughter of an emotionally remote father' (1988, p. 221). Elsewhere, King has also noted that Desdemona 'falls in love with Othello listening to his military stories. Unlike Phyllis, she asks for and is granted permission to accompany her soldier to war' (1991, pp. 231–2).

Three Notable Stories (TNS)

This hardback reprint of 'The Melancholy Hussar' is essentially the same as the *Bristol Times*. There are eighteen substantive differences between the two versions, and they all involve individual words, except for the transposition of two short phrases (*TNS* reads 'humility and modesty' and 'no longer paid him', where the *Bristol Times* has 'modesty and humility' and 'paid him no longer'). On all but five of the 18 occasions, it is the *TNS* variant which is transmitted to the story's first collected publication in *1894*. The five unique variants in *TNS* are all of a kind which could be compositorial errors (such as the omission of 'then' and 'seen', or the setting of 'dared' as 'dare'), and none of them renders a sentence unintelligible to an editor reading the copy for sense.

Three Notable Stories, then, is closer to *1894* in its words than the *Bristol Times*, but the reverse is true of their respective treatment of accidentals. There are some eighty differences between the two versions in their use of spelling, punctuation and styling, and the *Bristol Times* reading is found in *1894* on two-thirds of such occasions. It would therefore appear unlikely that Hardy read proofs for either of these two publications of the story, and neither of them served as copy text for *1894*.

The serial and the galleys of *1894*

The distinctive features of the serial version of the story in the *Bristol Times and Mirror* are best seen by comparison with the revised version of the story in its first collected form in the 1894 edition of *Life's Little Ironies*.

The first galley proofs of *1894* have survived (they are located in the Dorset County Museum), and the sheets of 'The Melancholy Hussar' bear the printers' date stamp 16 December 1893. Hardy revised the story in three distinct stages when preparing it for publication in *1894*. Most of the revisions (nearly seventy, of which thirty are substantive) were made when producing what was presumably a printers' copy from which the first galleys were set up. The next stage was Hardy's marginal emendation of these proofs (nearly forty revisions, of which half are substantive). These emended proofs must have been the basis of a second set of proofs, or revises, because *1894* has, on twenty occasions, a reading which is different from the emended galley proofs, and which must therefore have been introduced at a later stage. (Of these twenty alterations, half are substantive.)

The serial and the first galley of *1894*

The scene which underwent most revision for the first collected edition of the story is the execution of the hussars, which Hardy supplemented in *1894* by inserting six phrases which were lifted almost verbatim from the *Morning Chronicle* report which he had recorded in the 'Trumpet-Major Notebook'. 'Two priests' replace the single clergyman who accompanied the men in the serial, and the firing-party consists of 24 men, twice the previous figure. New information is that the condemned men are brought to the scene 'in a mourning coach' and are then 'marched along the front of the line' before being 'returned to the centre'. After their death, the regiments are 'wheeled in sections [...] in slow time' past their bodies. An entertaining revision to the scene is not directly caused by Hardy's reading of his *Morning Chronicle* note: in the serial, the regiments were drawn up in a square and the hussars were executed in the middle of it. Hardy must have realized that this formation would be rather dangerous for the soldiers standing behind Matthäus and Christoph, so he has them all standing in a line in *1894*. While Hardy may have borrowed these phrases from the newspaper account, he invented the most harrowing detail, the two coffins on which the condemned men kneel to pray and from which they are flung out upon their faces on to the grass.

All nine occurrences of 'Weymouth' were removed from the serial, but at different stages. Eight of them were replaced in the first galley by a phrase such as 'the royal watering-place' or 'his favourite sea-side resort'. On two occasions, however, 'Weymouth' became the fictional 'Budmouth', but the first galley also includes a reference to 'the Weymouth *bourgeoisie*', so that the real and the fictional placenames co-exist at this stage. Hardy's marginal revisions removed any reference to the place by either name. The topography is also altered in the first galley by the addition of a short paragraph describing the coastline:

> The spot was high and airy, and the view extensive, commanding the Isle
> of Portland in front, and reaching to St. Aldhelm's Head eastward, and
> almost to the Start on the west.

An identical coastline was evoked in 'A Tradition of Eighteen Hundred and Four': 'one of the little bays inside the Isle of Portland, between the Beal and St. Alban's Head' (St Alban's and St Aldhelm's Head are actual names for the same location). This description, too, was new for the 1894 edition of *Life's Little Ironies*, in which both stories were first collected, suggesting that Hardy was seeking to give a geographical as well as a historical unity to the volume's two Napoleonic tales.

Hardy added '*October* 1889' to the end of the story, which was the date (22 October) on which Hardy delivered the MS. to Tillotson's.

Galley revisions

During his revision of the proofs, Hardy added in the margin that Phyllis's home was a 'half farm half manor-house', which may have approximated more closely to the original house in Bincombe. The boy to whom Phyllis tells her tale had been 'a lad of sixteen' in the manuscript and the serial, but Hardy at this stage made him fifteen years old. This was Hardy's age when he was told the story in 1855, but it is unclear why he had previously permitted this minor inaccuracy or why he now wished to rectify it. Among a few other substantive revisions, the harbour from which Matthäus and his friend Christoph are going to sail is specified as being 'four miles ahead' of them from their meeting place in the highway. Christoph is identified as being an Alsatian when he is first mentioned in the story: this is important to establish that, like Matthäus, he is not a Hanoverian and therefore his desertion is mitigated.

One of Hardy's marginal emendations appears to have been ignored or overlooked. A description of Phyllis's sorrow as 'great' was altered to 'deep', but *1894* and later editions retain 'great' (*1894H* reads 'deep', for reasons described immediately below).

These emended proofs must at this stage have been sent to Harper & Brothers in New York to form the basis of *1894H*, since they are virtually identical in substantives. For the British edition, however, as has been mentioned, the proofs underwent a further revision, and the account given below of these second proofs is therefore an account of most of the differences between the British and American editions of 1894. For instance, there are eleven substantive occasions on which Hardy revised again the emended proof; *1894H*, however, retains the readings of the emended proof, showing that it was based on this intermediate stage of the galley.

One of these revises changed the time at which Humphrey Gould has arranged to meet his driver from 'ten o'clock' to 'half-past nine o'clock', for no apparent reason. Matthäus originally told Phyllis that his regiment would soon be 'leaving here', but this became the more dramatic and military 'striking camp'. Hardy also added that the Georgian watering-place was 'well-known', and he changed the spelling of Matthäus's place of birth in the register of burials from 'Sarsbruk' to 'Sarrbruk'. Other changes at this stage are very minor.

1894 Harper

There are some seventy differences in accidentals between *1894* and *1894H* (ignoring US spelling), all of which were no doubt caused by Harper's house-styling and editorial correction. There are three substantive variations not accounted for by Hardy's revises of the emended proof; one is Harper's printing of 'deep' described above, and the other two appear to be an editorial revision of 'uniform' to 'uniforms' and of 'soldier's acquaintance' to 'soldier acquaintance'.

1912 Macmillan Wessex edition

By reverting to the original serial title for the story's appearance in the Wessex edition, Hardy chose to omit the description of the Hussar as being a member of the German Legion. This change of title might reflect an uncertainty in Hardy about the exact status of the German Legion and its relation to the York Hussars. This doubt can be seen as early as the 'Trumpet-Major Notebook', where Hardy wrote 'Any descripn. of York Hussars. Are they same as German Legion' (Taylor, p. 156). Within the story, he continued to refer to the two military formations as if they were one and the same, but perhaps an element of doubt led him to decide in 1912 not to be quite so assertive of the Hussar's allegiance in the title. Such caution was well placed, for, as George Lanning has shown, there was no connection between the York Hussars and the King's German Legion, and they were not even in existence at the same time, the former being disbanded in 1802 and the latter being founded the following year. The two Germans were shot in 1801 and therefore they were members of the York Hussars.

There are only half a dozen differences between *1894* and the Wessex edition. The latter alters a misprint of 'Goold' to 'Gould' (p. 61), but also introduces one by printing 'conscience-stricken' as 'conscious-stricken' (p. 59). Another revision makes the topography consistent with the other volumes in the Wessex edition, so that a reference to 'the Isle of Portland' becomes 'Portland – the Isle of Slingers –' (p. 49). A typical stylistic revision sees Hardy substituting 'such a while' (p. 54) for 'so long' to avoid repeating that phrase in the following sentence.[6]

Notes

1 See Millgate, p. 300, Purdy, pp. 72–3, and *Letters*, I, 201.
2 Another of the entries in the Notebook refers to the *Morning Chronicle* of 2 March 1803 and reads simply: 'Breach of Promise & Elopement – interesting' (Taylor, p. 130). Kathryn King plausibly suggested that this note might be a source for the plot of 'The Melancholy Hussar', but she had not been able to locate the *Morning Chronicle* to check it (King, 1988, pp. 211–12).

   Hardy's note is a reference to a detailed account in the newspaper of a court case which covers three columns and is headed 'Breach of Promise of Marriage'. A Mr

Leeds claimed damages of £5000 from Elizabeth Cooke, *née* Cardinal, of Essex, who eloped with a sailor to Gretna Green, shortly after becoming engaged to Leeds. The court heard how Leeds had threatened to flog her and break her bones when they were married, and he had thrown a whip at her as a warning. He had also visited a brothel immediately after signing their marriage settlement and told his prospective father-in-law about it. When Cardinal not unreasonably eloped with her sailor, Leeds proposed to another woman three days later, and the verdict of the jury clearly shows that they did not believe he had suffered much distress: *'Damages One Shilling!!!'*

  Hardy obviously found the newspaper report 'interesting', but he does not appear to have used the information in any of his Napoleonic works and it is certainly not the source of 'The Melancholy Hussar'.

3 This note is located at the Harry Ransom Humanities Research Center in the University of Texas at Austin.

4 Ellis (1928), p. 398. Ellis first met Hardy in April 1913. See also Lowndes (1946): 'concerning Hardy's short stories, I remember feeling surprised to hear from him how many had been founded on fact. He particularly instanced "The Melancholy Hussar"' (p. 148).

5 Hardy seems to have deliberately departed from the entry he made in the 'Trumpet-Major Notebook', where the Hussars were said to have reached Guernsey. Perhaps Jersey had some special personal significance for him: as he wrote in the *Life*, 'the family, on Hardy's paternal side, [...] derived from the Jersey le Hardys who had sailed across to Dorset for centuries' (p. 9).

6 For the sake of a complete record, the other revisions to *1894* for the Wessex edition are as follows (*1912* is quoted first, and the pagination is that of *1912*): 'few minutes' pause/few minutes pause' (p. 64); 'firing party/firing-party' (p. 64).

CHAPTER 4

'The Withered Arm'

One of Hardy's favourite stories, 'The Withered Arm' was based on facts and superstitions which he had learned from his parents. His mother, Jemima, is the source of the details about conjurors and the effects of the incubus, while the hanging of Rhoda's son, who was 'only just turned eighteen, and only present by chance when the rick was fired', recalls his father's account of an incident in the 1830s. As Hardy told Newman Flower,

> My father saw four men hung for *being with* some others who had set fire to a rick. Among them was a stripling of a boy of eighteen. Skinny. Half-starved. So frail, so underfed, that they had to put weights on his feet to break his neck. He had not fired the rick. But with a youth's excitement he had rushed to the scene to see the blaze. [...] Nothing my father ever said to me drove the tragedy of Life so deeply into my mind.[1]

Jemima is also presumably the 'aged friend' mentioned in the 1896 Preface to *Wessex Tales* who had reminded him since writing the story that the incubus had oppressed the woman in daylight and not during a midnight dream.[2] Hardy seems to have been dwelling on Dorset superstition in September 1887, when he was writing the story, and also later that autumn, for the *Life* records several notes about local spells and folklore at this time, and the recollections of his mother and grandmother are also invoked (p. 211).

In September 1887 Hardy went walking in the Frome valley, the setting of 'The Withered Arm' and of 'The Waiting Supper', which he was also writing at this time. Towards the end of the month, he sent 'The Withered Arm' to *Longman's Magazine*, which had printed 'The Three Strangers' in 1883, but they rejected it as being too grim and unrelieved for a magazine read mostly by girls.[3] Within days of the rejection, Hardy submitted the unsolicited story to William Blackwood on 1 October:

> I take the liberty of sending you the MS. of a short story I have just written, which I think might suit Blackwood's Magazine. It is of rather a weird nature – but as the taste of readers seems to run in that direction just now perhaps its character is no disqualification. I may add that the cardinal incidents are true, both the women who figure in the story having been known to me. (*Letters*, I, 168)

Blackwood accepted 'The Withered Arm' later that month and Hardy wrote on 28 October to say that 'I am glad to hear that the story is likely to have the honour of a place in your magazine. It occurred to me, as it seems to have done to you, that the story had a Blackwood flavour about it – though not till I had finished writing it – which was what prompted me to send it up' (*Letters*, I, 169).

In March of the following year, he promised Blackwood that 'when I am again rambling in the country I must endeavour to find another weird subject for you. But the truth is that a really good tale of the sort comes but seldom, either to experience or invention' (*Letters*, I, 175).

The versions of the story which have textual significance are as follows:

Serial	*Blackwood's Edinburgh Magazine*, January 1888, pp. 30–48. Published anonymously. Hardy acknowledged payment of £24 on New Year's Day, 1888 (*Letters*, I, 171–2).
1888	*Wessex Tales*, 2 vols. (London: Macmillan, 1888), I, 55–126. Published at 12*s.* in an edition of 750 copies on 4 May 1888.
1896	*Wessex Tales* (London: Osgood, McIlvaine, 1896), pp. 63–104. Volume XIII in the Wessex Novels, the first uniform and complete edition of Hardy's works.
1912	*Wessex Tales* (London: Macmillan, 1912), pp. 67–108. Volume IX of the Wessex edition.

Hardy was always at pains to stress the factual nature of the tale, as in his initial letter of submission to Blackwood. For instance, shortly after its publication, he assured Lady Margaret Wallop that 'it is founded on fact. I have some more creepy ones in my mind: yes – creepier ones still!' and in 1904 he told Florence Henniker that it was 'largely based on fact'.[4] Rebekah Owen noted that Gertrude had a local original (Kathryn King provides the following useful summary of Owen's notes):

> Owen reports Hardy as naming the following elements in Gertrude's story as true: she dreamed that her arm was grasped by an enemy; it withered; she put up at the White Hart Inn when coming to the assizes; she 'took that remedy' (presumably the touching of the corpse); and eventually, though not at the jail, she died persuaded she was bewitched. 'I believe', noted Owen, 'I am safe in assuming that the connection of Rhoda and her son with Gertrude and her husband are "where fiction comes in"' (King, 1988, p. 183).

Hardy also revealed to Rebekah Owen that Davies was the name of the hangman, who was a family friend.[5] Of Conjuror Trendle, he told Hermann Lea in 1907 that 'I do not remember what his real name was, or rather, he is a composite figure of two or three who used to be heard of. I have a vague idea that Baker was the name of one, but cannot be sure' (*Letters*, III, 264). As early as 1872, Hardy made a memorandum about a conjuror who lived in Blackmoor Vale and who performed precisely the kind of divination which Trendle effects for Gertrude: 'he would cause your enemy to rise in a glass of water. He did not himself know your enemy's name, but the bewitched person did, of course, recognizing the form as the one he had expected' (Taylor, p. 12).

Serial

On 9 December, William Blackwood sent proof of the serial and noted that 'on margin of proof I have made a few suggestions for your consideration'.[6] Hardy replied two days later:

> I am much obliged for the proof, which I am now reading, & will return to you at Edinburgh. The oversights to which you kindly draw attention shall be corrected. One little change elsewhere has occurred to me – & I think you will consider it an improvement – that of making the farmer die a natural death, & as a chastened man, rather than by his own hand. If however you should think the latter more striking please restore the original text. (*Letters*, I, 170)

Blackwood agreed with Hardy's suggestion and he wrote on 30 December to say that he thought his revision was 'a decided improvement'. In the absence of the manuscript, it is impossible to know what alterations Blackwood himself had proposed.

Although 'The Withered Arm' was published anonymously in accordance with *Blackwood's* usual practice, Hardy made no effort to disguise its authorship, telling Blackwood that 'I fancy readers will detect me on account of the scenery of the story – that is, if they take the trouble – though readers are very obtuse in such matters' (*Letters*, I, 171). Hardy was pleased with its reception and told Arthur Blomfield on 18 January that 'if you are inclined for a neat thing in *weird* tales, read one of mine which appears in this months [sic] *Blackwood*. I myself thought nothing of it, but the papers say that it is very striking, & of course I am bound to believe them' (*Letters*, I, 173). He mentioned his 'little story' in a letter to Edmund Gosse at the end of January, saying that 'it attracted more notice than I expected – perhaps because it was unsigned – & an eminent critic wrote to me about it' (*Letters*, I, 173).

The critic was Leslie Stephen, who had written to say that he thought the story was weakened by a failure to explain the withering or to call it hallucinatory:

> I don't think that you have exactly hit off the right line of belief. Either I would accept the superstition altogether and make the wizard a genuine performer – with possibly some hint that you tell the story as somebody told it; or I would leave some opening as to the withering of the arm, so that a possibility of explanation might be suggested, though, of course, not too much obtruded. Something, *e.g.* might have happened to impress the sufferer's imagination, so that the marks would be like the stigmata of papists.
>
> As it is, I don't know where I am. I begin as a believer and end up as a sceptic.[7]

Hardy gave his opinion of Stephen's criticism during a conversation about the story with S.M. Ellis (Meredith's nephew) in April 1913. As Ellis remembers,

> It was at our first meeting that he told me *The Withered Arm* was founded on fact, and he agreed with me that a story dealing with the supernatural

should never be explained away in the unfortunate manner of Mrs. Radcliffe. Mr. Hardy added that Leslie Stephen wrote to him protesting that the mystery in this story should have been dispersed by a normal solution, which the author regarded as a dull and unimaginative example of gratuitous criticism.[8]

When Hardy came to revise 'The Withered Arm' for its first collected publication a month or two after Stephen's letter, he introduced five small revisions which question the validity of Rhoda's belief in her supernatural experience but which go only a very little way towards meeting Stephen's objections. For instance, the serial tells us that 'Rhoda Brook dreamed – if her assertion that she really saw, before falling asleep, was not to be believed', but *1888* alters the speculative 'if' to a dismissive 'since'. The next morning, she 'would not explain' in the serial to her son what the noise in her room had been (that is, she knows but will not say), whereas *1888* says she 'could not explain' (it is a mystery to her). When she learns from Gertrude that her arm started to hurt at the same hour as her own dream, the serial says that 'she could not understand the coincidence', but *1888* pours cold water on this enigma and replaces it entirely with the commonsensical reproof that 'she did not reason on the freaks of coincidence'. The serial asserts as fact that the outline of four fingers on Gertrude's arm is precisely where Rhoda had clutched the arm in her trance, but later editions say merely that 'she fancied that' it was so. Finally, Rhoda is said to have 'good reason' in the serial to be superstitious, but this was later changed to 'a haunting reason', implying that she is simply obsessed by her experience.

The serial is set in Stickleford (Tincleton), about five miles east of Casterbridge, but all later versions locate it in Holmstoke, which is a combination of the names of two actual villages, East Holme and East Stoke, some eight miles further east along the Frome valley.[9] No descriptive changes were made to the story and only the placename was altered, for no apparent reason. It would appear, then, that Hardy originally conceived of the action taking place in the dairyland west of Wareham, near East Holme and East Stoke, but confusingly called the location Stickleford, which elsewhere in his work (e.g., 'The Romantic Adventures of a Milkmaid') corresponds to Tincleton. 'Swenn' is used as the name of the river which in *Tess* became the Frome. Kathryn King says of the topography in general that Hardy

> locates the action [...] in relation to the Egdon Heath rather than to the river, as might be expected for a story that follows *Return of the Native*, but comes before the imaginative charting of the Frome and 'The Valley of the Great Dairies' that would wait until the development of the setting of *Tess*. (1988, p. 194)

1888 Macmillan

'The Withered Arm' is easily the latest of the five stories which Hardy collected to form *Wessex Tales*, being first published in serial form between five and nine years after the others. His first reference to the proposed volume is when he submitted it to Macmillan on 29 February 1888, just a couple of months after 'The Withered Arm' had first appeared. Shortly after Macmillan had accepted the proposal to publish the volume, Hardy wrote to William Blackwood on 10 March for permission to reprint 'The Withered Arm'. On 14 March, Hardy wrote again to thank Blackwood for his consent, adding that he agreed to the latter's proposal 'to include the same story in your "Tales"' (*Letters*, I, 175), but 'The Withered Arm' does not appear, in fact, to have been published in any of the *Tales from 'Blackwood'* volumes.

One small detail in the story indicates that Hardy might have been thinking of the collected volume and the sequence of its tales while he was writing 'The Withered Arm'. In the penultimate paragraph of the story, Farmer Lodge retires to Port-Bredy (this may have been added in the December revision of the ending in the serial proof), and thus the story as it stands in the collected edition leads into the following one, 'Fellow-Townsmen', which is set entirely in Port-Bredy. The two tales have a certain symmetry in the volume: in 'The Withered Arm', a mournful widower moves to Port-Bredy and stays for the rest of his life, while in 'Fellow-Townsmen' a relieved widower eventually quits the place for ever.

In addition to the alterations to the serial discussed above, Hardy took the opportunity to make about twenty other revisions to the story, even though he had first published it so recently, and most of these involve just an individual word or two. By far the longest of these changes is the insertion of a sentence to emphasize Gertrude's growing obsession with finding a cure for her withered arm: 'instead of her formal prayers each night, her unconscious prayer was, "O Lord, hang some guilty or innocent person soon!"' Her reaction to the entry of the corpse is also slightly altered: in the serial she 'half-fainted and could not finish', but *1888* makes the scene more dramatic, saying that it was as if she had 'nearly died, but was held up by a sort of galvanism'. Another new gothic detail is that the hangman uncovers the face of the corpse before laying Gertrude's arm across the dead man's neck.

1896 Osgood, McIlvaine

Hardy made a score of alterations for *1896*, none involving more than a phrase. The most prominent tendency is the introduction of half a dozen dialect forms to replace standard usage, so that 'brings', 'has' and 'are', for instance, become 'do bring', 'hav'' and 'be'. They are all in the first six pages of the story, as if Hardy was seeking to establish the sound of the dialect at the outset and then trusting the reader to imagine it.

Wessex topography is slightly altered. A reference to the Swenn valley, the name which Hardy originally gave to the Frome both in this story and in 'The Romantic Adventures of a Milkmaid', is omitted to make it consistent with the rest of the uniform Osgood, McIlvaine edition, where the river is called the Froom. The pool outside Casterbridge where Gertrude halts and sees the workmen erecting a scaffold at the jail is named for the first time as Rushy-pond, which is on the heath near Hardy's birthplace. Gertrude thus enacts a scene from Hardy's youth when he witnessed an execution at the jail through a telescope from the same spot (see *Life*, pp. 32–3).

Hardy removed an amusing piece of gallows-humour in creating this edition. In earlier versions, the hangman told Gertrude that he never left Casterbridge, and added 'though sometimes I make others leave'. This is replaced in *1896* by the mundane information that 'my real calling is officer of justice'. King suggests that Hardy wished to make the hangman, based on a friend of the Hardy family, more serious and professional, thus distinguishing him from the hangman in 'The Three Strangers', who is given to making grim jests about his occupation (King, 1988, p. 199; see also Weber, 1939, pp. 70, 71, quoted in n. 5 below). Finally, there are two revisions concerning Rhoda and Gertrude. The former is introduced to us as being 'fading' rather than 'faded', which seems a more appropriate description of a woman who is only thirty years of age. Gertrude fears that the mark on her arm may become 'an incurable wound'; this replaces 'a permanent blemish' which hardly sounded sufficiently serious to justify her trip to see the conjuror.

1912 Macmillan Wessex edition

There are another twenty differences between *1896* and *1912*, two-thirds of which are substantive. The most significant are two revisions which continue the process of asserting that Rhoda was asleep when she experienced Gertrude's nocturnal visit. Thus, a statement that Rhoda had 'seen her' in her chamber becomes 'dreamt of' her, and 'the scene' of that night becomes 'the dream-scene'.

The date of the hanging is altered from 'near twenty years' after 1813 to 'near twelve years'. As F.B. Pinion notes, this places it in the mid-1820s when there were many outbreaks of rioting and arson among agricultural labourers after the Napoleonic Wars.[10]

The many-forked stand on which the farm workers hang their pails is said for the first time to be made 'as usual' of the peeled limb of an oak-tree. Kristin Brady makes an excellent comment on this addition:

> The 'as usual' of this sentence was added in 1912 – an effort, it would seem, to emphasize the stand's traditional shape and use. The dairy is thus an emblem of its transitional time, exemplifying the beginnings of modern agricultural organization and management in its status as a rented farm, but continuing to appear 'old-style' in its appurtenances and in the garb of its workers – as well as in their superstitious beliefs. (Brady, p. 24)

Hardy here is the rural antiquarian, recording a vanished country practice and once again injecting the historical into his tale of the pastoral and the supernatural. Another historical detail may be introduced when Conjuror Trendle explains that he drinks a glass of grog 'at your expense', his only payment for his divination.

Hardy took the opportunity in 1912 to remove any possible ambiguity or inconsistency. For instance, in earlier editions the hangman had told Gertrude that 'you must get into jail' when there was to be a hanging, which makes it sound as if he is advising her to get herself arrested and locked up, so *1912* more clearly reads 'you must go to the jail when there's a hanging'. An inconsistency occurred when Gertrude was described in previous versions of the story as riding into Casterbridge on her 'mare'. This contradicts the information a couple of pages earlier that her husband had not kept his promise always to maintain a mare for her, so *1912* alters 'mare' to 'bearer'.[11]

Notes

1 Flower (1950), p. 92. Four years later, Hardy used the detail about putting weights on the boy's feet in his description of Jack Winter's hanging in 'The Winters and the Palmleys'. See also Hardy's letter to William Rothenstein in March 1912 (*Letters*, IV, 206).

2 This is presumably what Hardy meant when he told the Owen sisters that 'he learnt *all* the details and ending after he had published the story; in some respects they were more gruesome than in his version. Gertrude Lodge was sleeping on a hot afternoon, when she had this dream or nightmare that her arm was grasped by an enemy, or a witch'. He learned such details 'from a more authentic source than the first teller of it' (Weber, 1939, p. 70; see also Weber, 1952, pp. 66, 238).

3 C.J. Longman's letter of rejection, dated 27 September 1887, is in the Dorset County Museum.

4 *Letters*, I, 172, and III, 151.

5 Weber, 1952, p. 238. 'He is not the hangman of "The Three Strangers"; had not his characteristics' (Weber, 1939, p. 70; see also p. 71, where Hardy described him as '"quite another sort of man"').

6 Blackwood's letters quoted here are in the Dorset County Museum.

7 Maitland (1906), pp. 393–4.

8 Ellis, (1928), p. 397.

9 This is the explanation which Hardy gave Rebekah Owen; see Weber, 1952, p. 71.

10 See Pinion, ed., *Wessex Tales*, p. 375.

11 For the sake of a complete record, the other differences between *1896* and the Wessex edition which have not previously been mentioned are as follows (*1912* is quoted first, and the pagination is that of *1912*): 'milk streams/milk-streams' (p. 70); 'twilight/twilight,' (p. 71); 'evening/evening,' (p. 72); 'bright/bright,' (p. 72); 'faced/face' (p. 72; *1912* is a misprint); 'wired/caught' (p. 75); 'frame/frame,' (p. 80); 'slopes/hills' (p. 87); 'the mixture/them' (p. 89); 'Half a dozen/Half-a-dozen' (p. 91); 'to tell her husband privately/to privately tell her husband' (p. 98); 'wownd/place' (p. 103); 'woman/girl' (p. 105); 'corpse/copse' (p. 106; *1896* is a misprint).

CHAPTER 5

'Fellow-Townsmen'

If it is safe to assume that the stories in *Wessex Tales* were first published shortly after they were written, then 'Fellow-Townsmen' was probably composed at Upper Tooting in 1880, during the interval between *The Return of the Native* and *The Trumpet-Major*.

This story, like 'The Distracted Young Preacher' the previous year, was printed in the *New Quarterly Magazine* because of Hardy's friendship with its Dorset-born editor, Charles Kegan Paul, who was, 'after Leslie Stephen, the literary figure who did most to assist Hardy and advance his reputation at this still early period' of his career, as Michael Millgate puts it.[1] In October 1879, Hardy had published his review of Barnes's *Poems of Rural Life in the Dorset Dialect* in the *New Quarterly* (the only one he ever wrote), and the magazine had also printed in 1879 a long and generally favourable essay on his work, 'Mr. Hardy's Novels', the first extended survey of its kind. The critic was Mrs Sutherland Orr, and Hardy declared that he had 'nothing but the warmest expressions of gratitude to offer the writer' (*Letters*, I, 67). Hardy must have felt assured of a serious and sympathetic reception when writing 'Fellow-Townsmen' with all its unrelieved marital misery: while he observed the proprieties in preparing his story for the magazine public, the unrelenting grim irony remains constant throughout. Incidentally, Hardy's friendship with Kegan Paul may have contributed a detail to the story, as Kathryn King points out: the two men had first met at the Savile Club, and Kegan Paul had helped Hardy to obtain election to the club in June 1878, hence Lucy Savile's surname.[2]

Hardy had originally intended to serialize the story in America in the May 1880 issue of *Harper's New Monthly Magazine*, but it reached New York too late and was instead included in *Harper's Weekly*, for which Hardy received £40 in payment (see *Letters*, I, 72). In 1893, Hardy told Florence Henniker that '"Fellow-Townsmen" is one I thought rather good myself; but it is a story to write *after* you have drawn attention to your work, rather than to draw it with' (*Letters*, II, 33), and in 1904 he told her that she was correct to prefer 'Fellow-Townsmen' to 'The Three Strangers' because 'there is more human nature in it' (*Letters*, III, 151).

The versions of the story which have textual significance are as follows:

NQM   *New Quarterly Magazine*, April 1880, pp. 335–83.

HW   *Harper's Weekly*, 5 instalments, 17 April–15 May 1880, pp. 246–7, 262–3, 278–9, 294–5, 314–15. The content of each instalment was as follows: 1st: Chapters 1–2; 2nd: Chapters 3–5; 3rd: Chapters 6–7; 4th: Chapter 8; 5th: Chapter 9.

1880   *Fellow-Townsmen* (New York: Harper & Brothers, 1880). R.L. Purdy writes that 'while it was still running in their magazine, Harper & Brothers, using the same types, issued it in this separate edition, to forestall piracy. It was published at 20 cents (15 cents extra for flexible cloth) as No. 136 in Harper's Half-Hour Series at the end of April 1880' (pp. 30–31).

1888   *Wessex Tales*, 2 vols. (London: Macmillan, 1888), I, 127–247. Published at 12*s*. in an edition of 750 copies on 4 May 1888.

1896   *Wessex Tales* (London: Osgood, McIlvaine, 1896), pp. 105–72. Volume XIII in the Wessex Novels, the first uniform and complete edition of Hardy's works.

1912   *Wessex Tales* (London: Macmillan, 1912), pp. 111–73. Volume IX of the Wessex edition.

No manuscript of the story is known to have survived.

Serials

In 1910, thirty years after he had written the story, Hardy told the publisher John Lane that the American serial versions of 'Fellow-Townsmen' and 'The Distracted Young Preacher' 'are merely reprints from the magazines in which those stories appeared, are uncorrected, & were issued before copyright, – I think without my knowledge' (*Letters*, IV, 97). Hardy seems mistaken in at least one respect here, for the American serial of 'Fellow-Townsmen' in *Harper's Weekly* is not at all a reprint of the British serial. There are numerous minor substantive differences between the two serials, and it would appear instead that the American serial is an earlier version of the story, perhaps set from proofs, which Hardy later further emended before the story appeared in the *New Quarterly Magazine*.

Before examining the distinctive features of each of the serials, however, I would like to study their common elements which distinguish them from later collected editions. The most important alterations concern the whole of Chapter One, where events and scenes are different, and most of Chapter Two, in which the conversation between Barnet and Lucy reveals a previous relationship between them which, in the serial, was markedly less advanced than it was to become in later versions.

The action in the serials begins with Barnet violently banging his front door and walking round to Downe's house in the rain, where he finds his friend and family examining a pile of picture-books around a lamp-lit table. It must have been the sheer mawkishness and sentimentality of this domestic bliss which led Hardy to omit it entirely in later editions. Barnet walks round the room, touching the cheeks and patting the heads of the children, and then surveys this family group:

Though they could lay no special claim to elegance, they constituted a perfect scene of domestic cheerfulness and comfort, which Barnet seemed to recognise very clearly; for, with the privilege of an old acquaintance, he remained silently thinking for some time, while the children resumed their occupation of turning over leaves.

'How happy you are!' he said at length, half involuntarily. ''Tis a treat to come and see you, Downe, – you fortunate fellow!'

In the collected editions, the story begins with Barnet driving into town, where he meets Downe and gives him a lift home, forming a parallel with the ending of the story, where Barnet leaves the town forever. We do not witness the cosy domestic interior, and Mrs Downe speaks only eleven words, so that her presence is greatly diminished. She has barely featured in the narrative, so that her drowning in Chapter Four is not a distraction.

A cumbersome incident in the opening of the serials is a slightly ludicrous scene where Downe, who has a poisoned thumb, accidentally raps it on a table and appears to faint, and the ensuing fuss and wifely devotion (Mrs Downe kisses him 'a good half-dozen smacks') take up a couple of pages. This excessively obvious contrast with Barnet's own home life is made much more economically in later editions, where Downe slips on getting out of the carriage and lands on his knees, his wife helping him to his feet. The touching tableau is disposed of in ten lines.

The serials do not show Barnet returning home and receiving his wife's cold message that she is with her dressmaker and so he must dine alone. The importance of the addition of this scene to the collected editions is that it establishes a sharp contrast between the two wives and the two homes, and it proves that Barnet is being accurate in his description of his wife's haughty indifference to him. This establishes the basis for the irony of Barnet having to revive her after she has apparently drowned; in the serials, we have only Barnet's version of their marriage, and his hesitation to revive her seems simply callous because her conduct towards him has not been dramatized. Another consequence of these changes to the serial is pointed out by Kathryn King: 'the 88 revisions reverse the reader's point of view in regard to the settings: the Downe home is seen only from outside, and it is the cold, childless Barnet household that the reader enters' (1988, p. 118).

Barnet's visit to Lucy's cottage in Chapter Two is also largely altered in tone. In a sentence which later editions omit, the serials show Lucy as presenting a rather severe image: 'her hair was brushed plainly over her forehead, and her dress was black'. On entering her apartment, Barnet in the serials asks Lucy to give him her hand 'as an old acquaintance' and there is still no indication of the nature of their previous relationship. In the collected editions, however, he is much more forward and frank: 'you can give your hand to me, seeing how often I have held it in past days?', he begins, and later he explains that he has come, 'not to mince matters, to visit a woman I loved'. In the revised version, he moves quickly away from the servant who admits him so that he will not be recognized, an acknowledgement of his dubious behaviour as a married man that the magazine versions could not permit.

When Lucy and Barnet talk of their last meeting and the silence which followed it, it is clear that in the serials their relationship had been in a much less advanced state than it was later to appear. Lucy specifically states that there was 'no compact of any sort between us' and that 'there had been nothing said by you which gave me any right to send you a letter. [...] You had made me no promises, and I did not feel that you had broken any.' She later assumed that Barnet had met another woman who was 'more after your own heart than I was'. In later versions, her reasons for not writing to Barnet are quite different: she did not feel that she had said anything which required an explanation, she saw that his position was so much wealthier than her own and that the future Mrs Barnet was of such a good family. Money and class here conspire to drive the lovers apart (although Barnet ironically declares that it was 'destiny – accident' that separated them). Lucy also feared that she 'might have mistaken your meaning', which would imply that Barnet did at least make some kind of declaration. In the serials, she proudly says that he does not know if she would have accepted any proposal from him, but later editions add that 'at this his eye met hers, and she dropped her gaze. She knew that her voice belied her.' Their conversation, then, in its later versions reveals a greater degree of commitment on both sides; this is necessary to make Barnet's choice between reviving his wife or marrying Lucy a very real one, for he knows now that Lucy would accept him.

In all of these changes to the serials discussed so far, it is characteristic of Hardy's revisions that he showed great economy in adapting existing text, salvaging or rearranging whatever he could.

Harper's Weekly

The American serial appears to be an early and unrevised version of the story, probably set from proofs which were later altered for its appearance in *New Quarterly Magazine*. There are some sixty instances of substantive variants between the two serials, though none is longer than a sentence in length, and the first collected edition in 1888 always follows the British reading.

Barnet's friend, Downe, undergoes a change of name during the American serial. His first wife calls him Charles, but he later signs a letter as 'J. Downe', and his second wife calls him John (*NQM* corrects this so he is called Charles throughout). Another confusion in names is that *HW* has three characters who are all known simply as Jones (a tradesman, the architect and a wine-merchant). *NQM* erased the last of these three, but the tradesman's name was altered to Smith only in 1888. A further mistake is that Barnet's eyes are described as being both hazel and gray in *HW*, and *NQM* settles for the former colour.

HW has three instances of a characteristic Hardy revision, where he altered a word in order to avoid repeating it in the same or an adjacent sentence. For instance, in Chapter Two of the American serial, we learn that 'Charlson had been in difficulties, and to oblige him Barnet had put his name to a bill; and, as he had expected, was obliged to meet it when it fell due'. Hardy later altered 'obliged' to read 'called upon' in the British serial. Such typical changes are further evidence that *HW* is an early unrevised version of the story.

New Quarterly Magazine

Hardy added two new sentences to *NQM* to emphasize the irony of Barnet's marital position. When his wife leaves him, he reflects that 'it was for this that he had gratuitously restored her to life, and made his union with another impossible!', and, on receiving news of her death, he thinks that 'surely his virtue in restoring his wife to life had been rewarded!', just moments before learning that Lucy is about to marry Downe.

1888 Macmillan

The location of the story had previously been unnamed, but in *1888* Hardy introduced three references to Port-Bredy (Bridport), and the Black Swan Hotel was changed to the Black-Bull, nearer to the name of the actual Bull Hotel. The distance of the town from the railway junction in the later part of the story is said to be twenty miles in the serials, but *1888* alters this to a dozen miles, which is approximately the distance between Bridport and the junction at Maiden Newton.[3]

There are about thirty other substantive changes to the serial version, mostly involving only a word or two, and none longer than a short phrase. The title of the lord whom Mrs Barnet reveres and whose name she takes for her new house is altered from Kingdale to Ringdale, perhaps because Hardy felt that his original name indicated his aristocratic connections too obviously.[4] Hardy also took the opportunity to clarify a puzzle in the plot. In the serials, Barnet's servant says there are two letters for him and he gives him the first one announcing his wife's death and causing him much elation at the prospect of marrying Lucy. Only then does the servant hand over the second letter in which Downe declares that he is marrying Lucy that very morning. It is not at all clear in the serials why the servant did not give Barnet both letters at the same time, and the gap between Barnet reading them, which is necessary to allow his hopes to be briefly built up before they are bluntly demolished, appears highly contrived and mysterious. Hardy remedies this in *1888* by showing the servant deliver the first letter and then adding that 'he searched his pocket for the second'.

A few minor details are changed. Two of these concern the appearance of the aged Charlson when Barnet meets him in the town after many years. Charlson's shoulders were originally said to have a 'shine', but *1888* alters this to the appropriately unpleasant 'greasiness', and he is later said to be 'needy' rather than 'seedy', a typically economical revision which explains why Barnet gives him money (Hardy made an identical alteration to 'Interlopers at the Knap' in the same edition). In the serials, Charlson says that Mrs Barnet was a drowned woman 'as far as I was concerned', but *1888* alters this to 'as far as the world was concerned', implying, perhaps, that she was *not* beyond all hope of recovery in his medical opinion, but that he was willing to certify death in order to please Barnet, to whom he was in debt.

The serials gave the age of the man who told Barnet about the sailing accident as 37 years, but *1888* deletes this information, since his age is hardly relevant to the role he plays in the story. The sailing-boat lying at the water's edge was originally said to be 'prostrate', but this adjective would be more appropriate to the woman lying beside it and *1888* alters it to 'lying draggled'.

1896 Osgood, McIlvaine

1896 appears to introduce a misprint which is retained in later editions. Earlier versions of the story had described how open ground appeared between the houses on either side, the 'tract' on the right hand rising to a higher level. *1896* reads 'track', which makes sense but is not as appropriate as 'tract' in a description of the open ground.

When Barnet sees his wife and Mrs Downe driving past on their way to the shore, he resolves not to do anything that would hazard the 'promise' of the day. This replaces 'glory', and is more pertinent since the importance of the trip for Barnet lies in its future consequences (Mrs Downe's influence on his wife's behaviour) rather than in the trip itself. 'Promise' is also more ironic, given the fatal outcome of their sailing trip.

Among the sixteen other substantive changes which Hardy made to the previous collected edition, the distance to the nearest railway from Port-Bredy in the first part of the story is said to be merely 'many miles', replacing the earlier 'eighty miles'. The servant who conveys his wife's message to Barnet that she had dined early and hoped that he would excuse her joining him that evening was originally said to have 'repeated' her former words to him after further enquiries. In *1896,* however, she 'transmitted' them, making clear that his wife is responsible for the cold message and that the servant is merely relaying it. Finally, when Barnet proposes to Lucy after his long absence, she gives a 'forced' laugh, rather than the previously 'feverish' one which made her appear rather neurotic and highly-strung.

1912 Macmillan Wessex edition

There are only nine substantive changes for the 1912 Wessex edition, and they are of little significance. Hardy took the opportunity to remove an ambiguity which had been in all earlier versions. After Barnet has read the two letters announcing his wife's death and Lucy's marriage, we were previously told that a close watcher would have seen a horizontal line forming across Barnet's forehead 'which he had never noticed before'. This raises irrelevant questions: who is this watcher and how often has he observed Barnet? Or is the phrase instead saying that the watcher had simply failed to spot it before? *1912*'s 'which had never been seen before' (p. 157) removes these difficulties and is unambiguous.

After the accident, Barnet's wife is brought home unconscious and taken to her chamber. Previously, Barnet had then stood 'mutely regarding the bed', but this was changed in *1912* to 'regarding the shape on the bed' (p. 136). This is a double improvement, since it is his wife and not the bed which interests him, and 'mutely' seems redundant because he is alone with his unconscious wife and is hardly likely to address her.[5]

Notes

1 Millgate, p. 207.

2 See King, 1988, pp. 109–10 and *Letters*, I, 57.

3 Pinion (1989, p. 217) notes that the description of West Bay as 'a little haven, seemingly a beginning made by Nature herself of a perfect harbour ... famous' is a paraphrase of Holinshed's description in Hutchins.

4 Both names may partly be suggested by 'Knapdale', the name which Alexander Macmillan, the publisher, had given to his house. Macmillan was a neighbour of the Hardys in Upper Tooting, and they visited him (see Morgan, pp. 66 and 99, and *Life*, pp. 124, 125 and 149).

5 For the sake of a complete record, the other revisions to *1896* for the Wessex edition which have not previously been mentioned are as follows (*1912* is quoted first, and the pagination is that of *1912*): 'friends/friends,' (p. 112); 'drizzle from the sea/drizzle' (p. 113); 'roadside/roadside,' (p. 118); 'rough gravel/common road' (p. 118); 'embarrassment/embarrassment,' (p. 121); 'He slowly/he slowly' (p. 122); 'carriage/carriage,' (p. 135); 'his domestic/their domestic' (p. 136); 'completeness/complete form' (p. 137); 'harbour-road/harbour-road,' (p. 144); 'makes/make' (p. 144); 'book/roll' (p. 154); 'Then/then' (p. 154); 'town/town,' (p. 157); 'round/round,' (p. 158); 'no:/no,' (p. 159); 'tray/meal' (p. 170).

CHAPTER 6

'Interlopers at the Knap'

Hardy wrote 'Interlopers at the Knap' in Dorchester during the interval between *Two on a Tower* and *The Mayor of Casterbridge*. He seems to have completed it by January 1884, when he told a correspondent that 'I have nothing in hand at present beyond a story which will, I believe, appear in the English Illustrated' (*Letters*, I, 125). It was first published in May of that year, and a few days after its appearance he mentioned in a letter to Henry Atkinson that 'I am glad to hear that the little story was attractive enough to interest your listeners & yourself' (VII, 100).

The opening of the story is partly based on the journey which Hardy's father made from Puddletown to Melbury Osmond on the eve of his wedding in 1839, accompanied by James Sparks, Jemima's brother-in-law. Hardy told Rebekah Owen that 'it was my father who rode along ... and was obliged to climb the guide post and strike a light, finding nothing on the fingers of the post' (Weber, 1952, p. 238). Sally's house is based on the one in Melbury Osmond which had belonged to Jemima's ancestors, the Swetmans and Childses, and which is also depicted in the poem, 'One who Married above Him'. The name of the house, Kathryn King suggests, may derive from 'Knapdale', the name which Alexander Macmillan, the publisher, had given to his house in Upper Tooting, where he was a neighbour of the Hardys from 1878–81.[1] Hardy confirmed the setting in a letter of 1911 to Hermann Lea, who was preparing *Thomas Hardy's Wessex*: 'on looking over the story ('Interlopers') I think a general view of Melbury Osmond would be best, if any – the house I had in mind being quite swept away & the tree gone. [...] It is the only story in the whole series in which I was thinking entirely of Melbury Osmund [sic]' (*Letters*, IV, 164). As King notes, 'Interlopers' contains 'Hardy's earliest portrayal of the wooded "Hintocks" region [and] was written about two years before he began *The Woodlanders*' (1991, p. 239). As for the dating of the action, this is the only story in *Wessex Tales* where the time is not specified beyond a vague reference to 'some few years ago', but the reappearance of Darton in *The Mayor of Casterbridge* suggests that 'Interlopers' too can be placed around the middle of the nineteenth century.[2]

The versions of the story which have textual significance are as follows:

Serial	*English Illustrated Magazine*, May 1884, pp. 501–14.
1888	*Wessex Tales*, 2 vols. (London: Macmillan, 1888), II, 1–75. Published at 12s. in an edition of 750 copies on 4 May 1888.
1889	*Wessex Tales* (London: Macmillan, 1889). Macmillan reissued the collection in one volume in an edition of 1500

1896   copies in late February 1889. See Purdy, p. 60.

1896   *Wessex Tales* (London: Osgood, McIlvaine, 1896), pp. 173–215. Volume XIII in the Wessex Novels, the first uniform and complete edition of Hardy's works.

1903   *Wessex Tales* (London: Macmillan, 1903). Macmillan's reissue of *1896*.

1912   *Wessex Tales* (London: Macmillan, 1912), pp. 177–214. Volume IX of the Wessex edition.

No manuscript of the story is known to have survived.

English Illustrated Magazine and *1888* Macmillan

Many of the changes to 'Interlopers' at each stage of revision were topographical, and Pinion correctly observes that the topography of the story in the serial was more accurate than in later versions. At the start, for instance, Darton and Johns in the serial are said to be taking the 'north-west road' from Casterbridge, which 'is called' Holloway Lane, but in *1888* they are on the 'north road' which 'connects with' the Lane. The serial, as Pinion puts it, 'shows more clearly where the wrong road was taken and how The Knap was subsequently three miles off to the left'.[3] In the serial, Sally lives in 'the old-fashioned village of Hintock Abbas', but this is revised in *1888* to 'an old-fashioned village – one of the Hintocks (several of which lay thereabout)', perhaps to add an element of disguise and also to reflect the greater diversity of the Hintocks which Hardy had created in *The Woodlanders* since first publishing the story. Helena in the serial changes her dress in 'the Abbot's Barn', and Hardy may have had in mind the Abbey Barn at Cerne Abbas (seven miles north of Dorchester), whose Wessex name is Abbot's Cernel and which he had used as the model for the Great Barn in *Far from the Madding Crowd*. Phil explains to his mother that he had been given the parcel at Verton to deliver to Sally, and had caught up with his wife at the Abbot's Barn. Rebekah Owen identified Verton as Longburton (Weber, 1952, p. 238), which is on the same road as Cerne Abbas, but this means that Phil is approaching home from the north and has gone too far south for the road to Melbury Osmond when he reaches Cerne Abbas. Clearly, Hardy did not seek any close correspondence between Dorset and Wessex when he was preparing the serial. In *1888*, 'the Abbot's Barn' became 'the Lower Barn', perhaps in order to avoid suggesting Cerne Abbas. 'Verton', a name which Hardy does not appear to have used elsewhere, was changed in *1896*, for reasons which will be discussed below. The carrier who is bringing Sally's dress was said in the serial to have reached Verton from Casterbridge, which meant that he had gone north past Melbury Osmond, but in *1888* he sets out from Sherton Abbas, so that he is still heading towards Sally's home when he meets Phil and gives him the dress to deliver to his sister.

Mrs Hall in the serial uses 'ye' for 'you' on just one occasion, and this inconsistency is corrected in *1888*. Her reunion with her son Phil is made more dramatic in *1888* by the addition of her interjection, 'Oh, Phil!', the references to her 'sinking down confounded' and 'clasping her hands' in despair at the news that he has a wife and children, and his 'bitterly' offering to go away again. A description of Phil in the serial as 'seedy' becomes 'needy' in *1888*, a typically economic revision which is identical to one which Hardy made in 'Fellow-Townsmen' for the same edition. In the serial, Darton curiously omitted to explain the reason for his delayed arrival, but in *1888* he immediately tells Mrs Hall that 'we lost our way, which made us late'. The relatives to whom Helena applies for financial help after Phil's death were said in the serial to live in India, but they are later said to live in 'the north'.

1889 Macmillan one-volume edition

I am indebted to Kathryn King for the observation that Hardy made a revision for this one-volume edition. He wrote to Frederick Macmillan on 13 October 1888 that

> It occurs to me to ask if you think it worth while to print a cheap edition of the "Wessex Tales" – or to make a cheap edition of the same typesetting, so as to produce a companion volume to the 6/– edn of The Woodlanders.
>
> Or would this be an opportunity of trying a very cheap bookstall edition of the Tales, say at 2/– or 2/6. (*Letters*, I, 180)

Macmillan's one-volume edition of *Wessex Tales* is closely similar in format to their one-volume edition of *The Woodlanders*, published in September 1887.

King explains the publisher's reaction to Hardy's letter:

> Macmillan liked the idea, and immediately directed his printers to begin work setting up a one-volume edition. Hardy made one change. In Macmillan's letter book is a transcript of a note requesting that the name 'Holloway Lane' be altered: 'Holloway Lane is mentioned more than once in the Wessex Tale called Interlopers at the Knap – I think it occurs once more on the first page and again at the end – so that Long-Ash Lane may be substituted for all' (Macmillan Archives, British Library).[4]

Long-Ash Lane is the actual name of a stretch of the road between Dorchester and Yeovil. This change involved five substitutions and was of course made possible because the two names had the same number of characters. This would appear to be Hardy's first use of the actual name of the road.[5]

1896 Osgood, McIlvaine

Verton, as previously mentioned, was the original place where Phil obtained Sally's dress from the carrier, but Rebekah Owen pointed out to Hardy that it was unsuitable:

> With regard to the village of 'Verton' [...], Miss Owen identified it as Long
> Burton [sic], but noted that Hardy placed it in a wrong position with
> relation to King's Hintock for a man to pass through, plausibly, on arriving
> (say, at Southampton) from Australia. In the next edition of *Wessex Tales*,
> Hardy changed 'Verton' to read 'Evershead' (i.e., Evershot). (Weber, 1952,
> p. 238)

Weber believes that Hardy paid tribute to Rebekah Owen's help and he gives a
rather gushing explanation of the change to a character's name in this edition:
originally, 'the woman who "assisted at the dairy" [...] was named Susannah.
Then Hardy "fired" her, and installed Rebekah in her place. There she is to this
day. "Rebekah was the woman who assisted...." And in all truthfulness she did
assist' (1952, pp. 226–7; see also Weber, 1939, p. 72).

Hardy's other topographical revisions at this time introduced a greater
accuracy in the use of names and places. Now that Phil passes through
Evershead instead of Verton on his way home, he no longer stops at the 'Dog'
inn, as he had done in *1888*, but at the 'Sow-and-Acorn', a name which reflects
the actual Acorn Inn at Evershot and which had previously appeared in 'The
First Countess of Wessex' and *Tess*.[6] Another inn which is described differently
in *1896* is the one at which Helena's son is transferred into Darton's care: in
earlier versions it had been 'the "Pack-Horse," a roadside inn', but this now
became 'the "White Horse" of Chalk Newton', the real name of the inn at
Maiden Newton. (Hardy had been shown around the inn in September 1888: see
Life, p. 223.) However, the name of another inn is removed: Darton and Johns in
the serial and *1888* had stayed at the 'Sheaf of Arrows', but in *1896* the name is
replaced by various references to it as a little roadside ale-house half a mile from
Sally's house, and it is now behind rather than ahead of the two men (this
direction was to be reversed again in *1912*). There is more detail about Sally's
village in *1896*: in the previous edition, it had been described as 'one of the
Hintocks (several of which lay thereabout)', which was now revised to read 'one
of the Hintocks (several villages of that name, with a distinctive prefix or affix,
lying thereabout)'; this is a change which permits the revision later in the story of
'Hintock village-street' to 'Great-Hintock village-street'.

Dialect is occasionally altered in *1896*: Darton's friend, Johns, has half a
dozen extra non-standard forms, saying 'climm' (for 'climb'), 'have eat',
'natyves', 'o'' (for 'of'), 'ha'' (for 'have') and 'contrairy'. Sally, on the other
hand, loses a dialectal form, and says 'of it' instead of the earlier 'o't'. This
increasing divergence of the two characters serves in part to explain why she
rejects Johns as a suitor. There are a few other minor revisions: Long-Ash Lane
had previously been said to have once been a highway to Queen Elizabeth's
'court', but this was altered in *1896* to 'subjects' to avoid the possible ambiguity
of seeming to say that the Lane led to the queen's residence, rather than being a
highway for her courtiers. Finally, when Darton went to propose a second time to
Sally, he originally drank a glass of negus at the inn where he was staying; Hardy
may have felt that this drink (hot port and lemon, spiced and sweetened) was not
readily familiar to his readers, and it was changed in *1896* to the vague

description of Darton having 'something to drink'.

1903 Macmillan

Kathryn King notes one change to the story in Macmillan's reissue of *1896* in their Uniform edition: at the beginning of Part II, 'Great-Hintock' became 'King's-Hintock'. The alterations to 'Interlopers' in 1889 and 1903 were the only ones authorized by Hardy in those editions of *Wessex Tales*, a fact which 'attests to [his] unusual regard for topography in a story that is not in other respects especially distinguished' (King, 1988, p. 173; see also p. 175).

1912 Macmillan Wessex edition

Hardy took the opportunity when revising the story for the Wessex edition to provide further details about the White Horse Inn at Chalk Newton, noting that it was 'the fine old Elizabethan inn' and adding the footnote that 'it is now pulled down, and its site occupied by a modern one in red brick'. Hardy had inspected the 'White Horse' in October 1897 and written a report on its conservation for the Society for the Protection of Ancient Buildings (see *Letters*, II, 178–9), but the inn was demolished in 1900, so the increased prominence which he gives the building in 1912 seems to strike a note of antiquarian regret.

Other topographical revisions concern Long-Ash Lane and the neighbourhood of Sally's village. In earlier versions of the story, Darton and Johns walked along the straight Lane for several miles until 'it now took a turn' and began winding uncertainly for some distance. This is inaccurate, since the Lane is a Roman road, and so Hardy altered the phrase in *1912* to read 'they now left it for a smaller one'. It is this new track which is said to wind uncertainly. We also learn for the first time that Sally's house stood 'only a mile or two from King's-Hintock Court, yet quite shut away from that mansion and its precincts'.

Hardy took the opportunity in the Wessex edition to clarify the plot on a couple of occasions. When Darton and Helena first meet again, she now explains how she emigrated and ended up as Phil's wife: 'And he went to Australia, and sent for me, and I joined him out there', to which Darton replies, 'Ah – that was the mystery!' Another revision removes a statement that does not make sense: in earlier versions, Sally denies to Darton that she had heard of his alleged bankruptcy when refusing his last offer of marriage, and then adds, 'But if I had, 'twould have been all the same.' Sally seems to be saying that, if she *had* heard that he was bankrupt, she would *still* have refused him. In the Wessex edition, Hardy replaced this sentence with Sally's following comment: 'That you believed me capable of refusing you for such a reason does not help your cause.'

The name of Darton's farm hand who accompanies him and Johns on their trip to Sally's house is changed in *1912*, so that earlier references to him as Enoch and Nocky now become Ezra and Ezzy respectively. Hardy may have felt that Enoch, the name of the son of Cain, was rather too portentous for the witless worker, and he had anyway used the name for Geoffrey Day's keeper who was put in the stocks at the end of *Under the Greenwood Tree*. Ezra, which is Hebrew for 'help', may be more appropriate for the character's role in this story.[7]

Notes

1 King, 1988, p. 129. For details of Macmillan's house and the Hardys' visits, see Morgan, pp. 66 and 99, and *Life*, pp. 124, 125 and 149.

2 See Brady, p. 3, and King, 1991, p. 240.

3 Pinion, *Wessex Tales*, p. 375. Kay-Robinson notes that 'no route that one can work out, on map or terrain, brings one to a point that can be reconciled with the few details we are given about the site of the house' (p. 141).

4 King (1991), pp. xxi–xxii. None of Hardy's correspondence about this 1889 edition has survived, but he is known to have written to Macmillan at least twice regarding the change of placename. There is no direct record of the first letter, and the second is the one which is reproduced in Macmillan's letter book.

5 Hardy had written 'The First Countess of Wessex' in September 1888, but Long-Ash Lane is not mentioned in the serial version and was not introduced until 1891.

6 King suggests that Hardy changed the name of the inn to 'associate it with Tess's walk to Emminster when she breakfasts at a nearby cottage; see *Tess of the d'Urbervilles*, ch. 44' (1991, p. 241). Having moved the location of the inn to Evershead, however, Hardy may simply have wanted to be consistent with the earlier references to the Sow-and-Acorn.

7 For the sake of a complete record, the other revisions to *1896* for the Wessex edition which have not previously been mentioned are as follows (*1912* is quoted first, and the pagination is that of *1912*): 'hooked/curry-combed' (p. 179); ''ee/ye' (p. 180); 'town of Smokeyhole/great fireplace' (p. 181); 'sycamore tree/sycamore-tree' (p. 183); 'Sally's own/of course' (p. 192); 'onward/back' (p. 193); 'spit-and-daub/spit-and-dab' (p. 194); 'ahead/back' (p. 196); 'Sally's brother/this brother' (p. 199); 'civilisation/civilization' (p. 209); 'contradicted,/contradicted' (p. 211); 'under blue sky/out of doors' (p. 212); 'negative/negative,' (p. 213); 'up/up,' (p. 214); 'life/life,' (p. 214).

CHAPTER 7

'The Distracted Preacher'

'The Distracted Preacher' was the first of the *Wessex Tales* to be published. Little is known about the composition of any of these stories, but if one can assume that they were published shortly after they were written, then 'The Distracted Preacher' was probably composed at Upper Tooting in late 1878 or early 1879, in the interval between *The Return of the Native* and *The Trumpet-Major*. Indeed, as Kathryn King has plausibly suggested, it was Hardy's research into the Dorset history of the early years of the century for *The Trumpet-Major* which brought to mind his grandfather's smuggling activities at that time and which led to his interest in the next generation's illicit trade, as described in 'The Distracted Preacher' (1988, pp. 89–90).

The versions of the story which have textual significance are as follows:

NQM 'The Distracted Young Preacher', *New Quarterly Magazine*, April 1879, pp. 324–76.

HW 'The Distracted Young Preacher', *Harper's Weekly*, 5 instalments, 19 April–17 May 1879, pp. 320, 339–40, 360, 380, 399–400. The content of each instalment was as follows: 1st: Chapter 1 (part; as far as 'savored more of pride than of vanity'); 2nd: Chapter 1 (remainder) to Chapter 3; 3rd: Chapters 4–5 (part; as far as 'toward the point of contact'); 4th: Chapter 5 (remainder) to Chapter 6 (part; as far as 'Here be some of 'em at last!'); 5th: Chapter 6 (remainder) to Chapter 7.

1888 'The Distracted Preacher', *Wessex Tales*, 2 vols. (London: Macmillan, 1888), II, 77–212. Published at 12*s.* in an edition of 750 copies on 4 May 1888.

1896 'The Distracted Preacher', *Wessex Tales* (London: Osgood, McIlvaine, 1896), pp. 217–91. Volume XIII in the first uniform and complete edition of Hardy's works.

1912 'The Distracted Preacher', *Wessex Tales* (London: Macmillan, 1912), pp. 215–87. Volume IX of the Wessex edition.

A manuscript of 'The Distracted Young Preacher', not mentioned by Purdy, was sold at auction in 1973; it is now owned by a private collector and is unavailable for study.[1]

Hardy wrote a note on the factual background of 'The Distracted Preacher' for an amateur performance of the dramatized version of the story in 1911. The note is almost wholly reproduced in the Preface to the 1912 Wessex edition of *Wessex Tales*, and the only additional information it gives is that 'the details of the tale were related to the writer in his boyhood by one or two of those who were engaged in the business, being then old men'.[7] Hardy also told Catharine and Rebekah Owen in August 1893 that '"he knew one of the smugglers"' and that 'he had himself seen the hole into which, or out of which, the smugglers' apple tree was lifted. It was sometimes lifted when in full bloom' ('The preacher and his love-affair are "where fiction comes in"').[3] The smuggler whom Hardy knew might well be the man identified in the *Life* only as 'James S—', who 'worked forty years for Hardy's father, and had been a smuggler' (p. 170). This is a veiled reference to James Selby, of Broadmayne, Dorset, whose surname Hardy used for the narrator of 'A Tradition of Eighteen Hundred and Four', and who is no doubt the same man whom Hardy describes in the 1896 Preface as 'an old carrier of "tubs" – a man who was afterwards in my father's employ for over thirty years'. Selby, then, appears to be the 'informant' who told Hardy about lifting the apple tree out of its hole and who spoke of 'the horribly suffocating sensation produced by the pair of spirit-tubs slung upon the chest and back' (p. ix). Hardy was always keen to stress the tale's historical basis: for instance, in 1889, he told a correspondent that 'I have known several, now dead, who shared in the adventurous doings along that part of the coast fifty or sixty years ago', and, in a letter written in September 1896 to Bertram Windle, he stated that the story was 'founded on facts still traditional in the neighbourhood'. In 1911, Hardy confirmed the date of the story's events as being approximately 1830 (*Letters*, I, 204, II, 132 and IV, 188). Hermann Lea reports (perhaps on Hardy's authority) that the incident at Warmwell Cross, in which the excisemen were bound to the trees, was 'said to have been really enacted in the eighteen-thirties' (Lea, p. 162).

Hardy had several sources of information about smuggling exploits. One was George Nicholls, a retired coastguard and father of Eliza, whom Hardy courted in the 1860s. Another was Captain Joseph Masters, Hardy's landlord in Swanage in 1875–76, who used to tell him smuggling stories, as Hardy recorded in the *Life* (pp. 110–11). The most important source, though, was probably family anecdotes, for Hardy's grandfather, as he mentioned in one of his Memoranda notebooks in 1871, used to do a little smuggling, hiding the tubs in the cottage where Hardy grew up.[4] The same note records that, 'at a christening of one of their children' in 1805, Hardy's grandparents '"had a washing pan of pale brandy" left them by the smugglers to make merry with' (p. 9), a combination of liquor and religion which may have shown Hardy the potential for such ironic humour in his story. The memorandum also describes a large female smuggler named Mother Rogers who used to call at the cottage '& ask if any of "it" was wanted cheap. Her hugeness was caused by her having bullocks' bladders slung round her hips, in which she carried the spirits.'

In his 'Facts' notebook, Hardy wrote out a contemporary account from the *Dorset County Chronicle*, dated 5 August 1830, of the trial of three men for smuggling in Lulworth Cove.[5] Since Hardy copied this newspaper report perhaps five years after writing the story, he must have known some of its details earlier; for instance, he already knew that the surname of one of the three accused was Hewlett, since the name of the character Owlett in the story is, as Kathryn King notes, a conflation of 'owler', a traditional term for a smuggler, and 'Hewlett'.[6] The 'Facts' entry, however, certainly contributed to later revisions of the story; for instance, only in 1912 was Dagger's Grave mentioned as the site of the smugglers' rendezvous, a place referred to several times in the newspaper report, and only in the 1912 postscript is the smuggler's forename given as Jim (Hardy had found the full name of James Hewlett in the newspaper). Similarly, it was in 1912 that Hardy added the information near the end of the story that Owlett 'was caught, and tried with the others at the assizes; but they all got off' (p. 286). The 'Facts' entry ends with the words of the judge: 'the prisoners had shown great forbearance. Entered into their own recognizance for good behaviour, & were discharged.' Much of this finds its way into the penultimate paragraph of the 1912 Preface.[7]

In a letter of October 1911 written to T.H. Tilley, the Dorchester mayor and amateur actor, Hardy again reveals his use of the newspaper report:

> I find on referring to the notes I made for "The Distracted Preacher" that the "Preventive-men" (they were not called excisemen) each carried two pistols in his belt, which were fired to give the alarm; & then a blue-light was burnt.
> The smugglers carried heavy sticks. (*Letters*, IV, 186)

All of these details can be found in the 'Facts' notebook. In preparing the story for the 1912 Wessex edition a few months after his letter to Tilley, Hardy removed all 21 of the erroneous references to 'excisemen' and replaced them with 'preventive-men' or some other more accurate term; he also took the opportunity to insert a new clause after the description of the carriers as inoffensive men, adding 'even though some held heavy sticks' (p. 254).

Hardy's concern for historical accuracy in the story can be seen in another letter of the same period, written to one of the Dorchester actors: 'the character of the Customs-Officer, whom you personate in the play of "The Distracted Preacher", is given under his real name of Latimer, as told me forty years ago by one of the smugglers in his old age. I believe I am correct in stating that the Latimer buried in Osmington Churchyard, whose headstone you can see there any day, was the same man, though I have no actual proof of it' (*Letters*, IV, 190; Purdy and Millgate note, however, that the headstone is not visible now, nor has Latimer's name been traced in the parish registers).

Serials

In 1910, thirty years after he had written the story, Hardy told the publisher John Lane that the American serial versions of 'The Distracted Young Preacher' and 'Fellow-Townsmen' 'are merely reprints from the magazines in which those stories appeared, are uncorrected, & were issued before copyright, – I think without my knowledge' (*Letters*, IV, 97). Hardy's memory seems mistaken in at least one respect here, for the American serial of 'The Distracted Young Preacher' in *Harper's Weekly* is not at all a reprint of the British serial. There are numerous minor substantive differences between the two serials, and it would appear instead that the American serial is an earlier version of the story, perhaps set from proofs, which Hardy later further emended before the story appeared in the *New Quarterly Magazine*.

Before examining the distinctive features of each of the serials, however, I would like to study their common elements which distinguish them from later collected editions. In the serials, for instance, Lizzy speaks more in dialect, and there are four occasions when she addresses Stockdale as 'ye' or uses a form such as 'they be' when speaking with him (and two further occasions unique to *NQM*). All of these are altered in later versions, making her appear more refined, further removed from her fellow smugglers, and a more equal mate for the minister.

Two rather racy episodes involving Lizzy are less provocative in the serials than they were later to become. The first concerns her method of filling up a keg with water after she has drawn off some spirits for Stockdale's cold on the night of his arrival. In later versions, she produced a bottle of water, 'from which she took mouthfuls, conveying each to the keg by putting her pretty lips to the hole' (*1912*, p. 225); in the serials, however, she merely took the bottle, 'which she poured on the hole'. The other episode involves her disguise as a male smuggler, using her late husband's clothes. In the serials, she wears leggings rather than breeches, which perhaps is rather more decorous, and the serials also lack her comic and illogical excuses, when Stockdale catches her in disguise, that it is 'no harm, as he was my own husband' and that her dress is 'only tucked in!' (*1912*, p. 249; all these changes were first introduced in *1888*).

Some names and places are unique to the serials. For instance, Swanage, Ringstead, Lulworth and Weymouth appear under their real names, where *1888* changed them to the fictional Knollsea, Ringsworth, Lullstead and Budmouth, and the only fictional name in the serial is Nether-Mynton (altered to Nether-Moynton in *1896*); Gatrell observes that Hardy took the same attitude to place-names in the serial of this story that he did in *The Trumpet-Major* shortly afterwards, using an authentic environment to preserve the historical nature of the story's content (1988, p. 122). In addition, the names of two characters are given differently: Will Latimer was originally Jim in the British serial (*HW* did not give him any forename), while Susan Wallis, the girl who comes to ask Lizzy for some mustard, was called Sarah in both serials.

Harper's Weekly

The American serial has some unique numbers and quantities, and it alone gives the year of the action as 1835 (which, as we saw above, is historically inaccurate), where all other versions read '183–'. It calculates the celebrated population-puzzle of Nether-Mynton at 300 Episcopalians, 250 Dissenters and yet only 450 adults in total (the slightly different numbers arise because other versions give the quantities as so many scores of people). In *HW*, the smugglers hide 40 tubs in the church-tower and 80 in the orchard (compared to 30 and 70 tubs respectively in other versions). Nether-Mynton is said to be ten or twelve miles from Weymouth (perhaps twice the actual distance between the real place, Owermoigne, and Weymouth), which elsewhere is always said to be merely 'some considerable number of miles distant'. If Hardy was responsible for either of these variations in date and distance, then it would seem that he initially sought to give a slightly greater disguise to the historical events on which the story is based.

The list of places searched after lunch by the Customs men is slightly different in *HW*, and includes pump troughs, leafy ditches and new-turned garden soil. The revised list in the British serial is unified because they are all places associated with refuse, making the search uniformly unpleasant.

On the rare occasions when later editions include a *Harper's Weekly* variant rather than the British serial one (there are only five individual words so affected), it is because the American serial corrected an obvious misprint in the *New Quarterly Magazine* (for instance, standing *in* a chair, rather than on it), or else Hardy may have made late changes to the British serial proof and not copied them on to a duplicate proof which probably formed the basis of the first collected edition (which would explain, for instance, why Lizzy says 'be' instead of 'are' on two occasions found only in *NQM*).

New Quarterly Magazine

'The Distracted Young Preacher', like 'Fellow-Townsmen' in the following year, was printed in the *New Quarterly Magazine* because of Hardy's friendship with its editor, Charles Kegan Paul.[8]

The British serial added a substantial amount of new detail to the story as it was to appear in *Harper's Weekly*, and nearly all of the new material was retained in subsequent collected editions. The conflict which Stockdale feels between his roles as preacher and lover is sharply increased, and Lizzy's involvement in the smuggling is heightened, thus providing a greater obstacle to their eventual union.

In *NQM*, Stockdale is a much more conscientious and committed minister. On his arrival in Nether-Mynton, he wishes to radiate 'at once' to the surrounding chapels, and we learn that he had been 'brought up with a single eye to the ministry'. At the same time, though, he is also made a more committed and smitten lover: he is now described as 'the doomed young fellow', and even after he has made clear his disapproval of her role in hiding the tubs in the village, we quickly see 'his tenderness reasserting itself'. His fate seems sealed by the increasingly attractive appearance of Lizzy, his 'enkindling' landlady with a 'beautiful' forehead and 'eyes that warmed him before he knew it'. His distraction from his duties is such that he comes to wish that 'tutelary saints were not denied to Dissenters'.

Lizzy is more knowing and worldly-wise than the naive and sheltered Stockdale. When she takes him to the church on his first night to purloin some spirits, he observes ingenuously that there are some barrels under the stairs; in

HW she had confirmed his remark 'with seeming candor' but in *NQM* she speaks 'in an emphatic tone of candour that was not without a touch of irony'. Lizzy is made more involved in the smuggling: in *HW* she was merely 'engaged in' it but now she becomes 'excited by' it. When Stockdale says that he hopes she can soon see a way to end any conflict between her memories and her conscience, she replies 'Well, I don't just now', implying that she will continue her participation in smuggling. In the American serial, she says nothing at this point. Another addition is that Stockdale tells her 'heavily' that smuggling is a bad business, and the sea makes a 'moan' as he says it, reflecting his own mood (in *HW* the sea had merely made a 'noise'). Such is his more passionate regard for Lizzy in the British serial that his concern for her while the village is being searched is altered from mere 'uneasiness' to 'anxiety'.

Stockdale's answer to his own conflict between love and religious duty is to conceive of proposing to Lizzy when he has a respectable house with a varnished door 'and a brass knocker', this comic addition showing his utter ignorance of Lizzy's real needs and aspirations. Later, he again asks her to wait for him until 'I have a house'. He also says that he wants to take her away to some far-removed 'inland' county which he imagines is uncontaminated by smuggling, but the addition here serves to set up an ironic parallel, since the story repeatedly stresses that it is the inland areas which are the destination of the smuggled liquor, and without the inland market there would be no trade. Stockdale's supposed pastoral haven for his respectable marriage is merely the other side in the equation of supply and demand.

To add to Stockdale's problems, Owlett is a much more serious rival for Lizzy's hand in the British serial than he had been in *Harper's Weekly*. In *NQM*, Lizzy admits to Stockdale that Owlett had spoken of marriage to her 'every now and then' (this phrase is not in *HW*, where Owlett seems to have spoken of it only once), and their supposed engagement is more widely and firmly believed by the villagers in *NQM* than it is in *HW*: the former reads that 'it was generally understood that a quiet engagement to marry existed between her and her cousin Owlett, and had existed for some time' (compare the much vaguer plan in *HW*: 'it was becoming generally understood that a dim family arrangement to marry some day existed between her and her cousin Owlett'). It is not surprising to find Stockdale and Lizzy described in the British serial as 'the sad lovers', although the story retains its 'light dramatic character', as Hardy described it many years later (*Letters*, IV, 284).

Hardy's treatment of Lizzy's dialect in *NQM* is very subtle. Generally, she speaks standard English, apart from the occasional colloquialism in dialect. Her language places her in an intermediate position between the villagers and the 'correct' Stockdale, expressing her divided loyalties. There is one occasion, however, when her dialect reasserts itself: as Kathryn King puts it, 'the link between her love of smuggling and more colloquial language is nowhere better employed than in the monologue in which she passionately defends smuggling to the disapproving Stockdale, a speech which Hardy gave even greater colloquial freedom in the *New Quarterly* revisions' (1988, p. 97). In the following extract from the *NQM* version, brackets contain the standard English reading in *HW* which Hardy emended in proofs for the British serial:

> It stirs up one's dull life at this time o' [of] the year, and gives excitement, which I have got so used to now that I should hardly know how to do 'ithout [without] it. At nights, when the wind blows, instead of being dull and stupid, and not [never] thinking whether it do blow [blows] or not, your mind is afield [abroad], even if you are not afield [abroad] yourself; and you are wondering how the chaps be [are] getting on; and you walk up and down the room, and look out o' [of the] window.

This is the only speech by Lizzy in *NQM* which shows an increased use of dialect, in contrast to her more subdued language elsewhere. Her dialect here reveals that her true identity is found in the life of the village and in the smuggling, and Hardy left this monologue largely unchanged in later editions, although he removed even more dialect from her speech in other parts of the story. (There is one slight alteration to Lizzy's monologue in subsequent editions, the final 'be' reverting to the original 'are', but this may have been caused by Hardy omitting to note the *NQM* revision on a duplicate set of proofs, so that the restoration of the *HW* reading was inadvertent.)

The final sermon which Stockdale preaches before he departs is much more emotional in *NQM*:

HW	NQM
His sermon was a discourse on contraband trading, as she had expected; but none of his hearers perceived that it was particularly directed at Lizzy Newberry. Stockdale could not get on with it at all well in the face of her, and at one time nearly broke down.	The little building was full to overflowing, and he took up the subject which all had expected, that of the contraband trade so extensively practised among them. His hearers, in laying his words to their own hearts, did not perceive that they were most particularly directed against Lizzy, till the sermon waxed warm, and Stockdale nearly broke down with emotion. In truth his own earnestness, and her sad eyes looking up at him were too much for the young man's equanimity. He hardly knew how he ended. He saw Lizzy, as through a mist, turn and go away with the rest of the congregation; and shortly afterwards followed her home.

It is possible that a Harper's editor paraphrased this scene, which appears in the final column of the serial, in order to allow the story to finish at the foot of the page.

All the references to the male smugglers disguising themselves as women to rescue their tubs are new to the British serial, making a counterpoint to Lizzy disguising herself as a male smuggler earlier. Also new is the sabotage when the wheels drop off and the carts fall down while the barrels are being removed. A further addition is the sentence showing Latimer marking broad-arrows on vehicles and harnesses to commandeer them. The men who are hired by the excise officers to search the village are, for the first time, described as a 'formidable body' of men, and the smugglers' rescue of the tubs is a 'desperate' affair. A similar melodramatic addition is the news that Owlett suffered 'dreadfully' when he was later captured. One final curiosity is that, in *Harper's Weekly*, Stockdale and Lizzy wed at a registry office, but in the British serial Lizzy appropriately marries her distracted preacher in a chapel.

1888 Macmillan

For this first collected edition of 'The Distracted Preacher', Hardy made approximately sixty substantive alterations to the story as it had appeared in the *New Quarterly Magazine*, usually involving a single word or two at most. It is at this stage that Hardy introduced those changes to the serials which were described above: the removal of some dialect, Lizzy's method of filling up a keg, her disguise as a male smuggler in breeches, her comic and illogical defence of her clothing, and the change in names and places.

Six of the eight alterations to dialect serve to standardize Lizzy's speech still further (only two of the six restore *HW* readings). Especially notable are the five changes which involve the substitution of 'are' for 'be', which separates Lizzy even more from her fellow smugglers, who continue to use 'be'. Kathryn King helpfully summarizes Hardy's handling of dialect in this story: 'it would appear that, after first conceiving of Lizzy in somewhat genteel terms and then "dialectizing" her for the English serial version, Hardy decided in 88 to return to something closer to his original conception' (1988, p. 98).

Two rather amusing alterations needed to be made to the serial versions. When Stockdale wanted to reveal his presence to the person eavesdropping on Lizzy and Owlett, in the serials he stood up 'in the lighted room'. In *1888* Hardy altered this to read that Stockdale showed himself 'against the firelight', because he noticed that in the previous paragraph he had said that the candles were not yet lit. Later in the serials, the men searching the village were said to have 'pushed their noses' into places where the tubs might have been thrown, and there then follows a list of such places which includes mixens and cesspools. To prevent a disconcerting literal reading of his idiom, Hardy changed 'noses' to 'search'.

By far the most substantial alteration in *1888* is the addition of a sentence to explain why Latimer went around the village marking every vehicle and set of harness with chalk: 'The owner of every conveyance so marked was bound to give it up for Government purposes.' Another revision concerning Latimer is his description of the two women who tied him up as 'strapping', making it clear that he has not realized they were men in disguise'.[9]

1896 Osgood, McIlvaine

Hardy made a couple of dozen substantive changes to 'The Distracted Preacher' when including it in the first uniform edition of his work; most involve individual words, and the longest alteration is a phrase of three words.

The name of Lizzy's village was altered from Nether-Mynton to Nether-Moynton, making it sound more like Owermoigne, the village on which it was modelled. Lullstead became Lulstead Cove, which is closer to the spelling of the real Lulworth Cove. Finally, a reference to the real Bere became the Wessex Kingsbere. These changes show two opposite directions in Hardy's creation of Wessex topography: the real becomes fictional, while the fictional is made to correspond more closely to the real.

In *1896*, the list of occupations of those involved in the smuggling includes 'shoemakers', which replaces the earlier 'masons'. This may allude to Hardy's uncle, John Antell, and its possible significance is discussed below in the remarks on the Wessex edition. The rendezvous for the smugglers is moved from being 'at' Lulstead to 'near' it, making this consistent with the later information that they descended the cliffs 'not many hundred yards' from Lulstead Cove. A couple of changes see dialect being either introduced or made even more marked in the speech of the smugglers: 'seed' becomes 'zeed' and 'may' becomes 'mid', creating an even greater distance between their speech and that of Lizzy.

Stockdale is writing a sermon one night, and in *1896* we learn that it 'occupied him perfunctorily' for some considerable time, which replaces 'unintentionally occupied him'. The new reading shows him clearly to be a distracted preacher, while the earlier phrase could have been taken to mean that he was so absorbed in writing his sermon that he lost track of time.

When Lizzy and Stockdale are removing some liquor from the church on his first night, Lizzy tells him that the spirits are 'so 'nation strong' (replaces 'so burning strong'). Her oath, a euphemism for 'damnation', is a beautifully inappropriate thing to say to a preacher in a church, and it summarizes in a single word the forthcoming conflict between Lizzy the smuggler, associated here with liquor and damnation, and the pious Stockdale who offers himself as her salvation.

A description of the abstemious minister as being 'young' is removed in *1896*. As with the removal of the same adjective from the story's title when it was first collected, it would seem that Hardy increasingly wished to portray Stockdale as responsible and rather earnest, in contrast to Lizzy the daring and adventurous smuggler.

1912 Macmillan Wessex edition

The topography of Wessex is, as usual, defined more precisely and made consistent in the Wessex edition. Lulstead Cove is changed yet again and becomes Lulwind Cove, while Chaldon (a real place) becomes Shaldon. For the first time, the site of the smuggling is identified as Dagger's Grave, although its distance from the Cove remains a few hundred yards (the actual Dagger's Gate is about a mile away). The journey between Round Pond and Dagger's Grave takes fifteen minutes of brisk walking in *1912*, which is a much more realistic time to cover a mile than the hour which the walk took in previous versions of the story.

The name of the owner of one of the requisitioned carts is altered from Thomas Ballam to Thomas Artnell (p. 274), which appears to be an oblique reference to Hardy's uncle, John Antell, the Puddletown shoemaker (in *1896*, the occupations of some of the smugglers had been changed from masons to shoemakers). Perhaps Hardy made a private association between smuggling liquor and his uncle's alcoholism.[10] Kathryn King notes that Lizzy's tub-broaching tool is a shoemaker's awl and that the excisemen discover shoemakers' aprons, as well as the fact that Antell died in December 1878, around the time when Hardy began writing the story, but I do not know of any evidence to support her intriguing suggestion that Antell may have been involved in the smuggling in the 1830s (1988, pp. 102–3).

In *1912*, Lizzy explains to Stockdale about the tubs of spirit which have accidentally 'floated over' (p. 223) from France in the dark. This replaces her previous explanation that they had merely 'come over' and makes her attitude to Stockdale even more disingenuous and ironic. Later, Stockdale sees 'fresh' (p. 242) splashes of mud on her coat (replaces 'actual'); the new reading is more pertinent, since the fresh splashes show that someone has been walking in mud *recently*. Hardy also added the reference to her 'breeches' (p. 251) which Stockdale can see, making her disguise consistent with the reference to breeches a couple of pages earlier, which had been introduced in *1888*. Stockdale tells her that he would rather that she had 'scraped the streets' (p. 281) than been a smuggler; this replaces the slightly more decorous 'swept the streets' of previous versions, and Stockdale's preference for her scraping streets (removing horse-manure) shows a more extreme disgust at her smuggling. When he makes his final proposal to her, Lizzy was 'moved a little' (p. 281), which seems more in keeping with her spirited character than her response in earlier versions, where Stockdale's proposal left her 'trembling a little'. Finally, as with most of his revisions of the story, Hardy took the opportunity to diminish the dialect in Lizzy's conversation with Stockdale, and on the concluding page she says 'given' instead of the earlier 'gied'.

The postscript which tells how Lizzy actually married Owlett and emigrated to America was added in *1912*. Hardy must have known at least some of this information long before, since in previous versions Lizzy tells Stockdale that Owlett was settled 'in Wisconsin', a phrase removed in *1912*, presumably because it was made redundant by the factual note.[11]

Notes

1 Written in ink, the manuscript consists of 57 leaves, recto only. It was sold at Hanzel Galleries during the David Gage Joyce Sale, 23–24 September 1973 (Lot 106) and was purchased by Hamill and Barker. See Barbara Rosenbaum, *Index of English Literary Manuscripts*, 4:2 (London: Mansell, 1990), p. 151, and *Letters*, IV, 165.

2 'Mr. Hardy's Note on the Story', *The Three Wayfarers, The Distracted Preacher* (Programme, Dorchester Debating and Dramatic Society), Dorchester, 15–16 November 1911, p. [4].

3 Weber, 1952, pp. 83, 85, and Weber, 1939, p. 72: in the latter, Hardy is said to have remarked that he knew 'some' of the smugglers, not just one.

4 See Taylor, pp. 8–9.

5 'Facts' notebook, pp. 163–[166]. It is in the Hardy Memorial Collection at the Dorset County Museum. The 'Trumpet-Major Notebook', which Hardy began in 1878 while doing research for the novel, also contains a number of references to smuggling: see Taylor, pp. 120, 127–30.

6 See *Wessex Tales*, ed. King, p. 243.

7 Another of Hardy's notebooks, 'Poetical Matter', would appear to have contributed a detail to the story, as Kathryn King has observed (1988, pp. 61–2). On 19 January 1879, Hardy recorded a peaceful moment at home with Emma in Tooting: 'In the study firelight a red glow is on the polished sides & arch of the grate: firebrick back red hot: the polish of fireirons shines; underside of mantel reddened: also a shine on the leg of the table, & the ashes under the grate, lit from above like a torrid clime' (quoted in Millgate, p. 204). Hardy seems to have remembered this note when describing Lizzy's parlour at the start of the story: 'The fire-light shone out from the grate upon the side of the table, fluttering on the bulging portions of its legs, and gilding the under surface of the chimney-piece' (*HW*, p. 320). Perhaps Hardy introduced this description when revising proofs of the story shortly after making the notebook entry.

8 Edith Wharton, who first met Hardy around 1900, recalled that he once made the following comment about one of his stories: 'the editor of the Scottish magazine which had published his first short story had objected to his making his hero and heroine go for a walk on a Sunday, and obliged him to transfer the stroll to a week-day!' (*A Backward Glance*, p. 216). Perhaps Hardy was thinking of *Blackwood's Edinburgh Magazine* which had published 'The Withered Arm' in January 1888, but there is no such scene in that story. Rather, the episode in Part III of 'The Distracted Preacher' in which Lizzy and Stockdale go for a walk on an unspecified day seems to be the one to which Hardy was referring (although the *New Quarterly Magazine* was a London periodical). If Kegan Paul had objected to the walk on a Sunday, it might be relevant to note that he had been a clergyman for twelve years before he became a publisher.

9 The only substantial addition for *1888* not yet mentioned is Lizzy's remark that 'I go to burn the lugger off'. King suggests that this was 'withheld from the magazine readership as suggesting a familiarity with the smuggling argot that might appear unseemly in a heroine' (1988, p. 99).

10 See Millgate, pp. 34, 107–8, 348.

11 'Old' Owlett the smuggler is mentioned again in 'Enter a Dragoon', written in 1899 and set in the Mellstock of the 1850s, so, for the purposes of that story, he had not emigrated.

For the sake of a complete record, the other revisions to *1896* for the Wessex edition which have not previously been mentioned are as follows (*1912* is quoted first, and the pagination is that of *1912*): 'gi'ed/gied' (p. 218); 'head/head,' (p. 218); 'meal/meal,' (p. 220); 'walk/walk,' (p. 227); 'house/house,' (p. 230); 'Mr. Owlett./Owlett' (p. 233; all six later references to 'Mr. Owlett' involve this change); 'half a dozen/half-a-dozen' (p. 240); 'Lizzie/Lizzy' (p. 252); 'half offended/half-offended' (p. 252); 'on that/on, that' (p. 254); 'yards/yards,' (p. 261); 'canter/tramp' (p. 263); 'orchard/orchard,' (p. 266); 'orchard/orchet' (p. 269); 'enter/enter,' (p. 271); 'out they/out, they' (p. 272); 'went to/got to' (p. 286).

PART TWO

A Group of Noble Dames

A Group of Noble Dames

A *Group of Noble Dames* was first published by Osgood, McIlvaine on 30 May 1891 at 6*s*. in an edition of 2000 copies, and it marked the beginning of Hardy's association with the firm. All of the ten stories in the volume had previously appeared in serial form. The nucleus of *A Group of Noble Dames* is the six stories which had appeared in the 1890 Christmas Number of the *Graphic*, namely 'Barbara of the House of Grebe', 'The Marchioness of Stonehenge', 'Lady Mottisfont', 'The Lady Icenway', 'Squire Petrick's Lady' and 'Anna, Lady Baxby'. All six stories in their serial form were bowdlerized and altered in plot and detail, three of them especially so ('Mottisfont', 'Petrick' and 'Baxby'). The serialization of these six stories will be discussed separately below. When Hardy came to arrange the publication of *A Group of Noble Dames* in book form in early 1891, he added four more stories. Two of them, 'The First Countess of Wessex' and 'The Lady Penelope', were relatively recent, having been written in 1888–89, but the other two date from many years earlier and are among the first short stories which Hardy ever wrote: 'The Duchess of Hamptonshire' (under its original title of 'The Impulsive Lady of Croome Castle') was composed in early 1878, while 'The Honourable Laura' (as 'Benighted Travellers') was written in autumn 1881. The collection of stories in *A Group of Noble Dames* therefore represents some of Hardy's work in the short story form over a period of thirteen years from 1878 to 1891. In arranging the stories for this collected edition, Hardy slightly altered the sequence in which the six *Graphic* stories had appeared, for reasons which will be discussed in the individual chapters below. His aim in the volume as a whole was to place the stories in a contrapuntal structure, so that 'with few exceptions, each story can be seen as a repatterning or ironic refutation of the ostensible moral of the one preceding it' (Brady, p. 53).

Graphic

The changes to *A Group of Noble Dames* forced upon Hardy by the *Graphic* for reasons of propriety were, as Michael Millgate notes, 'painful and humiliating for a man of his years and standing',[1] and the whole episode was a foretaste of the difficulties with the same journal which Hardy encountered when he submitted *Tess* to them later in 1890.

The manuscript of the *Graphic* stories, together with that of 'The Lady Penelope', was presented by Hardy, through Sydney Cockerell, to the Library of Congress, Washington DC, in October 1911 when he was distributing his MSS. among various public collections. The bound volume of seven stories consists of

152 leaves, five of which are wholly or in part in Emma Hardy's hand. On a paper cover which has been bound in, Hardy wrote in blue pencil 'A Group of Noble Dames (3 missing) Original MS.' On the first page of text he wrote 'To these seven stories three others previously printed were also added – to make up the set of ten in the published volume.' As R.L. Purdy notes, the MS. was foliated and rearranged by Hardy to conform to the sequence of the stories in the collected edition of *A Group of Noble Dames*:

1–2	title-page and table of contents for 1891 Osgood, McIlvaine
1–73	'Preliminary', 'Barbara' and 'The Lady Caroline'
115–36	'Lady Mottisfont'
85–114	'The Lady Icenway' and 'Squire Petrick's Lady'
75–83	'Anna, Lady Baxby'
1–14	'The Lady Penelope'
137–8	conclusion

Two missing leaves, fos. 74 and 78, contained links which were cancelled and rewritten when Hardy was arranging the collected edition. The last leaf bears the date 'April, 1890', which refers to the six *Graphic* stories only.[2]

Hardy's first contact with the *Graphic* about *A Group of Noble Dames* was in a letter dated 28 March 1889 which Hardy sent to the editor, Arthur Locker, in which he enquired, 'Can you give me any idea how much you would be disposed to pay for the *Graphic* form alone of a Christmas story – same length as the "Romantic Adventures of a Milkmaid"? Also for the entire right to issue it simultaneously in periodicals throughout the world? I think I could write such a story some time next year.'[3] (Hardy was working at this time on *Tess of the d'Urbervilles*). Four days later, on 1 April, Hardy wrote again to Locker, saying that his price for a Christmas story of the proposed length would be £125, to include the *Graphic* right only, with Hardy retaining 'the right to print the story simultaneously in America or elsewhere abroad [...] also to issue it in book form at any time not less than a month after its appearance in the *Graphic*' (*Letters*, I, 189). On 8 April, Hardy told Locker with regard to the 'short novel', as he called it, that 'I do not like to pledge myself to be in time for next year's summer number; but I can certainly let you have it some time next year' (I, 190). Hardy appears at this stage to have considered the stories as constituting a single piece of work, and none of the six individual stories was ever published separately.

The next surviving reference to *A Group of Noble Dames* is five months later, on 1 September 1889, when Hardy again contacted Locker to say that 'I have much doubt as to the possibility of my getting the story written by January 1st. But I can do it later on in the year, for the Christmas number: or if you prefer it, the summer number following. I would undertake to send it in by July 1, if you decide for the Xmas number' (*Letters*, I, 198). Some time after this, Hardy was in touch with Locker again but the letter went missing and he wrote on 13 November to explain what the lost letter had proposed: 'the missing letter (if I recollect rightly) was a mere line to the effect that if you wished I would substitute a serial story for the short one. But as the date at which I could send in the short one suits you I will consider that as settled' (*Letters*, I, 201). In other words, Hardy had suggested that he substitute (evidently) *Tess* for *A Group of Noble Dames*. Five days later, he proposed terms to Locker for the serialization of *Tess*, which were accepted, so he was now under contract with the *Graphic* for two works simultaneously. This apparently caused Hardy some difficulty about the timescale of production, for he wrote to Locker on 29 November to suggest a modification in the date of the delivery of *Tess*: 'it has occurred to me for the first time that the interval to next September is very short for what I have to do, remembering the Xmas number (for which I have, by the way an excellent idea, or what seems like one) – & in the interest of the stories themselves I will ask you whether half the serial MS. for certain by the end of next Septr & the remainder in instalments onwards, would be soon enough, to begin in the July following? [...] I am extremely anxious that both stories should be good & well-considered, so that it is advisable to feel sure about time' (*Letters*, I, 203–4). On 10 January 1890, he wrote to Harper & Brothers in America, informing them that he had agreed to write a story for the *Graphic*'s Christmas number and offering Harper's the sheets of the same story (*Letters*, I, 207). Hardy told Locker on 26 February that Harper & Brothers had accepted his offer (*Letters*, I, 209).

Hardy was working on *A Group of Noble Dames* at this date, telling Locker on 5 March that 'I think I may be able to send the MS. of the Christmas number a month or two earlier than July. I am now engaged upon it – & shall not put it aside till finished' (*Letters*, I, 210). Two days later, Hardy described the contents of *A Group of Noble Dames* to Harper & Brothers:

> I may say that it is to be a Tale of Tales – a series of linked stories – of a somewhat different kind from the mass of my work of late, excepting The First Countess of Wessex, which comes near it in character. The scenes, which are numerous, will be laid in the old mansions and castles hereabouts: the characters are to be proportionately numerous, & to be exclusively persons of title of the last century (names disguised, but incidents approximating to fact). Like the Wessex-Folk stories, these may be divided easily into parts. The whole Tale of Tales will consist of 30,000 words. There is, of course, much more incident in a scheme of tales of this kind than in a single story of the same length; but I believe the result will be commensurate with the added labour.[4]

At least a couple of the stories, including 'The Lady Icenway', were completed by Easter 1890 (6 April), because Sir George Douglas, who was visiting Hardy at Max Gate that weekend, recalled that 'it was either on this or another night of the same visit that he himself read aloud two of the sketches from his "Group of Noble Dames", one of them being the slightly enigmatic story of the gardener and the lady'.[5] The stories were completed shortly after and Hardy notes his diary entry for 9 May 1890 in the *Life*: 'MS. of "A Group of Noble Dames" sent to *The Graphic* as promised.'[6]

It is at this stage that Hardy's problems began, as Simon Gatrell has shown in his excellent study of Hardy's textual history.[7] He did not hear from the *Graphic* for more than six weeks, during which time, it would appear, his stories had been set in type and proofs pulled, these being read by the *Graphic*'s directors, of whom the most influential would seem to have been William Luson Thomas, the *Graphic*'s founder. The sequence of events is confused at this point, as Simon Gatrell has demonstrated, since at least one of the key documents must be misdated or wrongly attributed.[8] Hardy appears to have received a letter from William Locker, Arthur Locker's son and assistant, on 20 June (see Hardy's letter of 30 July described later), but this has not survived (if it ever existed, since Hardy's reference to the letter of 20 June may be a mistake for 25 June, the date of a letter from William Locker which has survived). Hardy's diary entry, which he records in the *Life*, then notes that he had a distressing meeting with the *Graphic*'s editor three days later: 'June 23. Called on Arthur Locker at The Graphic office in answer to his letter. He says he does not object to the stories but the Directors do. Here's a pretty job! Must smooth down those Directors somehow I suppose.'[9]

The surviving letter which Hardy had received from the *Graphic* and which prompted his visit is not from Arthur Locker but from his son and assistant, William, and it is dated two days *after* the date which Hardy gives for his meeting at the *Graphic*'s office. Either Hardy's diary gives the wrong date for his meeting, or it mistakenly identifies which of the two Lockers he met at the office, or the date on William Locker's letter is an error. Whatever, the *Graphic*'s objections to all of the stories in *A Group of Noble Dames* are bluntly spelled out in William Locker's letter of 25 June:

> I have now read 'A Group of Noble Dames' and am sorry to say that in the main I agree with our Directors' opinion. In the matter of tone they seem to me to be too much in keeping with the supposed circumstances of their narration – in other words to be very suitable and entirely harmless to the robust minds of a Club smoking-room; but not at all suitable for the more delicate imaginations of young girls. Many fathers are accustomed to read or have read in their family circles the stories in the *Graphic*; and I cannot think that they would approve for this purpose a series of tales almost every one of which turns upon questions of childbirth, and those relations between the sexes over which conventionality is accustomed (wisely or unwisely) to draw a veil. To go through them *seriatim* –
>
> The Old Surgeon's story ['Barbara of the House of Grebe'] is, it is true, not the least what Mrs. Grundy would call 'improper', but its main incident is very horrible – just the sort of story an old surgeon might be expected to tell, but none the less unpleasant for that.
>
> The Rural Dean is, as is natural, a good deal milder ['The Lady Caroline']; but still insists rather more than is perhaps advisable upon the childbirth business.
>
> The Colonel's yarn is, of course, a mere anecdote; and would not suffer at all if some other ending were substituted for the discovery by Lady Baxby of her husband's vulgar amour.
>
> Similarly, all that wants cutting out in the Churchwarden's story is the suggestion at the end that Lady Icenway intended to raise up seed unto her second husband by means of her first.

But the tales of the Crimson Maltster ['Squire Petrick's Lady'], and of the Sentimental Member ['Lady Mottisfont'] seem to me to be hopeless – Frankly, do you think it advisable to put into the hands of the Young Person stories, one of which turns upon the hysterical confession by a wife of an imaginary adultery, and the other upon the manner in which a husband foists upon his wife the offspring of a former illicit connection?

I quite admit that if the stories were to be written they could not be better or more innocently done – But I still think it very unfortunate that they should have been written for a paper with the peculiar clientele of the *Graphic*; and I am sure we should not be justified in printing them as they stand.

Now, what do you propose to do? Will you write us an entirely fresh story, or will you take the 'Noble Dames' and alter them to suit our taste; which means slightly chastening 1, 2, 3 & 4; and substituting others for 5 & 6? Please let me have an answer at your earliest convenience; or, if you can call, I shall be in every day except Saturday from 11 to 1 & 3 till 5.[10]

Hardy quickly made changes as requested to all six stories. He must have submitted the revised manuscript to the *Graphic* by mid-July, for he wrote to his wife, probably on 24 July, that 'I think it is all right with the *Graphic* – as they really don't themselves know what it is I have written, apparently: one of the directors having read the 1st proofs in mistake for the second' (*Letters*, I, 215).

It was not only one of the directors, William Luson Thomas, who accidentally re-read the first proofs after Hardy had submitted the revised copy, but probably also the editor, Arthur Locker, as Hardy's letter to him of 30 July makes clear:

I am glad to say that on comparing the copy of the unrevised proof read by Mr Thomas (in mistake for the revised one) his marks thereon of passages for revision correspond almost exactly with changes I had already carried out in the revise which Mr Thomas has not seen, & which was the result of your son's original suggestions in his letter of June 20. So that there was nothing left for me to do beyond making a few additional changes in the wording – as shown in the revise herewith returned.

When Mr Thomas, & your assistant editor, read this, they will both see that their wishes have been complied with to the letter – & more.

Your idea, therefore, that I should write another story altogether, which I was quite prepared to do, seemed to be rendered unnecessary.

I can understand that owing to your coming to the matter after an absence, during which your son & myself had begun operations, the proofs must have been nearly forgotten by you, & I feel almost sure that you accidentally read a second time some of the original sheets. (*Letters*, I, 215–16)

Harper's Weekly

The simultaneous publication of the six stories in *Harper's Weekly* is especially significant because the American periodical issued the stories more or less as Hardy had originally written them and as they were to appear in the first book edition, with little of the Grundyan interference which the *Graphic* had displayed. Hardy, incidentally, received £74 for the *Harper's Weekly* publication.[11]

Sources

Five of the stories in *A Group of Noble Dames* have their origin in one of Hardy's favourite books, John Hutchins's *The History and Antiquities of the County of Dorset* (a copy of the four-volume 3rd edition was in Hardy's library): these stories are 'The First Countess of Wessex', 'Barbara of the House of Grebe', 'Squire Petrick's Lady', 'Anna, Lady Baxby' and 'The Lady Penelope'. As Kristin Brady rightly says, however, Hardy's use of his historical material indicates that 'his aim was not accuracy, but a particular symbolic configuration of events' (p. 85). Unlike the stories in *Wessex Tales*, which usually have their source in personal and oral reminiscences, *A Group of Noble Dames* is often rooted in 'diagrams on the pages of county histories' (*1912*, p. vii).

Rebekah Owen noted in her copy of the stories that

> All the Group of Noble Dames tales are true. (Mrs. Hardy says that Barbara of the House of Grebe is not.) Often Mr. Hardy has got traditions from old people who got them from old family servants of the great families, whose representatives now think that Mr. Hardy ought not to have published them. At least Lord Ilchester thought so of 'The First Countess of Wessex', though Lady Pembroke and other descendants of Betty (he knows eight) are quite pleased. One Lord R— (I forget) said to Mr. Hardy, 'It is all nonsense, you know, of Ilchester to feel so, and I shall tell him so' (Weber, 1939, p. 73).[12]

On 15 July 1891, Hardy told Lord Lytton that

> Of all the welcomes that have been accorded to the Noble Dames I value none more highly than that with which you have honoured them; & when I consider the compeers in real life that they must have encountered on their arrival at the brilliant centre whither they were dispatched, & your memories of the same, I feel that considerable good nature must have tempered your critical eye. I am truly glad however to know that any pleasure has been given by what is, I fear, rather a frivolous piece of work, which I took in hand in a sort of desperation during a fit of low spirits – making use of some legendary notes I had taken down from the lips of aged people in a remote part of the country, where traditions of the local families linger on, & are remembered by the yeomen & peasantry long after they are forgotten by the families concerned. Some day I must tell you how much truth there is in some of the tales, & the real names. (*Letters*, I, 239–40)

Michael Millgate notes that Hardy omitted to mention that one of these 'aged people' from whom he heard the traditions was his own mother, 'almost certainly a source for the tradition of the Ilchester family of Melbury House which was eventually worked up into "The First Countess of Wessex'" (p. 317).

1891 Osgood, McIlvaine: the first collected edition

Hardy wrote in the *Life* that 'At the beginning of January [1891] he was at home arranging *A Group of Noble Dames* for publication in a volume' (p. 243). He told Emma on 11 April 1891 that *A Group of Noble Dames* would be published 'about the first week in May' (*Letters*, I, 230), but it did not in fact appear until 30 May. After publication, Hardy wrote to Edward Clodd on 3 June to say that 'I am glad you like the book. Read the maltster's story ['Squire Petrick's Lady'] if you have time. Most of the tales are founded on fact' (I, 237). On 9 August, he told Louise Chandler Moulton that 'your opinion of the Noble Dames is one which, I need hardly say, I value very highly, coming from such a sympathetic critic' (I, 241), and he told an unidentified correspondent on 11 October that 'I am gratified to learn that the Noble Dames have found favour in your eyes. They have had their detractors as well as their champions' (I, 245). Hardy probably had in mind the review in the *Pall Mall Gazette* of 8 July which singled out 'Barbara of the House of Grebe' as 'a hideous and hateful fantasy' (see Purdy, p. 300). In his retort, published two days later, Hardy asserted that the tale-within-a-tale structure of the book had been intended to protect the reader by removing the action 'into a second plane or middle distance, being described by a character to characters, and not point-blank by author to reader', adding that 'A good horror has its place in art. Shall we, for instance, condemn "Alonzo the Brave"? For my part I would not give up a single worm of his skull.'[13]

In the 'Preliminary' to the serial version of the stories, the members of the Field and Antiquarian Club met 'at the Museum, an old chocolate-brick house of early Georgian date, with heavily moulded sash-bars, festooned chimney-pieces, deep cornices, and ponderous flights of stairs – doubtless the residence formerly of some opulent burgher'. This would seem to be the old museum in Trinity St, Dorchester, but in preparing the first collected edition Hardy moved the setting to a building which would appear to be the Dorset County Museum, which had opened in 1884. The Dorset Natural History and Antiquarian Field Club, of which Hardy was already a member, held meetings at the new museum.

1891 Harper

A Group of Noble Dames was published in America by Harper & Brothers early in June 1891. As Purdy notes (p. 67), this edition reproduced the headpiece and six of the seven illustrations by Alfred Parsons and C.S. Reinhart for 'The First Countess of Wessex' as they had appeared in *Harper's New Monthly Magazine* eighteen months before. All of the stories except 'Lady Mottisfont' have some minor substantive differences from the 1891 Osgood, McIlvaine edition, but these are almost certainly the result of compositorial error or editorial intervention. The only Harper's variant which is retained in the 1912 Wessex edition is one which occurs in 'The First Countess of Wessex' (see Chapter 8 on the story below).

1896 Osgood, McIlvaine: the Wessex Novels edition

Osgood, McIlvaine published *A Group of Noble Dames* in 1896 as Volume XV in their Wessex Novels edition, the first uniform and complete edition of Hardy's works. Plates of the original edition of 1891 were used. In a letter of 18 September 1894 to Frederick Macmillan, Hardy mentioned *A Group of Noble Dames* as one of four volumes in which he proposed to introduce 'very slight alterations' (see *Letters*, II, 63). The only changes to the stories for the 1896 edition of *A Group of Noble Dames* were the correction of the two misprints in 'The First Countess of Wessex' and 'The Honourable Laura' (see the respective chapters on these stories) which Hardy had noted in June 1891. Hardy also added a Preface, dated June 1896, and there was a frontispiece by Henry Macbeth-Raeburn, entitled 'King's-Hintock Court'. The Macmillan Uniform edition of *A Group of Noble Dames* was printed from the 1896 Osgood, McIlvaine plates, which Macmillan purchased from Osgood, McIlvaine's successors, Harper & Brothers (London). It was first published in 1903 and was reprinted in 1914, 1924 and 1934. The same plates were used for the Macmillan Pocket edition of *A Group of Noble Dames* in 1906: this was a thin-paper edition, priced at 2/6, which was reprinted six times between 1911 and 1928.

1912 Macmillan Wessex edition

A Group of Noble Dames was published as Volume XIV of the Wessex edition in 1912. It was set from a marked copy of a 1906 printing of the Macmillan Uniform edition. It had a frontispiece entitled 'Wintoncester Cathedral (in "Lady Mottisfont")', a reproduction of a photograph taken by Hermann Lea. Hardy wrote to Lea on 7 June 1912 about the frontispiece:

> The view of Winchester would do, though it is a little injured in its effect by the mass of chairs, & by being so mathematically central. But it is not worth while to go to take another. If however, you should be going, please take one rather aslant, giving a glimpse of an aisle, & of some of the very fine monuments. However, perhaps such a view is not possible. (*Letters*, IV, 220)

The photograph which was eventually used for the frontispiece was taken slightly to the right of centre, suggesting that Lea followed Hardy's instructions. However, neither the aisle nor the monuments are visible. Gatrell notes that the frontispiece is very similar to Hardy's own drawing of the cathedral, which appeared in *Wessex Poems* as an illustration to 'The Impercipient' (1988, p. 140). In a footnote to the letter to Lea, Hardy added, 'Although Wilton is a better picture I think we are bound to Winchester': Hardy probably rejected the notion of showing Wilton House because he had not even given it a fictional name in 'The Marchioness of Stonehenge'.

All of the ten stories were revised but the changes were minimal and did not affect the main outline of the plots.

Notes

1 Millgate, p. 305.

2 See Purdy, p. 64.

3 *Letters*, I, 189. The *Graphic* had published 'The Romantic Adventures of a Milkmaid' in 1883.

4 *Letters*, VII, 113. 'The First Countess of Wessex' had been published in *Harper's New Monthly Magazine*, December 1889. 'Wessex Folk' had been accepted for publication in the same magazine in March–June 1891 and was later collected as 'A Few Crusted Characters' in *Life's Little Ironies*. In 1893, during an interview with Frederick Dolman at Max Gate, Hardy conceded that 'I suppose I was wasteful' in the use of subject matter in *A Group of Noble Dames*, but added that 'it doesn't matter, for I have far more material now than I shall ever be able to make use of' (Dolman, p. 75).

5 Douglas, p. 30.

6 *Life,* p. 236.

7 Gatrell (1988), pp. 80–96, gives an invaluable account of Hardy's dealings with the *Graphic* when publishing *A Group of Noble Dames*. After an independent collation of the stories, I can confirm Gatrell's view that the 1968 University of Notre Dame doctoral dissertation, 'A Textual Study of Thomas Hardy's *A Group of Noble Dames*', by A. Macleod is often inaccurate and unreliable.

8 See Gatrell, p. 81.

9 *Life*, p. 237.

10 Letter in the Dorset County Museum; quoted in Gatrell, pp. 81–2.

11 Gatrell (1988), p. 235.

12 'Lord R—' may be Lord Rowton, with whom Hardy once lunched at Lady Pembroke's (see *Letters*, II, 53). Similarly, Hardy told an interviewer in late 1891 that 'the Noble Dames are mostly drawn from life' ('Hodge', p. 2).

13 'The Merry Wives of Wessex', *Pall Mall Gazette*, 10 July 1891, p. 2, quoted in Millgate, p. 316.

CHAPTER 8

'The First Countess of Wessex'

The primary textual interest of 'The First Countess of Wessex' is that the final quarter of the serial version was considerably changed for its first appearance in *A Group of Noble Dames*. The differences in the plot of the serial are of a type which suggest that Hardy bowdlerized it.

The versions of the story which have textual significance are as follows:

Harper's   *Harper's New Monthly Magazine,* 80 (December 1889), 20–43, with headpiece and three illustrations by Alfred Parsons and four illustrations by C.S. Reinhart.

1891   *A Group of Noble Dames* (London: Osgood, McIlvaine, 1891), pp. 1–59. This was the first collected edition of the story in the expanded *A Group of Noble Dames* which now included ten stories, of which 'The First Countess of Wessex' was 'Dame the First'. Published at 6*s.* in an edition of 2000 copies on 30 May 1891. It was the first volume of Hardy's work which Osgood, McIlvaine had published.

1891H   *A Group of Noble Dames* (New York: Harper & Brothers, 1891), pp. 1–68. Published early in June 1891.

1896   *A Group of Noble Dames* (London: Osgood, McIlvaine, 1896), pp. 1–59. Volume XV in the first uniform and complete edition of Hardy's works. Plates of the original edition were used, and 'The First Countess of Wessex' is identical in every respect to *1891*, except for the correction of a misprint.

1912   *A Group of Noble Dames* (London: Macmillan, 1912), pp. 3–51. Volume XIV of the Wessex edition.

R.L. Purdy notes that the manuscript of 'The First Countess of Wessex', written on 50 quarto leaves and signed by Hardy, was sold in New York by the Anderson Auction Company on 29 May 1906, and its current location is unknown.[1]

Hardy wrote the story in the autumn of 1888, and he told H.M. Alden in a letter of 7 September that 'I just send a line to let you know, as promised, that I am getting through the Christmas story, & hope to finish it in about ten days – when I will send it on to you through Mr Osgood – so that I think it will be in your hands by Oct 1'.[2] On 4 August 1889, he wrote to Osgood that 'I have not received any proofs of the Christmas story. I hope it will not be printed without my corrections, there being some rather important touches & deletions required, which would have been done in MS. but for the hurry of sending off' (*Letters*, I,

196).

The story concerns Elizabeth, wife of the first Earl of Ilchester, and Hardy noted that the fifth Earl 'was angry with me for putting a legend of his family into the First Countess of Wessex', although when he was staying at their home, Melbury House, in 1915 he mentioned to Sydney Cockerell that 'the family have now quite forgiven me' (*Letters*, III, 190, and V, 134). Millgate dismisses the story that the publication of *A Group of Noble Dames* 'led to a general ostracism of the Hardys, first by the families concerned and then by all levels of local society'.[3]

The serial had a headpiece and three illustrations by Alfred Parsons, and four further illustrations by C.S. Reinhart. The drawings by Parsons are all exterior views of the settings, while Reinhart's illustrate scenes from the story. Hardy and Parsons had together visited Melbury House, the model for King's-Hintock Court, in late January 1889. Rebekah Owen recorded that

> Some of the Horners [see 'Sources' below] did not like [Hardy's] portrayal, nor Mr. Alfred Parsons giving an exact delineation of Mells Park in *Harper's Magazine*. Mr. Hardy had told Mr. Parsons *not* to draw the house exactly, nor, indeed, at all. (Weber, 1939, p. 74)

Mells Park is depicted as 'Falls-Park', the home of Squire Dornell, and Parsons illustrated both it and King's-Hintock Court.

Sources

'The First Countess of Wessex' has the most fully documented historical basis of any of the *Noble Dames*. Squire and Mrs Dornell are based on Thomas Strangways-Horner (1688–1741) and his wife, Susannah (1690–1758), who succeeded to her Strangways family estate at Melbury. Their only child, Elizabeth (born February 1723), married Stephen Fox (1706–76; hence Reynard) in 1736, when she was just thirteen years of age. Hardy found his information in Hutchins's *History of Dorset*, and he gives most of the dates accurately: for instance, Reynard is said to be 30 years old at the time of his marriage, and Squire Dornell is 48 (see Hutchins, II, 663, 665, 667, 679). One slight change is that Betty is eighteen-and-a-half years of age when she is first pregnant, so she would be at most nineteen when she gives birth, putting the year at 1742, whereas Hutchins shows that Elizabeth's first child was born in 1743.

Following the death of her husband in 1741, Susannah is said to have 'spent the latter part of her life in acts of piety, charity, and generosity. She built, repaired, or ornamented several churches; contributed largely to several charitable foundations, and the augmentation of poor livings' (Hutchins, II, 665). Unlike her fictional counterpart, however, there is no hint that she performed such acts in pious memory of her husband. The couplet from Reynard's epitaph in praise of his manners and mind is an exact quotation from Stephen Fox's monument, as inscribed in Hutchins (II, 679), and Betty's description of Reynard as 'the best of husbands, fathers and friends' on his epitaph, which she erected as 'his disconsolate widow', is an accurate paraphrase of Fox's epitaph: 'as a small token of her great affection to the best of husbands, fathers, friends, his disconsolate widow inscribes this marble'.

Fox was created Lord Ilchester in 1741 and the Earl of Ilchester in 1756. Reynard's letter to Betty in which he tries to induce her to live with him says that he is about to be made a Baron and would be raised to an Earl in a few years. The Fox-Strangways appear to have had nine children, like the 'numerous family' of Betty and Reynard.

Hardy appears not to have known of historical facts which are not in Hutchins. Elizabeth's mother, for instance, did not oppose the union at any time, and Elizabeth began to live with her husband two years before her father's death (see Brady, pp. 85–6). Hardy's principal invention for his story is Betty falling in love with someone else during the years of her separation from Reynard. Millgate believes that Hardy's mother was almost certainly the source of the story's traditional elements.

Rebekah Owen noted in her copy of *A Group of Noble Dames* that

> Often Mr. Hardy has got traditions from old people who got them from old family servants of the great families, whose representatives now think that Mr. Hardy ought not to have published them. At least Lord Ilchester thought so of 'The First Countess of Wessex', though Lady Pembroke and other descendants of Betty (he knows eight) are quite pleased. One Lord R— (I forget) said to Mr. Hardy, 'It is all nonsense, you know, of Ilchester to feel so, and I shall tell him so'. [...]
>
> Mr. Hardy told me to-day, Nov. 12, 1896, that he has known eight of Betty's descendants, from whom he has learned little facts which – had he known them in time – he should like to have put into the story. One was that Betty was so tiny she could not reach the door-knob of her husband's room. He said he had gleaned from such sources as I state above much which had never been handed down in the respective families. Squire Dornell is very true to life; he was just such a man. (Weber, 1939, pp. 73–4)[4]

This account of his sources broadly resembles the one which Hardy gave to an interviewer, Frederick Dolman, in 1893. Asked whether it was true that most of the stories in *A Group of Noble Dames* derived from hearsay rather than printed records, Hardy replied,

> Nearly all. In this story of 'The First Countess of Wessex', the only fact which can be learned from the records – and it was this, of course, which first attracted my attention – is that the child was married at that age. That is given in the usual way; born in such a year, married at another date, twelve years later. The other facts in the story have been handed down by word of mouth from generation to generation. It is a singular fact that I am personally acquainted with eight ladies who are her direct descendants, and they are nearly all as piquant as she.[5]

In the first collected edition of the story, published a couple of years before this interview, Hardy had described Betty as being only twelve-and-a-half years old, but he made her thirteen years of age in the 1912 Wessex edition.

Harper's New Monthly Magazine

There are eight numbered sections in the serial, and the first six of these correspond with the divisions in the collected edition. Thereafter, the plot is radically revised and any appearance of impropriety is removed from the final quarter of the story. In the version which readers now know, Betty and Phelipson elope. He finds she has smallpox, and he abandons her on their return home. Reynard arrives and kisses her, despite her illness. Mrs Dornell later notices that Betty is pregnant, and she learns of Betty's secret meetings with her husband. None of this is in the serial: no elopement, no kiss, no secret meetings and, above all, no pregnancy. The serial version appears to have been thoroughly bowdlerized.

What Hardy gives us instead is a tale of melodrama and intrigue. Tupcombe, Squire Dornell's manservant, arrives at King's-Hintock Court to fetch Betty to her father, and he finds a ladder going up to Betty's chamber. Wrongly assuming that Reynard has arrived and is going to spirit Betty away, he moves the ladder so that anyone descending it will fall. Phelipson tries to climb out of the window and breaks his neck, whereupon Betty swoons at great length. Reynard and Betty are eventually reconciled, but the scene is not dramatized and her change of heart seems prompted solely by the news that her husband is to be an Earl one day. After she has learned this news, Hardy asks simply, 'What could a poor girl do?' Reynard's visit to her is glossed over in four lines and the story rushes towards a close: 'his stay was but short – a matter of an hour or so – rather to her surprise. But the division between them was bridged, and the rest was a mere question of time.'

The ages of some of the characters are slightly different in the serial. Betty, for instance, is described in the opening paragraph as being thirteen or fourteen years of age, but later versions say she is twelve or thirteen, making her an even younger child bride. Her lover, Phelipson, is sixteen, rather than fifteen, as he later became. Another difference is that Reynard, the husband, is less generous and more peremptory in the serial than in subsequent versions. For instance, there are several references to the notion of him 'claiming' his wife, as if she were a chattel. Thus, when the Squire confronts him in Bristol, Reynard declares that he must 'insist on claiming' his rights, where the first collected edition reads 'insist on maintaining' (*1891*, p. 33). When he first arrived in Bristol, he wrote to Betty's mother in the serial that he would come to carry off his wife 'in a day or two', but later editions talk of him arriving 'in a few days' (p. 24), showing him to be less insistent and impatient.

Mrs Dornell's bedroom is differently located in the serial, where it is said to be almost opposite Betty's, and by keeping her door ajar she can ensure that Betty does not escape. Betty's sense of imprisonment is made even stricter in later versions, where her mother's chamber is a sort of passage-room to the girl's apartment, and Betty would have to go through it in order to leave.

The opening paragraph of the serial places King's-Hintock Court in 'the beautiful White-Hart or Blackmore Vale' but this was altered in later versions to read 'our beautiful Blackmoor or Blakemore Vale'. The origins of the older name of White-Hart are explained in *Tess* (ch. ii): 'The Vale was known in former times as the Forest of White Hart, from a curious legend of King Henry III's reign, in which the killing by a certain Thomas de la Lynd of a beautiful white hart which the king had run down and spared, was made the occasion of a heavy fine.' Why did Hardy omit the older name from the first collected edition? Perhaps he felt that he could not use 'White-Hart' without adding an explanation of its significance, and he did not want to repeat information which he knew would be given in the opening instalment of *Tess*, which was to appear only five weeks after the publication of *A Group of Noble Dames*.

1891 Osgood, McIlvaine

This original collected edition of 'The First Countess of Wessex' is essentially the same as the one which we read now in the Wessex edition, and its distinctive features will be illustrated by my later remarks on the changes which Hardy made to it when revising it in 1912. *1891* gives the unbowdlerized version of the story, but it is impossible to determine whether Hardy restored the text as it appeared in the manuscript or whether he re-wrote the story for the collected edition.

The *1891* version of 'The First Countess of Wessex' introduced a curious contradiction which editors have overlooked and which has been contained in all subsequent collected editions of the story. The anomaly concerns the father of young Phelipson, the suitor whom the Squire favours as a husband for his daughter, Betty. In all versions of the story which were published during Hardy's lifetime, including the serial, the Squire supports Phelipson because he is 'the son of a dear deceased friend of his' (*1891*, p. 7). As we saw earlier, in the serial version of the story, Phelipson is killed when he falls and breaks his neck while climbing out of Betty's window. However, in preparing the story for *1891*, one of the many changes which Hardy made was that Phelipson does not die but, instead, he rejects Betty when he learns that she has contracted smallpox, and we are told eventually that 'young Phelipson had been packed off to sea by his parents' (p. 51). In introducing this later reference to Phelipson's father, Hardy forgot that he had earlier described him as dead and did not amend it accordingly.

1891 Harper

The first American collected edition has some 150 differences in accidentals from the British edition, ignoring US spelling. There are also fifteen substantive variants which would mostly seem to be the result of house editing.

The principal alteration is that the two notes which Mrs Dornell and Reynard write no longer have their characteristic Augustan appearance: the frequent capitalization is removed and two archaic spellings ('expir'd' and 'anger'd') are modernized. Further changes include an alteration of 'your Betty' to 'your daughter Betty' (p. 10), no doubt for the benefit of inattentive readers, and the printing of 'damn' as 'd–'. There are three instances of nouns which were singular in the British edition becoming plural in the American edition: 'solicitations', 'reasons' and 'misgivings'. The first two of these are unique to *1891H*, but the last one is retained in the 1912 Wessex edition (p. 39). One possible explanation of this variant might be that the singular reading was a marginal emendation which Hardy made to the proofs of *1891* but which he omitted to add to the proofs which were sent to Harper's or to the duplicate copy of them which he retained and which became the basis for later editions of the story.

1896 Osgood, McIlvaine

The misprint in *1891*, 'a sa misfortune' (p. 7), is corrected in *1896* to 'as a misfortune'. *1891H* had also corrected it. Edward Clodd had pointed it out to Hardy in June 1891 (see *Letters*, I, 238–9).

1912 Macmillan Wessex edition

The appearance of the two family homes is slightly changed for *1912*. Falls-Park (based on Mells Park, a manor house near Frome in Somerset) is said to have a Palladian front (replacing the earlier 'classic') and to date from the reign of the first Charles rather than the second. King's-Hintock Court is now 'many-gabled' (p. 6), which replaces the earlier 'battlemented' and identifies it more closely with Melbury House. Another factual change is that Betty is now just gone thirteen years of age at the time of her marriage; in *1891* she had been only twelve and a half years old.

The news of Betty's marriage to Reynard is broken to her father by Lord Baxby, who says, 'Well, Dornell – so cunning reynard has stolen your little ewe lamb?' (p. 9). In earlier versions, 'reynard' had been capitalized, but *1912* draws more obvious attention to the symbolic meaning of the bridegroom's name.

For the story's first appearance after 1900, Hardy remembered to change a reference in the opening paragraph to 'the last century', which became 'the eighteenth century' (p. 3), although he neglected to make the necessary update to the same phrase in the final paragraph of the story.

Reynard's letter announcing his imminent arrival to carry off Betty causes her much consternation. Her mother in *1896* manages to calm her by promising that she will 'instantly' send the letter to her father who will act to stop him. In *1912* 'instantly' is altered to 'speedily' (p. 22). Apart from deleting the third use of this word in less than a page, the change has the advantage of establishing an ironic verbal parallel which stresses Mrs Dornell's duplicitous conduct: she promises that she will 'speedily' forward Reynard's letter, but we learn her true intention in the next paragraph, which is that Reynard must be 'speedily' installed as Betty's husband.

The Wessex edition corrects an error in the chronology of the story as it appeared in *1896*. After Dornell's ride to Bristol to see Reynard, he returns home and grows increasingly anxious in the earlier edition as 'the week' drew on and Reynard's arrival to claim Betty approached. However, we learned earlier that Reynard was going to come the day immediately following his Bristol meeting with Betty's father, so a week is too long to await him. *1912* corrects the mistake by substituting 'the morning' (p. 31). (The serial, incidentally, had correctly said that 'the afternoon' drew on.)

The single scene which was most substantially revised is the final conversation between Betty and her mother about Betty's pregnancy. Mrs Dornell's opening reference to Betty's 'dear father' in *1896* becomes the 'dear deceased' (p. 46), which echoes a change earlier on the same page from 'your dear father' to 'your dear dead father', Hardy stressing the irony of Mrs Dornell regarding her late husband as dear only when he is dead.

Betty confesses in *1896* to having seen her husband a dozen times in the past year, but in *1912* she follows this with the further admission: ' – I mean quite alone, and not reckoning – ' (p. 47), making the dozen meetings much more intimate. A new admission is that their 'accidental' meeting at Abbot's-Cernel took place 'in the ruined chamber over the gatehouse', which makes the professed chance encounter appear in its true light as a secret assignation. The newly-added italics in Mrs Dornell's reference to the meeting as 'an *accident*' emphasize her scornful scepticism about her daughter's account of events.[6]

Notes

1 See Purdy, p. 65.
2 *Letters,* I, 180.
3 Millgate (1982), p. 317.
4 Lady Gertrude Frances Herbert, Countess of Pembroke, was the daughter of the eighteenth Earl of Shrewsbury. 'Lord R—' may be Lord Rowton, with whom Hardy once lunched at Lady Pembroke's (see *Letters,* II, 53). Hardy knew a number of Betty's descendants, such as the Earls of Ilchester and Agnes Jekyll.
5 Dolman (1894), p. 78.
6 The other revisions to *1891* for the Wessex edition are as follows (*1912* is quoted first, and the pagination is that of *1912*): 'Hell/H—' (p. 4); 'unawares/unawares,' (p. 11); 'peerage/title' (p. 12); 'acquaintances/acquaintances,' (p. 12); 'O/Oh' (p. 16; also found on pp. 17, 21 (twice), 25, 29, 36 and 48); 'accompany her mother/accompany her' (p. 18); 'visit/visit,' (p. 24); 'this commission/his commission' (p. 25); 'treble doze/treble dose' (p. 26; a misprint in the Macmillan edition, which correctly reads 'dose' two lines earlier); 'over the airy uplands and through/through the pleasant woodlands and' (p. 27); 'Cross-roads/cross-roads' (p. 32); 'whom my illness will hinder waiting for him/she'll have a reason for not waiting for him' (p. 32); 'hinder

Betty from following to/hinder Betty's departure for' (p. 33); 'Tupcombe knew/he knew' (p. 34); 'and followed behind/and walked on to the house' (p. 34); 'serious/serious,' (p. 36); 'desireable/desirable' (p. 36; yet the Macmillan edition reads 'desirable' on p. 45); 'grievously/seriously' (p. 37); 'father,/father' (p. 38); 'woefully/seriously' (p. 38); 'much misgivings/much misgiving' (p. 39); 'pit/speck' (p. 43); 'Red Lion tavern/Red Lion' (p. 47); 'fully sure/quite sure' (p. 50); 'I wondered what could have happened, and then/ [not in *1894*] (p. 47); 'figured frock/white frock' (p. 48); 'South-Wessex/Mid-Wessex' (p. 51).

CHAPTER 9

'Barbara of the House of Grebe'

'Barbara' was among the stories which were most severely altered by Hardy for their British serialization in the *Graphic*, though not in this case for reasons of sexual propriety but in order to minimize the cruelty of Uplandtowers's treatment of his wife. Three pages of the manuscript were omitted which showed him terrifying Barbara by making her confront the mutilated statue of her late husband, and this excision had the added bonus for the editors of the *Graphic* that Hardy thereby also removed most of the bedroom scenes from the story.

The versions of the story which have textual significance are as follows:

Graphic	'Barbara (Daughter of Sir John Grebe)', *Graphic*, Christmas Number (published 1 December) 1890, pp. 4–5, 8–9. It was the first one of the six stories entitled *A Group of Noble Dames* published simultaneously in this issue.
HW	'Barbara, Daughter of Sir John Grebe', *Harper's Weekly*, 29 November 1890, pp. 937–40. As in the *Graphic*, it was the first of the six stories in *A Group of Noble Dames*. *Harper's Weekly* published these stories in four weekly instalments (29 November–20 December) and 'Barbara, Daughter of Sir John Grebe' was the only story in the first instalment.
1891	'Barbara of the House of Grebe', *A Group of Noble Dames* (London: Osgood, McIlvaine, 1891), pp. 61–106. This was the first collected edition of the story in the expanded *A Group of Noble Dames* which now included ten stories, of which 'Barbara of the House of Grebe' was 'Dame the Second'. Published at 6s. in an edition of 2000 copies on 30 May 1891. It was the first volume of Hardy's work which Osgood, McIlvaine had published.
1891H	'Barbara of the House of Grebe', *A Group of Noble Dames* (New York: Harper & Brothers, 1891), pp. 69–120. Published early in June 1891.
1896	'Barbara of the House of Grebe', *A Group of Noble Dames* (London: Osgood, McIlvaine, 1896), pp. 61–106. Volume XV in the Wessex Novels, the first uniform and complete edition of Hardy's works. Plates of the original edition were used, and 'Barbara of the House of Grebe' is identical in every respect to *1891*.
1912	'Barbara of the House of Grebe', *A Group of Noble Dames* (London: Macmillan, 1912), pp. 55–92. Volume XIV of the Wessex edition.

The manuscript of the *Graphic* stories is extant. It was presented by Hardy, through Sydney Cockerell, to the Library of Congress, Washington DC, in October 1911 when he was distributing his MSS. among various public collections. As R.L. Purdy notes, the MS. was foliated and rearranged by Hardy, and 'Barbara' is numbered 6–53; each of the six stories was also independently foliated and 'Barbara' is numbered 1–47.[1]

Sources

Barbara is based on Barbara Webb (1762–1819), daughter and eventual sole heiress of Sir John Webb, who married Anthony Ashley-Cooper (1761–1811), fifth Earl of Shaftesbury, on 17 July 1786. She died in Florence, as did Hardy's Barbara. Hardy found many minor details of his story in Hutchins's *History of Dorset*, but the principal features of his plot (the first marriage to Edmond, his mutilation and her ill-treatment by her second husband) are all entirely invented.

In the manuscript, Barbara is occasionally called Mabella (see below), which was the name of Barbara Webb's great-aunt, according to the Webb pedigree in Hutchins (III, 298). Barbara Grebe's father is called Sir John, as was Barbara Webb's, and their baronetcy was created 'a few years before the breaking out of the Civil War': the Webb baronetcy was created in 1640. The story opens around 1780, when Barbara Grebe is barely seventeen years of age (like Barbara Webb). We learn that Barbara's blood, 'through her mother, was compounded of the best juices of ancient baronial distillation, containing tinctures of Maundeville, and Mohun, and Syward, and Peverell, and Culliford, and Talbot, and Plantagenet, and York, and Lancaster, and God knows what besides'. Barbara Webb also had a distinguished ancestry: Hutchins records that her maternal grandmother was a Talbot, a name which features in Hardy's otherwise invented lineage, and her mother was descended from the ancient barons of Mauley, the last of whom died in 1415. Barbara Grebe has many children in quick succession by Uplandtowers but only one daughter reaches maturity, whereas Barbara Webb appears to have had only one child, also a daughter: neither of them, therefore, produced a male heir. Barbara Webb's daughter married the Honourable Mr Ponsonby, who was later created Lord de Mauley, and Barbara Grebe's daughter, we learn, married the Honourable Mr Beltonleigh, who was later created Lord Welland in all versions of the story before the first collected edition in 1891, when his title became that of Lord D'Almaine. It is possible to conjecture that Hardy made this revision to echo the Norman sound of the historical title.

Uplandtowers is said by Hardy to be the fifth Earl, as was Barbara Webb's husband, and we learn that he succeeded to the title in only his twelfth year, his father having died 'after a course of the Bath waters'. The historical Earl of Shaftesbury was even younger, being only nine years of age when he succeeded to the title, and his father similarly died in Bath, according to Hutchins (see III,

594; Hardy's comment about the waters seems a comic invention). Uplandtowers had no living son and heir, and the title passed to his nephew, whereas Shaftesbury's title passed to his brother (the MP for Dorchester). A major departure from Hutchins's pedigree is that Uplandtowers outlives Barbara, whereas the Earl of Shaftesbury died some eight years before his wife. This change allows Hardy to introduce the irony of the once brutal Uplandtowers being unable to marry again, despite his lack of an heir, because his affections have become untransferable.

Rebekah Owen recorded that 'All the *Group of Noble Dames* tales are true [except that] Mrs. Hardy says that "Barbara of the House of Grebe" is not' (Weber, 1952, p. 238).

The manuscript

The manuscript has some forty uncancelled and unique substantive variants, which must presumably have been altered at the serial proof stage. Nearly all such instances are a matter of a word or two at most, and are of little significance.

Hardy was very uncertain about his heroine's name at first. He begins by calling her Barbara, but this is deleted and Mabella is substituted. This name in turn is cancelled and the deleted Barbara has dotted underlining to mark it for retention. However, after fo. 31, Hardy originally wrote Mabella most of the time and then substituted Barbara. The change was not decisive, however, for on fo. 35, he first calls her Mabella, then she is twice referred to later on the same page as Barbara first, and then Mabella again. Hardy's source for the story, Hutchins's *History of Dorset*, shows that Mabella was a Webb family name.[2]

Hardy's alteration of his heroine's name in one particular instance helps to establish that the manuscript, though heavily revised, was used as the printers' copy for the *Graphic*. On fo. 8, Hardy hyphenated the name Barbara, so that the first three letters were at the end of one line and the remainder at the start of the next. He then scored out the name heavily, substituted Mabella and later marked 'Barbara' for retention with dotted underlining. The printer misread the cancelled word as 'But Barbara', where 'But' is his attempt to decipher the manuscript's 'Bar-', the three letters at the end of the line. The misprint appears in both the serial publications.

Hardy initially had much uncertainty about Edmond's occupation and background. A couple of deleted lines show that at first he was to have been a landscape painter and then a 'hopeful yeoman', and that his father was to have been, in turn, a curate given to non-conformity who died poor, a farmer and a music-teacher. Hardy eventually settled on Edmond's father or grandfather being a glass-painter. Lowering Edmond's social status in this way serves to make the match with Barbara increasingly unsuitable and explains why he needs to be sent on a Grand Tour of Europe to compensate for his lack of education.

A cancelled paragraph in the manuscript shows that Hardy originally intended Barbara to learn of Edmond's death much earlier in the story, *before* her marriage, and her reaction to the news at that time was to be 'scarcely surprised' (fo. 34). In the revised version, she learns of his death years later, and, significantly, after she has had a year of loveless marriage to Uplandtowers, which has no doubt made her prone to revive her feelings for her first husband. The letter informing her of his death arrives just before his statue, and the coincidence helps to explain her passionate reaction to it. Unlike her blank response in the cancelled paragraph, she now feels 'passionate love for his memory |gentle pity for his misfortunes|' (fo. 38; both serials follow the manuscript). In revising the story for its first collected edition in 1891, Hardy restored part of the deleted reading, so that she feels 'passionate pity for his misfortunes' (p. 92), which better explains her intense reaction to the statue. By delaying the announcement of Edmond's death, Hardy makes Barbara's behaviour more credible and allows her to have gained a deeper and more mature sympathy for her first husband's suffering.

The sculptor who makes Edmond's statue was originally to have lived in Florence, but Hardy later moved him to Pisa (presumably at the serial proof stage, since the two references to Florence are uncancelled in the manuscript). Hardy may have made this change because Florence is where Barbara eventually dies and he wanted to prevent any melodramatic link between her death and the statue.

The manuscript shows that Hardy altered the story's timescale and topography in several instances. The eloping lovers were originally to have stayed away for six months, not six weeks as it later became. Hardy may have altered it after writing the next page, where his narrator gives a sardonic description of the descending scale of happiness experienced by such newly-wedded lovers, moving from bliss in the first week to being temperate and reflective by the end of the month. At this rate, if Hardy had not altered his original timescale, the lovers would have become suicidal by the end of six months. They return home, then, after six weeks and Barbara prepares to move into Yewsholt Lodge, which on its first mention in the manuscript was called Wood Park.

Following his return after injury, Edmond leaves his wife a note saying that he is going away but will return after one year to see what her feelings for him are. A cancelled few words show that originally he had ended by saying that he was leaving England for ever and would see her no more. The revision means that he can eventually be presumed dead when he fails to return as promised, thus allowing Barbara to marry Uplandtowers.

'Barbara' was the first story in the serial versions of A Group of Noble Dames, and the manuscript has a prologue introducing the members of the Wessex Field and Antiquarian Club who form the narrators and audience of the stories. This prologue is an adapted version of the ending of 'The First Countess of Wessex' as it appeared in the collected edition of 1891, where it immediately preceded 'Barbara'. A few deleted phrases in the manuscript show that Hardy originally thought to open the serial version of his six tales with 'The Lady Caroline (Afterwards Marchioness of Stonehenge)', to be told by the Rural Dean, but this story was eventually placed second.

Graphic

There are five principal ways in which Hardy altered 'Barbara' to please the directors of the *Graphic*. The most important one is the omission of three pages from the manuscript which describe Uplandtowers grilling Barbara about her love for him, putting the mutilated statue at the foot of the bed and terrifying his wife on three consecutive nights until she suffers a breakdown. In the *Graphic*, she sees the mutilated statue only once, when it is still in her own boudoir; she then faints, recovers and instantly swears her love for Uplandtowers. Her revulsion at the sight of Edmond when he returns is also notably toned down. These two changes make it difficult to comprehend the extreme transformation in her attitude to Uplandtowers after he has deformed the statue, since we no longer have his prolonged torture of her or her sense of horror at the injuries suffered by Edmond. Other alterations are that Uplandtowers is made a much more humane man, and there is no mention of his wish for heirs or of his wife's gynaecological history.

The most bizarre change is the moral improvement in the character of Lord Uplandtowers, making him less cruel and sadistic. For instance, he does not force her to look at the statue on three consecutive nights, and when she faints after first seeing the mutilated image of Edmond he tries to disperse her terrors by a laugh in her ear which is oddly compounded of 'causticity, solicitude, and brutality'. All other versions of the story read 'causticity, predilection, and brutality'. If he had possessed any solicitude for her, he would not have mutilated the statue in the first place. After Barbara's death, his affection for her is described in the *Graphic* as being 'strange, hard, selfish', the last adjective replacing 'brutal', which is justifiably used everywhere else. The new Lord Uplandtowers was no doubt less offensive to *Graphic* readers, but the story loses much of its Gothic savagery.

The *Graphic*'s account of Edmond's return to Barbara after the fire has disfigured him removes much of the sense of her revulsion. Three paragraphs describing her horror when he reveals his face and how she tries vainly to bring herself to look at him are omitted, so that there is no mention of her shuddering at the sight of 'this human remnant'. Edmond no longer asks her, 'Can you bear such a thing of the charnel-house near you?' Elsewhere in the scene, words such as 'hideous', 'horrified', 'repulsive' and 'mutilated' are removed, although they all appeared in the American serial, and, similarly, Barbara's assurance that 'I do not loathe you' becomes the weak 'I do not know you'.

Any reference to Uplandtowers's hope of an heir is deleted, so we do not learn of his dislike of the heir-presumptive, a remote relative, and he does not blame Barbara much that there was no promise of children yet. When he catches Barbara embracing the statue passionately, the manuscript has him say to himself, 'This is where we evaporate – this is where ~~the~~ my lhopes of al successor in the title dissolves – ha-ha!' (fo. 43). The *Graphic* replaces all this merely with 'This is treachery to the living!', omitting any sexual element in Uplandtowers' response.

Oaths and expletives are much more genteel in the *Graphic*. A reference by

Barbara's father to 'the devil' becomes 'the deuce', while Uplandtowers's 'D–her!', which he says twice on learning of Barbara's marriage to Edmond, was altered to 'Hang her!' Similarly, his 'By G–' became 'By Heaven', while the American serial has merely 'By –'. (Incidentally, it was only in 1912 that 'Damn' and 'God' were first printed in full.)

When Uplandtowers visits the tutor who had accompanied Edmond on his tour to learn about his accident, the details of the injuries which Edmond suffered are much less gruesome. The tutor drew a sketch of the 'dead man', rather than of the 'disfigured head' which is in all other versions, and Hardy omitted Uplandtowers's comment that Edmond had 'neither nose nor ears' after the fire (the further 'nor lips scarcely!' was not added until 1912). The resulting mutilation of the statue which the sketch allows Uplandtowers to carry out is also given in much less detail in the *Graphic*, and Hardy omitted the explanation that, in the words of *Harper's Weekly*, 'it was a fiendish disfigurement, ruthlessly carried out, and was tinted to the hues of life, as life had been after the wreck'. In the *Graphic* version, we can only imagine why the statue has such a devastating effect on Barbara.

After Barbara is cured of her love for Edmond, Hardy deletes the question of how fright could cause such a change in her, and, more importantly, he also omitted the following comment on her behaviour, which reads in *Harper's Weekly* as follows:

> The strange upshot was that the cure became so permanent as to be itself a new disease. She clung to him so slavishly that she would not willingly be out of his sight for a moment.

The *Graphic* directors probably felt that a woman's love for her husband, no matter how pathological, should not be described as a disease. As if to underline and presumably approve of her wifely devotion, the *Graphic* alone explains that Barbara would have no sitting-room apart from 'her husband's', where all other versions simply say 'his'. Similarly, the *Graphic* omits Barbara's exclamation, 'how could I ever be so depraved!', since the notion of feminine depravity must have seemed an oxymoron (it is also omitted in *Harper's Weekly*, but restored for the collected edition in 1891). This respectable Barbara is seen earlier in the *Graphic*, when she swears to the statue of Edmond that 'I am ever faithful to you, despite my seeming fickleness'. All other versions have her confessing instead to 'my seeming infidelity'.

Of Barbara's later life, we do not hear in the *Graphic* how 'little personal events came to her in quick succession – half a dozen, eight, nine, ten such events' (also omitted in *Harper's Weekly*) or how 'half of them came prematurely into the world, or died a few days old' (included in *Harper's Weekly*). Indeed, in the *Graphic*, we are not told that she had eleven children in eight years, as the manuscript has it, or ten children as it is in *Harper's Weekly*, but that she merely had 'several'. The *Graphic*'s squeamishness about matters of pregnancy means that it thus loses the story's final irony that Uplandtowers is frustrated in his wish for a male heir, despite fathering so many children.

One particular phrase caused Hardy a great deal of trouble, it would appear.

After Barbara's death, the Dean of Melchester preached a sermon, as the manuscript puts it, on the folly of 'lsensuousl love ~~of~~ lthroughl the eyes ~~& senses~~ merely' (fo. 51). *Harper's Weekly* followed the manuscript except for the omission of 'sensuous' (perhaps Hardy felt that serial editors were likely to confuse 'sensuous' with 'sensual'). The *Graphic*, however, reads 'love of the form merely', as if Barbara's physical fascination with Edmond was really just a kind of aesthetic appreciation. The first collected edition is an amalgam and extension of these different versions: 'sensuous love for a handsome form merely' (p. 105).

One occasion when the *Graphic* and *Harper's Weekly* share a variant reading but where the first collected edition follows the manuscript with a different reading suggests that *1891* was set from duplicate *Graphic* proofs on to which Hardy had not marked this particular revision to the serials. *1891* and the manuscript talk of Barbara's 'maid' (p. 67), while the serials call her the 'woman'.

One other variant reading suggests that Hardy may have checked the *Graphic* proof against the manuscript. The manuscript initially described the people who were hurt in the Venetian fire as 'senseless forms' but Hardy altered this to 'senseless bodies' (fo. 20). The *Graphic*, however, eventually printed the deleted manuscript reading, which Hardy must have restored at proof stage. *Harper's Weekly* is different again, calling them 'senseless sufferers'. It is this reading which Hardy must have written on to the duplicate proof, since *1891* follows *Harper's Weekly*. Once again we see Hardy differently revising copies of the same proof.

Harper's Weekly

The American serialization of 'Barbara' is very close to the manuscript version and shows only half a dozen instances of bowdlerization, involving a few words at most. There are none of the large cuts made to the *Graphic*. *Harper's Weekly* includes Uplandtowers's wish for an heir, though with a slightly different version of the manuscript, which says that 'he blamed her much that there was no promise of this, and asked her what she was good for' (fo. 37). *Harper's Weekly* omits the last clause, thus removing the taunt. Hardy was clearly aware, though, that he had to handle the issue of heirs sensitively in both serials. In the manuscript, when he catches Barbara kissing the statue, he exclaims to himself, 'This is where we evaporate – this is where ~~the~~ my lhopes of al successor in the title dissolves – ha-ha!' (fo. 43). As we saw earlier, the *Graphic* replaces all this merely with 'This is treachery to the living!', omitting any sexual element in Uplandtowers' response. *Harper's Weekly* reads instead, 'This is treachery to the living; this is where my hopes are wrecked. Ha, ha!' The manuscript is quite blunt in showing the sexual consequences for Uplandtowers of Barbara's continuing obsession with Edmond. While the *Graphic* inevitably forbids any such mention, *Harper's Weekly* does at least hint at it in the vague reference to 'my hopes'. As in the *Graphic*, the American serial omits Barbara's confession of depravity and the enumeration of the ten children which came to her in quick succession. In *Harper's Weekly*, when Uplandtowers first finds Barbara with the statue, she has her 'lips' on Edmond's; all other versions rather more primly read 'mouth'.

The presentation of Barbara's reaction to the disfigured statue is slightly different from the manuscript. For instance, *Harper's Weekly* does not describe the fascination which the statue exerts as 'horrid', and the American serial adds a couple of lines not found in the manuscript: on the third night, 'she laughed more and more, staring at the image, till she literally shrieked with laughter'. Since later editions retain this description of Barbara's hysteria, Hardy must have added it as a marginal addition to the proofs and copied it on to a set of duplicate proofs which were used as the basis for *1891*.

After the fire, Edmond is said to have been saved by the care of several 'eminent' surgeons in both the manuscript and *Harper's Weekly*. The *Graphic*, however, described them as 'skilful' and later editions in this instance follow the *Graphic*. One can see the point of the revision, since it is strictly the surgeons' skill and not their eminence which is relevant to saving Edmond. Perhaps Hardy noted this alteration on the *Graphic* proofs and on the duplicate set but simply forgot to copy it on to the proofs for *Harper's Weekly*.

The American serial has a handful of other unique substantive variants which have not yet been described, but they are all minor and can be explained as the work of a Harper's editor or compositorial error.

1891 Osgood, McIlvaine

The first collected edition has some seventy new substantive readings. Most of these are individual words, but there is one lengthy insertion of twelve lines describing Barbara's growing attachment to Uplandtowers at the end of the story. A quarter of the changes were made to the final couple of pages showing Barbara's avowal of love for her husband and its consequences.

The substantial addition occurs after Uplandtowers promises never to put the statue before Barbara's eyes again:

> 'Never', said he.
> 'And then I'll love you', she returned eagerly, as if dreading lest the scourge should be applied anew. 'And I'll never, never dream of thinking a single thought that seems like faithlessness to my marriage vow'.
> The strange thing now was that this fictitious love wrung from her by terror took on, through mere habit of enactment, a certain quality of reality. A servile mood of attachment to the Earl became distinctly visible in her contemporaneously with an actual dislike for her late husband's memory.
> (p. 103)

The main function of this addition is to stress that Barbara's new love for her husband has no real substance to it and is 'fictitious'. The reference to her apparent 'faithlessness' would also have been difficult to make in the earlier serials.

A further revision is to make Barbara's change of affection gradual. In previous versions, she had experienced 'a complete reversal of emotion' the moment she regained consciousness after her fainting fit. In *1891*, she has instead only 'a considerable change' (p. 102) on awaking, and the next morning her mood of attachment to Uplandtowers 'grew and continued when the statue was removed' (p. 103). Earlier this had read 'continued and the statue was removed'. This revision has two consequences. Firstly, the gradual alteration of her feelings appears more realistic than the magical transformation. Also, in the earlier versions the statue is removed as a reward for her continuing good behaviour, whereas in *1891* the removal of the statue *causes* her increasing affection, strengthening the link between her love for her husband and her revulsion at the deformed statue. Similarly, after recovering from her fit, Barbara bursts into tears and in *Harper's Weekly* Hardy had uniquely explained that 'his cruelty had not brought hatred, but love'. For *1891* this description of her love is premature and Hardy removes the whole sentence. Finally, the statue is not now removed the next morning, as it was in previous versions, but at some indefinite time in the future, again indicating a longer timescale to her change of feelings.

After her conversion to loving Uplandtowers, she is no longer in *1891* described as 'scared and beautiful' (her beauty is beside the point here) but as 'scared and enervated' (p. 104), stressing the extent to which her husband has worn her down to the point of emotional exhaustion, and the blame is placed even more firmly with Barbara's parents for the wasted potential of her life. Were it not for their ignoble ambition in wanting Barbara to marry well, her existence might have been developed to 'so much higher purpose' (p. 104), which replaces the weaker 'such higher purposes'.

The reunion between Barbara and the deformed Edmond becomes even more melodramatic than before, and there is an increased stress on her revulsion. She has 'ashy lips' (p. 84) rather than just 'parted lips', and she looks at 'this human remnant, this *écorché*' (p. 85), which replaces the earlier 'this human fragment'. Edmond acknowledges how 'your Adonis' has changed, where earlier he had described himself as 'your Apollo'; *1891* appropriately emphasizes that Barbara loved Edmond's physical form and not his virtuous character. Sympathy for Edmond's plight is enhanced by a new reference to him as Barbara's 'poor' (p. 87) husband. His hideousness is increased by a description of him as 'lopped and mutilated' (p. 89) where *Harper's Weekly* had merely said he was 'mutilated'. *1891*'s reading here is closer in fact to the manuscript's 'docked and mutilated'.

Many other features of the story are similarly made more grotesque or melodramatic. Indeed, the change of title to 'Barbara of the House of Grebe' may be intended to recall Poe's 'The Fall of the House of Usher' and its Gothic apparatus. Hardy's story indeed becomes markedly more lurid in *1891*. For instance, Edmond's mutilated statue is 'rendered still more shocking' (p. 98) by being tinted to the hues of life, and Barbara is forced to confront its 'cropped and distorted features' (p. 101), which replaces *Harper's Weekly*'s 'mutilated' and the manuscript's 'docked'. After Edmond's death, Barbara's grief took the form of 'passionate pity' (p. 92), not 'gentle pity' as it had formerly been, and *1891*'s new reading better prepares the reader for the strength of Barbara's extreme response to the statue when it arrives. Another new detail is that Uplandtowers began to explain about his little shrine 'when they were in the dark' (p. 101), no doubt to exaggerate the garish impact of the mutilated statue lit by candles on each side. Barbara's shrieking laughter is now followed by the dramatic pause of a moment of silence before her collapse. On regaining consciousness after her fainting fit, Barbara in *1891* for the first time is said to have kissed Uplandtowers 'with gasps of fear abjectly' (p. 103). She 'begged' him to take the statue away (replacing 'sobbed'), and when she says that she cannot endure recollection of Edmond, Hardy adds 'cried the poor Countess slavishly' (p. 103).

The period of Edmond's recuperation is lengthened and its stages are made more specific in *1891*. He was well enough to write to Barbara only 'after long weeks' (p. 78; *HW* had the vague 'in due time'), and the time drew on 'slowly' (p. 79; 'thus' in *HW*). In total, he is separated from Barbara for seventeen months, rather than the earlier sixteen, increasing the gap between the length of his absence and the brevity of their married life together.

Two or three minor changes may be noted. Edmond is described as 'plebeian' for the first time in *1891*, no doubt to emphasize his social inferiority to Barbara. Edmond tells his father-in-law that he would be happy to live at Yewsholt if it were no bigger than a sedan-chair; this replaces 'sentry-box' in all the earlier versions. Barbara's daughter became the wife of Lord Welland in the manuscript and serials, and this title was altered to Lord D'Almaine in *1891* and again to Lord d'Almaine in *1912*.

In the serial versions, 'Barbara' is the first of the six Noble Dames, but in this first collected edition it is second, preceded by 'The First Countess of Wessex'. These two stories form a natural contrast: in the first, a young girl is not allowed to marry the man of her choice but eventually finds happiness with the husband her mother has arranged for her, whereas in 'Barbara' the heroine does marry her chosen one but eventually ends up with the husband of her family's choice and finds only a very ambiguous love.

1891 Harper

There are ten substantive differences between the British and American 1891 editions of 'Barbara' in *A Group of Noble Dames*. All are individual minor words and could be explained as editorial revision at Harper's since they mostly involve relative pronouns. The first American collected edition also has some 125 differences in accidentals from the British edition, ignoring US spelling.

1912 Macmillan Wessex edition

Hardy made eleven short substantive changes to 'Barbara' when preparing the Wessex edition, but he made no major alteration to the story as it had appeared in *1891*. The extent of Edmond's injuries in the fire is increased, so that he has neither nose nor ears 'nor lips scarcely' (p. 85). This serves to underline that, when Barbara is kissing the lips of Edmond's statue, she is kissing what no longer existed in reality. Also, Hardy increased the number of years in which Barbara bore her eleven children from eight to nine, perhaps feeling that eight years was too quick to have so many babies, even if half of them were premature. Finally, Hardy overlooked the need to alter a reference to 'the end of the last century' (p. 56), now that it was being published for the first time after 1900 (he had made one necessary adjustment to a similar phrase in 'The First Countess of Wessex' but omitted to make another in that story).[3]

Notes

1 See Purdy, pp. 64, 65.
2 See Hutchins, III, 298.
3 For the sake of a complete record, the other revisions to *1891* for the Wessex edition are as follows (*1912* is quoted first, and the pagination is that of *1912*): 'Melchester;/Melchester:' (p. 55); 'Barbara and/Barbara, and' (p. 56); 'further/farther' (p. 57); 'by Heaven!/by G–!' (p. 59); 'up/up,' (p. 59); 'By God/By G–' (p. 60); 'Damn her!/D– her!' (p. 60, twice); 'sobs,/sobs.' (p. 61); 'extend/increase' (p. 66); 'support/follow' (p. 66); 'now/now,' (p. 72); 'dreadful/hideous' (p. 73); 'O/Oh' (p. 73); 'WIFE./WIFE' (p. 76); 'dozen/twenty' (p. 76); 'tenderness/love' (p. 81); 'her she returned to/her, she entered' (p. 83); 'further/farther' (p. 83); 'furthest/farthest' (p. 86); 'by God/by G–' (p. 87); 'O/Oh' (p. 87); 'facing/near' (p. 87); 'wax candle/wax-candle' (p. 88); 'O/Oh' (p. 88); yet/as yet' (p. 88); 'tightly/tightly,' (p. 90); 'd'Almaine/D'Almaine' (p. 90); 'or,/or' (p. 91).

CHAPTER 10

'The Marchioness of Stonehenge'

'The Marchioness of Stonehenge' is one of three stories in *A Group of Noble Dames* which have no known source (the others are 'Lady Mottisfont' and 'The Honourable Laura'). Shortly after it first appeared in collected form, Hardy was urged to dramatize it by Lord Lytton, to whom he wrote on 15 July 1891 that 'the possibilities of the Marchioness of Stonehenge as a play had not struck me, & I am glad to have your suggestion on the point. I am outside theatrical life, except very occasionally; but if any opportunity offers of putting the suggestion in practice I shall not fail to do so' (*Letters*, I, 240). The opportunity, however, never did arise. In 1907, he mentioned in a letter to J.M. Bulloch that he had been 'soundly rated' (*Letters*, III, 250) for inventing a plot in which a sweetheart adopts the child of her lover's wife.

The versions of the story which have textual significance are as follows:

Graphic	'The Lady Caroline (Afterwards Marchioness of Stonehenge)', *Graphic*, Christmas Number (published 1 December) 1890, pp. 9, 12. It was the second of the six stories entitled *A Group of Noble Dames* published simultaneously in this issue.
HW	'The Lady Caroline (Afterward Marchioness of Stonehenge)', *Harper's Weekly*, 6 December 1890, pp. 959, 962. As in the *Graphic*, it was the second of the six stories in *A Group of Noble Dames*. *Harper's Weekly* published these stories in four weekly instalments (29 November–20 December) and 'The Lady Caroline' began the second of these, followed in the same issue by 'Anna, Lady Baxby'.
1891	'The Marchioness of Stonehenge', *A Group of Noble Dames* (London: Osgood, McIlvaine, 1891), pp. 107–28. This was the first collected edition of the story in the expanded *A Group of Noble Dames* which now included ten stories, of which 'The Marchioness of Stonehenge' was 'Dame the Third'. Published at 6*s*. in an edition of 2000 copies on 30 May 1891. It was the first volume of Hardy's work which Osgood, McIlvaine had published.
1891H	'The Marchioness of Stonehenge', *A Group of Noble Dames* (New York: Harper & Brothers, 1891), pp. 121–43. Published early in June 1891.
1896	'The Marchioness of Stonehenge', *A Group of Noble*

Dames (London: Osgood, McIlvaine, 1896), pp. 107–28.
Volume XV in the Wessex Novels, the first uniform and
complete edition of Hardy's works. Plates of the original
edition were used, and 'The Marchioness of Stonehenge' is
identical in every respect to *1891*.

1912   'The Marchioness of Stonehenge', *A Group of Noble
Dames* (London: Macmillan, 1912), pp. 95–111. Volume
XIV of the Wessex edition.

The manuscript of the *Graphic* stories is extant. It was presented by Hardy,
through Sydney Cockerell, to the Library of Congress, Washington DC, in
October 1911 when he was distributing his MSS. among various public
collections. As R.L. Purdy notes, the MS. was foliated and rearranged by Hardy,
and 'The Marchioness of Stonehenge' is numbered 54–73; however, each of the
six stories was also independently foliated and 'The Marchioness of Stonehenge'
is numbered 1–20.[1] The final leaf, fo. 74, is missing; it contained links cancelled
and rewritten when the stories were collected in *1891*.

Manuscript

The manuscript shows a dozen uncancelled and unique substantive variants,
which must presumably have been altered at the serial proof stage. All such
instances are a matter of a word or two at most. The only one of note occurs
when Hardy described Caroline as having a 'reposeful life' (fo. 65) after she had
persuaded Milly to pass herself off as her husband's widow. This suggestion of
Caroline leading a peaceful existence does not tally with the previous paragraph
where we learned how a 'strange light, as of pain' (fo. 65), shot from her eye
when she saw Milly tending her husband's grave. Hardy changed 'reposeful life'
to 'smooth arrangement', which is what all printed versions read.

The story was originally called simply 'The Lady Caroline', and Hardy added
'afterwards Marchioness of Stonehenge' to the title as an interlineation after
completing the story. This is apparent because throughout the manuscript Hardy
originally referred to her as the Marchioness of Athelney, and then deleted this
and substituted Stonehenge. Athelney is a village north-east of Taunton in
Somerset, and Hardy does not appear to have used the name elsewhere. Kristin
Brady makes the interesting observation that the title is ironic, seeing it as
appropriate that 'those women who place rank above natural instinct – "The
Marchioness of Stonehenge", "Lady Mottisfont", and "The Lady Icenway" –
should bear the titles for which they sacrifice their sexual and maternal
passions'.[2]

In the manuscript, Caroline told Milly that she had married at 'the church of
St ~~Fridwell's in Exonbridge city~~ |Shastonbury Michael's in Bath city|' (fo. 63).
The first place seems to be a thinly veiled reference to St Sidwell's in Exeter
(later mentioned in the poem, 'The Carrier'). Shastonbury is one of the two
names which Hardy gave to Shaftesbury.

Caroline's reaction to the death of her husband in her chamber undergoes a significant modification in the manuscript:

> Her first feelings had undoubtedly been those of ~~regret for~~ |passionate grief at| the loss of him: her second thoughts were concern at her own position |as the daughter of an earl|. "O why, why, my ~~darling~~ |~~dearest~~| |unfortunate| husband, did you die in my chamber at this hour!" she said ~~passionately~~ |piteously|to the corpse. (fo. 58)

Originally, she was passionate not about his death but about its inconvenient location. Perhaps Hardy felt that this was portraying her too crudely as being obsessed with her social position, although the resulting change is balanced by the diminution of 'darling' and 'dearest' to the ironic 'unfortunate' (for whom?).

Some deleted but legible original readings show Hardy altering some slight details of the plot. The husband was at one time able to climb up to Caroline's bedroom not by means of a rope ladder, as it became, but by 'a portable ladder of ash wood, thin and light, but exceedingly strong' (fo. 56). This would seem likely to make him rather conspicuous, not to say suspicious, in the neighbourhood. Originally, Milly and the child were to have stayed in her father's cottage, rather than moving away, but this would have meant the boy would have surely got to know the identity of his real mother living nearby. As it is, Caroline settles a 'comfortable little allowance' on them; this had initially been a 'liberal allowance' (fo. 69), but Hardy needed to reduce it so that Milly had to make many material sacrifices to educate the boy, thus helping to ensure his preference for her over Caroline at the end of the story.

Graphic

Decorum obliged Hardy to make three main changes to scenes in the *Graphic* version of the story. These concern the husband's habit of visiting Caroline at night, the time of his death in her boudoir in the early hours of the morning, and the removal of any references to her pregnancy.

Hardy simply omitted altogether the description in the manuscript of how the husband would visit Caroline 'after nightfall' (fo. 56) by climbing up to her apartments, and his visit during which he dies takes place not 'one dark ~~evening~~ |midnight|' (fo. 57) but 'one evening'. The subsequent reference to one o'clock in the morning is also removed. Because the time of death has been made earlier, Caroline does not think to awaken her mother to enlist her help. Hardy presumably felt that the clandestine meetings would be less morally objectionable if they did not occur under the cover of deepest night.

References to pregnancy are omitted in the *Graphic*. For instance, when Lady Caroline is ordering Milly to return her wedding ring, she tells her that 'I am in a grief and a trouble I did not expect!' The *Graphic* then alters Caroline's whispered words of explanation about her pregnancy as they appear in the manuscript and all printed versions of the tale:

Manuscript [etc.]	Graphic
And Lady Caroline whispered a few words to the girl.	'My heart reproaches me so for having been ashamed of him, that I get no rest night or day.'
"O my lady!" said |the thunderstruck| Milly. "What <u>will</u> you do?" (fo. 66)	

Lady Caroline in the *Graphic* wants her ring back out of guilt, whereas elsewhere her motive is mere social respectability, which is consistent with her conduct throughout most of the story. She later claims in the *Graphic* that her wish to reclaim her husband is prompted by a dislike of deceit, rather than because she is pregnant:

Manuscript	Graphic
"I cling to him, & won't let him go |to such as you!| How can I, when he is the father of the babe that's coming to me?" (fo. 67)	'I cling to him, and won't let him go to such as you! How can I, honestly?'

The *Graphic* similarly omits Caroline's later comment that her claim to have been married would appear to be merely an invention 'to save me from disgrace' (fo. 68), as well as the reference to her feeling pity for Milly 'in spite of her own condition' (fos. 67–8). The first reference to the boy occurs when Milly comes home 'with an infant in her arms, the child of the marriage of Lady Caroline'. This unique description of the boy who has miraculously appeared in the story from nowhere is primarily concerned to remind the reader that he is not illegitimate, and that Lady Caroline is still respectable. Or is it, perhaps, a sign of Hardy's quiet protest at having to make all these ridiculous changes in the *Graphic* to conceal the pregnancy of a woman who is, he reminds us, legally married?[3]

Another change which may have been forced on Hardy is to the description of the newly-weds as 'both being supremely happy & content' (fo. 56), which in the *Graphic* becomes 'both being presumably happy and content', the implication being, as Gatrell observes, that 'they should be utterly miserable if they had any right feeling'.[4] The *Graphic* editors may have felt that supreme happiness and contentment were hardly a fitting punishment for a clandestine marriage to a social inferior, even one who has the good grace to drop dead within a month.

The tone of the threat which Lady Caroline makes to Milly is quite different in all three early versions of the story. She says that she will always be her father's friend if Milly agrees to pose as a widow, and in the manuscript she follows this merely with 'if not – well' (fo. 63). *Harper's Weekly* reads 'if not – well, the reverse', while the *Graphic* has 'if not – the reverse'. These three variations seem to move from the unstated to the reluctant to the downright blunt and hostile. Later collected readings have 'if not, it will be otherwise', which allows the threat to be unspecified.

Much of the final paragraph of the *Graphic* and *Harper's Weekly* versions is broadly similar to the ending of the 1891 version of 'Squire Petrick's Lady', which precedes 'Anna, Lady Baxby' in the collected edition, the next story in the serial publications.

Harper's Weekly

The American serial has five significant variants which are retained in subsequent collected versions of the story, although they are not found in either the manuscript or the *Graphic*. This is further evidence that Hardy sent a differently revised set of the *Graphic* proofs to the editors at *Harper's Weekly* and that he kept an emended copy including these American revisions which he consulted when composing the first book-edition in 1891.

In *Harper's Weekly*, Caroline's husband is made more menial and the social distance between them is increased:

> The young woman who rode fine horses, and drove in pony chaises, and was saluted deferentially by every one, and the young man who trudged afoot, and directed the tree-felling, and the laying out of fish-ponds in the park, were husband and wife.

The manuscript and the *Graphic* merely said that the young man 'walked', but 'trudged afoot' seems much less dignified, and opens up a stronger contrast between the pedestrian husband and Lady Caroline driving in her pony chaises. (Later collected editions seem to have introduced and perpetuated a compositorial error in printing 'trudged about'.) His fish-ponds are also much less impressive than the rather grand 'lake' whose construction he supervised in the manuscript and the *Graphic*.

1891 Osgood, McIlvaine

Hardy made numerous small changes to the story when collecting it in the first book-edition in 1891. The two incidents which show the most extensive revision are the young husband's moment of death and Caroline's means of disposing of the body.

The husband's sudden death is made more dramatic and is also more credibly and fully explained as being caused by his distress at the news that Lady Caroline has begun to have more regard for her social position than for him. The manuscript and the two serials had all given the same rather curt presentation of the scene, but Hardy took the opportunity in *1891* to add extra details. For the first time, we learn that Caroline's words to him that night had not only excited but also 'angered' him, and he sees that cold reason had come 'to his lofty wife'. His 'agitation' is such that he 'gasped, rose' and sank to the floor 'before he had gone another step' (p. 112). All the quoted words are new to *1891*. Where earlier versions of the story had simply explained at this point that the husband was 'liable to attacks of this kind', now Hardy explicitly states that he was 'liable to attacks of heart-disease' (later emended to 'heart-failure' in *1912*).

Lady Caroline's means of disposing of the body caused Hardy problems at all stages of composition. How could she have done it? In the manuscript and *Harper's Weekly*, she tied his hands together with a handkerchief, hauled up the rope ladder by which he had entered, attached the ladder to the handkerchief and lowered him down. In the *Graphic*, Lady Caroline's room was moved to the ground floor (no romantic climbing up to the beloved's boudoir there) so she just let him slide over the window sill. When he came to prepare *1891*, Hardy must have felt that lowering him out of the window on a rope ladder was an improbable feat for Lady Caroline to perform, so he makes her drag him down the stairs and then over the window sill. The upstairs chamber and the downstairs window in *1891* are, then, a combination of the two different versions of the scene as presented in the manuscript and the serials. Lest a reader is beginning to wonder where Caroline finds the strength for all this, Hardy adds the helpful reference to her being 'robust as she was' (p. 114). Incidentally, in *1891* Hardy mentions for the first time that not only did Caroline dress herself before leaving the house but that she also dressed her husband, making explicit the sexual nature of their meeting.

The narrator at the start of the story is given a stronger identity and character in *1891*, introducing more of his own opinions and experiences. In the opening sentence he talks of the classical mansion 'with which I used to be familiar', and he shortly after registers a greater sense of admiration for Robert South, whose sermons, he says, might be read 'much' more than they are, an appropriate sentiment for a rural dean. In drawing conclusions from his tale towards the end of the story, he is markedly less willing than in previous versions to make generalizations. For instance, in describing the effect on Lady Caroline of her son's rejection of her, he now says that 'it was in the perverseness of *her* human heart that his denial of her should add fuel to the fire of her craving for his love' (p. 127; my italics). 'Her' replaces 'the', which in the manuscript and serials had made his observation universally applicable. Similarly, when he wonders how much scorn a cottager such as Milly may show to a peeress, he says that 'in this case' it was not so little as may be supposed, cautiously limiting his answer now to the two individuals concerned.

Hardy made some refinements in *1891* to the confrontation between the two women and the son at the climax of the story, as he was to do again in *1912*. When the boy is asked to choose Milly or Caroline as his mother, 'his answer amazed and stupefied her [Caroline]' (p. 126). Such is the Lady Caroline's conceit that it had clearly never crossed her mind that her son could reject her. He then proceeds to refer to Milly as a 'dear devoted soul' (p. 126), emphasizing the contrast between the two women.

In *1891*, 'The Marchioness of Stonehenge' immediately precedes 'Lady Mottisfont' (they had been the second and sixth of the stories in the serials). Hardy thus juxtaposes a pair of tales about unwanted children which reach opposing conclusions about the endurance of adoptive love.

1891 Harper

The first American collected edition has some eighty differences in accidentals from the British edition, ignoring US spelling. There are also two substantive variants which would seem to be the result of house-editing. A reference to 'this country' becomes 'his country' because of the foreign audience, and 'Caroline' is altered to 'Lady Caroline' (*1891*, p. 120), which is what she is called throughout the rest of the story.

1912 Macmillan Wessex edition

The Wessex edition introduced 26 changes to *1891*, fifteen of which are substantive. The young husband dies of 'heart-failure' rather than 'heart-disease' (*1912*, p. 98), which seems a more likely cause of such a sudden death. Lady Caroline then plunges under the trees with the corpse, 'still dragging him by his tied hands' (p. 99), an additional explanatory detail which shows Hardy still trying to make the disposal of the body more credible.

When Caroline decides to tell Milly the story of her secret marriage, she arranges to meet her by the dead husband's grave at dusk, a solemn place and hour 'which she had chosen on purpose' (p. 102), which, arguably, shows Caroline as calculating the effect of her story on Milly, rather than being merely sentimental. Caroline tells Milly that she was married at the 'church of St. Something' (p. 102) in Bath; all earlier versions of the story had given the name of the church as St Michael, but Caroline's new ignorance of the name makes it all the more credible that nobody went to the church and checked Milly's claim to have been married to the dead man, since the location of the wedding was not known. It also gives a further reason why Lady Caroline cannot prove that her marriage took place before her pregnancy, because she does not know where to go to produce the register (p. 106).

The confrontation between the two women and the son at the end of the story is slightly altered in *1912*. The son tells Lady Caroline that he cannot love her because 'you were *once* ashamed of my poor father, who was a sincere and honest man; therefore, I am *now* ashamed of you' (p. 110; my italics indicate the new words in *1912*), which gives a greater rhetorical emphasis to his rejection of her. He had earlier kissed Milly and he now does as Caroline requests and kisses her too, '*but with a difference – quite* coldly' (my italics), the additional words in *1912* pointing the distinction between the two kisses.[6]

Notes

1 See Purdy, pp. 64, 65.
2 Brady, p. 91.
3 This change led Hardy to make another one in the next paragraph in the *Graphic*, so that we learn that there was no child of 'this' marriage to the Marquis of Stonehenge,

to distinguish it from the one referred to earlier.

4 Gatrell (1988), p. 92.

5 The three other occasions when *Harper's Weekly* and later collected editions differ from the reading in the manuscript and the *Graphic* are as follows (*HW* first, followed by MS./*Graphic*; pagination is that of *1891*): 'the Lady Caroline's nerves/her nerves' (p. 114); 'transfer to her/place her in' (p. 120); 'had moreover/having' (p. 123).

6 For the sake of a complete record, the other revisions to *1891* for the Wessex edition are as follows (*1912* is quoted first, and the pagination is that of *1912*): 'father/father,' (p. 95); 'the visit/that visit' (p. 97); 'staircase/stair-case' (p. 97); 'longer/longer,' (p. 97); 'O/Oh,' (p. 98, twice); 'solitary hour of one/hour of one' (p. 99); 'O/Oh' (p. 102); 'brooch/locket' (p. 103); 'O–but/Oh–but' (p. 105); 'child/babe' (p. 106); 'O, this/Oh, this' (p. 106); 'ostensible widow/widow' (p. 107); 'her own/her son' (p. 108); 'strong/strong,' (p. 109); 'heart/heart,' (p. 109); 'said the quartermaster/he said' (p. 110); 'O/Oh' (p. 110).

CHAPTER 11

'Lady Mottisfont'

'Lady Mottisfont' is one of three stories in *A Group of Noble Dames* which have no known source (the others are 'The Marchioness of Stonehenge' and 'The Honourable Laura'). The Countess may be modelled on an Italian contessa of great beauty whom Hardy met in Venice in 1887: as Hardy wrote in the *Life*, 'it is not known whether the Italian Contessa in *A Group of Noble Dames* was suggested by her; but there are resemblances'.[1] Sir Ashley Mottisfont's name derives from Ashley Down and Mottisfont Priory, north of Romsey, Hampshire, and his home, Deansleigh, is based on Broadlands, one mile south of Romsey. It was the birthplace and for long the home of Lord Palmerston. Fernell Hall, which the Contessa leases, is probably the former Embley House, two miles to the west (although Hardy places it further north by the river) and once the home of Florence Nightingale.

The versions of the story which have textual significance are as follows:

Graphic   *Graphic*, Christmas Number (published 1 December) 1890, pp. 16, 20, 24. It was the final one of the six stories entitled *A Group of Noble Dames* published simultaneously in this issue.

HW   *Harper's Weekly*, 20 December 1890, pp. 994–5. As in the *Graphic*, it was the last of the six stories in *A Group of Noble Dames*. *Harper's Weekly* published these stories in four weekly instalments (29 November–20 December) and 'Lady Mottisfont' was the only story in the final instalment.

1891   *A Group of Noble Dames* (London: Osgood, McIlvaine, 1891), pp. 129–52. This was the first collected edition of the story in the expanded *A Group of Noble Dames* which now included ten stories, of which 'Lady Mottisfont' was 'Dame the Fourth'. Published at 6s. in an edition of 2000 copies on 30 May 1891. It was the first volume of Hardy's work which Osgood, McIlvaine had published.

1891H   'Lady Mottisfont', *A Group of Noble Dames* (New York: Harper & Brothers, 1891), pp. 144–69. Published early in June 1891.

1896   *A Group of Noble Dames* (London: Osgood, McIlvaine, 1896), pp. 129–52. Volume XV in the Wessex Novels, the first uniform and complete edition of Hardy's works. Plates of the original edition were used, and 'Lady Mottisfont' is identical in every respect to *1891*.

1912   *A Group of Noble Dames* (London: Macmillan, 1912), pp. 115–33. Volume XIV of the Wessex edition.

The manuscript of the *Graphic* stories is extant. It was presented by Hardy, through Sydney Cockerell, to the Library of Congress, Washington DC, in October 1911 when he was distributing his MSS. among various public collections. As R.L. Purdy notes, the MS. was foliated and rearranged by Hardy, and 'Lady Mottisfont' is numbered 115–36; each of the six stories was also independently foliated and 'Lady Mottisfont' is numbered 1–22.[2]

'Lady Mottisfont' tells the story of Philippa, who marries Sir Ashley Mottisfont. Before their marriage, Sir Ashley informs her that he has a little girl dependent upon him called Dorothy. The child comes to live with them and Philippa dotes upon her. Dorothy is in truth the illegitimate child of Sir Ashley and the widow of an Italian count. Two or three years later, Dorothy's real mother turns up to claim the child, whom Philippa reluctantly hands over before she unsuccessfully attempts to drown herself, such is her desolation. Shortly afterwards, the Contessa decides to remarry and no longer wants Dorothy with her, but by then Lady Mottisfont has given birth to a son and she too refuses to look after Dorothy. The rejected child is sent to live with a poor cottager.

Manuscript

The manuscript shows five uncancelled and unique substantive variants, which must presumably have been altered at the serial proof stage. All such instances are a matter of a word or two at most.

The most interesting deletion concerns the timing of the final interview between Sir Ashley and the Countess when she tells him that she will not adopt Dorothy. Now this meeting takes place three days after Lady Mottisfont has given birth, but originally it was to have been three days *before*. The revised reading makes Philippa's refusal to adopt Dorothy herself appear the direct result of her now knowing that she has a child of her own.

The manuscript shows that the lawyer in Bath who contacts Sir Ashley about the Countess's wish to adopt Dorothy was originally to have been a doctor in Wintoncester (Winchester). The change of profession must have been made at quite a late stage in composition, since he was at first described as a doctor throughout the story. Perhaps Hardy made the change because adoption is more a legal than a medical matter.

The list of friends whom the Mottisfonts know in Bath at one time included the old Duke of Uplandtowers, who was possibly the father of Lord Uplandtowers in 'Barbara of the House of Grebe', but Hardy deleted his name and restored his original intention, the old Duke of Hamptonshire, who must be an ancestor of the mid-nineteenth-century Duke in the ninth story of *A Group of Noble Dames*.

Graphic

Hardy's bowdlerization of 'Lady Mottisfont' for the *Graphic* is the most thorough and damaging of any of the stories in *A Group of Noble Dames*. Obviously this tale of illegitimacy was sensitive material for the magazine's editors, and Hardy altered the Contessa from being Dorothy's mother to her aunt. The key change comes to the passage relating Lady Mottisfont's suspicions about the baby's true parentage. In the manuscript it runs thus:

> Lady Mottisfont, true to her promise, was always running down to the village during the following weeks, to see the baby whom her husband had so *mysteriously* lighted on during his ride home – concerning which a *remarkable* discovery she had her own opinion; but being so extremely amiable & affectionate that she could have loved stocks & stones if there had been no living creatures to love, she s uttered none of the |her| thoughts.
> (fo. 117; my italics indicate the words which were deleted in blue pencil, underlined with dots and marked 'stet' in the margin)

The *Graphic* replaces this with a lurid Gothic melodrama of financial skulduggery, hanging and suicide to account for Dorothy's origin:

> Lady Mottisfont, true to her promise, was always running down to the village during the following weeks to see the baby whom her husband had adopted.
>
> Lady Mottisfont did not at this time guess her husband's true relation to the child, the circumstances of which were rather remarkable. Before knowing Philippa, he had secretly married a young woman of the metropolis, of no position, daughter of a dealer in East India Stock; and a short time after the marriage this man was convicted and hung for forgery. The disgrace thereof made Sir Ashley reluctant to avow his marriage, since he had not as yet done so: his wife's hopes in her future were completely shattered; and soon after the birth of their child, in a moment of gloom at her husband's disgust with his alliance, she put an end to herself.
>
> She had an only sister, who, more fortunate, had wedded an Italian nobleman, and left England before her father's crime was known. On this account she was not available as protector of the baby, who was thus thrown entirely upon Sir Ashley's hands. But still he would not own her by reason of the said events; and thus it fell out that the child was handed over to the tender care of a villager as though she were a child of shame. (p. 16)

This alteration has two effects which ruin the story, but at least Hardy managed to get a wedding ring into his tale to satisfy the *Graphic*'s directors. Firstly, it is wholly out of character with the figure of Sir Ashley as he is presented elsewhere. In the *Graphic*, he is callous, proud, drives his first wife to suicide and discards his child, but the rest of the story shows him to be caring and sensitive about Dorothy and the welfare of Lady Mottisfont, whom he *saves* from suicide. Sir Ashley in the *Graphic* is played by two different actors. Secondly, by making the Contessa the child's aunt rather than her mother, Hardy entirely loses his study of the relative strengths of natural versus adoptive motherhood as the Contessa and Lady Mottisfont both fight for and then reject Dorothy. As Gatrell notes, Hardy must have made this destruction of his central themes with a cynical contempt for the *Graphic* and its readers.[3] There is a lovely irony in the *Graphic* when the narrator mentions the Contessa, 'whose name I will not mention, but whom the shrewd reader maay [sic] guess to be Dorothy's aunt'. Clearly, Hardy thought that a shrewd reader would not be buying the *Graphic*.

Other changes follow as a consequence of this fundamental alteration to the plot. For instance, the Contessa's father has to lose his fortune before he dies, and there are no references to the Contessa being wealthy and the target of schemers. This is presumably because Dorothy, as the now legitimate heir of the Contessa's dead twin sister, would also have inherited a large sum of money from her mother and so could have afforded better nursery provision than the kind cottager who looks after her can provide. The story would then have lost the pathos of its ending, in which Dorothy suffers chilblains and cold water.

There are two further blue-pencil deletions which have dotted underlining and are marked 'stet', and both concern indications of Dorothy's questionable paternity. The first occurs when Sir Ashley is telling Philippa about Dorothy for the first time. In the manuscript, Sir Ashley describes Dorothy as

> a little waif I found one day in a bed of wild thyme [*such was this worthy baronet's humour*] (fo. 116; my italics indicate the blue cancellation)

None of this appears in the *Graphic*, while *Harper's Weekly* omits the blue-pencil cancellation.

The other blue-pencil deletion describes how Philippa did not worry her mind about

> *the past* |Dorothy's possible| origin *of Dorothy on the paternal side* (fo. 118; my italics indicate the blue cancellations)

The *Graphic* replaces this with 'Dorothy's possible origin', which is a partly cancelled and wholly unstetted reading in the manuscript. It seems likely that Hardy deleted two of these three words after the proofs of the *Graphic* were set up which contain them. *Harper's Weekly* reads the same as the *Graphic*. Hardy restored only two of these four blue-pencil deletions when he came to collect the story in 1891, 'so mysteriously' and '[such was this worthy baronet's humour]'. The other two were abandoned and never appeared in print.

As in 'The Marchioness of Stonehenge', Hardy omitted any reference to pregnancy in the *Graphic*'s version of 'Lady Mottisfont', so we do not learn how Philippa 'was expecting to become a mother' (fo. 133), and we first learn of the baby three days after its birth when it drops by magic into the narrative.

The close of 'Lady Mottisfont' in both serials describes the audience dispersing; it is an earlier version of the ending of 'The Honourable Laura' which concludes *A Group of Noble Dames* in the collected edition, just as 'Lady Mottisfont' concludes the serial publication.

Harper's Weekly

The version of 'Lady Mottisfont' which appeared in *Harper's Weekly* follows the manuscript very closely, and there is none of the bowdlerization which afflicted the *Graphic*. *Harper's Weekly* has eleven variant readings which do not appear in either the manuscript or the *Graphic*, but only four of these are wholly retained in later editions (presumably because Hardy noted these changes on a duplicate set of *Graphic* proofs which he retained and which became the basis of the 1891 collected edition). In the opening paragraph, the narrator describes the kind of love which 'arises from such companionship', replacing the awkward 'accompanies such companionship', as it reads in the manuscript and serial. Similarly, it is in the American serial that the Contessa first says to Sir Ashley that to everyone 'but ourselves' Dorothy is merely a child in whom she has taken an interest. When Lady Mottisfont goes outside to attempt suicide, Sir Ashley looks for her and 'discerned her form in the park', which replaces 'tracing her form into the park' in the manuscript and *Graphic*. Finally, Lady Mottisfont at one point 'thought' how much Dorothy had come to mean to her, instead of 'thought of'.

Hardy appears to have given the second sentence of the story much attention at each stage of composition. The manuscript describes how the interior of Wintoncester Cathedral allows one to walk nearly 'three hundred steps westward'. To this phrase the *Graphic* added 'amid the magnificent tombs' which *Harper's Weekly* altered to 'amid those magnificent ecclesiastical tombs and royal monuments', anticipating the reference later in the sentence to the graves of kings and bishops. Subsequent collected editions follow the *Graphic*, but with the change of 'the' to 'those' found in *Harper's Weekly*, so Hardy must presumably have marked at least this part of the American variant on to duplicate proofs.

When Sir Ashley proposes to Lady Mottisfont, the manuscript and *Graphic* say that he did so 'as elegantly' as if he had been taught it in Enfield's *Speaker*. In *Harper's Weekly*, Hardy expanded the phrase to read 'in discourse as full of elegance', but later editions follow the earlier reading. There are five other similar instances in the story where *Harper's Weekly* has an independent alteration, all quite minor and no more than three words in length.

1891 Osgood, McIlvaine

In *1891*, the first collected edition, 'Lady Mottisfont' immediately follows 'The Marchioness of Stonehenge' (they had been the sixth and second of the stories in the serials). Hardy thus juxtaposes a pair of tales about unwanted children which reach opposing conclusions about the endurance of adoptive love.

Hardy here appears much more relaxed in his hints at Dorothy's illegitimacy, and Sir Ashley tells Philippa before they are married that he had found her 'in a patch of wild oats' (p. 132), replacing the previous 'in a bed of wild thyme', which is more oblique and contains a rather strained pun on 'time'. (This was omitted entirely, of course, from the *Graphic*.) This is part of a pattern of increasingly frank revisions which continued in the Wessex edition of the story in 1912.

Minor changes see Hardy increasing the Contessa's beauty, Philippa describing her as 'so' good-looking (p. 147). The Contessa spells out to Philippa the reason why she cannot adopt Dorothy as she had planned: 'But my marriage makes it too risky!' (p. 148). Sir Ashley shows even more regard for Dorothy in *1891*. When he takes her for a walk to break the news that she cannot live with either of her two mothers, he first 'sat down on the root of an elm and took her upon his knee' (p. 149) before telling her. He now says aloud to her that 'you who had two homes are left out in the cold'; in earlier versions he had said it 'to himself', which makes Dorothy's following question about not being able to go to London with her pretty mamma seem telepathic.

Hardy made three changes to the final sentence of the narrator's tale. The Forest where Dorothy's husband repaired the old highway is given its real name of the New Forest. Her husband is described for the first time as a worthy man 'of business' (p. 151) to stress that Dorothy found much greater happiness in the commercial class than she ever did with either of her aristocratic parents. Finally, Dorothy herself, who had previously been referred to as just 'she' here, becomes 'the poor girl', a suitable note of pathos with which to end a tale narrated by the Sentimental Member.

There are eight other changes of minor significance, usually involving an individual word.

1891 Harper

The first American collected edition has some sixty differences in accidentals from the British edition, ignoring US spelling. There are no substantive variants.

1912 Macmillan Wessex edition

Hardy undertook practically no revision to 'Lady Mottisfont' as it had appeared in the 1891 Osgood, McIlvaine edition when he came to prepare the Wessex edition of the story, and there are only four new substantive variants in *1912*. The most interesting occurs in the final paragraph, where Hardy altered a reference to the Contessa as Dorothy's 'other mamma' to 'real mother' (p. 132). Hardy obviously felt no wish to hide behind a euphemism any longer and took the opportunity to announce the Contessa's true status as frankly as possible. At this point in the *Graphic* version, incidentally, Hardy had described her as a 'devoted aunt', a comparison which brings out the true ravages of the bowdlerized version.

One variant is a rare example of a misprint in *1912*. The Contessa is said to have enquired about her daughter 'at Gayton' (p. 121) instead of 'of Gayton' which all the earlier versions read. They are correct, since Gayton is the lawyer's name and not his place of residence.[4]

Notes

1 *Life*, p. 203.
2 See Purdy, pp. 64, 65.
3 Gatrell (1988), p. 90.
4 The other revisions to *1891* for the Wessex edition are as follows (*1912* is quoted first, and the pagination is that of *1912*): 'sent/sent us' (p. 118); 'widow lady/widow-lady' (p. 119); 'time:/time;' (p. 120); 'well-being/wellbeing' (p. 121); 'the girl/she' (p. 124); 'pulpit/pulpit,' (p. 125). There are also five instances of the 'O/Oh' alteration (pp. 119, 120, 121, 123, 131).

CHAPTER 12

'The Lady Icenway'

'The Lady Icenway' was first published at Christmas 1890 as one of the six bowdlerized tales in the *Graphic* which were collectively titled *A Group of Noble Dames*. The changes to *A Group of Noble Dames* forced upon Hardy by the *Graphic* were, as Michael Millgate notes, 'painful and humiliating for a man of his years and standing',[1] and the whole episode was a foretaste of the difficulties with the same journal which Hardy encountered when he submitted *Tess* to them later in 1890.

The versions of the story which have textual significance are as follows:

Graphic	*Graphic*, Christmas Number (published 1 December) 1890, p. 13. It was the fourth of the six stories entitled *A Group of Noble Dames* published simultaneously in this issue.
HW	*Harper's Weekly*, 13 December 1890, pp. 981, 984. As in the *Graphic*, it was the fourth of the six stories in *A Group of Noble Dames*. *Harper's Weekly* published these stories in four weekly instalments (29 November–20 December) and 'The Lady Icenway' began the third of these, followed in the same issue by 'Squire Petrick's Lady'.
1891	*A Group of Noble Dames* (London: Osgood, McIlvaine, 1891), pp. 153–69. This was the first collected edition of the story in the expanded *A Group of Noble Dames* which now included ten stories, of which 'The Lady Icenway' was 'Dame the Fifth'. Published at 6*s.* in an edition of 2000 copies on 30 May 1891. It was the first volume of Hardy's work which Osgood, McIlvaine had published.
1891H	*A Group of Noble Dames* (New York: Harper & Brothers, 1891), pp. 174–90. Published early in June 1891.
1896	*A Group of Noble Dames* (London: Osgood, McIlvaine, 1896), pp. 153–69. Volume XV in the Wessex Novels, the first uniform and complete edition of Hardy's works. Plates of the original edition were used, and 'The Lady Icenway' is identical in every respect to *1891*.
1912	*A Group of Noble Dames* (London: Macmillan, 1912), pp. 137–49. Volume XIV of the Wessex edition.

'The Lady Icenway' tells the story of Maria Heymere and a gentleman of Dutch extraction called Anderling. They marry and emigrate to South America, but during the voyage Anderling confesses that he is already married. Maria leaves him and, posing as a widow, returns to England, where she gives birth to their son. She shortly after marries Lord Icenway. Anderling discovers that his first wife has died and he comes to ask Maria to marry him legally, not knowing that she is now Lady Icenway. She makes him swear never to reveal his existence and to go away, but he secretly obtains a job as a gardener on her husband's estate so that he can see his son. She allows him to remain on the premises when she discovers this. More than two years later, Lord Icenway is filled with anxiety about the lack of an heir and begins to scorn his wife. Lady Icenway visits her first husband in his cottage to suggest the idea of him fathering another child by her and passing it off as Lord Icenway's heir, but Anderling is sick and dying. Lady Icenway ends by wishing that she had thought of her plan sooner.

The manuscript of the *Graphic* stories is extant. It was presented by Hardy, through Sydney Cockerell, to the Library of Congress, Washington DC, in October 1911 when he was distributing his MSS. among various public collections. As R.L. Purdy notes, the MS. was foliated and rearranged by Hardy, and 'The Lady Icenway' is numbered 85–114; however, each of the six stories was also independently foliated and the second page of 'The Lady Icenway' is numbered 7, indicating that its opening six pages were reduced to the single first page which now survives, some time after the story was finished.[2] It is unlikely that this alteration was the result of the *Graphic*'s pressure to bowdlerize the text, since the parts of the story to which they objected occurred at the end.

At least a couple of the stories in *A Group of Noble Dames*, including 'The Lady Icenway', were completed by Easter 1890 (6 April), because Sir George Douglas, who was visiting Hardy at Max Gate that weekend, recalled that 'it was either on this or another night of the same visit that he himself read aloud two of the sketches from his "Group of Noble Dames", one of them being the slightly enigmatic story of the gardener and the lady'.[3] The stories were completed shortly after and Hardy notes his diary entry for 9 May 1890 in the *Life*: 'MS. of "A Group of Noble Dames" sent to *The Graphic* as promised.'[4]

Unlike most of the stories in *A Group of Noble Dames*, the incidents in 'The Lady Icenway' have no historical source. The germ for 'The Lady Icenway' may possibly be found in a note which Hardy made in his 'Memoranda, I' Notebook as early as 1873:

> A good story or play might run as follows: A certain nobleman, a widower, has one son, a young man now lying at the point of death. The nobleman his father is an old man, in great trouble that there will be no heir in the direct succession. Son dies. Among his papers are found a girl's letter – the letter of a girl whom the son had begged his father to keep from want, as he had seduced her. The father finds that she is going to have a child. He marries her, parting from her at the church door. He obtains an heir of his own blood.[5]

More interesting than this initial conception of the story are the changes which Hardy makes to it, some seventeen years after, in order to produce 'The Lady Icenway', where it is the wife's idea, not the nobleman's, to produce a fake heir, with the added irony that she is not able to carry out her plan because of the premature death of her first husband.

Manuscript

The surviving manuscript is a printers' copy. It has some fourteen unique uncancelled readings which appear in no published version, but these are mostly individual words ('of', 'that', 'since', for instance) of little significance which could be economically altered in proofs with Hardy's characteristic minimum of interference to the type. The longest such variant reading exemplifies this tendency precisely, the manuscript's 'a child by him' (fo. 92) becoming the *Graphic*'s 'a child of his' without any disturbance of the surrounding type.

Several cancelled but legible features of the manuscript are significant. The Wessex name for Winchester was twice given as Westchester before being replaced by the now familiar Wintoncester, a change made apparently late in the composition of the story. The next tale in the manuscript, 'Lady Mottisfont', has 'Wintoncester' appearing unaltered in its opening line, thus confirming the chronology of Hardy's composition of these two stories.

Lord Icenway's home, Icenway House, is shown on Hardy's map of Wessex to be north-east of Winchester and is twice described in the story as being 'beyond' Winchester, but the first '‖beyond‖' (fo. 90) in the manuscript replaced a 'towards', indicating either that Hardy was uncertain of the house's precise location or that he was initially attempting to disguise it and prevent any too exact equation of his story's setting with the real Herriard House. One final detail concerning Wessex topography is that Exonbury (Exeter) was originally Exbury.

The manuscript shows a sign of Hardy increasing Anderling's devotion to Maria. After Anderling's confession of bigamy, Hardy originally wrote that Anderling would agree to anything she proposed for the restitution of one whom he adored so deeply, 'short of yielding life itself' (fo. 89), before altering it to the phrase which was to appear in all published versions: '‖even to the‖ yielding ‖of‖ life itself'.

Minor alterations within the manuscript show Hardy slightly reducing the length of time between the marriage of Maria and Anderling and his confession of bigamy by making the newly-weds stay only a fortnight in London before sailing to South America, rather than the month which he initially wrote. Anderling is staying at a friend's '‖mansion‖' when he first meets Maria, thus raising his social position, whereas originally Hardy had written 'house' before deleting it (fo. 86). Anderling is described as having a temperament that was '‖amorous‖', which replaces 'ardent' (fo. 86). When he begins working as a gardener for Maria's husband, he is there for a week or two before Maria meets him, longer than 'a day or two' (fo. 97) which Hardy had first written.

Graphic

The ironically titled *Graphic* demanded a couple of deletions from 'The Lady Icenway' concerning hints of extra-marital sex and illegitimacy. Hardy's three quite substantial cuts near the end of the story turn 'The Lady Icenway' from a tale about a woman hoping to use her bigamous first husband to produce a fake heir for her second into a sentimental story about a woman wishing that she had stayed free to re-marry her first husband.

The earliest deletion of a substantial passage from the manuscript is made in blue pencil, and it does not have black, dotted underlining marking it for retention (presumably in the first book-edition), as have some blue-pencil cancellations in other stories. The deleted passage occurs when Lady Icenway is visiting her dying husband and whispers her suggestion to him about his fathering a child by her which she can pass off as her husband's heir:

> Then on an impulse she whispered |some| words to him – blushing as she had blushed in her maiden days.
>
> He shook his head, "Too late" with a faint, wan smile. [...] "Time was... but is not no longer. is not now". (fo. 99)

Simon Gatrell has argued plausibly that such unstetted blue cancellations as this one were made voluntarily *before* Hardy submitted the stories to the *Graphic*, presumably in an attempt to anticipate their objections.[6] If this is the case, then this passage in 'The Lady Icenway' would not have been in the first proofs, and thus it is also absent from the *Harper's Weekly* version which would have been set from these first *Graphic* proofs. Perhaps Hardy felt that the passage was showing Maria's plan to get pregnant too frankly and that it would be more likely to be accepted for serial publication in its chastened form. The whole passage, despite not being stetted, is restored in slightly altered form in the 1891 collection of *A Group of Noble Dames*.

Another omission from the manuscript concerns Lord Icenway's desire for an heir and reads as follows:

> It was |a matter| of great anxiety to him that there should be a lineal successor to the title, & no sign of that successor appeared. One day he complained to her quite roughly of his fate. "All will go to that dolt of a cousin!" he cried. "I'd sooner see my name & place at the bottom of the sea!"
>
> The lady soothed him, & fell into thought, but & did not recriminate. But (fo. 98)

This passage is uncancelled in the manuscript and therefore the omission must have been made at a late proof stage. It appears in *Harper's Weekly*, and therefore must have been in the first *Graphic* proof from which the New York version was set. In itself, the passage is innocent enough and Lord Icenway's resentment of the lack of an heir and his rough treatment of his wife could, in the *Graphic* version of the tale, be left to stand as sufficient motivation for Lady Icenway turning back to her first love, but Hardy may have felt that any reference to producing an heir might have cast an ambiguity over her subsequent relations with her first husband.

The third and final substantial alteration to the manuscript in the *Graphic* concerns the ending of the story, where Hardy was obliged to rewrite rather than simply delete. The following two passages occur in the manuscript and the

Graphic respectively after Lady Icenway has told her husband that the dead man's wife (that is, herself) has erected a church memorial to him, being all the more sorry after his death that there were differences between them.

Manuscript	*Graphic*
"And lgol ruinlingl herself by this lexpensivel marble affair."	She was sorry, truly; and often felt that she might have done better by remaining free to avail herself of her first husband's offer of reparation by re-marriage than by hastily wedding a churlish second.
"She is not poor, they say."	
As Lord Icenway grew older he became crustier & crustier, & whenever he set eyes on her boy by her ~~first~~ lotherl husband he would burst out morosely saying "'Tis a very odd thing, my lady, that you could oblige your first husband, & couldn't oblige me."	
"Ah – if I had only ~~reflected~~ lthought of itl sooner!" she murmured.	
"What?" said he.	
"Nothing, dearest," replied Lady Icenway. (fo. 100)	

The passage in the manuscript is undeleted, and therefore, like the previous deletion described, Hardy must have altered it in the *Graphic*'s proofs. It appears largely unchanged in *Harper's Weekly*. These alterations, especially the changed ending, make the *Graphic* version a quite different story to the one which Hardy had intended. In the *Graphic*, Maria is merely regretting her first husband's death. There is no hint of any impropriety, and she visits her husband's cottage out of concern for his welfare and not with any intention of explaining her plan to get pregnant. The *Graphic* version loses the whole point of interest in the story.

Harper's Weekly

The *Harper's Weekly* version of 'The Lady Icenway' is not bowdlerized like the *Graphic* and is therefore much closer to Hardy's original conception of the story. Nevertheless, it differs in several respects from any other printing of the tale and is a unique version.

Principally, *Harper's Weekly* lacks two substantial passages which are present in the manuscript, the *Graphic* and all subsequent collected editions. The first describes Anderling's emotions when he began to live in the cottage adjacent to his wife and child, and it reads in the *Graphic* as follows:

> Owing to his loneliness, all the fervour of which he was capable – and that was much – flowed now in the channel of parental and marital love – for a child who did not know him, and a woman who had ceased to love him.

The second passage deleted in *Harper's Weekly* is an account of the Bookworm's concluding reaction to the tale he has just heard. The *Graphic* gives it thus:

> It was true his wife was a very close-mouthed personage, which made a difference. If she had spoken out recklessly her lord might have been suspicious enough, as in the case of that lady who lived at Stapleford Park in their great-grandfathers' time. Though there considerations arose which made her husband view matters with much philosophy.
>
> A few of the members doubted the possibility of this.

Why are these two passages omitted in *Harper's Weekly*? One cannot eliminate the possibility of compositorial error or even a revision by Hardy to the proofs which he sent. The most likely explanation, however, is the wish by Harper's to end the instalment precisely at the foot of a page, which is where the end of the next story in that week's issue, 'Squire Petrick's Lady', occurs. The unique excision of the two passages in 'The Lady Icenway' and of a further passage in 'Squire Petrick's Lady' allows Harper's to end at the foot of a page and thus avoid beginning the subsequent item in mid-page. It is notable that the instalments of 'A Group of Noble Dames' in the previous two issues of *Harper's Weekly* had also ended at the foot of a page, indicating Harper's apparent house policy on pagination.

There are two other variants in *Harper's Weekly* which may both be significant. The first concerns Anderling's view of Maria as 'the mother of his child' (p. 981) which in the manuscript read 'the mother of a child by him' (fo. 92) and in the *Graphic* read 'the mother of a child of his'. Subsequent collected editions all follow the *Graphic* reading. The second variant is Anderling's reaction to Maria when she holds up a finger warning him not to kiss their sleeping son: 'But why not?' (p. 981), he asks her in *Harper's Weekly*, which is substantively the same as the manuscript. The *Graphic*, however, reads 'But O, why not?', and all subsequent versions of the story follow the *Graphic* reading (with an oh/O variation). The first of these variants may be an editorial change at Harper's, while the second one may be a serial proof revision by Hardy which he did not copy on to the set which he gave *Harper's Weekly*.

1891 Osgood, McIlvaine

Hardy noted in the *Life* that 'At the beginning of January [1891] he was at home arranging *A Group of Noble Dames* for publication in a volume' (p. 243).

The alterations which Hardy made to the serial versions of the story when preparing the 1891 Osgood, McIlvaine edition of *A Group of Noble Dames* were also included in the Harper edition of that year.

The most important change is that all three of the bowdlerizations in the *Graphic* are restored, using virtually the exact wording of the manuscript. Similarly, the two excisions which had probably been made in *Harper's Weekly* for reasons of space are reintroduced.

The story's narrator, the Churchwarden, is made to speak more colloquially, three times saying 'o'' (pp. 155, 156) which replaces the 'of' in the manuscript and serials. This continues a trend begun when the serials had made the same alteration to one 'of' in the manuscript (fo. 88). Similarly, he talks of 'folk' rather than the more formal 'families' (p. 156).

Details of the characterization of Anderling are slightly changed. When confessing his bigamy to Maria, he embraces her in a very 'tearful' (p. 157) manner, rather than a 'warm' one as he had in the manuscript and serials, and he tells her that he had hoped and 'prayed' (p. 157) that his first wife was dead, whereas earlier he had merely 'believed' that she was dead. He later becomes self-denying 'as a lenten saint' (p. 161), which replaces the previous 'to asceticism', and Maria makes him swear to make her any 'amends' (p. 161) she chooses rather than any 'reparation', which perhaps mistakenly suggested the possibility of reconciliation.

The most detailed changes are to the memorial which Maria erects to her late husband's memory at the end of the story. In *1891* she desires to erect some 'tribute' (p. 168) rather than a 'monument' as it had been in the manuscript and serials. She now plans a 'stained-glass window for the church' (p. 168) instead of the 'mural tablet of marble' which she had 'directed to the church mason'. This entails a further change, making her husband read 'the legend on the glass' (p. 168), which replaces the words 'from the monument'. The window is to be a 'ruby-and-azure glass-design' (p. 168), and not the 'marble affair' it had been in the manuscript and *Harper's Weekly* (the phrase was cut from the *Graphic*).

The final paragraph of the story has four changes introduced in *1891*. The description of the crimson maltster as '*ventru*, and short in stature' (p. 169) is new, and he proceeds to give 'the instance before alluded to' of Squire Petrick's Lady (replacing what had previously been described as merely 'an instance'). He confesses that he has never known 'many' of the nobility (previously 'much'), and the final sentence is a wholly new addition: 'To his style of narrative the following is only an approximation' (p. 169).

1891 Harper

'The Lady Icenway' in the 1891 American edition of *A Group of Noble Dames* has one unique variant reading. Anderling is said to be 'not knowing or ever having seen' (p. 184) his son. All other versions read 'not knowing or having ever seen' him (*1891*, p. 165). This would seem to be the result of in-house editing at Harper's.

There are some sixty differences in accidentals between the two 1891 editions of the story, no doubt caused by house styling. In all cases (except for a single comma), subsequent editions follow the London edition.

1912 Macmillan Wessex edition

Hardy made thirteen substantive alterations to the version of 'The Lady Icenway' in Osgood, McIlvaine's edition of 1891 when preparing the Wessex edition of 1912. All of these are reproduced in the 1912 Harper edition.

An interesting change is geographical. Maria Heymere and her new husband sail from England to Paramaribo, on the north coast of South America, en route to his plantation in Guiana. Early versions of this story say that they 'crossed the Line' during their voyage and that they were 'right under the Line in the blaze o' the sun'. In the Wessex edition, however, we learn that the pair had only 'drawn near the Line' and that they were 'right under the tropical blaze o' the sun' (pp. 139–40). When preparing the Wessex edition, Hardy must have consulted an atlas and discovered that Paramaribo is in fact four hundred miles north of the Equator, and therefore the lovers would not have crossed the Line on a voyage from England.

The most significant alteration occurs during the meeting between Maria and the dying Anderling in his cottage, when she reveals to him her plan for conceiving an heir. Their conversation is made much more explicit than it was in *1891*. For the first time, Maria in *1912* tells him that he must get well because *'There's a reason'*, and he replies, 'Ah – why did you not say so sooner?' (p. 148). She tells him that she has been hard with him 'hitherto' (p. 148), implying that she will not be hard with him henceforth. It is hardly the case, however, that a reader of *1891* would have failed to grasp the point before these changes.

Two other substantive alterations merit comment. When Lady Icenway is telling her husband about Anderling's 'wife' (that is, herself) after his death, she says that the wife was 'never' (p. 148) seen visiting him at his cottage; all earlier versions had her saying that she was 'seldom' seen, and *1912* is more accurate, since Maria knows full well that she only visited Anderling the once. Another change occurs at the end of the story when the crimson maltster is introducing the next Noble Dame, Squire Petrick's Lady. He begins by saying that her lord might have had reasons for being suspicious of her, but considerations arose which made him view matters with much philosophy. Hardy then writes that 'A few of the members doubted the possibility of this *in such cases* ' (p. 149; my italics). The last three words are new to *1912*, and they prevent one from reading the sentence as if the members are doubting whether husbands could view *anything* with 'much philosophy'.[7]

Notes

1 Millgate, p. 305.
2 See Purdy, pp. 64, 65.
3 Douglas, 'Thomas Hardy: Personal Reminiscences', *Gleanings in Prose and Verse*, ed. Oliver Hilson (Galashiels: A. Walker, 1938), p. 30.
4 *Life,* p. 236.
5 Taylor (1978), p. 14.

6   Gatrell (1988), p. 85. See, however, the chapter below on 'Squire Petrick's Lady'.

7   For the sake of a complete record, the other revisions to *1891* for the Wessex edition
    are as follows (*1912* is quoted first, and the pagination is that of *1912*):
    'orphan/orphan', (p. 137); 'slow voyage/voyage' (p. 139); 'that he would/and that he
    would' (p. 140); 'further/farther' (p. 140); 'a second marriage/a re-marriage' (p. 141);
    'when not/when, not' (p. 141); 'against her/against her,' (p. 142); 'O/oh' (p. 145);
    'son had/son, had' (p. 145); 'intelligence/intelligence', (p. 146); 'my lord's stepson/his
    stepson' (p. 147); 'barony/title' (p. 147); 'had as yet appeared/appeared' (p. 147); 'O,
    you/Oh, you' (p. 148); 'Time was/Time was!' (p. 148); 'said./said,' (p. 148);
    'memory/memory,' (p. 148); 'O yes/Oh yes' (p. 148).

CHAPTER 13

'Squire Petrick's Lady'

Hardy's short story, 'Squire Petrick's Lady', was first published at Christmas 1890 as one of the six bowdlerized tales in the *Graphic* which were collectively titled *A Group of Noble Dames*. Of all the stories which the *Graphic* wanted altered, 'Squire Petrick's Lady' suffered the greatest changes.

The versions of the story which have textual significance are as follows:

Graphic	*Graphic*, Christmas Number (published 1 December) 1890, p. 16. It was the fifth of the six stories entitled *A Group of Noble Dames* published simultaneously in this issue.
HW	*Harper's Weekly*, 13 December 1890, p. 984. As in the *Graphic*, it was the fifth of the six stories in *A Group of Noble Dames*. *Harper's Weekly* published these stories in four weekly instalments (29 November–20 December) and 'Squire Petrick's Lady' ended the third of these, preceded in the same issue by 'The Lady Icenway'.
1891	*A Group of Noble Dames* (London: Osgood, McIlvaine, 1891), pp. 171–86. This was the first collected edition of the story in the expanded *A Group of Noble Dames* which now included ten stories, of which 'Squire Petrick's Lady' was 'Dame the Sixth'. Published at 6*s.* in an edition of 2000 copies on 30 May 1891. It was the first volume of Hardy's work which Osgood, McIlvaine had published.
1891H	*A Group of Noble Dames* (New York: Harper & Brothers, 1891), pp. 191–206. Published early in June 1891.
1896	*A Group of Noble Dames* (London: Osgood, McIlvaine, 1896), pp. 171–86. Volume XV in the Wessex Novels, the first uniform and complete edition of Hardy's works. Plates of the original edition were used, and 'Squire Petrick's Lady' is identical in every respect to *1891* (including the repetition of a misprint of 'through' for 'though' on p. 174), except for the loss of a comma at the end of a line on p. 182, apparently as the result of plate-batter.
1912	*A Group of Noble Dames* (London: Macmillan, 1912), pp. 153–64. Volume XIV of the Wessex edition.

The manuscript of the *Graphic* stories is extant. It was presented by Hardy, through Sydney Cockerell, to the Library of Congress, Washington DC, in October 1911 when he was distributing his MSS. among various public collections. As R.L. Purdy notes, the MS. was foliated and rearranged by Hardy, and 'Squire Petrick's Lady' is numbered 102–14; however, each of the six stories was also independently foliated and 'Squire Petrick's Lady' is numbered 1–13, with two leaves, fos. 109 and 110, having passages written on the verso.[1]

In the version of the story which readers now know, Squire Petrick believes he has a baby son, Rupert, but his wife confesses on her death-bed that he is really the offspring of the Marquis of Christminster. Petrick tries to ignore the child as he grows up, but the boy's natural charms win him over, and he comes to be genuinely proud of Rupert's aristocratic lineage and his wife's admirable discrimination in choosing a Marquis as the father of her child, rather than a mere Petrick who would simply have spawned yet another in the line of miserable scriveners and usurers who made up the family ancestry. Deep is Petrick's disappointment, then, to learn from his wife's physician that her family was prone to delusions, and his enquiries confirm that her confession could not possibly be true. The boy is, alas, only his own son, after all.

Sources

Old Timothy Petrick derives from Hutchins's account of Peter Walter, who 'acquired an immense fortune' in the first half of the eighteenth century as 'steward to the Duke of Newcastle, and other noblemen and gentlemen'.[2] Like Petrick, Walter's son predeceased him and he entailed his estate to his eldest grandson and male issue. Other similarities between the two men are that Walter's heir was his namesake, and he had another grandson called Edward, who married Harriet, daughter of Lord Forrester (Hardy's Edward married Harriet, daughter of a viscount). Walter, too, died in his eighties within a short time of making his last will (his will is dated 26 December 1744 and he died the following year, aged 83). Petrick's insistence on inspecting every acre of a property before purchasing it has its source in Hutchins:

Peter Walter	Timothy Petrick
Peter Walter would not lend money or buy without seeing every acre: for, said he, 'I live on bread and butter, and milk porridge; and it must be land that maintains the cows for this: whereas none of the stock companies have a single cow'. (III, 671)	It is said that when he bought an estate he would not decide to pay the price till he had walked over every single acre with his own two feet, and prodded the soil at every point with his own spud, to test its quality.

However, Hardy can be seen to be making some of the facts deriving from Hutchins less historically accurate in his story. For instance, the MS. originally said that Petrick had 'two or three' (fo. 103) grandsons, but Hardy deleted the last two words to leave Petrick with only two grandsons, unlike the historical Walter, who had three. The first occasion when Petrick is mentioned in the MS. after the title shows that Hardy originally wrote the name as Peters before deleting it and inserting Petrick (fo. 102), a probable slip perhaps, revealing Hardy's recollection of Walter's first name, Peter, rather than a deliberate decision to change the surname of his character from Peters to Petrick, since the latter stands unaltered in the title and elsewhere in the MS. There is no basis in Hutchins for the alleged adultery or the rejection of the son, which are entirely fictional: Peter Walter's eldest grandson died and left a fifteen-year-old daughter.

Deletions in the manuscript

At one point in the story, Timothy is thinking of his son as the little 'bastard', but Hardy cancels this and then inserts 'wretch' before deleting this and substituting 'fellow' (fo. 107), which is what all printed versions read. Gatrell explains this change thus:

> In context, the first seems the most appropriate, as well as being accurate so far as he knows; and the final reading is really too weak for the situation in which it is made. But Hardy must have known that 'bastard' would not have gone down too well with any of the magazines in which he was likely to find a home for the stories. Why 'wretch' was turned into 'fellow' I cannot guess; it seems simply a misjudgement.[3]

The alteration is not one of those blue-pencil cancellations discussed later, which were made with the *Graphic*'s directors specifically in mind. Rather, it seems an example of Hardy's self-censorship in the course of composing the story, before he submitted it.

A change in topography can be seen in the MS. Annetta's doctor who tells Timothy about the family's tendency to delusion is said to come from, successively, Melchester, Bath, and Budmouth, before Hardy finally settles on Weymouth (the last three placenames are all insertions). The real placename is retained for both serials, then Hardy introduces the uniform Wessex name of Budmouth for *1891*.

Uncancelled words in the manuscript

The MS. has some twenty instances of uncancelled words or phrases which were never to appear in any printed version. Most are individual words of little interest (e.g., 'by', 'him', 'so', 'when'), but the fact that they are unique to the MS. suggests that, while Hardy may have consulted it when creating the first collected edition of 'Squire Petrick's Lady', it was not the printers' copy for *1891*, which often retains a serial substitution for the MS. variant.

Some of the unique readings are significant: for instance, the MS. makes it more certain than any other version of the story that the Marquis could not have been the father of Annetta's child, as she deludedly believed. *Harper's Weekly* says only that the Marquis went abroad 'some time' before Annetta's marriage while *1891* and all other published versions say that he went 'the year' (*1891*, p. 183) before, which certainly makes it less likely that he could have been the father, but not absolutely so. The MS., though, is quite specific, saying that the Marquis went abroad 'two years' (fo. 112) before she married. The later versions make it more plausible that Annetta *could* have fooled herself into thinking she was the mother of the Marquis's child if she had seen him just before her marriage.

Another unique variant occurs in a passage which was deleted but marked for retention. The family of the Marquis whom Annetta claimed to have loved is said in the MS. to be older in origin than in later versions of the story, dating from 'the wane of the middle ages' (fo. 110^v) rather than beginning in 'the Restoration of the blessed Charles' (*1891*, pp. 180–81; this alteration to the MS. was made in *1891*, since both the serials omit the passage entirely). Perhaps Hardy wanted to create an irony that the family whom Timothy worships so much is relatively nouveau, ennobled barely a century before the events described in the story, but in doing so he creates a historical anachronism: if the family had been created only in 1660, at the time of the Restoration, they could not have been painted by Vandyke, as Hardy claims later in the paragraph, because he died in 1641. There is no anachronism in the MS., but Hardy needed to have removed the reference to Vandyke when he made the family newer. The other painter of the family who is mentioned, Lely, is valid because he did not die until 1680.

Graphic

The version of 'Squire Petrick's Lady' in the *Graphic* is quite unlike the story with which most readers today are familiar, for it was thoroughly bowdlerized. The *Graphic* version has no hint of extra-marital sex, and therefore Annetta's delusion about the Marquis being the father of her child, and indeed any reference at all to the Marquis, are removed. Instead, Annetta confesses that her child had died shortly after its birth in London and she had exchanged her child for a poor woman's living one, born about the same day.

The ending of the story especially is entirely rewritten. The boy attempts to borrow money by means of a forged letter, and the father is disillusioned to see that the ancestral traits of felony are showing forth in the son:

> But the happiness of Timothy was now at an end: he saw in this deed of his son additional evidence of his being one of his own flesh and blood, but it was evidence of a terrifying kind. The evil habits of his ancestors were coming to the front in him; the felony of his great-uncle in tampering with a document; his own trick in substituting one will for another were repeated in the boy at such an early age that it was probable he would excel in such arts in the course of time.

As Simon Gatrell comments, 'so we have the dubious hypothesis advanced, that ability in forging documents is an inheritable faculty'.[4] Petrick wishes that his wife's delusion had been true, and he ends by telling the boy that he 'ought not to be' related to him. The *Graphic* version is thus an entirely different tale, and it is difficult to find much in it to redeem this mildly ironic story of a disappointed father.

The most fascinating feature of the manuscript of 'Squire Petrick's Lady' is the deletion of many passages in blue pencil, which occurs also in two other stories in the manuscript of 'A Group of Noble Dames', namely 'The Lady Icenway' and 'Lady Mottisfont'. These blue-pencil deletions are of four kinds: (i) deleted in blue but with no indication that the deleted passage was to be retained at a subsequent stage – presumably the first book-edition in 1891 (one passage); (ii) deleted in blue, marked for retention by a 'Stet' in the margin and with black, dotted underlining or a vertical row of dots in the margin, but nevertheless appearing largely unchanged in both *Harper's Weekly* and *1891* (two passages); (iii) deleted in blue, marked for retention as before, *wholly* appearing in *1891* but only *partly* in *Harper's Weekly* (four passages); (iv) deleted in blue and never appearing in any printed version (one short phrase).

At what stage were these blue cancellations made, and for whom were they intended? Simon Gatrell distinguishes between the stetted and unstetted deletions, arguing that the unstetted ones in the MS. of 'A Group of Noble Dames' were made before Hardy even submitted the stories to the *Graphic* in a voluntary attempt to pre-empt precisely the kind of objections which were made, while the stetted ones are Hardy's response to the request for cuts and changes which the *Graphic* demanded.[5] This is a perfectly plausible interpretation, but I take a different view, believing that all the blue cancellations were made simultaneously, *after* Hardy learned of the *Graphic*'s objections. The unstetted cancellations seem to me to be so slight and to involve such relatively inoffensive material that Hardy cannot have thought that they would affect a magazine's decision whether to accept the stories or not.

There is no consistent practice underlying Hardy's marking of blue deletions. For instance, it is not the case that blue cancellations are excluded from the *Graphic* but are wholly included in *Harper's Weekly*. There are many parts of the MS. which are not marked in blue but which nevertheless do not appear in the *Graphic*, while substantial parts of some blue deletions are omitted from both the *Graphic* and *Harper's Weekly*. Certainly it would appear that the surviving MS. was not printers' copy for the revised *Graphic* proofs, since it contains only some of the deletions and none of the additions which Hardy made for the *Graphic*.

The surviving MS. may well have been printers' copy for the first *Graphic* proofs which caused such dismay when read by the directors. One possible interpretation of what happened next could be that Hardy then made the bowdlerizations to the proofs themselves, revising differently a duplicate set of *Graphic* proofs which were to become the *Harper's Weekly* version of the story, and then, for his own record, inconsistently marking some, but not all, of the *Graphic* changes on to his original MS., so that the blue cancellations are for his own benefit and were never seen by a printer. The key common element, though, is that all blue deletions, stetted or unstetted, were restored for *1891*, with some slight changes.

Three consecutive blue deletions have angry annotations against them which are similar in import:

> [N.B. The above lines were deleted against author's wish, by compulsion of Mrs Grundy, as were all other passages marked blue.]

> [Deleted solely on account of the tyranny of Mrs Grundy]

> [N.B. This was deleted only on account of the tyranny of Mrs Grundy] (fos. 108, 109^v, 110^v)

The handwriting in which such notes were made is markedly different from the accompanying text and the marginal 'Stet', being much smaller and cramped in character and suggesting that they were not made contemporaneously. It is possible that Hardy made them as a historical record of the circumstances in which the story first appeared when he was arranging for the manuscript to be delivered to the Library of Congress in 1911, some twenty years afterwards.

The main unstetted blue cancellation comes after we are told that the child born to Timothy and his wife had been baptized Robert (by which name he is called in the *Graphic*, although he is known as Rupert in *Harper's Weekly* and all subsequent versions). The passage had originally read:

> & her husband had never thought of it as a name of any significance, till, now, he learnt by accident that before her marriage she lAnnettal had been desperately enamoured *of the young Marquis of Trantridge* lChrisminsterl, *son of the Duke of Hamptonshire*. Robert was his name. (fo. 107: italicized words were not deleted in blue pencil)

The name of the seat of the young Marquis would appear to be Hardy's first version of the placename which would figure so prominently in *Jude*. 'Chrisminster' is an interlined replacement for Trantridge, and Simon Gatrell argues that it would therefore seem to be a deliberate spelling, which Hardy may have thought of as being pronounced with a short 'i'.[6] It is ultimately impossible to determine this, but my own conjecture is that it is probably a mis-spelling, for reasons which arise from the origin of the name. I do not recall seeing it stated before that Christminster as a name for Oxford would appear to derive from a combination of *Christ* Church, the Oxford college, and the fact that Christ Church's chapel is also Oxford's Cathedral, hence *minster*. This in itself is a fairly arcane way of referring to Oxford. Even as Christminster (as it was eventually called in *1891* and subsequent versions) it is impossible to equate the place with Oxford from this solitary first reference to it in *A Group of Noble Dames*, so why would Hardy feel the need to disguise the name further by omitting the 't' and also, as a result, changing the pronunciation?

Following the blue-pencil deletion of the above passage, the explanation of the origin of the child's name appeared in *Harper's Weekly* in the following form:

> and it was the name of the young Marquis of Chrisminster, son of the Duke of Hamptonshire.

This gives the undeleted part of the passage in the MS., although the *Graphic* omits even this much. The first edition of *1891* expands it thus:

> and her husband had never thought of it as a name of any significance till, about this time, he learnt by accident that it was the name of the young Marquis of Christminster, son of the Duke of Southwesterland, for whom Annetta had cherished warm feelings before her marriage. (*1891*, pp. 177–8)

1891 largely restores the blue deletion but also incorporates the gist of the *Harper's Weekly* reading, though altering the placenames, and Hardy then adds for the first time the clause that Annetta 'cherished warm feelings' for the young Marquis before her marriage, a rather prim substitute for the manuscript's original description of how she had been 'desperately enamoured' of him, which seems a more accurate account of the degree of emotion which caused her delusion. In this instance, *1891* is thus an amalgam of the manuscript before and after the blue pencilling had occurred, with a later additional layer of wording.

The short phrase which is cancelled in blue, marked 'Stet' and underlined with dots yet which never appeared in any printed version is a description of the son, called Robert in the manuscript, as being 'lof the ducal line of Robertsl' (fo. 110). Perhaps Hardy eventually omitted it because, of course, it is only a delusion that the boy is related to the Duke.

In preparing the *Graphic* version, Hardy's principal practice was simply to delete large passages of offending material that appear (mostly undeleted) in the manuscript. The best part of seven successive paragraphs in the middle of the story describing Petrick's respect for his wife's aristocratic tastes in choosing a Marquis as her lover and his contempt for his own miserable ancestry are left out. Hardy's typical economy in revising, however, is apparent when, right in the middle of this lengthy omission, he still manages to salvage for the *Graphic* a four-line passage showing Petrick's thought that 'So far [...] from cutting off this child from the inheritance of my estates as I have done, I should have rejoiced in the possession of him' (fo. 109). This is compatible with the *Graphic*'s version of events, since Petrick is simply here growing to like the boy after all, and regretting that he had disinherited the child he thinks is a changeling. Hardy does not replace this large central deletion with any new material in the *Graphic*; only at the beginning and end of the story does he rewrite, adding three passages totalling ten lines near the start, and a lengthy new passage of some thirty lines at the close. Even then, he manages to incorporate ten short phrases from the manuscript into the *Graphic* rewrite.

Harper's Weekly

The *Harper's Weekly* version of 'Squire Petrick's Lady' is virtually a cul-de-sac off the main route of the text's transmission, except in some few important respects. It is much less bowdlerized than the *Graphic* version and gives more or less the story as readers know it today. However, it contributed little of unique importance to later stages in the text's history. There are approximately thirty instances of individual words or phrases (ignoring for the moment the alteration of a character's name) and seven substantial passages where *Harper's Weekly* differs from the manuscript, and in all but a handful of individual words or phrases the collected edition of *1891* either retains the manuscript reading or rejects both alternatives and introduces a new reading.[7]

Perhaps the key contribution which *Harper's Weekly* made to future stages of the text is that the child of Petrick is called Rupert for the first time, rather than Robert as he was in the manuscript and the *Graphic*, and it is this name which is retained in later versions. This change from Robert to Rupert required the alteration of only two letters and did not disturb surrounding text, so it could easily have been done at a proof stage. However, why was Hardy concerned, apparently, not to disturb the Harper's type-setting? Did he make these changes not on a duplicate copy of the *Graphic* proofs which he sent to Harper's to have set in proof (in which case any changes to the surrounding text would have been irrelevant, since Harper's would have been resetting the text anyway), but on a proof set up by Harper's from the *Graphic* proof and sent to him for correction? There is no evidence that Hardy saw proofs for *Harper's Weekly*, though.

There are six substantial omissions from the manuscript in the *Harper's Weekly* version, some of which were probably the result of Hardy seeking to pre-empt any American criticism of the silly kind which he had received from the *Graphic* by voluntarily self-censoring what he presumably regarded as the most candid or potentially offensive passages. The six omissions are given in the manuscript as follows:

(i)   her husband had never thought of it as a name of any significance, till, now, he learnt by accident that before her marriage ~~she~~ |Annetta| had been desperately enamoured (fo. 107; blue-pencil unstetted deletion in MS., mostly restored in *1891*)

(ii)   Had he been of low blood like myself or any of my relations she would hardly have deserved the harsh ~~treatment~~ |measures| that I have meted out to her & her offspring; how much less, then, when such plebeian ~~instin~~ tendencies were furthest from her soul! The man ~~she~~ |Annetta| loved was noble, & (fos. 108–9; part of a blue-pencil stetted deletion in MS., mostly restored in 1891)

(iii)   He is of pure stock on one side |now| at least, whilst in the ordinary run of affairs he would have been a commoner to the bone (fo. 109; part of a blue-pencil stetted deletion in MS., mostly restored in 1891)

(iv)   & the probability that some of their bad qualities would have come out in a child of his loins to give him sorrow in his old age, turn his black hairs grey, & |his| grey hairs white, & cut down all the timber |& Heaven knows what-all,| had he not, like a skilful gardener, changed the sort; (fo. 109$^\text{v}$; part of a blue-pencil stetted deletion in MS., mostly restored in 1891)[8]

(v)   So much was he interested in the boy |in this new aspect| that he now began to read up [chronicles of the illustrious house ennobled as the Dukes of Hamptonshire] from their very beginning in the wane of the middle ages till the year of his own time (fo. 110$^\text{v}$; part of a blue-pencil stetted deletion in MS., mostly restored in 1891. *Harper's Weekly* replaces the whole omission with 'He took pleasure in reading up [chronicles ...]'.)

(vi)   To think how he himself, too, had sinned |in this same matter of a will| for
this mere |corporeal| reproduction of a wretched old uncle whose very name
he wished to forget. The boy's |Christian| name, even, was an imposture and
an irony, ~~One day the lad knocked at his study door~~ for it implied hereditary
force ~~& talent~~ |& brilliancy| to which he plainly would never attain. The
consolation of real sonship was always left him, certainly; but he could not
help saying to himself "Why cannot a thing be itself & something else
likewise!" (fos. 113–14; not deleted in MS., and mostly restored in 1891.
The fact that, unlike the other omissions above, this one was uncancelled in
the MS. may mean that *Harper's Weekly* deleted this paragraph near the end
of the story to ensure that that week's instalment of *A Group of Noble
Dames* could finish at the foot of a page)

All six passages were similarly omitted in the *Graphic*. The deletions may well
have been made on the duplicate of the *Graphic* proofs which Hardy presumably
sent as copy for *Harper's Weekly*.

The American serial has a unique three-line insert at the start of the next
week's instalment, describing how there was a short silence, 'during which the
company reflected on the disappointments of pedigree, as exemplified in the
Crimson Maltster's narrative'. Hardy presumably added this as a link to remind
his American readers of the previous week's tale; there is no trace of it in the
manuscript, and no need for it in the *Graphic*, where *A Group of Noble Dames*
was issued in one single instalment.

There are six instances of individual words or phrases in *Harper's Weekly*
which are not in the manuscript or the *Graphic*, but which are retained for the
first edition of the collected *Noble Dames* in 1891 (not including the
Robert/Rupert change). It is plausible to deduce that Hardy marked these six
readings on to a master set of proofs which he kept and which became the basis
for *1891*. The six are as follows (*1891* pagination):

Harper's Weekly & 1891	*MS. & Graphic*
the earlier will (p. 182)	that earlier will
ducal family (p. 182)	powerful family (MS.; not in *Graphic*. This variant may have appeared in the *Graphic* proof and been deleted for the British serial).
He delicately inquired (p. 183)	delicately inquiring (MS.) delicately enquiring (*Graphic*)
he, the physician (p. 183)	as he, the physician
at such a physical crisis (p. 183)	|at such a time|

eyed his noble countenance (p. 185)   leyed himl (MS.; not in *Graphic*. This variant may have appeared in the *Graphic* proof and been deleted for the British serial along with the rest of the ending)

It may be significant that the first five of these changes are consecutive and that there are no intervening variants in *Harper's Weekly* at this part of the story which do not appear in *1891*, as if Hardy had suddenly decided to begin marking any revisions on to the duplicate set of proofs from which *1891* was later set before resuming his normal practice of not recording them.

There are, however, many more variant readings in *Harper's Weekly* (some sixteen in total) which are unique to it and do not reappear in subsequent collected editions of the story, presumably because Hardy marked these alterations only on the proofs which he sent to America and did not make a note of them elsewhere. These revisions which are marooned in *Harper's Weekly* are undoubtedly authorial and may well indicate Hardy's first intentions for the serial which were overlooked and left stranded under the pressure of meeting the disturbing demands of the respectable elders at the *Graphic* to censor the story.

All such variants are a matter of a phrase at most, and do not alter the general import of the story as we know it today. Many of these variants are contractions of the MS. reading, with the result that the tendency of the *Harper's Weekly* version is towards a terser, less discursive discourse. For instance, where the MS. and *1891* describe how Squire Petrick believes that his son 'was by nature, if not by name, ~~the~~ lal representative of' (fo. 108) one of the noblest houses in England, *Harper's Weekly* condenses the phrase so that it reads simply that he 'represented' the noble house. A typical example of the variants in *Harper's Weekly* is afforded by a comparison of the following three readings, which show Squire Petrick reflecting proudly on his wife's discriminating taste in loving a Marquis:

MS.	*Harper's Weekly*	*1891*
To choose ~~as her lover~~ the immediate successor in that ducal line – it was grandly conceived! (fo. 108)	The immediate successor in that ducal line; it was grandly conceived.	To fix her choice upon the immediate successor in that ducal line – it was finely conceived! (p. 179)

The reading in *Harper's Weekly* is a shorter, intermediate version, omitting the first two words of the MS. which *1891* then replaces in expanded form. The MS. passage was blue-pencilled for the *Graphic*, and the omission of 'as her lover' probably shows Hardy's attempt at self-censorship in the course of composing the story. (Incidentally, the change of the adverb in the *1891* reading may have been caused by a wish to avoid a rather obvious pun about the child being 'grandly' conceived by a Marquis.)

The solitary occasion on which Hardy gives an additional detail to *Harper's Weekly* which is found in no other version occurs when Petrick notices his son's eye beginning to acquire the expression of the 'demoralized' orb of a particularly objectionable cousin of his own.

There is evidence of what appears to be editorial intervention at Harper's office. Timothy Petrick is described as the 'eldest' of two grandsons in all versions of the story except in *Harper's Weekly*, which has the strictly correct comparative 'elder'. Hardy's slip is explained by the manuscript originally stating that Timothy was one of two 'or three' grandsons, which would have made 'eldest' correct if 'or three' had not been subsequently deleted. There is a similar substitution of 'calmer' for 'calmest' in the *Harper's Weekly* version of 'Anna, Lady Baxby'.

On one occasion, the manuscript and *Harper's Weekly* have a common variant reading which is not transmitted to *1891*, which instead prefers a reading first introduced for the *Graphic*. Squire Petrick is angry with himself for liking the child and swears in 'rather loud whispers' (fo. 107 and *HW*, p. 984), as it says in the MS. and *Harper's Weekly*. The *Graphic*, however, talks of 'long loud whispers', which is what all subsequent versions read. Either the proofs of the *Graphic* printed 'long' and Hardy changed it back to the MS. wording for the American serial proofs, or else he altered the *Graphic* proofs from 'rather' to 'long' and noted the change on the duplicate proofs which formed the basis of *1891*, omitting to make the same change on the proofs sent to Harper's. This indicates that the *Graphic* version, for all its bowdlerized contortions, nevertheless can transmit its own independent textual significance.

1891 Osgood, McIlvaine

Hardy noted in the *Life* that 'At the beginning of January [1891] he was at home arranging *A Group of Noble Dames* for publication in a volume' (p. 243). This was the Osgood, McIlvaine edition, the first collection of all ten stories in *A Group of Noble Dames*. In the rearranged sequence of *1891*, 'Squire Petrick's Lady' is placed sixth, whereas it was the penultimate one of the six published serially. As Kristin Brady has observed, its new central place in *1891* is important precisely because it is the only story in the volume which is *not* concerned with the aristocracy or nobility:

> Appropriately located at the centre of *A Group of Noble Dames*, it portrays the extent to which the common man can be corrupted by the romantic illusion he has learned to share with his social betters: the belief that there is a 'glory' and a 'halo' (162) surrounding the aristocracy. For both the nobleman and the commoner, the effects of such a misconception are especially destructive because their victims are children, born into a society which confuses their lineage with their humanity. (pp. 75–6)

In *1891* and in subsequent editions, 'Squire Petrick's Lady' stands as the final one of a central block of four consecutive stories dealing, in part, with the child as victim. The clarity of this structure was lost in the serial publications because the four stories involved were printed second, fourth, fifth and sixth.

There are more than sixty substantive readings which first appear in *1891*, ranging in length from individual words to a four-line insert. In the case of a dozen of these variant readings, however, it is impossible to tell precisely at what stage Hardy made the revision, since they occur in passages which were omitted from both the serial publications, and therefore they may possibly have been in the *Graphic* proof before being deleted.

The four-line insert occurs after the doctor has told Petrick that the family of his late wife had been prone to delusions, and he realizes that his wife's confession of infidelity was false:

> 'You look down in the mouth?' said the doctor, pausing.
> 'A bit unmanned. 'Tis unexpected-like,' sighed Timothy (p. 183).

As Kristin Brady notes, Petrick's implicit self-hate is vividly dramatized by this new dialogue: 'preposterously, Timothy is "unmanned" by the fact that he has not been cuckolded' (p. 75).

A number of revisions work to make the narrator of *1891* more colloquial, as befits the style of the crimson maltster. Thus 'antecedents' (MS., *HW*) becomes 'beginnings' (p. 175), 'to exclude' (MS., *Gr, HW*) becomes 'to dish' (p. 176), 'plebeian tendencies' (MS.) becomes 'grovelling tastes' (p. 179), 'corollary' (MS., *Gr, HW*) is now 'afterclap' (p. 179), 'them' (MS., *HW*) is ''em' (p. 179) and, finally, 'corporeal' (MS) is 'fleshly' (p. 184). Hardy is not consistent in this wish to simplify the narrator's idiom, since on occasions he makes him use more formal language. For instance, 'to fall' (MS., *Gr, HW*) becomes 'to devolve' (p. 181) and 'beginnings' (MS., *HW*) is changed to 'paternity' (p. 178). This last revision affords a clue that Hardy might possibly have consulted the manuscript when revising the story for *1891*: the reference in the latter to the child's 'paternity' (p. 178) restores a reading that had been deleted in the manuscript.

A couple of revisions demonstrate Hardy's textual husbandry and his reluctance to discard anything once it was written. Petrick's thought that his wife's choice of the Marquis as her lover was 'grandly conceived' (MS., *HW*) is changed to the reflection that it was 'finely conceived' (p. 179) in *1891*, but Hardy recycles the gist of the original adverb by altering the previous sentence from 'She was a woman of noble instincts, after all' (MS., *HW*) to 'She was a woman of grand instincts, after all'. Similarly, in *Harper's Weekly* Petrick thanked God that he had not acted as 'other usurers' sons' would have done on learning of their wives' infidelity; in *1891*, this phrase becomes 'other meanly descended fathers' (p. 180), but Hardy retains the notion of usury by altering the start of the sentence so that Petrick reflects ruefully on 'the miserable scriveners, *usurers*, and pawnbrokers that he had numbered among his forefathers' (pp. 179–80; my italics indicate the *1891* addition).

Characteristically, it would seem, Hardy gave special attention to the opening and closing sentences of the story. At the start, he makes three alterations to the first sentence, changing 'require' to 'need', 'prince of mortgagees' to 'trump of mortgagees' and 'skill in obtaining possession' to 'skill in gaining possession' (p. 173). At the end of the narrator's tale, the father's response to his son's reasonable query how he can expect him to resemble the Marquis when he is not related to him is different; in *Harper's Weekly,* Hardy had written, '"Then you ought to be?" grumbled his father', but *1891* is more emphatic in its description of Petrick's ironic disappointment in his son: '"Ugh! Then you ought to be!" growled his father' (p. 185).

Again at the end of the story, Hardy slightly changes Petrick's response to his son. In *Harper's Weekly*, Rupert knocks at the door of his father's study and announces himself by name. His father replies:

> 'I'll Rupert thee, you young impostor! Say only poor commonplace Timothy?'

In *1891*, however, he replies:

> 'I'll Rupert thee, you young impostor! Say, only a poor commonplace Petrick!' (p. 185)

In the earlier version, for Petrick to tell Rupert to call himself Timothy is to say that the boy merely takes after his father and grandfather, both called Timothy. The alteration for *1891* widens this dismissal to include the whole clan of Petricks, such as the objectionable cousin and the fraudulent uncle.

A couple of topographical revisions can be noted. The Duke of Southwesterland, the father of the Marquis whom Annetta claims is the father of her child, was previously known in the manuscript and *Harper's Weekly* as the Duke of Hamptonshire, an old name for Hampshire. Perhaps Hardy altered it here to avoid any possible confusion with a later story in the collected edition, 'The Duchess of Hamptonshire' (the two stories had not previously been published together). The only other occasion when Hardy used the name is in the final scene of *Jude*, when the sounds of a Duke of Hamptonshire receiving an honorary degree in the Sheldonian float into the room where Jude lies in his coffin. Finally, it is only in *1891* that Hardy described the physician who reveals the nature of Annetta's delusion as belonging to the Wessex town of Budmouth; all previous versions of the story placed him in its real equivalent of Weymouth.

The closing comments on the story from the listeners are mostly new for *1891*, although the bulk of the final three sentences is salvaged from the ending of 'The Marchioness of Stonehenge' in the *Graphic*, which there preceded 'Anna, Lady Baxby', as 'Squire Petrick's Lady' does in *1891*.

1891 Harper

The American publication of 'Squire Petrick's Lady' in *A Group of Noble Dames* has about thirty-five differences in accidentals from the Osgood, McIlvaine edition (ignoring US spelling), and these are mainly matters of punctuation. Otherwise, the two texts are virtually identical. Harper's corrects the misprint of 'though' as 'through' (p. 174) in Osgood, McIlvaine, but introduces two of its own, printing 'at last' as 'as last' and 'art' as 'arts' (pp. 197, 200). This latter variant is probably a compositorial error, rather than editorial intervention, as is the unique use of 'to it' in the maltster's regret that he could not tell another story 'with a sufficiently moral tone to it to suit the club' (pp. 205–6) where *1891* reads 'in it'. The only other substantive variant is in the phrase 'a voice like the Marquis' (p. 205), replacing *1891*'s 'a voice like the Marquis's'. Harper's reading may well be editorial in origin.

1912 Macmillan Wessex edition

There are eleven revisions to 'Squire Petrick's Lady' for the 'definitive' Wessex edition of 1912, eight of which are substantive.

In the manuscript and *1891*, Petrick rejoices in his son's illegitimacy: 'He is of pure stock on one side at least' (p. 179). In *1912*, for the first time, he delights in his son being instead descended from 'blue stock' (p. 158). Perhaps 'pure' had acquired for Hardy a set of particular and deliberately contentious meanings since he had used it in the subtitle of *Tess*, 'a pure woman', and he did not think it appropriate here to raise again the issue of 'purity', especially in a context of illegitimacy. 'Pure' as he had previously used it in 'Squire Petrick's Lady' seems to be associated solely with aristocratic heritage, and Hardy may have feared that such a limited meaning might have reduced its resonance in *Tess*, where her noble ancestry is the least of Tess's claims to purity.

The passage describing Petrick's gratitude to his wife for being unfaithful undergoes a gradual expansion over the years, as a comparison of various versions shows. Petrick is considering his awful relations and the probability that his son might well have inherited their characteristics but for his wife's action:

MS. He considered [...] the probability that some of their bad qualities would have come out in a child of his loins to give him sorrow in his old age, turn his black hairs grey, & |his| grey hairs white, & cut down all the timber |& Heaven knows what-all,| had he not, like a skilful gardener, changed the sort (fo. 109^{v}; deleted and stetted).

HW He considered [...] how his descendants would now be saved from the taint of those ancestral qualities, which might have turned his black hairs gray and his gray hairs white.

1891 He considered [...] the probability that some of their bad qualities would have come out in a merely corporeal child, to give him sorrow in his old age, turn his black hairs gray, his gray hairs white, cut down every stick of timber, and Heaven knows what all, had he not, like a skilful gardener, minded his grafting and changed the sort (pp. 179–80).

1912 He considered [...] the probability that some of their bad qualities would have come out in a merely corporeal child of his loins, to give him sorrow in his old age, turn his black hairs gray, his gray hairs white, cut down every stick of timber, and Heaven knows what all, had he not, or rather his good wife, like a skilful gardener, given attention to the art of grafting, and changed the sort (pp. 158–9).

Only in *1912* do we get the reference to the loins for the first time, and also new is the mention of his 'good wife', as Petrick, in a delicious afterthought, generously acknowledges that he had in fact nothing at all to do with the ingenious idea of his wife making a cuckold of him, and her ensuing infidelity renders her 'good' in his eyes.[9]

Notes

1 See Purdy, pp. 64, 65.

2 See Hutchins, III, 671–2. There appears to be some confusion about Walter's surname, which is given as 'Walters' in Brady and 'Walker' in the New Wessex edition of *A Group of Noble Dames*. His correct name is Walter.

3 Gatrell, p. 84.

4 Gatrell, p. 88.

5 Gatrell, pp. 83–5.

6 Gatrell, p. 84.

7 This is ignoring those unique uncancelled words in the MS., described above, which were never in any printed version and which were probably deleted before or at the first proof.

8 *Harper's Weekly* does not simply delete this but replaces it with the following: 'and how his descendants would now be saved from the taint of those ancestral qualities, which might have turned his black hairs gray and his gray hairs white'. Out goes the manuscript's reference to loins.

9 For the sake of a complete record, the other revisions to *1891* for the Wessex edition are as follows (*1912* is quoted first, and the pagination is that of *1912*): 'furthest/farthest' (p. 158); 'historical perspective/perspective' (p. 159); 'and whose boasted pedigree on one side would be nothing to his Rupert's after all/whose boasted pedigree on one side would be nothing to his Rupert's' (p. 160); 'beloved Rupert of the aristocratic blood/beloved Rupert' (p. 160); 'dispossessed;/ dispossessed,' (p. 160); 'incontestable/incontestible' (p. 161); 'his son physically/his son' (p. 162).

CHAPTER 14

'Anna, Lady Baxby'

'Anna, Lady Baxby' was first published at Christmas 1890 as one of the six bowdlerized tales in the *Graphic* which were collectively titled *A Group of Noble Dames*. 'Anna, Lady Baxby', however, was far from being the most seriously bowdlerized of the tales, though the significant changes to it in the *Graphic* version show Hardy's willingness to meet the periodical's demands for propriety.

The versions of the story which have textual significance are as follows:

Graphic	*Graphic*, Christmas Number (published 1 December) 1890, pp. 12–13. It was the third of the six stories entitled *A Group of Noble Dames* published simultaneously in this issue.
HW	*Harper's Weekly*, 6 December 1890, pp. 962, 964. As in the *Graphic*, it was the third of the six stories in *A Group of Noble Dames*. *Harper's Weekly* published these stories in four weekly instalments (29 November–20 December) and 'Anna, Lady Baxby' ended the second of these, preceded in the same issue by 'The Lady Caroline'.
1891	*A Group of Noble Dames* (London: Osgood, McIlvaine, 1891), pp. 187–98. This was the first collected edition of the story in the expanded *A Group of Noble Dames* which now included ten stories, of which 'Anna, Lady Baxby' was 'Dame the Seventh'. Published at 6*s.* in an edition of 2000 copies on 30 May 1891. It was the first volume of Hardy's work which Osgood, McIlvaine had published.
1891H	*A Group of Noble Dames* (New York: Harper & Brothers, 1891), pp. 207–17. Published early in June 1891.
1896	*A Group of Noble Dames* (London: Osgood, McIlvaine, 1896), pp. 187–98. Volume XV in the Wessex Novels, the first uniform and complete edition of Hardy's works. Plates of the original edition were used, and 'Anna, Lady Baxby' is identical in every respect to *1891*.
1912	*A Group of Noble Dames* (London: Macmillan, 1912), pp. 167–74. Volume XIV of the Wessex edition.

The manuscript of the *Graphic* stories is extant. It was presented by Hardy, through Sydney Cockerell, to the Library of Congress, Washington DC, in October 1911 when he was distributing his MSS. among various public collections. As R.L. Purdy notes, the MS. was foliated and rearranged by Hardy, and 'Anna, Lady Baxby' is numbered 75–83; however, each of the six stories was also independently foliated and 'Anna, Lady Baxby' is numbered 1–9.[1] The final leaf, fo. 84, is missing; it contained links cancelled and rewritten when the stories were collected in *1891*.

Sources

In 1896, Hardy described 'Anna, Lady Baxby' as 'a traditional tale, mostly fact', which was set at Sherborne Castle (*Letters*, II, 132). Anna is based on Lady Anne Russell (died 1696), who was married to George, Lord Digby (1612–76, later Earl of Bristol). Her brother was William Russell (1613–1700), Earl of Bedford, who led the parliamentary forces which besieged Sherborne Castle (Sherton) for five days in September 1642, during the Civil War. Many of the story's details are taken directly from Hutchins's *History of Dorset*:

> While the Earl of Bedford besieged the castle, tradition reports that the wife of George, Lord Digby, son of the Earl of Bristol, his sister, was then at the lodge. He sent a message to desire her to quit it, as he had orders from the Parliament to demolish it. She immediately went on horseback to his tent, at the camp now called Bedford's Castle, and told him, 'if he persisted in his intention, he should find his sister's bones buried in the ruins', and instantly left him; which spirited behaviour in all probability preserved it. (IV, 269)

In Hutchins, Anna is occupying the lodge, the newer castle built by Sir Walter Raleigh across the lake, but Hardy moved her to the older castle, no doubt for dramatic effect. Otherwise, Hardy follows Hutchins's account closely: details of Bedford's 7000 troops, the site of the siege on the north side of the castle and his retreat towards Yeovil are all historically accurate. Lady Baxby's words to her brother are virtually a quotation of Hutchins: 'you will find the bones of your sister buried in the ruins'. Hardy, however, dramatizes their meeting at much greater length, and Anna's later political conversion to the parliamentary cause and her treatment of her husband are wholly fictional.

Hardy's contrast between the personalities of Lord Digby and Bedford has its basis in Hutchins:

> Though these lords were probably friends (they were brothers-in-law) when they sat for their portraits in one piece, their characters were exceedingly dissimilar. Lord Bedford was honest, sincere, and moderate; and so far from being a bigot to party that he often fluctuated, yet still with a view to preserving the balance of the constitution, and without even being suspected of acting from self-interest or ambition. Lord Bristol, with brighter parts, was rash, enterprising, full of art, and by no means steady to the principles of honour, nor firm to those of religion. Both distinguished themselves by personal bravery; but Bristol's restless ambition and subtlety only sullied his reputation. Bedford's integrity and temper carried him to the grave with honour at the great age of 87. (II, 789)

The manuscript

The manuscript of 'Anna, Lady Baxby' has some eight uncancelled readings which are unique to it. These are mostly a matter of an insignificant word or two, but a couple of variants are worth noting. The estrangement between Anna's family and her husband's is said to have 'resulted upon her marriage |into this family|' (fo. 75), where all published versions say that it 'resulted from hostilities with her husband's family' (*1891*, p. 190), allowing the inference that the estrangement between the two families is of recent origin, dating from their opposition during the Civil War. The manuscript gives a more interesting reading, showing that the antagonism is purely familial, not political, and hinting that the Civil War is, in this instance at least, merely the external public projection of existing personal conflicts.

Another variant occurs when Anna discovers her husband's intended infidelity. In the manuscript, she changes in an instant from a 'timorous truant' (fo. 82) to a strategic wife. Later versions talk of her being the 'home-hating truant' (*1891*, p. 195), making it clear that Anna is running away from her husband and not from any imminent physical danger to herself from the destruction of her home. There had been nothing 'timorous' about her defiant return to the castle earlier in the story, daring her brother to demolish it.

Graphic

Hardy's changes to the story for the *Graphic* remove the wanton woman with whom Lord Baxby has made an assignation and which his wife discovers. Instead, when Anna is creeping out of her house to join her brother, she overhears some plotters discussing how they have bribed her maid to tell her that her brother is ill in order to entice her to his camp, after which they can storm the castle and kill her husband. She defies them and despises them (although here in her own name, not that of Lord Baxby) before returning to her bed, waking her husband and confessing all in a fit of wifely contrition. The treacherous servant is drummed out of the castle, with her gown turned inside out. There is nothing of the scene in which Anna ties her husband's hair to the bedpost, since here he is not threatening to stray. These *Graphic* changes do not ruin the story but simply make it something quite different. Anna's motive for returning to her husband is not sexual, as elsewhere, but political and proud, a matter of domestic loyalty rather than jealousy.

Hardy made these alterations simply by deleting two substantial passages near the end of the story and adding fresh material in their place. There are also half a dozen unique substantive variants elsewhere in the tale; for instance, only in the *Graphic* does Anna bar the door of the turret on returning to her husband, but only in this version does she need to, since there is here a physical threat to his safety outside. None of the other changes to individual words alters the action in any way.

The close of the story in the *Graphic*, when the listeners comment on it, is an adapted version of the end of 'Lady Mottisfont' in the collected edition, introducing 'The Lady Icenway', which follows 'Anna, Lady Baxby' in the serial.

Harper's Weekly

The version of 'Anna, Lady Baxby' which appeared in *Harper's Weekly* largely follows the manuscript and is therefore close to the story which we know today.

There is evidence of what appears to be editorial intervention at Harper's office. When Anna is with her brother, she is described as being 'the calmest of the two' in all versions of the story except in *Harper's Weekly* which has the strictly correct comparative 'calmer'. (There is a similar substitution of 'elder' for 'eldest' in the *Harper's Weekly* version of 'Squire Petrick's Lady'.) *Harper's Weekly* has two other unique variant readings which seem editorial in origin: 'she was still' instead of 'she still was', and 'have I thought' in place of 'that I have thought'.

Like the *Graphic* ending, *Harper's Weekly* has the adapted version of the end of 'Lady Mottisfont'.

1891 Osgood, McIlvaine

In making the first collected edition of *A Group of Noble Dames*, Hardy made only a handful of very minor alterations to the version of 'Anna, Lady Baxby' as it had appeared in *Harper's Weekly*. For instance, a 'you' becomes 'ye' in the speech of the girl waiting for Lord Baxby at the end of the story, and the entreaty of Anna's brother to 'stay with me' becomes 'abide with me'.

There are only two additions of any note. The first occurs when Anna tells her husband that he should not be supporting 'the lying policy of the King (as she called it)' (p. 194). The parenthesis is new, and it shows Hardy giving increased characterization to his narrator, the Colonel, who would no doubt not support Anna's attack on the monarchy. The second occurs when Anna tells the waiting girl how she despises her and all her 'wanton tribe' (p. 196), the new adjective frankly stating the sexual transgression which Anna's husband had contemplated.

1891 Harper

The first American edition of the story has two dozen differences in accidentals from the 1891 British edition. It also has two substantive variants: 'that I have thought' becoming 'have I thought', and 'the voice' becoming 'her voice' (*1891*, pp. 192, 195). Both changes are probably editorial.

1912 Macmillan Wessex Edition

Hardy made only one substantive alteration to the version of 'Anna, Lady Baxby' in Osgood, McIlvaine's edition of 1891 when preparing the Wessex edition of 1912. When Anna is about to creep out the house to join her brother, we learn that 'her husband still slept the sleep of the weary, well-fed, and well-drunken, if not of the virtuous' (p. 173). The last two words had previously read 'the just' which Hardy perhaps felt might be understood as a criticism of Lord Baxby's royalist sympathies. His inability to sleep the sleep of the virtuous, however, is clearly a comment only on his moral conduct as a husband, which his wife is shortly to discover.[2]

Notes

1 See Purdy, pp. 64, 65.
2 For the sake of a complete record, the other revisions to *1891* for the Wessex edition are as follows (*1912* is quoted first, and the pagination is that of *1912*): 'history that,/history, that' (p. 167); 'Why, O/Why, oh' (p. 169); 'Marquis/Marquis,' (p. 170); 'approach/approach,' (p. 172); ''ee/ye' (p. 173); 'lying down/lying down,' (p. 173).

CHAPTER 15

'The Lady Penelope'

Very little is known about the composition of 'The Lady Penelope', although it was presumably written not long before its first publication in 1890.

The versions of the story which have textual significance are as follows:

Serial   *Longman's Magazine*, January 1890, pp. 279–87.

1891   *A Group of Noble Dames* (London: Osgood, McIlvaine, 1891), pp. 199–214. This was the first collected edition of the story in the expanded *A Group of Noble Dames* which now included ten stories, of which 'The Lady Penelope' was 'Dame the Eighth'. Published at 6*s.* in an edition of 2000 copies on 30 May 1891. It was the first volume of Hardy's work which Osgood, McIlvaine had published.

1891H   *A Group of Noble Dames* (New York: Harper & Brothers, 1891), pp. 218–33. Published early in June 1891.

1896   *A Group of Noble Dames* (London: Osgood, McIlvaine, 1896), pp. 199–214. Volume XV in the Wessex Novels, the first uniform and complete edition of Hardy's works. Plates of the original edition were used, and 'The Lady Penelope' is identical in every respect to *1891*.

1912   *A Group of Noble Dames* (London: Macmillan, 1912), pp. 177–88. Volume XIV of the Wessex edition.

The manuscript of 'The Lady Penelope' is extant. It was presented by Hardy, through Sydney Cockerell, to the Library of Congress, Washington DC, in October 1911 when he was distributing his MSS. among various public collections. As R.L. Purdy notes, the MS. was foliated by Hardy, and is numbered 1–14; 'The Lady Penelope' and the six stories which appeared as *A Group of Noble Dames* in the *Graphic* are bound together in the order in which they appeared in the first collected edition of 1891.[1]

Sources

Hutchins's *History of Dorset* gives the following account of Lady Penelope Darcy, who married Sir George Trenchard as his second wife in the early years of the seventeenth century:

> The second wife was heiress to the estate of her mother, Mary, countess of Rivers, daughter of Sir Thomas Kitson, of Hengrave, knt. Sir George dying soon after his marriage, she remarried Sir John Gage, of Firle, co. Sussex,

bart. by whom only she had issue; and being again left a widow, she then married William Hervey, of Ickworth, bart. She was courted by her three husbands at one time; but quarrels arising between them, she artfully put an end to them, by threatening the first aggressor with her perpetual displeasure; and humourously told them, that if they would be quiet and have patience she would have them all in their turns, which at last actually happened. (III, 329)

Lady Penelope is not identified by name at this point in Hutchins, so Hardy must have discovered it by consulting the Trenchard family pedigree (III, [326]). One modification which Hardy made to Hutchins is that his Lady Penelope has a child only by her third husband, and it is a stillborn one: she has a child, that is, only by the husband she loves best, and its death anticipates the tragic end of her final marriage. There is, of course, no hint in Hutchins of any malicious gossip about the death of her husbands.

In a letter to Bertram Windle on 28 September 1896, Hardy identified Wolverton House near Dorchester as 'the scene of the traditional story of "The Lady Penelope"' (*Letters*, II, 131).

Manuscript

The manuscript is the printers' copy for the *Longman's* serial, although it is not a fair copy, having numerous alterations, especially on the first page. It has nine uncancelled readings which do not appear in the serial and were presumably altered at the proof stage. Six of them are instances of a single word being substituted for another, often of the same length to avoid disturbing type (e.g. 'good' replaces 'fair', 'churlish' replaces 'knightly' and 'skulking' replaces 'sneaking').

Deleted passages in the manuscript show that Lady Penelope was originally to have been a neighbour of the Drenghards, not merely visiting the locality, and she was to have had only a father, and not just a mother, as it later became. Hardy's revision is in part historically accurate, in that Lady Penelope Darcy's mother, Mary, lived until 1644, although her father, Earl Rivers, also lived until about 1639. Lady Penelope's first husband, Sir George Drenghard, was initially described as the youngest of her three suitors, but Hardy altered this to make him the eldest.[2] Two further alterations show Hardy hastening Lady Penelope's third marriage; Lady Penelope is a widow for only eleven months (not fifteen, as the manuscript originally read) before Sir William resumes his courtship of her, and it is only a month or two later that he begins to urge her to marry him (initially he had waited two or three months). The shortened timescale helps to explain the criticism of Lady Penelope at the end of the story for her 'unseemly wantonness' in marrying three men in rapid succession.

Longman's Magazine

In addition to altering the uncancelled manuscript readings at proof stage, Hardy also took the opportunity to make four additions to the story, ranging in length from a single word to a clause of eight words. Five of these thirteen variants occur in the first page of the manuscript.

In the MS., Hardy described how the Countess, Penelope's mother, 'found ~~his~~ |the| door besieged by her suitors |wherever she went|' (fo. 1), but the serial says instead 'that suitors seemed to spring out of the ground wherever she went'. While the new reading perhaps gives a better image of Penelope's ability to summon suitors as if by magic, the manuscript's description of her being besieged is closer to what are presumably the Homeric associations of her name.

Hardy took the opportunity in correcting the serial proofs to increase the maliciousness of the gossip which hounds Lady Penelope to her death. In the manuscript, people had whispered that the death of her first husband was 'doubtless natural' (fo. 11), but in *Longman's* this becomes 'possibly natural', and she thus comes under suspicion for the death of both her husbands. This change perhaps explains why Hardy made it clear earlier in the story that Sir George died 'of his convivialities', a phrase not in the manuscript.

Of the other three additions to the serial, the only significant one is the information that Sir John, the second husband, has moved into Lady Penelope's house, 'his being but a mean and meagre thing'. This emphasizes that Sir John has very much the better of the bargain, making his cruel taunts that she was a prize not worth winning even more unjustified.

1891 Osgood, McIlvaine

The first collected edition of 'The Lady Penelope' in *A Group of Noble Dames* would appear to have been set from an emended duplicate set of serial proofs. This is indicated by a wording in the opening paragraph where *1891* restores a manuscript reading which had been altered in the serial. The manuscript and *1891* both explain how Lady Penelope's mansion has lost the fair estate which once belonged 'to its lord'; the serial, however, had said 'to it'. One explanation of this variant is that Hardy omitted to note the serial revision on the duplicate set of proofs, so that *1891* retains the manuscript wording. All the other alterations to the serial proofs, however, would appear to have been marked on the duplicate set, since they all appear in the collected edition of the story, albeit sometimes revised further in 1891.

1891 has two insertions totalling eight lines in length, and both concern the rumours which surround Lady Penelope and the death of her second husband. Sir William overhears the following new dialogue between the two basketmakers:

> 'A cupboard close to his bed, and the key in her pocket. Ah!' said one.
> 'And a blue phial therein – h'm!' said another.
> 'And spurge-laurel leaves among the hearth-ashes. Oh-oh!' said a third. (p. 211)

A little later, the narrator explains why the rumours were bound to reach Lady Penelope: 'it was impossible that they should not; the district teemed with them; they rustled in the air like night-birds of evil omen' (p. 212). The rumours are now said to be 'so' thick in the atmosphere around her. In preparing *1891*, Hardy took pains to dramatize and elaborate the suspicions surrounding Lady Penelope, and this better motivates Sir William's estrangement from her, since we now know exactly what he has heard.

Another addition to the story in *1891* is the information near the beginning that 'she was of the purest descent; ah, there's seldom such blood nowadays as hers!' (p. 202). Such a comment on pedigree helps to link the story to most of the others in the newly-collected volume, and it gives the narrator more characterization as his own views obtrude. In *1891*, he is identified for the first time as the Man of Family immediately after the story's title.

Hardy changed the spelling of the family name of Lady Penelope's first husband. In the manuscript, Sir George's family had been the Drenc-hards, in the serial they were the Drenchards and now in *1891* they are the Drenkhards. The latest spelling makes clearer their reputation for hard drinking.

The separation of Lady Penelope and Sir William is slightly altered in *1891*. Their estrangement is described as 'ghastly' (p. 211), and Lady Penelope appeals to Sir William as 'oh my dear husband' (p. 213) when declaring her innocence, giving the scene more pathos. The rumours which led to her death are described in the manuscript and serial as a 'wicked scandal', and as a 'vile scandal' in *1891*.

The final six-line paragraph linking 'The Lady Penelope' to the following story is of course new to its first appearance in collected form.

1891 Harper

There are some thirty differences in accidentals between the 1891 British and American editions of the story (ignoring US spelling). There are also three substantive variants, all of which may be either compositorial error or editorial in origin.[3]

1912 Macmillan Wessex edition

There are a dozen differences between *1891* and the 1912 Wessex edition of 'The Lady Penelope', of which four are substantive. The lengthiest revision concerns a description of Lady Penelope's estate and 'the high road which then gave entrance from the north' (p. 183) which replaces *1891*'s 'the high road which then skirted the grounds on the north', presumably to give greater topographical precision. The house itself is said at the opening of the story to be 'somewhat reduced' (p. 177) from its original size, where *1891* had described it as being 'much reduced'.

The reverend Vice-President had concluded the story in *1891* by saying that

Lady Penelope's fate should be clearly recognized as a 'punishment' for her wantonness, but the Wessex edition replaces this with 'chastisement' (p. 188), which perhaps gives a slightly less vindictive view of her death as the work of a vengeful Providence.[4]

Notes

1 See Purdy, p. 64.

2 I have been unable to discover the dates of birth of Lady Penelope Darcy's husbands.

3 The British 'had place' (p. 202) became 'had taken place' in *1891H*; 'and she said' (p. 203) became 'as she said', and 'her widowhood' (p. 204) became 'the widowhood'.

4 For the sake of a complete record, the other revisions to *1891* for the Wessex edition are as follows (*1912* is quoted first, and the pagination is that of *1912*): 'James/James,' (p. 177); 'towers/towers,' (p. 181); 'O/oh' (p. 182); 'will know/wooll know' (p. 182); 'By God/By G–' (p. 182); 'O/oh' (p. 187); 'physician/physician,' (p. 187); 'Sir John/Sir John,' (p. 187); 'Vice-President/Vice-President,' (p. 188).

CHAPTER 16

'The Duchess of Hamptonshire'

'The Duchess of Hamptonshire' was the second short story which Hardy wrote (after the uncollected 'Destiny and a Blue Cloak' of 1874), and the first one he published in England. It is also one of his most textually complicated tales. He wrote 'The Impulsive Lady of Croome Castle', as it was originally called, in Sturminster Newton in early 1878, while he was completing work on *The Return of the Native*. Six years later, he substantially altered it, although the outline of the plot remained the same, and then published it in America under the title 'Emmeline'. The story was first collected in *A Group of Noble Dames* in 1891, and for the first time it was called 'The Duchess of Hamptonshire': this edition of the story combines different parts of the two earlier published forms.

The versions of the story which have textual significance are as follows:

Light	As 'The Impulsive Lady of Croome Castle', *Light*, 6 April (pp. 7–8) and 13 April (pp. 51–2) 1878. The division occurred at the end of Part First, when Hill leaves Emmeline in the shrubbery.
HW	As 'The Impulsive Lady of Croome Castle', *Harper's Weekly* (New York), 11 May (pp. 370–71) and 18 May (p. 394) 1878. The division is the same as above.
Independent	As 'Emmeline; or, Passion versus Principle', *Independent* (New York), 7 February 1884, pp. 26–8. Like the previous versions, this is divided into Part First and Part Second.
1891	'The Duchess of Hamptonshire', *A Group of Noble Dames* (London: Osgood, McIlvaine, 1891), pp. 215–35. This was the first collected edition of the story in the expanded *A Group of Noble Dames* which now included ten stories, of which 'The Duchess of Hamptonshire' was 'Dame the Ninth'. The story is not divided into sections in this or subsequent editions. Published at 6s. in an edition of 2000 copies on 30 May 1891. It was the first volume of Hardy's work which Osgood, McIlvaine had published.
1891H	'The Duchess of Hamptonshire', *A Group of Noble Dames* (New York: Harper & Brothers, 1891), pp. 234–55. Published early in June 1891.
1896	'The Duchess of Hamptonshire', *A Group of Noble Dames* (London: Osgood, McIlvaine, 1896), pp. 215–35. Volume XV in the Wessex Novels, the first uniform and complete edition of Hardy's works. Plates of the original edition were used, and 'The Duchess of Hamptonshire' is identical in

every respect to *1891*.

1912   'The Duchess of Hamptonshire', *A Group of Noble Dames* (London: Macmillan, 1912), pp. 191–206. Volume XIV of the Wessex edition.

A bound manuscript of 'Emmeline' is currently located in the Pierpont Morgan Library, which acquired it in 1909.

The origin of part of the story may lie in an incident which Hardy's brother-in-law told him. Caddell Holder, who was married to Emma Hardy's sister, was once a curate in Bristol during an outbreak of cholera, and, as Hardy recalls in the *Life*,

> He related that one day at a friend's house he met a charming young widow, who invited him to call on her. With pleasant anticipations he went at tea-time a day or two later, and duly inquired if she was at home. The servant said with a strange face: 'Why, Sir, you buried her this morning!' He found that amongst the many funerals of cholera victims he had conducted that day, as on every day, hers had been one. (p. 161)

The first surviving reference to the story is to the version that became 'Emmeline'. On 16 October 1883, Hardy replied to John Bowen, assistant editor of the New York *Independent*: 'I have received your letter of the 14th Sept., together with a copy of the Independent. I will take your offer into consideration, & let you know as soon as possible if I can send you a story, such as you describe, on the terms proposed' (*Letters*, VII, 98). As we shall see later, it may be very significant that Bowen had sent Hardy a copy of the *Independent*, which would allow him to gauge the interests and outlook of the audience which he was being invited to address.

The three different titles of the story indicate the three distinct versions in which it existed, first in 1878 (the English publication in *Light* is effectively identical to the American *Harper's Weekly*), then in 1884 in the *Independent*, and finally in 1891 in the first collected edition. What is the relationship between these three versions? Purdy notes that 'the version of 1884 is much the longest (and may be the earliest), as the version of 1878 is the shortest' (pp. 63–4). Purdy is correct about the respective lengths of the three versions, but his conjecture about the order in which they were composed is mistaken. A close study of the manuscript of the 1884 publication shows that the sequence of publication is the same as the sequence of composition: the earliest version was the first to be published, and the *Independent* was an augmented and revised version which Hardy prepared in 1884. He then combined parts from these two earlier versions to produce the collected edition in 1891: the 1878 version was the basis for the first part of the story in the collected edition (up to the point when Hill leaves Emmeline in the shrubbery), while the 1884 version provides the bulk of the second part.

Why might Hardy have wished to alter and augment the story for the *Independent*? This New York title was a leading Congregational newspaper, and in his later dealings with it Hardy always showed himself to be very aware of its religious outlook. For instance, in November 1885 he offered to serialize *The*

Woodlanders in it, and was careful to emphasize that its 'moral tone will be unexceptionable', repeating in a letter of February 1886 that 'the tone of the story' was 'of a kind which I think would suit your readers'. Five years later, he proposed to write the story that became 'The Doctor's Legend': 'as it would be specially written I would do my best to keep it in harmony with the general tone of The Independent (with which I am familiar.)'. In 1900, he sent the newspaper one of Florence Henniker's stories and recommended it to the editor because it had 'a moral which was as sound as it was unobtrusive'.[1] It seems likely, then, that Hardy would have been especially careful not to give offence to the editor or readers of the *Independent* when submitting a story about a curate in love with a married woman, and many of the unique features of the 1884 version are, as we shall see later, examples of the kind of self-censorship which Hardy performed elsewhere. For instance, there is no physical contact between the two lovers in 1884, and generally Hardy seems to have striven to produce a story that has the earnest clarity of a moral allegory, and the new subtitle, 'Passion versus Principle', reassures its readers from the outset of its lofty tone.

Light and *Harper's Weekly*

The serial publications of 'The Impulsive Lady of Croome Castle' in *Light* and *Harper's Weekly* are substantively identical.

R.L. Purdy gives an account of the English serial:

> *Light: A Journal of Criticism and Belles Lettres* (London) was a short-lived weekly founded by Robert Buchanan. Fiction was printed in an independent *feuilleton*, 'Belles Lettres', and these were collected and reissued monthly as *Light Magazine*. Hardy's story appeared in the first two numbers, simultaneously with the opening instalments of Trollope's 'The Lady of Launay'. The British Museum has the only file I know of. (p. 63n)

These two versions of 1878 uniquely locate the story in the parish of Croome. In the *Independent* this becomes Stroome and in *1891* it is called Batton.[2]

This 1878 version is the shortest of the three, and therefore it is best defined by what it does not contain. The first part of the story here will be familiar to readers of the collected edition in *A Group of Noble Dames*, since Hardy largely restored the 1878 version. Sir Byng has 5000 acres (as he does in the *Independent*) which increases to 10,000 in 1891. We learn nothing of what her husband taunted Emmeline with (we learn most in the *Independent*, and *1891* retains some of those details). In general, we discover most about her suffering in the *Independent*, less in *1878* and least in the collected editions. For instance, *1878* has Emmeline telling Hill that 'two days ago he shut me up in an attic in the middle of the night, and there was nothing for me to sit upon, and I was chilled and wretched'. The *Independent* retains this but Hardy deleted it in *1891*. The entire paragraph which describes Sir Byng being smitten by the sight of Emmeline and declaring to himself that he wants to marry her is not in *1878*, and it first appeared in *1884*.

The second part of the story in the collected edition, beginning with Hill's voyage to America, is largely based on the *Independent*, so the 1878 version will be unfamiliar to most readers. It is similar to later versions in its plot, but is shorter and lacks several details which appear for the first time in the *Independent*. For instance, it does not mention Hill officiating at a funeral on board the ship at the time it happened, so the later versions have a much stronger sense of retrospective irony. In *1878*, Hill does not write 'Lines to an Unfortunate Lady', another ironic touch introduced later to stress the pathos of addressing poems to a woman who, we eventually learn, has long been dead. We do not see him talking to his acquaintances and omitting the episode involving Emmeline, which is not described as being 'of towering importance to himself'.

The chronology of the story is slightly different in *1878*: Hill learns of Sir Byng's death five months after it occurred, and he cannot get free of his engagements for a further six, whereas in later versions he learns the news seven months after and is detained for a further four. *1878* does not have his reflection that 'old times will revive with the cessation of her recent experience, and every day will favour my return'. It also omits the information that Lady Saxelbye likes the villagers to enjoy themselves and often has them at the castle, leading Hill to think that she is 'kind-hearted, as always!', an ironic note since he does not yet know that Emmeline is dead. In the final paragraph, the narrator states that Hill never returned to England after he left; later versions merely say that he departed with no intention to return.

Independent: the manuscript

The surviving manuscript of the 1884 version of the story, entitled 'Emmeline; or Passion versus Principle', is written on 25 leaves of ruled paper. Purdy describes it thus:

> Though printers' MS., it is cleaner than was common with Hardy at this time and there are comparatively few alterations, suggesting it was largely copied from an earlier draft. The sub-title seems to have been an afterthought. (p. 65)

The evidence that the sub-title was a later addition is that 'Emmeline' is centred at the top of the page and has its own double underline. The sub-title was then written to the right of this and separately double-underlined. The MS. does appear to be copied from an earlier draft (presumably written shortly before): not only, as Purdy notes, is it cleaner than normal, but there are also numbers in many of the left-hand margins, in an irregular sequence from 2 to 16, which might indicate the leaves on which the material being copied appeared in the earlier draft.

The MS. reveals that the 1884 version derives from the earlier one of 1878. There are five occasions when Hardy began to write out the 1878 reading but then deleted it and continued immediately to the right of the deletion with the reading that was to appear in *1884*. This indicates that he made these revisions while copying out the draft. As an example, the opening sentence of the third paragraph of the story in the MS. reads

> This ~~pleasant~~ |edifying| gentleman's ~~castle stood~~ |personal| appearance was somewhat impressive (fo. 2)

In the 1878 versions, the paragraph begins 'This gentleman's castle stood', but in the MS. Hardy deleted the last two words and followed the deletion with the reading which was to appear in *1884*. Elsewhere in the MS., there are twelve other instances which show him deleting an 1878 reading and substituting above it the 1884 one. There are also fifteen interlineations which add a new 1884 reading to a passage which is the same as in *1878*.

There are eight substantive differences between the MS. and the *Independent*. All appear to be either misprints or compositorial misreadings: for instance, the MS. 'shutter' and 'sprouted' (fo. 3) appear in print as 'shuttle' and 'spurted'. This would suggest that Hardy did not see proofs of the *Independent*. The second part of the story in the MS. is substantively identical to that which appeared in the *Independent*, with the exception of two words (and the obvious misprint of 'wrote him to' instead of 'wrote to him'): the MS. reads 'experiences' and 'statements' (fos. 19, 22) which both appear as singular nouns in *1884*. Since they also appear as singular in the collected edition of 1891, Hardy must have consulted a printed copy of the story when preparing it, rather than the MS.

Two additions to the MS. in another hand are both printed in the *Independent*. Below Hardy's name on the first leaf is inserted 'Author of "A Pair of Blue Eyes," "Two on a Tower," etc.', the latter being his most recent novel in 1882, and at the end is written 'Shire-Hall Place, Dorchester, England', Hardy's home from June 1883 till June 1885.

Independent

The first part of the story in its collected form, with which readers are now familiar, is largely the same as in the 1878 versions. The expanded version of the first part in the 1884 *Independent* has a number of unique features: sympathy for Emmeline is increased and her conduct is both more blameless and more understandable, while her father and husband are painted more critically. The key scene in the story, the meeting between Emmeline and Hill before his emigration, is especially revised to make it a quite innocent affair. Finally, the church and religion are portrayed in a kinder light. All of these features are revisions which Hardy might have undertaken to make the story more acceptable to the *Independent*.

Emmeline is more saintly in *1884*. For instance, we learn that she has a 'shortcoming', but this is only her ignorance of her own beauty, so that her one failing seems perversely to be an absence of vanity. In all other versions we learn nothing of Hill's courtship of her, the narrator dismissing it with 'particulars of the courtship remained unknown then and always'. In the *Independent*, however, we learn details of it which are much to the credit of both lovers:

> Attracted at first by her reverential attitude at church, he silently observed
> her long before making any advances; where and when the advances were
> made, and how their distant acquaintanceship ripened into warmer relations,
> is not precisely known, so extremely reserved and shy were both the young
> people in their conduct through the affair.

The narrator proceeds to imagine the accidental 'encounters by dale and down'
which Hill engineered to sustain his 'tender fancy'. Their courtship is a tale of
pastoral piety and chivalric discretion, in even greater contrast here to the
coarser baronet which the *Independent* has just introduced. (In the serial
versions, incidentally, the Duke was called Sir Byng Saxelbye.)

In the 1878 versions, we do not learn any details of her husband's behaviour
before she decides to meet Hill in the shrubbery, so that her actions at this stage
seem to be prompted solely by love for him, but the *Independent* gives many
details of her husband's cruelty to her (none of the following quotation is in
either of the 1878 versions, and italics indicate those parts of it which Hardy
retained in the first collected edition in 1891):

> But as he [Sir Byng] was a rough man, so he was a careless man. *At first he*
> *would taunt her* with *her folly*, threaten her with all kinds of severities for
> daring to think *of that milk-and-water parson*, as he knew she did think of
> him, and then, with some coarse allusion, leave the room and go to his dogs
> and horses. *But, as time went on*, the scenes between them *took a more*
> *positive* shape – not on her side, for she was quietness personified, but on
> the part of Sir Byng. *He would not believe her assurance that she had in no*
> *way communicated with her former lover*, or *he with her, since their parting*
> *in the presence of her father.* He told her flatly that he knew she was
> deceiving him, that no woman would speak the truth in such circumstances,
> and many other cruel things of the sort *which need not be detailed.* Then,
> for the first time, this gentle woman seemed to form a resolution of a
> different nature from the course she had hitherto preserved with religious
> scrupulousness.

The last two words, Hardy perhaps felt, would placate any offence to his pious
readership in the *Independent*. She is here exonerated of any blame and Sir Byng
is wholly responsible for forcing her to seek escape.

In all other versions, the lovers meet two months after the wedding, but in the
Independent she suffers for 'a few months' before Sir Byng's cruelty makes her
contact Hill, and they have both remained scrupulously principled during that
period. When they do meet, they 'impulsively approached each other; but they
restrained the impulse, as if with pain'. In all other editions, they 'leapt together
like a pair of dewdrops on a leaf', so the *Independent* reading removes any
indiscreet physical contact, as well as removing the most poetical touch in the
story.

The *Independent* again gives unique details of her suffering to justify her
need to escape. When they meet after her marriage, her first words to him are "'I

scarcely dare say," she answered in broken tones. "But I have nerved myself to this, and I will speak. Oh! Alwyn, it grieves me that I should wound and distract you by letting you know my misery. I would not have done so, had I perceived any other course possible.'" In all other versions, her first words are 'You are going to emigrate', giving us the immediate impression that her wish to see him has been caused not by her misery but by the thought that she is losing a lover. A little later, she again stresses her suffering, uniquely talking of 'the unutterable extremity of sending for you. Listen, Alwyn. Yet I can hardly say what – what I want to say. But if you only knew what I have suffered before coming to this, you would understand me.' This sounds equally like a plea from Hardy to his devout American readers, and at least she has the good grace to recognize the enormity of her proposal to run away. Indeed, the future which she conceives for them is very respectable: 'I wish you merely to watch over me – to give me a little assistance and protection after my escape – no more'. She then invokes divine sanction for her plan: 'it might be honestly done. God knows it might, seeing how wretched I am.'

The curate's rejection of her plea is markedly more decisive and pious in the *Independent*. He tells her 'in a dry, firm voice' that she must not go with him because it would be 'a terrible sin', and his scrupulous rectitude is even more prominent than in other versions: 'Honor and virtue above all things', he declares, and he informs her that 'your good name, your purity' are more precious than her life or her happiness. He begins his final address to her by acknowledging her 'suffering' heart yet again as an extenuation of her proposal, but says that it would be contrary to God's law, 'which it is my life's duty to uphold'. Perhaps Hardy hoped that his model curate would provide a moral authority to his tale which would conquer any scruples at the *Independent* about Emmeline's impropriety.

Religion has a prominence in this version of the story which may have been especially geared to the *Independent*'s readership. For instance, our attitude to Hill and to Emmeline's father, Mr Oldbourne, may be shaped by their respective qualities as preachers: when Hill delivered a sermon, 'the people were less interested in the subject of his discourse than in his manner of delivering it', whereas Oldbourne's sermons were 'mathematically divided into the time-honored first, secondly, and thirdly; and it is said that, during the life of his wife, this angularity of character in him led to no small amount of unhappiness in her'. The religious failings of most of the Saxelbyes are stressed: they had knelt in their church for generations, 'with and without hypocrisy', and in the *Independent* Hardy specifies that it is the 'other Saxelbye dames' who in their time have counted their rings, fallen asleep or laughed at the congregation. The devout reader is being asked to sympathize with Emmeline, married against her will into this ungodly family.

Sir Byng is a much more prominent, and much more unpleasant, character in the *Independent* than he is elsewhere. We learn, for instance, how his family acquired his baronetcy:

> it is said that the title was originally won by his ancestor rendering timely
> assistance in a court intrigue during the reign of the first George. Religion

and social morality were, as is well known, at a pretty low ebb at that date; and it is therefore quite probable that the services of the first baronet reflected less credit upon him as a worthy gentleman than as an adroit time-server.

This information in the opening paragraph, never repeated in any other version of the story, immediately introduces the theme of religion and the unprincipled nature of the Saxelbye family. It also establishes an ironic parallel between the time-serving Saxelbye, who is rewarded for his worldliness, and the religious Hill, who waits patiently so many years for Emmeline, only to learn that she has been dead all along. The unrighteous thrive in this version. Sir Byng himself is a coarse boor: 'his highest intellectual aim was to preside at agricultural dinners of the jovial kind, where the speeches turned on the wildest country sports, practical jokes, feats in steeplechasing, and the latest coursing events', and we learn why he defends the 'ancient amusements' of cock-fighting and bull-baiting: '"Beasts suffer that men may dine," he would say. "Why shouldn't they suffer that men may laugh and sport and disperse dull care?"' This more brutal portrayal of Sir Byng mitigates Emmeline's flight and perhaps motivates it better than in the other versions. In the *Independent*, Emmeline's charms had 'unfortunately' been noticed by Sir Byng; in other versions, this 'unfortunately' is transferred to describe the relationship which had arisen between Emmeline and Hill. The other versions, that is, take a more worldly and conventional stance, judging her love for Hill to be regrettable, while the *Independent* sees the attraction of the rich but reprobate baronet to be worse than the love of a respectable curate.

Alwyn Hill is presented in contrast to the baronet as a principled man. In the conversation between the bell-ringers, one of them defends Emmeline and Hill thus:

> 'I don't believe she knows where he is gone to any more than we. Mr. Hill was not a man to force his memory upon her in any underhand way, when he decided to leave her, that she might not be hated by her father. He's a quiet, modest young fellow; but mind you that underneath that there's a good deal of strict, fair and square dealing even with people that don't deal so with him.'
>
> 'Well, she's the one that will suffer most, if suffering there be in the business. Think of him she will at first, but 'tis to be hoped she won't do so long. For what's the odds, after all? Anything, says I, for a quiet life.'

Hill's ability to stand up for himself was presented earlier in the *Independent*, which uniquely gives details of his quarrel with Emmeline's father:

> Mr. Oldbourne accused the young fellow of attempting to undermine his daughter's happiness treacherously and by stealth, instead of asking his approval at the first; and Alwyn Hill replied in words too hasty for prudence, and too cutting to be forgiven. The gentle Emmeline could do nothing between them; and Alwyn Hill went away, his indignation against her father almost supplanting, for the moment, his tenderness toward herself.

In the second part of the story as it appeared in the *Independent*, there are only two notable unique features. The first is that we learn a further reason why Hill felt unable to continue in America as a minister of religion: he was 'still guided by that vigorous conscientiousness which some would have called puritanical self-abasement'. This is a sentiment which seems specifically designed to appeal to the New England Congregationalists who would be reading the story in the *Independent*. The other variant concerns the final paragraph; in the *Independent*, Hill does not confide his story to anyone before he emigrates again, presumably back to America.

1891 Osgood, McIlvaine

In preparing the collected edition of 'The Duchess of Hamptonshire' in 1891, Hardy collated the two serial versions of 1878 and 1884. The first part of the story, up to Hill leaving Emmeline in the shrubbery, is based on the first section of the 1878 version, and the second part closely follows the expanded version of the 1884 *Independent*. However, Hardy in each part includes variant readings from the other version not being copied at that point. Perhaps Hardy wished to restore the original version of the first part of the story because he regarded the *Independent* version as having been voluntarily bowdlerized for a specific audience.

In *1891*, Sir Byng is elevated to the status of a Duke for the first time, and Emmeline's father becomes the Honourable Mr Oldbourne, in keeping with the rank of the other characters in the volume. Following his marriage to Emmeline, the Duke is described as the 'august' husband, rather than merely as the 'new' one, stressing again the increased social gap between him and Hill. In the second paragraph, Hardy deleted a striking simile describing the castle which had appeared in both previous versions: 'from the high road it appeared set against the tangled boughs of the trees and over the dark lawns like a camellia in a raven head of hair'. In 1891, the housemaids who stalk the corridors of the castle at the fire-lighting hour are called 'ghostly' for the first time.

The opening four sentences of the second paragraph, describing the Duke's personal appearance, derive from the *Independent*, as does the account in the following paragraph which explains how Oldbourne's 'white neckcloth, well-kept gray hair, and right-lined face betokened none of those sympathetic traits whereon depends so much of a parson's power to do good among his fellow-creatures'. Hardy continues the critical presentation of the curate by retaining the *Independent*'s statement that 'his procedure was cold, hard, and inexorable' in separating Hill and Emmeline.

In the second part of the story, a key sentence describes Hill's decision to become a teacher:

> Distracted and weakened in his beliefs by his recent experiences, he decided
> that he could not for a time worthily fill the office of a minister of religion,
> and applied for the mastership of a school.

While the second part of the story largely follows the *Independent*, this sentence derives from the 1878 version, with the exception that 'could not for a time' is the *Independent* reading (*1878* had said that he could 'no longer' be a curate). This small revision shows the detailed collation of the two earlier versions which Hardy undertook when he came to prepare the 1891 collected edition. The only other feature of the second part which derives from *1878* and not *1884* is the description of Hill confiding his story to an old friend before he left the town. In 1891, Hardy adds that the identity of the dead woman was never publicly disclosed and that the friend in whom Hill confided was 'grandfather of the person who now relates it to you'. Previously, the story had not had a narrator, but in *A Group of Noble Dames* the story is related by the Quiet Gentleman, and Hardy also adds the final two paragraphs describing his audience's response.

In *A Group of Noble Dames*, 'The Duchess of Hamptonshire' is placed as the penultimate story, possibly because, like the final one ('The Honourable Laura'), it had first been published a decade before the other stories in the volume.

1891 Harper

The American edition has some forty differences in accidentals from the Osgood, McIlvaine edition of 1891, ignoring variations in US spelling, and there are three substantive variants which would appear to be editorial or compositorial. For instance, the 'gentler sex' becomes the 'gentle sex', and news of Emmeline's illness on board the ship causes alarm among 'the passengers', instead of 'all the passengers' in the British edition. There is no indication that Hardy read proofs for the Harper edition.

1912 Macmillan Wessex edition

The only substantive variation between the Wessex edition and the 1891 Osgood, McIlvaine occurs in the following sentence, which reads thus in *1891*: 'Who shall wonder that his mind luxuriated in dreams of a sweet possibility now laid open for the first time these many years? for Emmeline was to him now as ever the one dear thing in all the world.' In the Wessex edition, Hardy changes the first 'now' to 'just' (p. 200), no doubt to avoid repetition.[3]

Notes

1 *Letters*, I, 138, 141, 220, and II, 205.
2 F.B. Pinion notes that '"Batton Castle" appeared on Wessex maps before 1912 (and it is still shown on the smaller map) at a point which suggests Tottenham House, south-east of Marlborough. The fictional name resembles that of the historic neighbouring borough of Bedwyn' (New Wessex edition, p. 379). Denys Kay-Robinson, however,

suggests that '"Batton" is very like a Hardy substitution for Badminton, and Badminton is very near Castle Combe' (p. 256). See also *Letters*, IV, 175.

3 There are seven differences in punctuation and styling between the two editions: in the following list, the Wessex edition reading is given first and the pagination is that of *1912*: 'ago/ago,' (p. 191); 'incontestably/incontestibly' (p. 191); 'parish church/parish-church' (p. 191); 'O/Oh' (p. 197, twice); 'further end/farther end' (p. 202; 1912 however reads 'farther' later on the same page); 'majority,/majority' (p. 206).

CHAPTER 17

'The Honourable Laura'

'The Honourable Laura' was first collected as the final story of *A Group of Noble Dames*, published by Osgood, McIlvaine in May 1891. It had twice been published previously in serial form ten years earlier, under the title 'Benighted Travellers', making it one of Hardy's earliest stories, and even after it had been collected it was again published serially in 1903 under its original title.

The versions of the story which have textual significance are as follows:

HW   'Benighted Travellers', *Harper's Weekly*, 10 December 1881, pp. 826–7, and 17 December 1881, pp. 858–9. The division occurred at the end of the first of the story's five numbered chapters, which correspond to the breaks in the collected editions.

BWJ   'Benighted Travellers', *Bolton Weekly Journal* (*Christmas Leaves* supplement), 17 December 1881, p. 1. Five numbered chapters, as *HW*.

1891   'The Honourable Laura', *A Group of Noble Dames* (London: Osgood, McIlvaine, 1891), pp. 237–71. This was the first collected edition of the story in the expanded *A Group of Noble Dames* which now included ten stories, of which 'The Honourable Laura' was 'Dame the Tenth'. Published at 6s. in an edition of 2000 copies on 30 May 1891. It was the first volume of Hardy's work which Osgood, McIlvaine had published.

1891H   'The Honourable Laura', *A Group of Noble Dames* (New York: Harper & Brothers, 1891), pp. 256–92. Published early in June 1891.

1896   'The Honourable Laura', *A Group of Noble Dames* (London: Osgood, McIlvaine, 1896), pp. 237–71. Volume XV in the Wessex Novels, the first uniform and complete edition of Hardy's works. Plates of the original edition were used, and 'The Honourable Laura' is identical in every respect to *1891*, except in two instances: plate-batter has caused a comma to be lost at the end of a line on p. 257, and *1896* corrects *1891*'s mis-spelt 'icthyosaurus' in the story's final sentence, an error which Hardy had noticed in June 1891 (see *Letters*, I, 238–9).

Sphere   'Benighted Travellers', *Sphere*, 2 May 1903, pp. 111–12, 114, and 9 May 1903, pp. 133–4, 136, with two illustrations by Bernard Partridge. The division occurred at

the end of the second chapter. Five numbered chapters, as
HW.

1912   'The Honourable Laura', *A Group of Noble Dames*
(London: Macmillan, 1912), pp. 209–36. Volume XIV of
the Wessex edition.

The manuscript is not known to have survived.

Serials

The intention of this section is to trace the evolution of the story through its three
serial versions and to describe their relation to the 1891 edition of *A Group of
Noble Dames*. Throughout this part, I shall refer to the story by its serial title,
'Benighted Travellers', not only because I am discussing the periodical versions
but because, in the serials, the Honourable Laura is not Honourable and she is
not even called Laura, but Lucetta.

The chronology of serial publication is highly misleading, since the text's
chain of transmission is the exact reverse of the sequence in which the versions
were published. As I hope to demonstrate later, the last version to appear, in the
Sphere, is in fact the earliest of the three versions to have been written, while
Bolton Weekly Journal is intermediate and *Harper's Weekly* is closest to *1891*.

While each of the three serial versions has minor substantive variant readings
which distinguish it from the others, they nevertheless as a group share common
features which are lacking or were altered in later editions of the story as it was
published in *A Group of Noble Dames*. For instance, the names of characters are
different; in the serials Laura was called Lucetta (Hardy perhaps changed it
because he had meanwhile used the name prominently in *The Mayor of
Casterbridge*), and her lover was Smittozzi, not Smithozzi (as he was to be
called in *1891*).[1] Lord Quantock is a mere squire in the serial, his elevation to the
peerage not occurring until the story was collected and made consistent with
most of the other aristocratic tales of *A Group of Noble Dames*. For the same
reason, Lucetta is plain Mrs Northbrook at the end of the story.

The location of the story in the serials is different. In *1891*, the Prospect Hotel
is located near the 'wild north coast of Lower Wessex' (p. 239), but in the serials
it is 'on the verge of one of the most picturesque glens in Great Britain'. There
are no references to cliffs, creeks or headlands in the serials, where the primary
attraction of the site is a ruined castle. Clearly, the scene is inland and its
location unidentified. The topography and placenames of Wessex are also
altered in later collected versions. In the serials, Lucetta and James are married
at St Mary's, Portpool, rather than Toneborough (Taunton), as it later became.
Portpool is probably an early fictional name for Bridport, which has a St Mary's
church and is called Port-Bredy in later Wessex works. In *1891*, Laura and
Smithozzi set off after the attempted murder to Cliff-Martin (Coombe Martin),
which is six miles away, and Smithozzi departs from there by coach after Laura
has escaped from him. In the serials, Lucetta and Smittozzi head for Portpool,
seven miles away, and Smittozzi possibly leaves from there by steamer. In *1891*,

he manages to get out of the county, but in the serials he gets out of the *country*.

The main substantive differences between the serials and the later publications concern the site of the intended duel between Smittozzi and Northbrook and the former's attempt to murder his rival. There are no cliffs in the serials, so Northbrook is pushed from a wooden bridge as he is crossing a cataract. A few other minor variants are worthy of note. The 'Ha! ha!' of the two men making grim comedy on the verge of going out to their duel is not in any of the serials, and the same is true of Laura's avowal to her husband that she is 'innocent of the worst' (p. 261) in eloping with Smittozzi, by which she presumably means infidelity, a typical example of what is probably Hardy's self-censorship when producing serial fiction.

Hardy sold the story in 1881 to Tillotson's Newspaper Fiction Bureau, which 'ran a very active syndicated fiction business at this period, purchasing serial rights from authors and then selling the stories to magazines and, especially, provincial newspapers both at home and abroad'.[2] Tillotson & Son had their office in Bolton, Lancashire, and they owned several local newspapers, the chief of which was the *Bolton Weekly Journal*, hence the appearance of Hardy's story there. Through their agency, the story was to be widely reprinted in later years, particularly in provincial newspapers. 'Benighted Travellers' was the first of four short stories and a novel which Hardy was to sell to them over the next eleven years.[3]

Hardy had written to Tillotson & Son on 29 July 1881 to say that 'I should be very happy to write you a short Christmas story for your supplement. My price would be six guineas per 1,000 words for the newspaper right to the same in the United Kingdom only – or eight guineas if American and Australian newspapers are also included.'[4] After some apparent negotiations over the price, Hardy wrote again on 10 August 1881 and accepted Tillotson's terms but with what is, for the purpose of this study, an important condition: 'I will write a Christmas story of between 4,000 and 8,000 words at the price of seven pounds per 2,000, provided you send me proofs of the same early enough for publishing simultaneously in America.'[5] These were the proofs which were ultimately to be used to set up the story in *Bolton Weekly Journal* and *Harper's Weekly* in New York, and they will be discussed in detail later in this chapter.

Both the *Bolton Weekly Journal* and the *Harper's Weekly* versions of the story show signs of some revision at proof stage and thus they constitute later versions of the story than the one which Hardy initially sold to Tillotson & Son. The version of 'Benighted Travellers' which approximates most closely to this earliest Tillotson version is in fact the one published in the *Sphere* in 1903, which is known to be unrevised and which therefore represents most nearly the version first purchased by them. It was unrevised by Hardy because he wanted nothing to do with the *Sphere* publication, but they proceeded to publish it despite his wishes, obtaining the serial rights from Tillotson's (each instalment of the *Sphere*'s serialization ends with '*Copyright in the U.S.A. by Tillotson & Son*').

Early in 1903, Clement Shorter, the editor of the *Sphere*, must have written to Hardy to inform him of his plan to reprint 'Benighted Travellers', for Hardy replied on 22 January that 'I put a clause in nowadays to prevent the sale of my old stories in that way'.[6] Hardy would not condone the *Sphere*'s publication because, as he rightly foresaw, readers would assume that it was a recent piece of writing, instead of one which was now more than twenty years old, and a week after the serial ended he was obliged to write the following letter to the *Athenaeum* to disown the *Sphere*'s publication:

> As I receive inquiries concerning my 'new story' in the *Sphere* for May 2nd and 9th, will you allow me space to say that, so far from being new, it is a resuscitated old story which appeared in a country journal nearly twenty years ago, and that I am in no way responsible for its publication as if new?
>
> I make this an opportunity of reminding inexperienced writers of fiction that, in disposing of 'serial rights' in their productions, they should take care to limit the time during which such rights may be exercised.[7]

Three days after the *Athenaeum* letter, Hardy wrote again to Shorter: 'I judged that my telling you that I had reprinted the story in one of my volumes (A Group of Noble Dames) would be sufficient to stop you. I improved it a little in reprinting so that I did not particularly wish to have the 1st version revived. But my "annoyance", if any, was with the syndicate people for taking what seems to me to be an unfair advantage of the words "serial right" that most authors use without realizing that they may be acted on 20 years after.'[8]

The *Sphere* version contains two errors, one of which is repeated in *BWJ* and the other is repeated in *HW*. The first error in the *Sphere* is that, on the first appearance in the story of the father Charles and the husband James, Hardy transposes their names before reverting to what he calls them elsewhere. *BWJ* corrects this but the error still stands in *HW*. The second mistake in the *Sphere* is Hardy's misquotation of Shakespeare. In the *Sphere*, we learn that husband James may be recalling the familiar words of Brabantio in *Othello* with reference to Othello's wife: 'She hath deceived her father, and will thee.' This is corrected in *HW* to 'She has deceived her father, and may thee.' The error remains in *BWJ*. The importance of these two slips for our understanding of the chain of transmission will be considered shortly.

BWJ differs substantively from the *Sphere* on fifteen separate occasions, including one misprint of 'he' for 'she' which appears for the first and last time. All of these variants are a matter of a word or two at most. *HW* in turn retains twelve of *BWJ*'s fifteen revisions and variant readings: it corrects the he/she misprint but fails to notice *BWJ*'s correction of the names which had been transposed in the *Sphere* when Charles and James first arrived.

In addition to the twelve revisions mentioned above, *HW* makes a *further* fourteen alterations to *BWJ*, so that it is even further removed from the *Sphere*. One of these new variants is probably a compositorial error at Harper's New York office, since it is unique to *HW*. The error occurs in the following sentence: 'Not a track or rut broke the virgin surface of the white mantle that lay all along it, all marks left by the lately arrived travellers having been speedily obliterated [...].' The first 'all' appears in no other version of the story and was probably prompted by a compositor skipping ahead to the same word shortly afterwards.

This error, then, is not passed on to *1891*, nor is the mistake in *HW* about Charles/James. There are two further occasions when Hardy revised the wording yet again when preparing *1891*, but otherwise all of *HW*'s variant readings are retained in *1891*.

What version of the text did Hardy use when establishing *1891*? It cannot have been a published copy of *HW*, since it would then be likely that the 'lay all along' reading would have been transmitted, as might the mistake about Charles/James. The following hypothesis is offered as one way of explaining the known facts of the serial differences and takes into account aspects of Hardy's working practices which have been observed in his revision of other texts.

The syndicate copy purchased by Tillotson's was used by them to make a first set of proofs for *BWJ*. Hardy revised these proofs to create the version of the story that subsequently appeared there. At this revision stage, he noticed the transposition of forenames, and corrected them, so that this error does not appear in *BWJ*. However, he did not detect the he/she misprint or the misquotation of Shakespeare.

Hardy, it may be posited, had two duplicates of these *BWJ* proofs, one of which was to be sent to *HW*, and the other retained for his own record. On to this pair of duplicate proofs, he tried to copy, firstly, the changes he had made for the *BWJ* version of the story. Hardy, though, as we know from the evidence of other works such as *Two on a Tower* and elsewhere in *A Group of Noble Dames*, had great difficulty in revising identically two copies of a text.[9] As a result, he wrote the revision of the transposition of names on to his own copy but not on the one to be sent to *HW*.

In preparing the proofs for *HW*, Hardy made about a dozen *further* revisions, in addition to those he had already copied on to them from the *BWJ* proofs, and he marked these new alterations on to his own duplicate copy. At this stage he spotted the Shakespeare error, corrected it and noted it also in the copy which he retained. Why not alter it in the *BWJ* proofs, or add all the other new revisions? Perhaps he had already sent them off to Tillotson. The same would apply to the he/she error which he detected at this stage.

The 'lay all' was perhaps a compositorial error at Harper's and therefore never occurred in any other version. Certainly there is no evidence that Hardy received proofs for *HW*. It would not have been in his retained copy of proofs and so would not be transmitted.

The duplicate proofs which Hardy retained are, by this account, the basis for *1891*. On to these proofs he had recorded the transposition of names when preparing the *BWJ* version, and later he added the he/she correction and the revision of the Shakespeare quotation, so that all three of these appear correctly in *1891*.

A comparison of variants in accidentals in the serial versions supports this view of the priority of *Harper's Weekly* in the chain of transmission. It would appear that Hardy made many alterations to accidentals when preparing proofs of *HW* and that he marked these in his own retained copy. One obviously has to be very cautious in discussing the significance of accidentals, but it can be noted that, where *1891* is faced with a choice between the reading of *HW* and that of

BWJ, 1891 is four times as likely to follow the *HW* reading (there are just under 250 instances where such a difference between the two occurs).

1891 Osgood, McIlvaine

The principal changes made to the story for its first collected edition have been described above in the discussion of the serials' distinctive features.

Hardy ennobled Laura and her father in *1891* to make the story consistent with most of the other tales of Noble Dames, and the new title, 'The Honourable Laura', is, like 'The First Countess of Wessex', one of the few in the volume which is not to some degree ironic: as Kristin Brady comments, Laura is 'distinguished not only by a formal designation of her social status but also by the virtue she finally acquired'.[10]

In the serials, the squire describes Captain Northbrook as 'the only male relative I have left'. When the squire is converted into Lord Quantock in *1891*, however, he says that Northbrook is merely 'the only male relative I have near me' (p. 248). If Hardy had not made this alteration, then Northbrook would have inherited the title, and Laura's loyalty and patience in waiting for him to return might have made her seem merely worldly and mercenary, another Noble Dame sacrificing her life to be the wife of a Lord. As it stands, however, her selfless and sincere repentance is rewarded and 'The Honourable Laura' closes on a truly happy note, this final story in the volume being the only one to do so apart from the opening tale, 'The First Countess of Wessex'. Such blissful symmetry to *A Group of Noble Dames* is ironic in that it belies the eight tales of envy, greed, misery and malice which intervene between the first and final stories.

1891 Harper

There are seven substantive differences between the American and British editions of 1891, and all of them are individual words (such as 'that', 'had', 'up' and 'as') which could be accounted for by editorial revision at Harper's office.

Excluding US spelling, there are one hundred differences in accidentals, half of which are caused by Harper's greater use of commas.

1912 Macmillan Wessex edition

The principal change for the Wessex edition is that Hardy reverts to the serial name, Signor Smittozzi, for the baritone with whom Laura elopes; he had been called Smithozzi in the editions of 1891. Also at this stage Hardy gives new information about him which establishes that he is clearly a fraud: he is ironically described as being a distinguished 'Italian' (previous versions of the story had said that he was merely an 'alien') who had come into the world 'as the baby of Mr. and Mrs. Smith' (p. 215). His surname is now shown to be a bogus affectation.

Hardy altered the description of the waterfall over which Smittozzi pushes Captain Northbrook; in *1891* it had been 'little' but now it is said to be 'lofty' (p. 222), which is more consistent with the earlier information that it was eighty or a hundred feet high. Finally, a reference to the squire as 'the old man' is changed to 'the uncle' (p. 214), which seems less disrespectful now that he has risen to become Lord Quantock.

Notes

1 The 1912 Macmillan Wessex edition reverts to the serial name for this character.

2 *Letters,* I, 93n. See also Purdy, pp. 340–41.

3 As Purdy notes, the others were 'A Mere Interlude' (1885), 'Alicia's Diary' (1887), 'The Melancholy Hussar' (1890) and *The Pursuit of the Well-Beloved* (1892). Tillotson's contract with Hardy for *Tess of the d'Urbervilles* was subsequently cancelled; see Purdy, pp. 71–3.

4 *Letters*, I, 93.

5 *Letters*, I, 93. Publication in *Harper's Weekly* was arranged through J.B. Lippincott Co., a Philadelphia publishing firm: see *Letters*, I, 97.

6 *Letters*, III, 48; see also III, 60–61.

7 'Serial Rights in Stories', *Athenaeum*, 16 May 1903, p. 626.

8 *Letters*, III, 60.

9 See Gatrell, p. 94.

10 For the sake of a complete record, the other revisions to *1891* for the Wessex edition are as follows (*1912* is quoted first, and the pagination is that of *1912*): 'lingered/lingered on' (p. 209); 'conjectures/conjectures,' (p. 212); 'once more to withdraw/to once more withdraw' (p. 212); 'was disclosed, [...] hotel,/[...] hotel, was disclosed' (p. 215); 'entered/entered,' (p. 215); 'opened/opened,' (p. 215); 'affair./affair!' (p. 219); 'O/Oh' (p. 220; three more examples of this change on pp. 221, 225 and 228); 'further and further/farther and farther' (p. 222); 'way/way,' (p. 224); 'moments,/moments' (p. 224); 'further/farther' (p. 224); 'so in/so, in' (p. 226); 'learnt/learned' (p. 227); 'recovery/recovery,' (p. 227); 'trouble/trouble,' (p. 230); 'further/farther' (p. 232); 'sight/sight,' (p. 232).

PART THREE

Life's Little Ironies

Life's Little Ironies

Hardy's first reference to *Life's Little Ironies* is in a letter to Florence Henniker, when he told her in October 1893 that he had been 'hunting up the tales I told you of ("Two Ambitions" being one of them). They are now fastened together to be dispatched to the publisher' (*Letters*, II, 38). In assembling the stories for the single volume, Hardy made substantial revision to the serial version of all the stories. Copy was sent to the publisher, Osgood, McIlvaine, in October 1893. A couple of days before Christmas of that year, he jocularly complained to Lena Milman about his work on the volume: 'My proofs wander away to Scotland out of pure festivity, it seems, before they come to me from London' (II, 45; the pages were being printed by the Edinburgh firm of R. & R. Clark). This set of marked galley proofs is now located in the Dorset County Museum and they are dated December 1893. Alan Manford has succinctly summarized the importance of the proofs in the development of the text:

> The proofs contain numerous instances of revision to both substantives and styling in all the stories: of the 301 Osgood, McIlvaine printed pages 76 per cent contain a revision of some kind, 27 per cent have revisions to both substantives and styling, 22 per cent have revisions to substantives alone, and 26 per cent to styling alone. Furthermore (excluding the two stories later transferred to *Wessex Tales*) there are some 15 instances spread across six stories where the first edition text does not reproduce exactly what is marked in the galley proofs: several of these are probably later authorial revisions, made with others at the page-proof stage. (1996, p. xxxii)

Hardy expected *Life's Little Ironies* to be published at the end of January 1894, 'as soon as the Harper's can get the American edition ready' (II, 44), and as late as 15 January he was telling Florence Henniker that the book would appear 'at the end of the month' (II, 48). However, as Purdy notes, the publication date was first announced as being 16 February 1894: the British Library copy bears this accession date, and the book is listed among the publications of the week in the *Spectator* and the *Athenaeum*, 17 February. Even then, *Life's Little Ironies* did not finally appear until 22 February: 'in view of the exceptionally large demand, the first edition being sold out a week in advance, publication was postponed until a second edition could be prepared. The book profited by the great success of *Tess*, then in its twenty-third thousand, and there were 5 large editions (more properly, impressions) before the end of May' (Purdy, p. 85). This first edition of *Life's Little Ironies* was published by Osgood, McIlvaine at 6*s.* in an edition of 2000 copies.

An American edition of the book was published by Harper & Brothers in March 1894, on which Hardy received a 15 per cent royalty on the retail price of all copies sold (see *Letters*, II, 47).[1] The text was reset, and a letter from Harper & Brothers to Osgood, McIlvaine dated 28 December 1893 indicates that it was probably prepared from proofs of the English first edition: 'We have received a few slips of this collection of Mr. Hardy's short stories and are preparing to formally publish the volume at the close of next month. [...] We have no doubt that Mr. Hardy wishes us to publish the volume, as the proofs are marked by him with our name' (quoted in Manford, 1996, p. xxxiii). Since the proofs for the British edition underwent a further revision, any second galley revisions are missing from the American edition.

This first edition contained the following nine stories: 'The Son's Veto', 'For Conscience' Sake', 'A Tragedy of Two Ambitions', 'On the Western Circuit', 'To Please his Wife', 'The Melancholy Hussar of the German Legion', 'The Fiddler of the Reels', 'A Tradition of Eighteen Hundred and Four' and 'A Few Crusted Characters'. For the 1912 Wessex edition, as will be discussed later, 'An Imaginative Woman' was added to the volume and two stories, 'A Tradition of Eighteen Hundred and Four' and 'The Melancholy Hussar of the German Legion', were transferred to *Wessex Tales*. Most of the stories which appeared in the first collected edition date from the latter half of 1890 and the early months of 1891, after the work on *Tess* and *A Group of Noble Dames* was mostly completed. 'The Fiddler of the Reels', however, was not composed until 1892, and 'A Tradition of Eighteen Hundred and Four' dates back to the summer of 1882, when Hardy was finishing *Two on a Tower*, so the whole collection covers a period of approximately a decade. As Norman Page has noted, this volume of stories explores an alternative fictional world to that of the Wessex novels (1996, p. xii). In the stories, the foreground is populated by outsiders who are usually urban professionals, replacing the world of rural occupations and traditional crafts: 'the social order represented by church, manor-house, farm, cottage, and village inn gives way to the seaside lodgings, the railway hotel, the suburban villa' (Page, 1996, p. xiii). Since the majority of the stories are modern and urban, Hardy came to feel that two of them did not fit very easily with the others and, as we shall see later, he transferred them to a different volume when he came to prepare the Wessex edition of *Life's Little Ironies*.

On the day after the first English edition appeared, Hardy wrote to John Lane, who was about to publish Lionel Johnson's *The Art of Thomas Hardy*, and asked him not to reveal for the moment the original serial publications of the stories in the volume:

> such information so soon after the publication of the book is likely to injure the sale. The lending libraries are on the alert to trace stories in such cases, & pacify subscribers by handing over the periodical in which a tale in demand – or portion of it – has been issued, as I know from personal experience. If therefore you will say [...] that some of them have appeared in periodicals, but in a modified & Bowdlerized form, & no more for the present, I shall be glad. Six months hence I will help you to trace them all, with pleasure. (*Letters*, II, 51)

In a letter to Emma on 3 March 1894, Hardy quoted a favourable press comment about the volume:

> The Speaker to-day quotes one of the candid sentences from "Life's Little
> I." & adds – (*apropos* of women's novels, like *Keynotes*, &c) "so that the
> old hands know a thing or two as well as the young 'uns." (*Letters*, II, 52)

That morning, the *Speaker* had quoted part of a sentence from 'On the Western
Circuit' in a review article entitled 'French Literature': 'This "crowning, though
unrecognized, fascination" of which Mr. Hardy speaks – the fascination of a
triumphant seducer for the she-animal.' Another comment in the press by
William Archer, however, caused Hardy much concern: Archer had protested in
a letter to the *Daily Chronicle*, published on 4 May 1894, about the boycotting
of George Moore's *Esther Waters* by W.H. Smith & Son, noting that those who
believed that 'morality consists in the discouragement of sexual impulse, or even
of its unlicensed manifestations [...] should clamour for "Esther Waters," and
demand the suppression of "Life's Little Ironies"'. Archer also remarked that
Hardy had 'introduced into English fiction a note of sensuality from which
"Esther Waters," at any rate, is entirely free'. Hardy came to the defence of the
volume by asking Edward Clodd and Lady Jeune to write to the *Daily Chronicle*,
and their letters appeared on 5 May and 8 May respectively, Lady Jeune
commenting that she could not recall one story in the book 'that can offend the
most sensitive morality' (see *Letters*, II, 56). On 9 May, Hardy wrote to Archer
and told him that 'I have not the least feeling in the matter of your criticism in
the D.C., for though I thought "sensuousness" or "passionateness" or something
of the sort would have been free from the stigma which has come to be attached
to "sensuality" I knew that you were perfectly conscientious in your remarks, as I
thoroughly believe you to be in all your expressed opinions, however much I
may disagree with them' (II, 57). Hardy's comment in a letter to Clement Shorter
on 31 May that 'I did not send the notes, as on second thoughts it seemed better
to let the subject drop' (II, 59), is probably another reference to the Archer
controversy.

Life's Little Ironies was reprinted from the 1894 plates as volume XIV in
Osgood, McIlvaine's edition of the Wessex Novels in 1896, and Hardy added a
Preface, dated June 1896, which contained some observations on the source of
'The Melancholy Hussar' and the model for Parson Toogood in the tale of
'Andrey Satchel'. This Preface was not reprinted in the Wessex edition in 1912
but it is now readily available in Manford's edition of the stories (1996, p. 219).
A frontispiece by Henry Macbeth-Raeburn was also added in 1896, entitled 'A
View in "Melchester"'. The Macmillan Uniform *Life's Little Ironies* was printed
from the 1896 Osgood, McIlvaine plates, which Macmillan purchased from
Osgood, McIlvaine's successors, Harper & Brothers (London). It was first
published in 1903 (but without the 1896 Preface) and was reprinted four times
between 1909 and 1928. The same plates were used for the Macmillan Pocket
edition of *Life's Little Ironies* in 1907: this was a thin-paper edition, priced at
2/6, which was reprinted ten times between 1910 and 1928.

A European edition of *Life's Little Ironies* was published by Bernhard
Tauchnitz of Leipzig in 1894, and Manford notes that it was a resetting based on
the Osgood, McIlvaine text (1996, p. xxxiii). Similarly, the Macmillan Colonial
Library edition of 1895 was printed from the Osgood, McIlvaine plates.

In preparing the Macmillan Wessex edition of 1912, Hardy made an important change to the volume's contents: he removed 'A Tradition of Eighteen Hundred and Four' and 'The Melancholy Hussar of the German Legion' to *Wessex Tales*, where, as he says in the Prefatory Note, 'they more naturally belong'. At the same time, he transferred 'An Imaginative Woman', which had previously been published in the 1896 Osgood, McIlvaine edition of *Wessex Tales*, to *Life's Little Ironies*, which is 'more nearly its place, turning as it does upon a trick of Nature, so to speak'. (The Macmillan Archives show that the publishers were negotiating these changes with the printers throughout May 1912.) The result of these alterations was to make the stories in *Life's Little Ironies* more consistently contemporary and those in *Wessex Tales* more traditional. Hardy chose to place 'An Imaginative Woman' at the beginning of the volume, and this might indicate the special emotional importance which the story had for him and which is discussed in the chapter on it below. For the Wessex edition, Hardy added a new Prefatory Note dated May 1912 which explains his reasons for altering the contents of the volume. The printers' copy for the Wessex edition was probably a composite of dismembered copies of Macmillan Uniform editions of *Life's Little Ironies* and *Wessex Tales* (for 'An Imaginative Woman'), into which Hardy had written revisions. There was a frontispiece entitled 'The White Hart at Casterbridge'.

A limited signed edition of Hardy's works, the Autograph edition, was published in America by Harper's in 1915. Hardy read proof for the five volumes in the Autograph edition which were copyrighted in the United States and so had to be reset, and these included *Life's Little Ironies* and *A Changed Man*. Manford observes that the former contains all the Wessex edition revisions, and that any variants appear to be compositorial (1996, p. xxxiv). The Autograph edition was reissued in 1920 as the Anniversary edition, whose four illustrations may have originated with Hardy. *Life's Little Ironies* was published as volume XIV of the Macmillan Mellstock edition of 1920, but Manford records that Hardy did not make any revisions to it and he did not read proofs (1996, p. xxxiv).

Notes

1   Harper & Brothers Contract Book 6 contains the firm's letter to Osgood, McIlvaine of 28 December 1893, explaining that the first proofs of the volume had arrived without prior correspondence with Hardy but that they would be pleased to publish it and pay a 15 per cent royalty. Hardy wrote to McIlvaine to confirm this arrangement on 9 January 1894.

CHAPTER 18

'An Imaginative Woman'

The manuscript of 'An Imaginative Woman' was presented by Hardy to Aberdeen University Library in 1911 when he was distributing his MSS. among various public collections. Aberdeen University had conferred on him the honorary degree of LLD in April 1905, his first academic distinction. This chapter will study the changes in the manuscript which indicate the evolution of the story, the subsequent three publications of it which have textual significance, and in addition it will offer some observations on the important contribution which Hardy's friendship with Florence Henniker made to the writing of the work, as revealed by the MS. This story had a special place in Hardy's affections, perhaps because of its association with her, and during a conversation at Max Gate in August 1909 with Walter Peirce, an American enthusiast, Hardy remarked that 'of his stories, his favorite was *An Imaginative Woman*, "the best piece of prose fiction I ever wrote"' (Peirce, p. 194).

The three published versions of 'An Imaginative Woman' which have textual significance are as follows:

PMM   *Pall Mall Magazine*, II (April 1894), 951–69. Seven illustrations by Arthur Jule Goodman.

1896   *Wessex Tales* (London: Osgood, McIlvaine, 1896), pp. 1–32. Volume XIII in the Wessex Novels, the first uniform and complete edition of Hardy's works.

1912   *Life's Little Ironies* (London: Macmillan, 1912), pp. 1–31. Volume VIII of the Wessex edition.

The MS. of 'An Imaginative Woman' is written in black ink on 31 leaves, two of which have insertions written on versos to be inserted in the text on the recto. It is bound in three-quarters brown morocco and is still in its brown paper cover with the title written in blue pencil. As we shall see, it is extensively revised, especially on the opening few leaves and at the end, but some pages show barely any alteration. Although it is apparently the first draft of the story, it was used as the printers' copy from which the serial was initially set in print, because the names of four compositors are written in the margin of fos. 1, 5, 9, 14, 19, 24 and 30. However, there must have been extensive revision to the proofs of *PMM*, since the serial shows about seventy alterations to the MS., plus all the occasions on which the poet's surname is changed from Crewe to Trewe (the significance of this alteration will be discussed in connection with the role of Florence Henniker).

The transmission of the text is clear. The story was first collected in *1896*, and Kristin Brady plausibly suggests a reason why 'An Imaginative Woman' was included in Osgood, McIlvaine's edition of *Wessex Tales* instead of their *Life's*

Little Ironies, where it would have seemed naturally to belong:

> *Life's Little Ironies* was produced from Osgood, McIlvaine's own first
> edition plates, but since they had not previously published *Wessex Tales*,
> new plates had to be made for that volume – thus making it possible to add
> an entire story at the beginning without much additional work.[1]

1896 was not, however, simply a reprint of the serial, for there are approximately
fifty substantive alterations to *PMM*. Most interestingly, eleven of these are
changes which restore the readings of the MS. Thus, it would seem either that
Hardy collated *PMM* with the MS. in revising the story for *1896*, or that these
eleven *PMM* readings were proof revisions which Hardy did not copy. 'An
Imaginative Woman' was subsequently collected in *1912*, the Wessex edition of
Life's Little Ironies. For *1912*, Hardy altered five individual words in *1896*, and
made five additions to it, ranging in length from a single word to a whole
sentence. He also restored two words, 'of Solentsea', which had been scored out
in the opening sentence of the MS. and which had been omitted from published
versions until now, nearly twenty years after the story was written; again, this
will be seen to relate to the influence of Florence Henniker on the story.

   Hardy undertook to write a story of 6000 words for *Pall Mall Magazine* on
26 March 1893, but added that 'I hope they don't want the story just yet? as I
have nothing ready or thought of'.[2] He accepted £100 for the story, and assured
his agent that it would be 'quite a proper story, of course'.[3] On 13 July, he writes
that 'I will set about the P.M.M. story as soon as possible' and on 14 September
he announces that the story is completed.[4] It was intended to be a contemporary
tale, as shown, for instance, by the description of the photograph of the unnamed
Duke and Duchess in Trewe's room, which is almost certainly a topical reference
to the wedding of the Duke of York (later George V) and Princess Mary of Teck
on 6 July.

Florence Henniker

In the *Life*, Hardy notes 'December [1893]. Found and touched up a short story
called "An Imaginative Woman".'[5] The story would appear to have been initially
written in August and September 1893, while the key event in Hardy's
conception of Ella Marchmill and many incidental details of the story was his
first meeting with Florence Henniker three months earlier, on 19 May in Dublin.
A study of the MS. and subsequent versions of the text reinforces the importance
of her influence on the story.

   It has often been recognized that certain features of 'An Imaginative Woman'
recall Mrs Henniker: for instance, as Evelyn Hardy and F.B. Pinion note, 'the
Solentsea where the heroine stays is Southsea; like Mrs Henniker, she is
interested in Shelley's poetry [and] her husband, like Mrs Henniker's, was most
unpoetical and connected with the weapons of war'.[6] The MS. shows that four
times on the first leaf Hardy originally wrote 'Marchfold' as Ella's surname
before altering it to Marchmill, perhaps to strengthen the similarity between the

names of Ella Marchmill and Florence *Ellen* Hungerford Henniker, *née Mil*nes. Her beloved poet is throughout the MS. called Robert Crewe, not Trewe as he later became in all published versions. *Crewe* has associations with Florence Henniker because her uncle was Lord Crewe whose home was Crewe Hall in Cheshire. Other incidental details of the story which might have been prompted by the friendship with her are the photograph of Trewe which Ella takes to bed (in his second letter to her Hardy apologizes for forgetting to give her a photograph[7]) and the lock of Trewe's hair which Ella requests after his death (Mrs Henniker's father possessed a lock of Keats's hair). Perhaps even Hardy's awareness that he and Mrs Henniker narrowly missed meeting each other thirteen years earlier may lie behind the series of frustrated meetings which punctuate the story.[8]

Florence Henniker and her husband had lived on South Parade, Southsea, for the previous year, and Robert Trewe had lived on New Parade, Solentsea, for less than two years. Both houses faced the sea, and it would seem that the house in which Ella Marchmill stayed is modelled on Mrs Henniker's.[9] Most curiously, Hardy sought to remove any emphasis from the location of the story in Solentsea/Southsea. The opening sentence of the MS. originally set the story at the 'watering-place of their choice' and this was revised to the '|well-known marine| watering-place of their choice |of Solentsea in Upper Wessex|'. Hardy then deleted 'of Solentsea', and this modified sentence is what *PMM* and *1896* read. Only in *1912* did Hardy immediately identify the story as being set in Solentsea. In other versions of the story, the first reference to the name of the town occurs more than two-thirds of the way through, after the Marchmills have left it.

1912 is the occasion when Hardy moved 'An Imaginative Woman' to *Life's Little Ironies*: that is, as he moves the story from *Wessex Tales*, he curiously locates it more prominently in Wessex. As with the change of Crewe's name to Trewe, it is possible that Hardy felt the story would be too obviously associated with Mrs Henniker and therefore sought to give less prominence to its setting in her town; only twenty years later did he feel able to restore his original wording of the MS.

Hardy seems to have felt in 1893 that the story might be too clearly identified with Mrs Henniker unless he tried to disguise some of the parallels. He may have been prompted to do so by a desire to conceal his romantic feelings about her from Emma Hardy, or by a wish not to embarrass Mrs Henniker publicly. However, another occasion when Hardy considered using Solentsea in a story might suggest a further possible motive.

'An Imaginative Woman' would appear to have been written about August or September of 1893. In the early autumn of that year, Hardy was also collecting and revising the stories which would appear in *Life's Little Ironies*, to be published in 1894 by Osgood, McIlvaine. One of these was 'On the Western Circuit', a story originally published in the *English Illustrated Magazine* and *Harper's Weekly* in 1891. Hardy took the opportunity to revise it when preparing for its publication in *Life's Little Ironies,* and these revisions resulted in the galley proofs of the volume. The galley proofs have survived and are now held in the Dorset County Museum. They show a host of revisions to the magazine versions of the story, but the one which concerns us here is the honeymoon destination of Raye and Anna. In the *English Illustrated Magazine* and *Harper's Weekly*, they were to have honeymooned in Tunbridge Wells, but the galley proof has them going instead to Solentsea. Hardy emended this in the margin to 'Knollsea' (Swanage) which is what eventually appeared in *Life's Little Ironies*. Solentsea therefore only ever appeared in the galley proof of the story and was never in any published version. The proof page containing the first of these Solentsea/Knollsea variants bears the printers' date stamp for 12 December 1893, which is also the month when Hardy was preparing the proofs of 'An Imaginative Woman' for its magazine appearance. That is, in the same month Hardy deleted references to Solentsea from two of his stories which he had inserted only two or three months earlier.

The reasons for the timing of these changes can be explained by reference to the developments in Hardy's relationship with Mrs Henniker. After a very intense beginning to the relationship on his part, Hardy soon appears to have tried to act and write more circumspectly after seeing that his feelings for her were not reciprocated, so that, in a letter of 10 September 1893, he ends by saying that 'You may be thankful to hear that the *one-sidedness* I used to remind you of is disappearing from the situation. But you will always be among the most valued of my friends, as I hope always to remain one at least of the rank & file of yours' (*Letters*, II, 31). The alterations which Hardy made to the two stories in the early autumn revealed the romantic associations which Solentsea had acquired for him, and for that reason they needed to be undone when December arrived, by which time their relationship was on a determinedly platonic level. Solentsea as a honeymoon destination was certainly not a place to be mentioned any longer, and it could not be prominently announced as the holiday home of a married woman besotted with a poet, which would have displayed all too clearly the elements of fantasy and role-reversal which contributed to the writing of 'An Imaginative Woman'.

Manuscript

The MS. shows that two scenes caused Hardy particular trouble, and they were to be revised also in all three published versions: they were the depiction of Ella in bed with the photograph of Trewe, and the ending, where Ella's husband calculates the date of his child's conception and decides that she had been unfaithful.

Hardy's general tendency in revising this tale over the years was to remove or tone down any words or scenes which might have indicated some kind of sexual or passionate basis to Ella's obsession with Trewe, and this tendency can be seen in the MS. itself. When Ella is in bed with Trewe's photograph, an erased passage can be seen to describe how she has 'almost a guilty sense that she had the poet actually present with her' (fo. 16; this is a blue-ink deletion described more fully below). In the serial, her husband finds the photograph under the pillow, but originally, in another cancelled passage, Ella 'softly drew up her foot, & pushed the ~~pho~~ picture down as far as she could reach with her toes' (fo. 17; another blue-ink deletion). Trewe cannot get any further into her bed than that, and Hardy must have felt that this was inappropriate for his conception of the story. Indeed, Hardy continuously worked to remove references to 'bed' from the story: *PMM* omits three which are in the MS. (even thoroughly innocuous ones as in Marchmill's remarks to Ella, 'Not in bed yet?' and 'I didn't know you had gone to bed' [fo. 16]), and *1896* omits a further one.

The longest omission from the MS. in all later versions of this incident was to be a fascinating passage, undeleted in the MS., which shows Ella trying to persuade her husband to sleep in another room that night, presumably so that she can be alone with 'Trewe', and it is an episode which anticipates Sue Bridehead's behaviour in *Jude*, albeit for quite different motives. In the serial, Marchmill has returned home unexpectedly and says, 'I've had a good feed, and I shall turn in straight off. I want to get out at six o'clock to-morrow if I can. ... I shan't disturb you by my getting up.' In the MS., however, the ellipsis is filled by the following passage:

> |He passed through into the ~~adj~~ dressing-room communicating, & she c^d. hear him pulling off his clothes.| She wondered which of the ~~bed~~rooms he was going to occupy, & finding that he showed no sign of withdrawing she said,
>
> "That is a comfortable little bed in the ~~other~~ |upper| room, |isn't it?| ~~I am rather fatigued.~~"
>
> ~~Is it?~~ "O yes". |he replied.| "Well no, it isn't. It is so beastly narrow [...]".
> (fo. 17)

The serial then adds the following three lines not found in the MS.:

> 'Sure you're not ill?' he asked, bending over her.
> 'No – only wicked!'
> 'Never mind that'. And he stooped and kissed her.

Only *1912*, however, continues this scene with Marchmill's comment that 'I wanted to be with you to-night', showing that he is not so neglectful of Ella as she believes. These emendations demonstrate Hardy's tendency at each stage of revision to make the husband slightly more sympathetic.

The ending of the story is different in each of the four versions of the text. In the MS. Hardy initially scored out Marchmill's mistaken belief that his wife '<u>did</u> play me false' (fos. 30–31) and also his calculation of dates ('I'm damned if I didn't think so [...] week in August') and then immediately wrote them out again. Incidentally, in the MS. (and the serial), Hardy adds after 'I'm damned if I didn't think so' the parenthesis '(he never did before, by the way)', which he must later have come to regard as too intrusive a narrative comment.

In a letter to Sir Douglas Straight, the editor of the serial, Hardy wrote on 20 January 1894 that

> I have deleted the passage; which I do quite willingly: & may as well say once for all – in case I shd write again for you – that I always give editors

carte blanche in these matters: as I invariably reprint from the original copy
for the book-form of my novels. If there is anything else (I have not
observed anything myself) please use your judgement freely.[10]

Hardy does not identify the bowdlerized passage, but the only substantial part of
the story which is omitted from the serial and which is found both in the MS. and
1896 is at the ending. In the MS. it reads as follows:

Then she <u>did</u> play me false with that fellow at the lodgings. / Let me see ...|-
the dates –| the last |second| week in August. .... the third week in May. ...
|Yes;| Exactly. .... (fo. 31)

1896 restored this passage, with the single alteration of the final word to another
'Yes'. Obviously Marchmill's calculation of gestation must have been rather too
clinical for the editor of the *Pall Mall Magazine*. It is impossible to tell whether
Straight was responsible for the omission from the serial of any of the other
words and phrases which were restored to *1896*.

Hardy continued to revise the ending in both *1896* and *1912*. The former adds
more evidence for Marchmill to reach his false conclusion about the boy's
paternity, as if Hardy were keen to make his mistake more credible: we learn that
'the dreamy and peculiar expression of the poet's face sat, as the transmitted
idea, upon the child's'. In *1912*, Hardy gives Marchmill even firmer evidence for
his error: 'By a known but inexplicable trick of Nature there were undoubtedly
strong traces of resemblance to the man Ella had never seen.' Hardy's revisions
to the ending do not seem to improve on the MS. version. He was obviously
trying to give a proper motivation to Marchmill's mistake and to make it seem
more plausible and realistic, but the effect is instead to give us a narrator who
endorses the superstition that a child's features can be determined by the
experiences of a parent. He also obscures the ending's real irony, which is that a
story about an imaginative woman becomes a story about an imaginative man
ready to believe his own fancies and reject his own son. The irony would have
been heightened if Hardy had given *less*, not more, physical evidence to justify
his mistake.

There are a few more points to observe about the MS. before leaving it to
examine later versions. The story was originally entitled 'A Woman of
Imagination' but this is scored out in favour of the present title. This change
gives more prominence to Ella's imaginative faculty and less to her gender: it is
to be a story more about imagination than a woman. She is more than just a
'breeder' (fo. 7) of her kind (published versions all read 'mere multiplier').

Hardy's narrator appears to be more intrusive and ironic than he is in later
versions. We have already seen his sardonic dismissal of Marchmill's comment
that he had always suspected his wife had been unfaithful, and a similar ironic
tone can be seen in his initial description of Marchmill's business of
manufacturing guns as a 'trade of tender humanity' (fo. 2; deleted in the MS.).
Further irony, as well as Hardy's irritation at reviewers, may be seen in his
description of Trewe's verses and their reception: Hardy originally said that
Trewe 'wrote sonnets in the loosely-rhymed Shakespearian fashion, which he
ought not to have done' (fo. 7). After alterations and insertions in the MS. this

passage became 'wrote |perpetrated| sonnets in the loosely-rhymed Shakespearian |Elizabethan| fashion, which |every right-minded reviewer said| he ought not to have done'. In the first instance, the criticism of Trewe is obviously meant to be ironic, but, perhaps fearing he would be misunderstood and taken literally, Hardy makes his mockery of the reviewers and their conformity more direct, removing the irony.

Hardy's description of Ella having a 'volatile' (fo. 3) cast of soul is found in none of the published versions, while Marchmill in the MS. is described as 'uncongenial' (fo. 6) rather than 'commonplace' as it later became in print. Trewe's age is given as about 31 or 32, and Ella is herself over thirty, but a deleted phrase in the MS. suggests that Hardy originally conceived of her as being 'seven or eight' (fo. 13) years younger than him. Making Ella older is compatible with Hardy's inclination in revising to make her more irresponsible. For instance, the MS. and the serial describe her as 'youthful' (fo. 14) in nature whereas later versions alter this to 'immature'. *1896* and *1912* also omit an earlier description of her 'childish' (fo. 13) eagerness when asking the landlady whether she would regard Trewe as handsome. Similarly the MS. shows her as a '|sympathetic| young woman' (fo. 27), but all later versions omit 'young'.

Finally, the MS. shows a small number of additions and deletions which were made with other writing materials: pencil, blue ink and violet crayon. They would appear to have been made after the completion of the rest of the MS. The pencil and crayon alterations are insubstantial and seem to indicate that Hardy merely used whatever writing equipment was nearest to hand at the time. The blue-ink revisions, however, are possibly different in nature and will be discussed more fully later.

The two pencil revisions occur on fos. 1 and 2. The first replaces a reference to 'Mr & Mrs William Marchfold|mill|' with 'They'. The second alters 'littlest' to 'smallest'. The three crayon revisions are on fos. 14, 15 and 29. The first changes 'though' to 'but' to avoid repeating 'though' in consecutive sentences. A more substantial revision occurs on the next leaf in a description of Ella's thoughts and feelings, which

> her husband, |distinctly lacked –| perhaps luckily for himself, |considering
> that he had to maintain her provide for family expenses| distinctly lacked.
> (fo. 15)

The words in violet crayon are the first 'distinctly lacked' and 'provide for family expenses', and the deletions are also in crayon. Being presumably a late revision to the passage, they reveal that Hardy wanted to remind us again that the infatuated Ella has a 'family' of three small children. The third crayon revision occurs near the end of the story, when Marchmill asks Ella if she is still thinking about that 'poetical friend or rival of yours' (fo. 29). Hardy must have come to feel that Marchmill would be unlikely to consider the dead Trewe as his wife's 'rival' in poetry, or to know that she had once regarded him in such a light.

The blue-ink revisions are more numerous and are concentrated in the scene in which Ella is in bed with Trewe's photograph. There is, however, one isolated blue-ink revision which occurs earlier on fo. 9: Ella's curiosity about Trewe is said to give her an 'indescribable ~~self~~ |consciousness |of personal ~~of sex~~-interest rather than literary|'. That is, Hardy first described her 'self-consciousness', then her 'consciousness of sex-interest' and finally her 'consciousness of personal interest'. Hardy used blue ink to delete 'of sex-' and to insert 'of personal', and this immediately suggests that he was bowdlerizing the phrase and marking it by the colour of the ink for restoration at a subsequent stage of publication. This is also possibly the reason for all the other blue-ink revisions which we shall examine below, but it should be noted that none of them was ever restored.

The other blue-ink alterations all occur on fos. 16–18, in the scene portraying Ella in bed with Trewe's photograph. The first is a reference to her feeling that she is 'permeated by him' (Trewe), which Hardy revised to 'permeated by his spirit', a more ethereal and arguably less physical form of possession. This was followed by another blue-ink deletion of the obviously indecorous statement that Ella had 'almost a guilty sense that she had the poet actually present with her' (fo. 16) in bed. On the next leaf, Hardy similarly deleted a paragraph of five lines which described Ella hiding the photograph in her bed:

> There ~~would~~ |might| have been nothing remarkable in his finding the photograph lying on the table or |outside the| bed, but it might have struck him as odd to find it inside; at any rate ~~she~~ |Ella in her sensitiveness| fancied so; ~~accordingly she~~ |& she| softly drew up her foot, & pushed the ~~pho~~ picture down as far as she could reach with her toes.

All of this was heavily scored out in blue, and the same pen was used to replace the paragraph with the statement that 'While her eyes followed his movements Ella softly stretched out her hand and pushed the photograph under the pillow.' (This change necessitated other minor revisions to the following paragraph.) A further apparent bowdlerization on this leaf is the blue deletion of Marchmill's exclamation on finding the photograph: 'Three in a bed'. The final blue-ink revision occurs on fo. 18, where a reference to Ella's 'affection' for Trewe is altered to 'admiration'.

The serial and *1896* Osgood, McIlvaine

The serial has ten readings which are unique to it; all but one are single words and are of little significance (e.g. 'dilated' for MS. 'spoke'). The only interesting one is a quaintly chivalrous alteration; all other versions of the story describe how women reach an age when the 'vainer' ones among them shrink from receiving a male visitor except with their backs to the window or with the blinds half down. *PMM*, however, replaces 'vainer' by 'more sensitive'.

We do not know when Hardy made his alterations to *PMM* in preparing *1896*, but it must have been at or about the time that he was completing *Jude*. In this light, it is interesting that the most substantial revisions he made to *PMM* concern generalizations about the nature of marriage. Out, for instance, went the early observation that the Marchmills 'were less |distinctly| an ill-assorted than an un-assorted couple' (fo. 1). Ella's motive for marrying is explained more acerbically in *PMM*, where we learn that she did not think about her husband's occupation before marrying (italics in the following quotation indicate the words omitted from *1896*): 'the necessity of getting life-leased, at all cost *to heart or conscience, which well-trained young women of moral and enlightened countries are duly taught by their high-principled mothers,* kept her from thinking of it at all'.[11] Hardy was not, however, toning down his mordant views on marriage for he was quite capable of a lovely revision such as the following succinct reversal of phrasing: *PMM*'s 'in the natural course of passion, under conditions which the wit of civilisation has ingeniously devised for its extinction, her husband's love for her had not survived' becomes in *1896* 'in the natural way of passion under the too practical conditions which civilization has devised for its *fruition* [...]' (my italics). Similarly, when the Marchmills return from visiting Trewe's grave, the serial tells us how they travelled in silence, since it was one of those 'dreary situations' that occur 'in married life', but *1896* adds the ominous clause 'which words could not mend'.

In revising *PMM*, Hardy took the opportunity to introduce a pun on Trewe/true. In *1896*, Marchmill has been considering his wife's claim that he neglects her and he unwittingly tells her, 'I've been thinking of what you said, Ell: that I have gone about a good deal and left you without much to amuse you. Perhaps it's true.' The pun would not have worked in the MS., of course, since Trewe was called Crewe there. Other alterations continue that process whereby Ella is seen in a more critical light; when she thinks how wicked she is to be infatuated with Trewe when she has three children, *1896* reminds us that she has a husband as well. As we saw earlier, Hardy sought to play down the romantic aspects of her 'relationship' with Trewe, and where the serial described him as someone 'for whose person she was now absolutely love-sick', in *1896* the last word is replaced by the much more decorous 'attached'.

1912 Macmillan Wessex edition

In preparing *1912*, perhaps the most significant decision which Hardy made was to move 'An Imaginative Woman' from *Wessex Tales* to *Life's Little Ironies*; as he explained in the Prefatory Note, he regarded the latter volume as being 'more nearly its place, turning as it does upon a trick of Nature, so to speak', this 'trick of Nature' being exactly the phrase which Hardy added to the ending of *1912*. Other changes to the text, apart from those already discussed, are minor and seem to have been done simply to make the plot clearer or more consistent. For instance, Ella tells her husband that Trewe's photograph must have been swept into their bed from the *mantelpiece*, where Hardy had earlier described it as standing, and not from the table, which all earlier versions of the story said. Similarly, for the first time, Hardy in *1912* identifies the Marchmills as living in a *midland* city; this makes it feasible for Trewe to pass through on his way from North Wales to Solentsea. Until *1912*, the only other reference to the town had located it vaguely as a 'thriving city northwards' of Solentsea, which, from the south coast, is not a very helpful direction! Nothing better illustrates Hardy's attention to detail and his indefatigable revisions throughout the evolution of 'An Imaginative Woman'.[12]

Notes

1 Brady, p. 186.
2 *Letters,* II, 5.
3 *Letters*, II, 7.
4 *Letters*, II, 22, 32.
5 *Life*, p. 276.
6 *One Rare Fair Woman: Thomas Hardy's Letters to Florence Henniker, 1893–1922,* ed. Evelyn Hardy and F.B. Pinion (London: Macmillan, 1972), p. 38n.
7 *Letters*, II, 11.
8 See *Letters*, II, 22–3.
9 See Hardy and Pinion, p. 6n.
10 *Letters*, II, 48.
11 As with all these omissions from the serial discussed at this point, the reading in *PMM* is the same as the MS. 'Moral and enlightened' had originally read 'humane & civilized' (fo. 2) in the MS. before the latter phrase was deleted.
12 For the sake of a complete record, the other revisions to *1896* for the Wessex edition are as follows (*1912* is quoted first, and the pagination is that of *1912*): 'the well-known/a well-known' (p. 3); 'since nobody/that nobody' (p. 8); 'envy/envy,' (p. 8); 'the servant replied, and/[not in *1896*]' (p. 14); 'Next/Then' (p. 16); 'eyes described/eyes, described' (p. 16); 'landlady/landlady,' (p. 16); 'aside/aside,' (p. 17); 'door/door,' (p. 18); 'O,/O;' (p. 19); 'their city/the city' (p. 22); ' 'Behold/ "Behold' (p. 22); 'lattice,'/lattice,"' (p. 22); 'condition/condition,' (p. 29); 'to the man Ella had never seen/[not in *1896*]' (p. 31); 'August/August.' (p. 31).

CHAPTER 19

'The Son's Veto'

Hardy remarked in 1896 that 'The Son's Veto' was his best short story, according to Rebekah Owen.[1] He had written it in 1891 in London, from where he had written to Emma Hardy on 16 April that he was 'engrossed in the matter of a story which shall have its scene in London – I am going out looking about on that account now'.[2] Part of the story, though, recalls an earlier stay in London in 1888, when the Hardys' bedroom faced on to Kensington High Street and they were liable to be disturbed in the early hours of the morning by the noise of the market wagons making their way in from the country to Covent Garden: as Hardy noted in the *Life*, 'July 7. One o'clock a.m. I got out of bed, attracted by the never-ending procession as seen from our bedroom windows Phillimore Place. Chains rattle, and each cart cracks under its weighty pyramid of vegetables.'[3]

The manuscript of 'The Son's Veto' has survived and is located at the Fondation Martin Bodmer in Geneva. The published versions of the story which have textual significance are as follows:

Serial   *Illustrated London News*, Christmas Number (published 1 December), 1891, pp. 20–21, 25, with two illustrations by A. Forestier.

1894   *Life's Little Ironies* (London: Osgood, McIlvaine, 1894), pp. 1–23. Published at 6s. in an edition of 2000 copies on 22 February 1894.

1894H   *Life's Little Ironies* (New York: Harper & Brothers, 1894), pp. 3–21. Published in March 1894.

1896   *Life's Little Ironies* (London: Osgood, McIlvaine, 1896), pp. 1–23. Volume XIV in the Wessex Novels, the first uniform and complete edition of Hardy's works. Plates of the first edition were used.

1912   *Life's Little Ironies* (London: Macmillan, 1912), pp. 35–52. Volume VIII of the Wessex edition.

In addition, the galley proofs of *1894*, showing Hardy's marginal emendations, are extant; they are now in the Dorset County Museum.

The manuscript

The manuscript contains sixteen leaves, and there is, as Purdy notes, evidence of a considerable excision towards the end of the story: the last seven centimetres of the penultimate page have been cut out, and about 3.5 cms are missing from the top of the final page.[4] Alan Manford has remarked that 'the reason for this is not apparent, but Hardy may have removed this section because it had been written in his wife's hand' (1996, p. xxx). The manuscript is very close to the serial version of the story; in both, for instance, Sam was called Ned, and Aldbrickham was Oldbrickham. Very little was added to the MS. for the serial. The village of Gaymead is not said in the MS. to be 'near the town of Oldbrickham', as it is in the serial, and indeed the name of Gaymead does not appear in the MS. until near the end of the second section of the story. It is the serial which first tells us in the second sentence that Sophy's long locks 'composed a rare, *if somewhat barbaric*, example of ingenious art' (my italics indicate serial's addition to MS.). One other difference between the MS. and all printed versions of the story occurs in the description of the lame Sophy 'sliding' (fo. 12) downstairs by the aid of the handrail, as the MS. puts it near the start of section three. All other versions read 'sidling', and this looks like a case of a misprint either being overlooked in successive revisions or else being adopted after the event. Certainly the MS. reading seems a much more appropriate term to describe Sophy's action.

The serial and the galley proofs of *1894*

The first galley proofs of *1894* have survived (they are held in the Dorset County Museum), and the sheets of 'The Son's Veto' bear the printers' date stamp 1 and 4 December 1893. An analysis of the proofs shows that Hardy made the alterations to the serial version at three distinct stages when preparing the story for publication in *1894*. The bulk of the revisions were made when preparing a revised copy of the story which was used to set up the galley proofs. The next stage is Hardy's marginal emendation of these proofs. These emended proofs must have been the basis of at least a second proof, or revises; these have not survived but their existence can be posited because, on six occasions, *1894* has a reading which is different from the emended galley proofs and which must have been introduced at a later stage.

Hardy's marginal emendations are 30 in number, of which 22 are substantive. These emended proofs must at this stage have been sent to Harper & Brothers in New York to form the basis of *1894H*, since they are largely identical in substantives. For the British edition, however, as has been mentioned, the proofs underwent a further revision, and the account given later of these second proofs is therefore in part an account of some of the differences between the British and American editions of 1894. Crucially, there are three substantive occasions on which Hardy revised again the emended proof; *1894H*, however, retains the readings of the emended proof, showing that it was based on this intermediate stage of the galley.[5]

Firstly, to describe the alterations and additions which Hardy made to the serial in preparing for the first printing of the galley proofs. His principal aim seems to have been to highlight the urban/rural contrast, emphasizing the fatal influence of London on Sophy and the fertility of her native Gaymead. For the first time, we hear how her husband ends up in a 'well-packed' (p. 11) cemetery, making London even more a place of pervasive death, and there is more antipathy to the metropolis in Sophy's description of London schools as 'wretched holes' (p. 16), while the house-façades which had been 'tawny' in the serial are now 'drab' (p. 12). Hardy also adds the detail that the vegetable carts are 'moving in an urban atmosphere' (p. 14).

By contrast, the fecund appeal of Gaymead is much heightened to balance this presentation of grim London. Consider, for instance, the following examples of Hardy's alterations to the serial in his description of the procession of country carts passing to Covent Garden:

Serial	*1894*
cabbages, carrots, turnips, built up in pyramids and frustums with such skill that a rope was sufficient to secure the whole load	waggon after waggon, bearing green bastions of cabbages nodding to their fall, yet never falling, walls of baskets enclosing masses of beans and peas, pyramids of snow-white turnips, swaying howdahs of mixed produce – creeping along behind aged night-horses, who seemed ever patiently wondering between their hollow coughs why they had always to work at that still hour when all other sentient creatures were privileged to rest (p. 13)
it was soothing to watch them when depression and nervousness hindered rest	it was soothing to watch and sympathize with them when depression and nervousness hindered sleep, and to see how the fresh green-stuff brightened to life as it came opposite the lamp, and how the sweating animals steamed and shone with their miles of travel (pp. 13–14)

As Kristin Brady puts it well in her comment on how Hardy expanded his original diary note about the carts, quoted at the start of this chapter, 'the clichéd "pyramid of vegetables" is expanded to include "bastions" and "swaying howdahs", giving the commonplace scene a curiously exotic quality. At the same time, the unspecified vegetables of the note are given a particularity which adds a striking visual clarity: in the light of the street-lamp, cabbages, beans, peas, and "snow-white turnips" are "brightened to life" in a vision that appears to Sophy's eyes like a transfiguration.'[6] To this I would only add that such an expansion of the diary note was not part of Hardy's original conception of 'The Son's Veto' but first occurred two years after he had initially written the story, and some five years after he had first witnessed the scene in Kensington High Street. Sophy's attraction to the sight of the waggons and her renewed affection for Sam put her clearly on the side of nature, stressing her blighted life, through having to live in town, and showing her to be 'a child of nature' (p. 12), which was another *1894* addition to the serial.

This cornucopia of nature is carefully balanced by the addition of the urban detritus lying around at the school cricket match; in *1894*, we read for the first time of the 'great coaches under which was jumbled the *débris* of luxurious luncheons; bones, pie-crusts, champagne-bottles, glasses, plates, napkins, and the family silver' (p. 20).[7] Hardy is clearly beginning to see this contrast between the rural Sophy and the urban son as the central thematic symmetry of his story.

In setting up the galley proofs, Hardy made Ned/Sam a more persistent suitor, and he altered the chronology of the story. In the serial, after the son's veto of the marriage at Christmas, the matter was 'dropped for three years', but the galley expanded this to read 'dropped for months; renewed again; abandoned under his repugnance; again attempted; and thus the gentle creature reasoned and pleaded till three long years had passed. Then the faithful Sam revived his suit with some peremptoriness' (p. 22). In the margin of the galley, Hardy increased 'three' years to 'four or five'. In the serial, then, Ned made no further effort to persuade her, so it is unclear why the son, three years later, has to make his mother swear not to marry him. The galley increases Randolph's opposition and his 'repugnance' at the prospect of the marriage, and it makes the duration of their waiting that much greater.

It is at this stage also that Hardy elaborates on the scene near the end of the story where the son, Randolph, makes Sophy swear never to marry Sam. In the serial, he 'made her swear before a little cross and shrine in his bed-room that she would not wed Edward Hobson', but the version of 'The Son's Veto' with which we are now familiar expands this to read, 'taking her before a little cross and altar that he had erected in his bedroom for his private devotions, there bade her kneel, and swear that she would not wed Samuel Hobson' (p. 22).[8] Making her kneel serves to increase the mock piety of this gesture, and the detail about Randolph's private devotions emphasizes the decidedly private *self*-devotion which the son has in his wish for her not to marry Sam. To stress that the boy is motivated solely by social ambition, it is at this stage that Hardy adds the comment that he 'cared exclusively for the class' (p. 20) which his school friends belonged to.

'Ned' was changed to 'Sam' when setting up the galley, probably because 'Ned' is also used in 'The Fiddler of the Reels' later in the volume (see Manford, 1996, p. 234). 'Oldbrickham' became the familiar 'Aldbrickham' (Reading), the first and only use of the name outside *Jude* (where it is spelt 'Aldbrickham' in the manuscript). Other revisions made in preparing the galley include the alteration of the serial's observation that 'her once cherry cheeks grew lily-pale' when Sophy lives in the city. The galley replaces this with the note that she 'wasted hours in braiding her beautiful hair, till her once cherry cheeks grew to pink of the very faintest', and Hardy altered 'cherry' and 'grew' in the margin to, respectively, 'apple' and 'waned' (p. 10). Sam gives Sophy an ironic reminder that she had once turned him down, saying to her in the galley that he would never forget her, 'notwithstanding that she had served him rather badly at one time' (p. 18; not in serial). Finally, at the very end of the story, the son who drives past the mourning Sam is described not just as 'a young cleric', as he was in the serial, but has become 'a young smooth-shaven priest in a high waistcoat' (p. 23), unctuous and dressed in the clothes of his class, a fitting final reminder of how he had vetoed his mother's happiness for the sake of his social ambitions.

Of the marginal additions made to the galley, the longest tells us how, at the time of the annual cricket match at Lord's, 'Mrs. Twycott felt stronger than usual: she went to the match with Randolph, and was able to leave her chair and walk about occasionally' (p. 19). Hardy obviously felt the need to explain how the normally infirm Sophy could manage to promenade around the ground a few lines later. Another change occurs when Sophy is explaining to Randolph that Sam is not what he would regard as a gentleman. In the serial, she says this 'firmly', but Hardy alters this to 'timidly'. This is much more plausible, for if she had been capable of speaking *firmly* to her son, she obviously would not have been so subject to his wishes throughout the story.

Other marginal alterations include increasing the length of Sophy's marriage from more than thirteen years to more than fourteen (p. 10). Her son had earlier in the story been described as being twelve or thirteen years of age, so the 1894 revision removes any possible ambiguity about the timing of her marriage. Finally, Hardy works to make his characterization of the Reverend Twycott more realistic, adding that Sophy is the only one of the servants with whom the parson came into immediate 'and continuous' (p. 8) relation, making the likelihood of his wanting to marry her more credible, since she is the only member of his household whom he sees, and he now sees her all the time.

There are some sixty differences between *1894* and *1894H*, including the six which have been described as resulting from the second proof of *1894*. Of these sixty differences, there are eight substantive variants, which suggests that there was mild editorial intervention and compositorial error at Harper's. For instance, the musical event which Sophy attends at the start of the story is termed in *1894H* a 'programme' (p. 4), rather than a 'recital' as elsewhere, and at the end of it she leaves the 'garden' (p. 4; 'gardens' in all other versions). All the substantive differences are of quite minor significance: for instance, the waggons going to Covent Garden bear pease, not peas, in Harper's edition.[9]

1912 Macmillan Wessex edition

The 1912 Wessex edition is identical to *1894* except in seven instances. Of the three substantive variants, only one seems of interest. Where *1894* explains how Sophy often could not sleep, and so would 'rise in the night or early morning and look out upon the then vacant thoroughfare' (p. 13), in *1912* we learn that she rises '*to* look out' (p. 43, my italics), giving to her early rising the deliberate purpose of seeing the country waggons passing by and stressing her longing for the way of life they represent for her.[10]

Notes

1 See Weber, 1952, p. 114.

2 *Letters,* I, 232.

3 *Life*, p. 219. See also Millgate, p. 290. The Hardys had taken lodgings at 5 Upper Phillimore Place, part of a terrace on the north side of Kensington High Street, in late June 1888, and they stayed there until 16 July.

4 See Purdy, p. 83. I am grateful to Dr Hans E. Braun, Director of the Bibliotheca Bodmeriana, for this information and for kindly providing a copy of the manuscript. The excised passage is the one which is printed as 'Parleyings were attempted through the keyhole [...] anything the worse in the world' (pp. 21–2) in the 1894 London edition.

5 The differences between, on the one hand, the emended galley and *1894H*, and, on the other, *1894*, are as follows (the galley and *1894H* reading is given first; pagination is that of *1894*): 'bearings/bearing' (p. 6); 'every early morning/early every morning' (p. 13); 'Chok/Chok'' (p. 16); 'shrine/altar' (p. 22). In addition, there are two differences between the emended galley and *1894* where *1894H* reads the same as the London edition, probably as the result of house editing at Harper's in New York: 'home,/home' (p. 5); 'father,/father!' (p. 22).

6 Brady, pp. 107–8. Brady also points out how the emphasis on the suffering of the horses is significant since it brings to light Sophy's own capacity for sympathy.

7 'Bones, pie-crusts' was a marginal addition to the proofs, making the '*débris*' even more prominent.

8 The galley reads 'shrine' for 'altar' here, so this change is an example of a revision at the stage of the second proofs. *1894H* reads 'shrine'.

9 The two substantive differences not yet described are 'things proceeded quietly again' (p. 8; 'things went on quietly again' in *1894*), and 'no expense had been or would be spared' (p. 10; 'no expense had been and would be spared').

10 For the sake of a complete record, the other revisions to *1894* for the Wessex edition are as follows (*1912* is quoted first, and the pagination is that of *1912*): 'hat/hat,' (p. 35); 'bandstand/bandstand,' (p. 35); 'O/Oh' (p. 38); 'O yes/Oh, yes' (p. 38); 'He was seen still less/He was still less seen' (p. 39); 'under her window/under the window' (p. 45).

CHAPTER 20

'For Conscience' Sake'

A study of the evolution of 'For Conscience' Sake' in its published forms shows that Hardy revised it at every opportunity when preparing to collect it for the first time in *Life's Little Ironies* (1894), and it was revised yet again when he was arranging the 'definitive' Wessex edition of 1912. These alterations show Hardy's continuing attention over a period of twenty years to the most meticulous details of characterization and plot, style and tone.

The published versions of 'For Conscience' Sake' which have textual significance are as follows:

Serial	As 'For Conscience Sake', *Fortnightly Review*, 49 (March 1891), 370–82.
1894	'For Conscience' Sake', *Life's Little Ironies* (London: Osgood, McIlvaine, 1894), pp. 27–50. Published at 6*s.* in an edition of 2000 copies on 22 February 1894.
1894H	'For Conscience' Sake', *Life's Little Ironies* (New York: Harper & Bros, 1894), pp. 22–43. Published in March 1894.
1896	'For Conscience' Sake', *Life's Little Ironies* (London: Osgood, McIlvaine, 1896), pp. 27–50. Volume XIV in the Wessex Novels, the first uniform and complete edition of Hardy's works. Plates of the first edition were used.
1912	'For Conscience' Sake', *Life's Little Ironies* (London: Macmillan, 1912), pp. 55–74. Volume VIII of the Wessex edition.

The manuscript

The manuscript of 'For Conscience' Sake' is extant. It probably dates in composition, like most of the other stories in *Life's Little Ironies*, from the latter half of 1890 and the early months of 1891, when work on *Tess* and *A Group of Noble Dames* was largely completed. The 24 leaves of cream paper are a fair copy of the story used to set up the serial publication, although there are a number of alterations within the MS., and there are also a number of variations between it and the serial. Hardy, incidentally, received the sum of £17 for the serial.[1] The manuscript was donated to Manchester University Library in October 1911. The manuscript is described by R.L. Purdy, and Alan Manford has fully discussed the alterations within it.[2]

The MS. shows that two characters originally had different names. Hardy twice wrote or began to write Leonora Frankland's surname as 'Falkland' before correcting himself (fos. 9, 18). Elsewhere, her name is given correctly, which suggests that 'Falkland' appeared in the draft version and he had decided to change the name before he began copying. The Doctor's name on fo. 5 was originally 'Benton', but Hardy cancelled this and wrote 'Bindon' immediately after it on the same line and then went back and altered an earlier reference to 'Benton' on fo. 2. However, he overlooked another 'Benton' on the same leaf, which must have been corrected later at the serial proof stage. This change in the Doctor's name, therefore, seems to have occurred to Hardy when he had copied as far as the fifth leaf: 'Bindon' appears in an unrevised form on fo. 6.

Millborne originally says that he came from 'Exonbury, in Lower Wessex' (fo. 3), but the name of the town was changed to Toneborough (Taunton). Since Hardy seems to have always planned to have Leonora and her daughter living in Exonbury (later references to it are unaltered), he must have realized that she would be unlikely to stay in her home town after the birth of her illegitimate daughter and try to pass herself off as a widow, so she has to come to Exonbury from somewhere else, hence the change to Toneborough as her and Millborne's town of origin. Hardy did not notice until he was preparing the collected edition of the story in 1894 that he needed to alter the Wessex region as well as the name of the town, since Toneborough is in Outer Wessex, not Lower Wessex. Another change of place is that their holiday was originally to have been at Brighton, but this became Cowes (fos. 15, 16), revised again in the collected edition to the Isle of Wight and the Island, a curious combination of the actual placename and the Wessex one.

Hardy can be seen to have changed the source of Millborne's wealth. Originally, he had 'risen to be manager, & in course of time a post of responsibility; & having been fortunate in his private investments, had retired from a business-life somewhat early' (fo. 2). In the revised version, it is his father who had been fortunate in his investments, and his death allowed Millborne to succeed to an income. This means that Millborne has profited by not marrying Leonora, for, we learn later, he told her they would have to live in 'dire poverty' if they married, presumably because his father would have disinherited him. At the start of the story, fortune seems to have favoured Millborne and he can afford to indulge the luxury of his guilty conscience.

Millborne's attitude to Leonora and his daughter undergoes a slight refinement, and he describes his lover as 'the poor victim' rather than 'the poor thing' (fo. 4), as it originally read, showing his increased appreciation of her plight. While copying Millborne's conversation with Bindon, Hardy introduced the former's comment, 'But I have never ~~seen~~ |set eyes on| her since our original acquaintance, & should not know her if I met her' (fo. 4). With regard to Frances, Hardy at first wrote that 'her father had been grievously disappointed in the young girl' (fos. 15–16), but Hardy altered this to read that 'the young girl had not fulfilled her father's expectations of her'. While this suggests a markedly less critical attitude towards Frances, the primary reason for changing the original wording was to avoid echoing a phrase from the previous sentence, where we had learned that the failure of Frances and Cope to marry would cause 'grievous disappointment' to one or both of them.

The social position of the two women is carefully modulated in the MS. For instance, Millborne urges Leonora to marry him because it would remove her from 'this business' (fo. 14) of teaching, a phrase which replaces 'this profession' and slightly lowers her class position, making the doubts of Cope's friends about the Franklands being beneath him more understandable. Following Leonora's marriage, Hardy wrote that 'the social lift that the ~~ladies had~~ two women had derived from the alliance was considerable' (fo. 15). The change from 'ladies' to 'women' enacts the very effect which the sentence describes, since 'ladies', presumably, do not require the social lift which 'women' do.

The quality of music which Leonora's pupils achieve is drastically changed in the MS. At first, Hardy referred to the fragmentary gems of classical music 'as produced by the young people' (fo. 9), which would appear to praise their playing, but he altered the description to 'as ~~produced~~ |interpreted| by the young people |of twelve or fourteen|', which makes any 'pleasure' in being able to hear their music all along the street highly ironic. When she is not teaching, Leonora raises funds for 'sending petticoats to the Lunar savages' (fo. 8), as it originally read, but Hardy strengthened the satire by changing it to 'making happy savages miserable & other such ~~Christian~~ enthusiasms of this Christian country'.

The tone of the narrator at the end of the story is much less intrusive. Originally, he had introduced his information about Millborne's secret whereabouts by grandly saying that 'We who know everything may as well admit, however, that shortly [after...]' (fo. 24). Hardy cancelled this and wrote instead, 'But ~~had~~ a searching inquiry ~~been made it~~ would have revealed that soon [...]', which, as Manford succinctly notes, is both more objective and less objectionable.

The largest alteration to the MS occurs in the final paragraph, where one sentence described how Millborne lived in exile, 'burdened with weariness of life' (fo. 24). In revising this passage, Hardy deleted the final word and replaced it with a lengthy marginal insertion (written in ink over erased pencil):

> [weariness of] his fellow creatures – ever answering negatively, as he sat and smoked among men, the inquiry in the <u>Hippolytus</u>: "What reserved person is not hateful? – and in the sociable is there any charm?"[3]

In Euripides' play, Hippolytus acknowledges that there is a great deal of charm in the sociable, but the misanthropic and world-weary Millborne cannot agree. However, Hardy deleted the entire marginal addition when preparing the serial proofs, possibly because he felt that the context of the allusion to Hippolytus was confusing and contradictory. The chastity of Hippolytus angered Venus: by disagreeing with Hippolytus, is Millborne saying that one should be the opposite of the chaste Hippolytus, which is hardly the moral that he has learned by the end of the story? For the *Fortnightly Review*, Hardy substituted the following passage:

> [burdened with] the heavy thought which oppressed Antigone, that by honourable observance of a rite he had obtained for himself the reward of dishonourable laxity.

This is one of two dozen substantive revisions which Hardy made to the serial proofs. Most of the revised readings in the serial are also present in the collected edition of 1894, but there are six occasions (usually involving just a word or two) where the unrevised MS. reading is present in *1894*. This might be because Hardy did not copy these six revisions to the serial on to a duplicate copy of the serial proofs which he retained and which became the basis for the collected edition. (Some of these six changes are discussed below.)

Serial

The *Fortnightly Review* has a number of unique readings which are not repeated in the later published versions. For instance, Millborne explains in the serial how he came from 'Toneborough, in Lower Wessex' (p. 371), where later versions correctly locate Toneborough (Taunton) in Outer Wessex. The reason for this slip is that in the MS. Hardy had originally written 'Exonbury, in Lower Wessex', before changing the name of the town but omitting to alter its Wessex region.

Each of the three sections in the serial is prefaced (as in the MS.) by an announcement of its location: respectively, 'Sherton Street, W.', 'High Street, Exonbury' and 'London Again'. Hardy perhaps came to feel that such information was redundant, as the change of scenes is made quite clear in the story. In the serial, Sherton Street, where Millborne lives, has a distinctly Wessex flavour to its name, especially when we learn that it leads into Casterbridge Square. In later versions, Hardy retained only actual street names such as Oxford St and Bond St, no doubt thinking that fictional placenames in London were incongruous in a story which is otherwise contemporary and realistic.

The galley proofs of *1894*

The next significant document in the chain of transmission is the first galley proofs of *1894*. Formerly in the possession of Hardy's sister, Kate, they are now held in the Dorset County Museum. The sheets of 'For Conscience' Sake' bear the printers' date stamp 5 December 1893. An analysis of the proofs shows that Hardy made the alterations to the serial at three distinct stages when preparing the story for publication in *1894*. The bulk of the revisions were made when preparing a revised copy of the serial which was used to set up the galley proofs. The next stage is Hardy's marginal emendation of these proofs. These emended proofs must have been the basis of at least a second proof, or revises; these have not survived but their existence can be posited because, on a number of occasions, *1894* has a reading which is different from the emended galley proofs and which must therefore have been introduced at a later stage. I shall indicate, where significant, whether the alterations under discussion were introduced for the first proof stage, or were written by Hardy in the margin of the first proof, or were added to the second proof.

When revising the serial version of the story in order to set up the first galley proof of Life's Little Ironies, Hardy appears to have worked from a duplicate copy of the serial proofs on to which he had copied most, but not all, of the serial proof revisions which appeared in the Fortnightly Review. There are six occasions when, apparently, Hardy did not make a copy of the serial revisions (either by accident or intent), with the result that the earlier reading of the MS. appeared in the first galley. Of these six MS. restorations, the most interesting is when Leonora is explaining to her daughter why she married Millborne: 'he kept on about his conscience and mine, till I was bewildered, and said Yes!' (1894, p. 46). In the serial, she had spoken not of 'conscience' but of 'honour' as motivating Millborne to marry the mother of his daughter after twenty years, but the revised reading is obviously much more appropriate to the story's title. Another reversion to the MS. occurs in the description of Leonora's feelings after she has had to tell her daughter that her new husband is her father. In the MS. and 1894 we learn of Mrs Millborne's 'irritation' (1894, p. 46), but the serial talked of her 'desolation'. If the 1894 reading was a conscious choice, Hardy perhaps felt that, in a short paragraph which also describes their 'anguish' and 'ghastly failure', a reference to 'desolation' had made the scene too melodramatic in the serial.

The character of Millborne undergoes one subtle but significant alteration at this first galley proof stage by the reappearance of a MS. reading. In the serial, we learn how and why he decides to leave his wife and daughter and abandon the scheme which he had planned to make amends to them and which had turned out so ruinously: 'the bitter sense of blighting their existence at length became so impassioned that one day Millborne calmly proposed to return again to the country' (p. 381). This clearly states that it is Millborne himself whose moral conscience prompts him to reach the decision to leave, but it is a curious, contradictory sentence, with Millborne being so 'impassioned' that he 'calmly' offers to leave. 1894 offers a much more consistent and satisfying scene by reverting to the original MS. wording: 'the bitter cry about blighting their existence at length became so impassioned that one day Millborne calmly proposed to return again to the country' (p. 47). This makes more sense, for now it is the women who are 'impassioned' and he who 'calmly' leaves. More importantly, it is the bitter cry of the women, and not his own remorseful realization, which finally makes him see the need for him to leave. He thus maintains to the end that lack of independent insight, that moral blindness and opacity which led him to concoct the scheme of reparation in the first place.

One final minor restoration of a MS. reading for 1894 at the end of the story serves to underline the tale's ironic theme. In the serial, Hardy described how Millborne, reading over the English papers in his exile in Brussels, saw the announcement of his daughter's marriage: 'She had become Mrs. Cope' (p. 382). In 1894, this was altered to read 'She had become the Reverend Mrs. Cope' (p. 49), which is what the MS. had originally read. The man who attempted to right a wrong by marrying the woman he had seduced and deserted twenty years before finds that his daughter can only find respectability if he abandons them again, and the stress on Frances's status as the wife of the upright curate highlights his own position at the end, living a twilight life of drunken anonymity. The story enacts a neat inversion of conventional assumptions about the relative social standing of the seducer and the wronged woman. It is he who is, as it were, disgraced and who must retire abroad to permit his wife and daughter to maintain and reinforce their respectability.

The next stage of revisions concerns Hardy's marginal emendations to the first proof, the most interesting of which is the revision of the serial's description of how Leonora gave musical recitals to raise funds for 'making happy savages miserable, and other such enthusiasms of this Christian country' (p. 374). This was now altered to read 'bewildering happy savages, and other such enthusiasms of this enlightened country' (*1894*, p. 34). This change serves to emphasize one of the principal themes of 'For Conscience' Sake' which, as Kristin Brady has described it, is that of 'the moral "bewilderment" that accompanies conventional life, in which 'intuitive' and 'utilitarian' judgements about matters of conscience are often confounded'.[4] The deletion of the ironic reference to the 'Christian' country may have been because Hardy felt that it was too unsubtle or that the story was already sufficiently anti-clerical in its portrayal of the decidedly secular and conventional curate.

Among a couple of other marginal emendations worthy of note is the comment that, after he has married, Millborne can no longer relax, 'reposeful in the *celibate's* sense that where he was his world's centre had its fixture' (*1894*, p. 47; the italics indicate the insertion), the new word being an ironic epithet for a man who has been conscience-stricken by his seduction of Leonora. Another emendation concerns the state of mind which Millborne reaches at the end of the story; instead of being burdened by a 'bitter thought' (p. 382), as he was in the serial, he now has merely a 'heavy thought' (*1894*, p. 49), making him, arguably, react less emotionally to the lessons he has learnt, which would be in keeping with his generally muted and dispassionate characterization.

The serial's description of the Reverend Cope as 'smoothly-shaven' was altered to 'scantly-whiskered' (*1894*, p. 39), which is similar to Hardy's original conception of him in the MS. as having 'sandy whiskers' (fo. 13; the phrase was deleted in the MS.). This change was probably necessitated by Hardy's revision to the final sentence of the previous story, where the young curate of 'The Son's Veto' was now described as 'smooth-shaven' in *1894* (p. 23). To avoid having a smooth-shaven curate in two successive stories, Hardy reverted to his deleted conception of the Reverend Cope.

From a study of other stories in *Life's Little Ironies*, Hardy is known at this stage to have sent these emended proofs to Harper & Brothers in New York to form the basis of *1894H*. For the British edition, however, the proofs underwent a further revision, but in the case of 'For Conscience' Sake' there were no late substantive alterations. There are nine differences between the emended proofs and *1894*, but they involve only such features as hyphens, capitalization, an exclamation mark and the substitution of 'O' for 'Oh'. It is impossible to tell if they are authorial.

1894 Harper

The stories in the Harper edition were set up from the emended galley proofs, which were then further revised to produce *1894*. However, as explained in the previous paragraph, there were no substantive additions to 'For Conscience' Sake' at the second proof stage. There are, however, two unique substantive variants in *1894H*, which are probably editorial in origin. Millborne recalls his promise to Leonora which he made 'some' twenty years ago (p. 23), so that the date in the Harper edition is thus only approximate. Later, Millborne questions Leonora about her daughter's lover: '"Who is he?" asked Mr. Millborne' (p. 33), in which 'asked' is a pedantic substitution for 'said' elsewhere.

1912 Macmillan Wessex edition

1912 has some thirteen differences from *1894*, of which six are substantive. Leonora, for instance, is made to appear slightly older: 'she was thin, though not gaunt, *with greying hair*' (p. 62: italics indicate new words), and Hardy captures her hesitation and surprise better when Millborne arrives and says he wants to marry her: '*I – fear* I could not entertain such an idea' (p. 63). When Frances tells Leonora that her lover had asked if her mother were related to her new husband, Frances watched closely for the effect of her words on her mother, '*which was a distinct one*' (p. 69). At the end of the story, Leonora becomes the 'absolute *mistress*' (p. 73) rather than the absolute owner of a comfortable sum in personal estate which Millborne has settled upon her.[5]

Notes

1 See *Letters*, I, 230.
2 Purdy, p. 83, and Alan Manford (1990), 89–100.
3 This is not T.A. Buckley's translation in *The Tragedies of Euripides*, 2 vols. (London: Bohn, 1850–53), which Hardy at one time possessed.
4 Brady, p. 113.
5 For the sake of a complete record, the other revisions to *1894* for the Wessex edition are as follows (*1912* is quoted first, and the pagination is that of *1912*): 'upheld/upheld,' (p. 55); 'Millborne's/Millborne's,' (p. 55); 'the street/his street' (p. 55); 'vividly,/vividly.' (p. 57: misprint in *1912*); 'or sitting room/or sitting-room' (p. 60); 'get/gain' (p. 62); 'well dressed/well-dressed' (p. 62); 'O/Oh,' (p. 68); 'Frances asked/she asked' (p. 69).

CHAPTER 21

'A Tragedy of Two Ambitions'

Hardy wrote 'A Tragedy of Two Ambitions' in the summer of 1888 in Dorchester, just before beginning work on *Tess*. The *Life* notes, '[August] 19. Sent a story to H. Quilter. By request, for his Magazine, entitled "A Tragedy of Two Ambitions".'[1] The previous month, Hardy had begun to write 'The Melancholy Hussar' with the intention of sending it to Harry Quilter, the editor of the *Universal Review*, but then, on 24 July, he wrote to Quilter:

> Now the question has occurred to me:– suppose you do not want a tale of that sort for your very modern review? I have in my head a story of a different character – embodying present day aspirations – i.e., concerning the ambitions of two men, their struggles for education, a position in the Church, & so on, ending tragically. If you much prefer the latter sort of thing I will abandon the first – though that is the most advanced, & could be sent in a week or ten days. The other would take a little more time, as it exists at present only in the form of half a dozen notes.[2]

Hardy's proposal was evidently accepted, for on 1 August he wrote to Edmund Gosse that 'I am at present up to the elbows in a cold blooded murder which I hope to get finished in a day or two'.[3] 'A Tragedy of Two Ambitions' was published in the *Universal Review* the following December, while 'The Melancholy Hussar' was published in the *Bristol Times and Mirror* in 1890.

The published versions of 'A Tragedy of Two Ambitions' which have textual significance are as follows:

Serial   *The Universal Review*, December 1888, pp. 537–60, with six illustrations by George Lambert.

1894   *Life's Little Ironies* (London: Osgood, McIlvaine, 1894), pp. 53–86. Published at 6*s*. in an edition of 2000 copies on 22 February 1894.

1894H   *Life's Little Ironies* (New York: Harper & Bros, 1894), pp. 44–75. Published in March 1894.

1896   *Life's Little Ironies* (London: Osgood, McIlvaine, 1896), pp. 53–86. Volume XIV in the Wessex Novels, the first uniform and complete edition of Hardy's works. Plates of the first edition were used.

1912   *Life's Little Ironies* (London: Macmillan, 1912), pp. 77–105. Volume VIII of the Wessex edition.

The manuscript of 'A Tragedy of Two Ambitions' was donated to Manchester University Library in October 1911. It is described by R.L. Purdy, and Alan Manford has fully discussed the alterations within it.[4]

The manuscript

The manuscript of the story is a fair copy in Hardy's hand. It consists of 36 leaves numbered 1–36 in the top right corner of each leaf. There are numerous minor revisions which Hardy made during the copying. The first leaf has two alternative titles bracketed together, with the rejected one, 'The Shame of the Halboroughs', cancelled underneath 'A Tragedy of Two Ambitions'. As we shall see, there is evidence that Hardy decided on this choice of title at a late stage of composition.

The majority of the revisions within the MS. arose because of Hardy's decision to alter the occupation of Halborough senior from miller to millwright. Hardy made this change in the course of copying, and it is not until fo. 12 that he wrote 'millwright' in unrevised form. It was presumably at this stage that he altered the earlier descriptions of him, so that, for example, 'the white clothes of a miller' became 'the ~~white~~ |light| clothes of a ~~miller~~ |country tradesman|' (fo. 2). The results of the father's drunken fecklessness are also consequently changed; thus, 'No bran ready for Dairyman Kench, the bakers out at Anglebury waiting for their flour' became, after the appropriate deletions, 'No |stones dressed for Miller| Kench, the |great wheel| out at Anglebury waiting for |new float-boards|' (fo. 2). Similarly, 'Already dealers sent their corn elsewhere & only one set of millstones was |now| kept going, though the mill contained two. Already he found a difficulty in meeting his liabilities, & appeared in the markets only at uncertain intervals' was changed to 'Already ~~dealers~~ |millers| ~~sent~~ |went| ~~their corn~~ |repairs & renewals| elsewhere |for their gear, ~~parts of~~| & only one ~~millstone~~ |set of hands| was now kept going, though ~~the mill contained~~ |there were formerly| two. Already he found a difficulty in meeting his ~~liabilities, & appeared in the markets only at uncertain intervals~~ |men at the week's end, & though they had been reduced in number there was barely enough to do for those who remained|' (fo. 4). Originally, his wife had been rather mundanely 'killed by the damp of the mill-stream', but Hardy took the opportunity afforded by the need to change this to make her death the ironic result of her efforts to finance her sons' education, so that she now dies '|worn out by too keen a strain towards these ends|' (fo. 3).

The first leaf of the MS. has an unrevised reference to the 'master-millwright's house'. Since all other references to the millwright between fos. 2 and 13 are revisions, this would suggest that the first leaf is a fair copy made after the rest of the surviving MS. Further evidence of this is that the first word on fo. 2 ('slight') is interlined, indicating that Hardy did not quite manage to fit the whole of the original first leaf into the new one when making his fresh copy. If fo. 1 was rewritten after the remainder of the MS., it would appear that Hardy's final choice of title for the story was made at a very late stage of composition, even after he had produced this relatively clean copy of the first leaf.

One slight revision lowers the father's character still further. On his arrest for disorderly conduct, we were originally told that the one saving grace of the incident had been that, 'as far as it appeared, the millwright had withheld his name' (fo. 23), as if he still had some regard for his family name and his children's reputation, but Hardy altered this passage so that only a newspaper error prevented his identification: 'ꞁthe millwright's name had been printed as Joshua Alburyꞁ' (in a serial proof revision, the surname was said to have been printed as 'Alborough'). Hardy might have introduced this press inaccuracy because he realized that the father could have withheld his name at the time of his arrest but not at his subsequent trial.

Rosa's education is subtly altered in the MS. Originally, she was sent off 'to as good a school as the limited means at their command would afford' (fo. 4), but this was revised to her being placed 'ꞁunder as efficient a tuition at a fashionable watering-place as theꞁ means at their ꞁdisposal could commandꞁ'. A later description of the school as 'good' was changed to 'ꞁhigh-classꞁ' (fo. 7). Both revisions serve to accentuate the social ambition behind the boys' scheme for educating their sister.

A couple of revisions allow Narrobourne to be identified as the actual West Coker. Halborough senior originally announced that he was planning to pass through 'Sherton' on his way from Fountall Gaol (Wells) to Narrobourne, but this was altered in the course of copying to 'the ꞁinterveningꞁ town of Ivell' (fo. 25). Yeovil lies on the direct route from Wells to West Coker, whereas Sherton (Sherborne) is a little to the east of it. The sons later encounter their father on 'the hill' (fo. 26) which was altered to 'ꞁHendcomeꞁ hill' in the MS. The first collected edition of the story identified it as 'Hendford Hill', the real name of a hill leading south-westward out of Yeovil towards West Coker.

Two expletives are cancelled in the MS. Cornelius exclaims 'Just God' (fo. 29) when his father falls in the water, which is a too obviously exultant and outspoken response to the accident, especially for a divinity student. Similarly, a disillusioned Joshua later says 'Damn the Church, she is [...]', which became 'ꞁTo tellꞁ the ꞁtruth, theꞁ Church is' (fo. 36). This revision would appear to be a bowdlerization which also served to remove the unsubtle criticism of Joshua, whose oath so blatantly condemned him from his own lips.

The presentation of the father's drowning is improved by the deletion of a statement, probably to have been attributed to Joshua: 'To think he should just have been resolved upon ruining us all, should have pronounced my disgrace with such exultation' (fo. 30). To have had one of the sons say this while they were waiting for their father to drown would perhaps have been too explicit and heartless in what is already a very callous scene, and Hardy chose instead to portray the relatively silent complicity of the brothers, who understand each other perfectly well without words at this point.

Minor details of plot are revised. Fellmer's late wife was at first said to have died 'after a brief married term of a few months' but this was altered to 'ꞁin the year ~~shortly~~ after her marriage, at the birth of a fragile little girlꞁ' (fo. 15). When Mrs Fellmer first meets Rosa, Hardy originally wrote that she expected to see 'a Dorcas, Rhoda, or Tryphena', but he altered this to read 'a Dorcas, ꞁMartha, orꞁ Rhoda ꞁat the outsideꞁ' (fo. 18). All four names would have served as biblical models of good works, but perhaps 'Tryphena', the name of Hardy's cousin, had acquired personal associations for him. (Incidentally, the change in the sequence of names ensures that the new order remains alphabetical). At the end of the story, Rosa was originally described as the 'late' (fo. 32) curate's sister, but this adjective was deleted. Joshua has moved to another parish, and so is strictly the 'late' curate, but perhaps Hardy decided only at this stage that he would be replaced by his brother, Cornelius, thus making the description of the 'late' curate redundant and confusing (the information about Cornelius taking the vacant curacy is given at the end of the next paragraph).

Serial proof revisions

There are 43 occasions when the serial has a different reading from the MS., and these revisions must have been introduced at the serial proof stage. They mostly involve individual words and are quite minor. Two revisions, however, are worth noting. Hardy deleted the last four interlined words of the following description of the brothers: 'their two rather harsh faces had softened directly they began to speak of their sister, whom they loved more ambitiously than themselves, lif that were possiblel' (fo. 7). The revision serves to remove the outspoken criticism of the brothers and maintain the subtle, balanced depiction of their predicament. The other significant revision to the manuscript at this stage occurs on the final leaf where the serial added Cornelius's comment about seeing his dead father often: '"I see him every night", Cornelius murmured. "Ah, we read our *Hebrews* to little account, Jos! Ὑπεμεινε σταυρον, αισχυνης καταφρονησας. To have *endured* the cross, *despising* the shame – there lay greatness!"' (pp. 559–60). This ending is again altered for the 1894 edition and its significance will be discussed later.

Only one of the MS. variants appears in the collected edition of 1894: a reference to the father as 'old' Halborough, making clear which of the family is speaking, is in the MS. and *1894* but not the serial, and it was added as a marginal emendation to the galley proofs of *1894*. It would appear, then, that the galleys of *1894* were set up from a revised copy of the serial.

The galley proofs of *1894*

The first galley proofs of *1894*, which were formerly in the possession of Hardy's sister, Kate, are now held in the Dorset County Museum. The sheets of 'A Tragedy of Two Ambitions' bear the printers' date stamp 6–8 December 1893. An analysis of the proofs shows that Hardy made the alterations to the serial at three distinct stages when preparing the story for publication in *1894*. The bulk of the revisions were made when preparing a revised copy of the serial which was used to set up the galley proofs. There is no evidence that Hardy consulted the MS., as he did with, for example, 'On the Western Circuit', because there are no occasions when he restored a previously rejected MS. reading to the galley.[5] The next stage is Hardy's marginal emendation of these proofs. These emended proofs must have been the basis of at least a second proof, or revises; these have not survived but their existence can be posited because, on a number of occasions, *1894* has a reading which is different from the emended galley proofs and which must therefore have been introduced at a later stage. I shall indicate, where significant, whether the alterations under discussion were introduced for the first proof stage, or were written by Hardy in the margin of the first proof, or were added to the second proof.

There are two substantial additions to the serial at this first proof stage. One of them concerns Joshua's list of the qualities needed to succeed in the Church. In the serial he had said merely that 'people must believe in you, first of all, as a gentleman, with all their heart and soul and strength' (p. 545). Hardy supplemented this for *1894* so that it now reads thus:

> people must believe in you, first of all, as a gentleman, secondly as a man of means, thirdly as a scholar, fourthly as a preacher, fifthly, perhaps, as a Christian, – but always first as a gentleman, with all their heart and soul and strength. (p. 65)

Kristin Brady explains precisely Hardy's reasons for strengthening the list of obstacles which the brothers must overcome: 'the analysis of Victorian society implicit in this complaint, however unedifying Joshua's unquestioning acceptance of it may sound, defines his difficult position: he and his brother are victims of circumstances that prevent their advancing, except by hypocrisy'.[6]

The other major addition to the serial at this stage concerns the walking-stick of the drowned man which the brothers find has grown into a silver poplar at the end of the story. This detail recalls the Dorset legend about Heedless William, the drunken mail-van driver who ran off the road and drowned in the pond which now bears his name; his whip was said to have stuck in the ground, taken root and become an ash tree.[7] The four paragraphs from 'Why see – it was there I hid his walking-stick' to 'they could not bear to look at it; and they walked away' (p. 86) are new to *1894*. The silver poplar brings together many of the biblical motifs of the story and recalls Aaron's rod, the staff which turned into a snake and proved to the pharaoh that Aaron and Moses were priests of the true God. Kristin Brady again gives a succinct account of the significance of these additions at the end of the story:

> With the 1894 addition of the sapling symbol to the story, Cornelius's exclamation, 'Ah, we read our *Hebrews* to little account, Jos!' comes all the more naturally: the flowering poplar reminds him of Aaron's rod and of what it symbolizes in the biblical text he had so painstakingly translated. This memory leads him to the Epistle's special praise of the New Testament priest who must distinguish himself, like Christ, by enduring the cross, while despising its shame.[8]

All of these additions to the story's conclusion serve to underline through appropriately biblical allusions the utter failure of the brothers' priestly vocation.

When revising the first galley, Hardy made some sixty marginal emendations, of which half are substantive. Although they are nearly all minor changes and involve only a word or two, they nevertheless show Hardy's meticulous regard for the finest nuances of his story. A typical alteration, for instance, concerns Joshua's comment to his brother that 'I don't know why, but when I feel even too sleepy to read a novel I can translate'; obviously realizing that if a man is too sleepy to read he will fall asleep rather than start translating Greek, Hardy alters 'sleepy' to 'dreary' in the margin (*1894*, p. 58).

Another marginal alteration at this stage makes Joshua slightly less smug than he had been in earlier versions, so that we read now of his 'satisfaction' (*1894*, p. 71) at his successes in his new parish of Narrobourne, rather than his 'exultation'. We also learn that his father had 'cajoled' (*1894*, p. 79) his mother rather than 'deceived' her into having a child before their marriage. The presentation of the father's drowning which the brothers passively allow to happen is altered in one important respect: in earlier versions, the father had shouted 'feeble words' when crying for help, but Hardy alters this to 'gurgling words' (*1894*, p. 80) which the brothers cannot help hearing are the sounds of a drowning man, thus heightening their culpability in not acting to save him.

These emended proofs must at this stage have been sent to Harper & Brothers in New York to form the basis of *1894H*, since they are virtually identical in substantives.[9] For the British edition, however, the proofs underwent a further revision, and the following account of these second proofs is therefore an account of the differences between the British and American editions of 1894.

There are eighteen differences between the emended proofs and *1894*, of which eight are substantive. Changes here include increasing the amount of money which the mother has saved as necessary for the boys' university education from £700 to the more realistic, and impressive, sum of £900. The name of the place where the brothers meet their drunken father shortly before his death is changed from the fictitious Hendcome Hill to the real Hendford Hill, a topographical revision which strengthens the identification of the Narrobourne of the story as West Coker, south of Yeovil.

1912 Macmillan Wessex edition

The 1912 Wessex edition of *Life's Little Ironies* makes eleven further alterations to 'A Tragedy of Two Ambitions'. The most interesting is the addition of a sentence which had not been in any earlier versions: when the father falls in the water and is drowning, the brothers hesitate to rescue him and, we now read for the first time, 'In their pause there had been time to save him twice over' (p. 100). Later, their sister Rosa explains how she heard a man's cry at that time when she was sitting in the manor house, and the 1912 addition that the cry was 'in the distant meadow' (p. 103) makes it more credible why she was unable to tell whether the man was calling her name.[10]

Notes

1 *Life*, p. 276.

2 *Letters*, I, 178.

3 *Letters*, I, 179.

4 Purdy, p. 83, and Alan Manford (1990), 89–100.

5 There is one insignificant exception to this: the MS. and *1894* both read 'old Halborough' (*1894*, p. 78), whereas the serial omitted the adjective.

6 Brady, p. 117.

7 See Denys Kay-Robinson (1972), p. 59.

8 Brady, p. 118.

9 There are three minor substantive differences between the emended proofs and the New York edition which were probably the result of in-house editing or compositorial error; *1894H* reads 'saw-mill' (p. 45; all other versions read 'saw-mills'), 'the waves of the ocean' (p. 48; 'the waves of ocean') and 'prospect' (p. 64; 'prospects').

10 For the sake of a complete record, the other revisions to *1894* for the Wessex edition are as follows (*1912* is quoted first, and the pagination is that of *1912*): "ee/ye' (p. 85; two more instances on p. 98); 'the churchyard/churchyard' (p. 88); 'O/Oh' (p. 89); 'gipsy wife/wife' (p. 92); 'service/lessons' (p. 95); 'and neighbour's wife/and his wife' (p. 101); 'further/farther' (p. 101).

CHAPTER 22

'On the Western Circuit'

Thomas Hardy presented the manuscript of his short story, 'On the Western Circuit', to Manchester Central Public Library in 1911.[1] The story had been written in the latter half of 1890 or the early months of 1891,[2] and the history of its composition, serialization and collected publications is especially complex because Hardy introduced important alterations to the text at each stage of its transmission. The most interesting and extensive of these revisions concern the story's bowdlerization for the serial versions and Hardy's later partial restoration of his original conception of the story.

All versions of 'On the Western Circuit' except the serials tell the story of how a young illiterate maid, Anna, becomes pregnant by a barrister, Charles Raye, and persuades her married employer, Edith Harnham, to write letters to Raye in Anna's name, unknown to him. As Norman Page paraphrases the remainder of the story, Edith 'finds herself pouring her deepest feelings into the letters and forming a close if one-sided attachment to the young man whom she has seen only once and briefly. It is not until he has married the girl [...] that the truth emerges, and he finds himself, like his true correspondent, "chained" for the rest of his days to an incompatible spouse.'[3] This tale of looming illegitimacy and vicarious infidelity was bowdlerized for the serial versions, with Edith becoming a respectable widow and Anna merely a young maiden pining for her lover in London.

In conversation with Vere H. Collins on 19 August 1922, Hardy mentioned that he had consulted a judge, Sir Francis Jeune (husband of his friend, Lady Mary Jeune), before publishing the story:

> When I had written the story I gave it to Sir Francis Jeune to read for fear I had gone wrong in the legal details. Jeune returned the MS. to me and said that the only mistake I had made was in saying that Ray's [sic] absence at the next assize town was not noticed. (You remember he remained behind.) Jeune said that it would have been noticed, but that I could make it all right by saying that he had to stop on for an arbitration case. That's why I put this in. Some years later I told another judge – Cave, I think – about it, and said how glad I was I had not fallen into a pitfall. I read him out the passage. He said that the introduction of the arbitration case was quite unnecessary: no one would have noticed his absence. (Collins, pp. 77–8)

The manuscript which Hardy showed Jeune must have been an early draft, because the extant MS., a fair copy, explains at the end of Section I that Raye was 'detained in Melchester by a small arbitration' (fo. 7). Hardy first met Sir Lewis William Cave, a judge on the Western Circuit, when he dined with him in Dorchester in November 1891 during the Dorset Assizes of that autumn (see

Life, p. 251, and *Letters*, I, 247). It might well have been on such an appropriate occasion (rather than 'some years later') that Hardy discussed his story with him, especially as it was only a few days before its first publication; in any event, Cave died in 1897, so Hardy had several later opportunities to alter the phrase about Raye's arbitration case if he wished, but it remained in all editions of the story.

The published versions of 'On the Western Circuit' which have textual significance are as follows:

EIM *English Illustrated Magazine*, December 1891, pp. 275–88, with four illustrations by Walter Paget.

HW *Harper's Weekly*, 28 November 1891, pp. 946–8, with one illustration by W.T. Smedley.

1894 *Life's Little Ironies* (London: Osgood, McIlvaine, 1894), pp. 87–122. Published at 6s. in an edition of 2000 copies on 22 February 1894.

1894H *Life's Little Ironies* (New York: Harper & Brothers, 1894), pp. 76–106. Published in March 1894.

1896 *Life's Little Ironies* (London: Osgood, McIlvaine, 1896), pp. 87–122. Volume XIV in the Wessex Novels, the first uniform and complete edition of Hardy's works. Plates of the first edition were used.

1912 *Life's Little Ironies* (London: Macmillan, 1912), pp. 109–37. Volume VIII of the Wessex edition.

In addition, a revised typescript which was the printers' copy for the serials is in private ownership, and the galley proofs of *1894,* showing Hardy's marginal emendations, are located in the Dorset County Museum.

The manuscript

An excellent description of the Manchester manuscript and the changes which Hardy made in the course of writing it is given by Alan Manford. It consists of 33 leaves, numbered 1–32, with an additional leaf, 9a. There is a passage of eight lines written on the verso of fo. 9 and marked for insertion on the recto (see my comments on the typescript below). It is not, as Purdy implies (p. 83), the printers' copy for any of the printed versions of the story, for reasons which will be explained later. Below the story's title, 'On the Western Circuit', are two deleted ones: the earliest title is 'The Amanuensis', which Hardy probably rejected because it is not an accurate description of Edith's role, in that she does much more than merely write down Anna's words. The next title was 'The Writer of the Letters', and we know from the evidence of the typescript (see below) that Hardy deleted it only at a late stage of composition. Both of these rejected titles foreground Edith's role in the story, but the title which Hardy eventually chose moves the emphasis towards Raye, and this is in line with changes to the end of the story (discussed more fully below), where an additional final leaf allows Raye, not Edith, to speak the closing words.

Hardy sent the story to the literary agent, A.P. Watt, in early September 1891 to arrange its simultaneous publication in Britain and America,[4] but the extant manuscript could not have been used as the printers' copy for either of the serialized versions since there was so much bowdlerization in the latter. This intermediate printers' copy is extant but is not available for study: it presumably includes all the alterations for the bowdlerized passages, of which there is no indication at all in the MS., but Hardy also took the opportunity to revise many other aspects of the story, for numerous readings in the MS. are unique to it. Often these are quite minor revisions but they reveal Hardy's scrupulous re-writing for the serial versions; for instance, in the first sentence in the MS. the time of year is given as 'one |dark| October evening' whereas all other versions read 'an October evening'. The serial versions, therefore, were not altered only to accommodate the bowdlerization but frequently differ from the MS. elsewhere.

The most substantial reading which is unique to the MS. is a passage of five lines on fo. 22 describing Edith's frame of mind when writing to Raye on Anna's behalf. The serials (and the MS.) explain how Edith 'replied from the promptings of her own heart and no other', and the MS. continues

> the telepathetic these effusions being stimulated |strengthened vitalized| by the assumption that the conditions of her relationship with him were those of Anna's. They produced a fresh response from the barrister, full of all the cherishing assurances natural likely to allay the anxiety of a young thing who had such claims upon him. as Anna

This passage could have stood innocently enough in the bowdlerized serials, for Edith would then have been imagining herself as being in love with Raye, rather than being pregnant by him. Hardy chose not to restore it in either of the 1894 versions, the first collected publications of the story, and there are many other instances when Hardy rewrote the bowdlerized passages rather than simply restoring MS. readings.

There are no indications in the MS. of any of the numerous bowdlerizing revisions which needed to be performed for the serials, possibly because Hardy made all such changes in a later copy of the story which was used to set up the serials' typescript. The first such revision occurs on fo. 5, where a reference to 'Mrs Harnham' is supplemented in the serials by the information that she 'was a young widow-lady', and later in the same paragraph Hardy added an allusion in the serials to 'the loss of Mr. Harnham some fifteen months ago'. Such a length of time obviously allows Edith a seemly period of mourning before she becomes infatuated with Raye, but it also avoids the delicious ethical dilemma of whether a recent widow should not be writing on mourning stationery, even if she is signing the letters with someone else's name (Hardy himself was to use such stationery for just over a year following the deaths of his mother in 1904 and his first wife in 1912). The length of widowhood in the serials permits Hardy to observe the proprieties, however tongue-in-cheek he may have been. A consequence of Edith being a widow rather than a wife was that Hardy had to remove all references to her husband, and he chose instead to make him her uncle, but the ease with which he achieved this straightforward substitution reveals a great deal about the marital relationship in the unbowdlerized versions of the story.

Since Anna does not become pregnant in the serials, her relationship with Raye is quite different from the other versions of the story. Raye engages in a harmless flirtation with her, and Edith initially concocts the letters merely to maintain his interest in Anna and save her from a broken heart. For instance, in the manuscript Raye indulges in what he regards as a 'harmful passion' and 'much he deplored it' (fo. 12), but in the serials he is simply indulging a 'passing fancy' for her, and we learn that 'much he deplored trifling with her feelings for the sake of kisses upon her red lips'. The revised nature of their relationship obliged Hardy both to omit MS. readings and to create new ones. Thus, there is no need in the serials for Raye to feel that 'he could not absolutely desert her' (fo. 12), since he is not committed to her in any way, while the serials' description of 'a flirtation which had so unsettled the pretty little creature' would have been impossible in the manuscript, where Anna's condition is so much more serious. Since the serial version omits Anna's tearful confession of pregnancy, Hardy needed to find another reason for Edith to become so concerned about her welfare: she is distressed to see 'how the girl's happiness hung on this quickly matured attachment' and realizes that it is imperative 'to keep the young man's romantic interest in Anna alive' (this replaces the more pragmatic MS. reading: 'to keep the young man faithful', fo. 20). Edith's excuse in the serials, that she deceived Raye to 'save such a simple girl from misery', hardly justifies 'ruining' him, whereas in the MS. she acted more reasonably 'to save the honour of such a simple girl' (fo. 29).

Deletions within the manuscript reveal Hardy's changing conception of the story in the course of composition. Originally, there was a greater emphasis on the physical nature of the relationship between Raye and Anna: on fo. 12, Hardy twice in the same paragraph cancelled the information that Raye 'had caressed her', suggesting that he had been keen to use the phrase but had thought better of it almost immediately (he replaced the two deletions with '|& feeling a violent fancy for her had|' and '|had in brief, won her entirely|'). Lower down the same leaf, there is a blunt summary of Raye's seduction of her which was later deleted: 'However, the thing was done.' The most significant deletion, though, occurs at the foot of fo. 31, where Hardy wrote 'The End' before cancelling it and adding the eight lines on the final leaf, fo. 32. Originally, the story was to have concluded with Edith saying

"Ah:– my husband. I forgot I had a husband!" ~~she whispered.~~ |murmured she.| "Yes. ~~She~~ |Anna| is married," ~~Mrs Harnham replied~~ |she–added|. (fo. 31)

The new ending shows Raye and Anna in the train compartment on their way to their honeymoon, and the last words of the story are now Raye's explanation of what he is doing: "'Reading over all ~~your~~ |those| tender letters to me |signed 'Anna'|'" (fo. 32). The deletion and insertions here capture precisely the pathos of his position: the letters are not *hers*, but merely bear her name, as she now bears his, indissolubly. This revised ending lends an ironic symmetry to the story: Edith begins by being unhappily married, and all that her 'impassioned dream' (fo. 31) has achieved is to ensure the same fate for Anna and Raye.

The scene on the train invites sympathy for Raye, perhaps for the first time, and Hardy seems to have wanted to end the story on a note of resigned stoicism. The closing words were at one time to have been 'in the voice of a hopeless man' (fo. 32), but they were deleted so that the MS. now ends with the unemotional 'he replied', which gives no melodramatic expression to his feelings (this was altered again in published versions: see 'Preparing the galley proofs of *1894*' below). The increased sympathy for Raye is also assisted by the insertion of Edith's acknowledgement on the previous leaf that '|I have ruined him! [...] I have ruined him|', which is in turn an echo of her interlined comment to him that '|you are ruined|' (fo. 30; perhaps Hardy intended Raye to be an ironic reversal of the 'ruined maid'). Raye's response to her again illustrates his stoical indifference: '"|What matter!" he said shrugging his shoulders. "It serves me right|."' This new and repeated reference to Raye being 'ruined' probably led Hardy to omit from all published versions an earlier phrase which stands uncancelled in the MS.: Anna is said to be delighted to have 'her reputation saved' (fo. 31), but this stark contrast between the 'saved' Anna and the 'ruined' Raye is too simplistic and makes her seem callous.

The typescript

The printers' copy for the serials is a revised typescript which is not currently available for study. It was sold at Sotheby's in 1988 and remains in private ownership in the United States. The Sotheby Sales Catalogue for 15 December 1988 reproduces a short extract of eleven typed lines which seems to indicate that the TS. was a direct copy of the MS., which Hardy then revised by marginal or interlined alterations. The catalogue gives the following description of the TS.:

HARDY (THOMAS) TYPESCRIPT, WITH AUTOGRAPH REVISIONS, BEING THE PRINTER'S COPY, OF HARDY'S SHORT STORY "ON THE WESTERN CIRCUIT", the original deleted title reading "The Writer of the Letters", occasional autograph revisions, deletions and insertions throughout, some extending to several lines and one whole page (numbered 27-28) autograph, the typescript bearing printer's cast-off marks and the names of various compositors, with inky finger marks also indicating use as printer's copy, *43 pages, 4to, one page trimmed to half-size, stab holes, marginal dust-staining on a few pages where exposed, c.1891-1894*

[...] Hardy's autograph insertions here also support Purdy's comment about the manuscript in Manchester, that "both the mistaken holding of Mrs. Harnham's hand and the final glimpse of Anna and Raye appear to have been afterthoughts". Hardy's autograph additions here contain some of the sentences which were not deemed suitable for the original periodical publication ("... She wished she had married a London man who knew the subtleties of love-making as they were evidently known to him who had mistakenly caressed her hand...", "... she had still remained a woman whose deeper nature had never been stirred..."). (p. 55)

The catalogue is mistaken in its assertion that these last two additions did not appear in the serials, and it is further mistaken in suggesting that 'She wished she had married a London man' was not originally in the MS., but it does at least confirm that the rest of the two sentences were indeed autograph additions to the TS.

The TS. was purchased by David J. Holmes, a book-dealer of Philadelphia, who later sold it to Howard Lakin of Lakin & Marley Rare Books, Mill Valley, California. Mr Lakin has kindly informed me that the TS. has no pagination or date, and that it shows 'numerous and substantial autograph changes throughout [...]. In total, 38 of the 43 pages in this slightly worn and soiled but extraordinary manuscript bear Hardy's deletions and insertions.' A facsimile of the TS. is in the British Library (RP 4044), but access to it was reserved until January 1996, and will still require the permission of the owner.

The Sotheby catalogue's extract of eleven typed lines and their marginal or interlined revision describes the moment when Raye unwittingly holds Edith's hand in the belief that it is Anna's (the catalogue does not reproduce what are presumably the first 33 words of the lengthy insertion, apparently because they are written in a column too far to the left of the page to be accommodated in the facsimile):

> other than smile at the accident; but neither spokel, [...] also knew that from the position of the girl he had no other thought than that the imprisoned hand was Anna's. ~~Not con~~ What prompted her to ~~not be~~ [?] ǁrefrain fromǁ undeceiving him she could ~~not~~ ǁbarelyǁ [?] hardlyǁ tell. ~~Presently~~, Not content with holding the hand, he ǁplayfullyǁ ~~put two~~ ǁslipped twoǁ of his fingers inside her glove, against her palm. Thus matters continued till the pressure lessened, butǁ Several minutes passed before the crowd thinned sufficiently to allow Mrs Harnham to withdraw.
>
> "How did they get to know each other, I wonder?" she mused as she retreated. "Anna is really very forward - and he very nice."
>
> She was so greatly struck with the young barrister's manner, voice, ~~or winning quality of some sort~~ ǁwith the fascination of his touchǁ, that instead of re-entering the house she turned back again and observed ~~them~~ ǁthe pairǁ from ~~an unseen~~ ǁa screenedǁ nook. Really she argued (being little ~~more experienced~~ ǁless impulsiveǁ than Anna herself) [p. 55]

Hardy then noted most of these revisions at the appropriate point in the MS. by making a fair copy of them in pencil, either as interlineations or, in the case of the lengthy one, as an addition to the verso of fo. 9. The only alteration in the TS. extract which he did not copy on to the MS. in this way is the change of 'them' to 'the pair'. This allows us to see an important feature of the manuscript which Alan Manford's 1990 study, written before the TS. was known to be extant, could not have described: at least some (and possibly all) of the manuscript's many pencilled revisions are copies of the changes which Hardy had previously made to the TS. These pencilled revisions might reasonably be seen as a group of simultaneous changes representing a later stage in the story's evolution, made after the MS. was completed and the TS. was revised. Studied cautiously in this light, such pencil insertions in the MS. might allow us to recover some of the changes which Hardy made when revising the TS. We cannot, however, recover *all* such changes in this way, because (as we saw with the substitution of 'the pair' for 'them') not all of the TS. revisions were copied into the MS.: for instance, of the two autograph additions described in the Sotheby catalogue, only the first was copied.

There are about a score of pencil additions to the MS., and none of them involves bowdlerization, which suggests that such changes had already been made to the copy of the story from which the typescript was prepared. Indeed, some of the pencil revisions indicate for the first time a physical basis to Edith's fascination with Raye, giving a new and more daring dimension to her feelings which had been made possible precisely *because of* the bowdlerization, as if Hardy were trying to take advantage of the need to change her from a wife into a widow: now that she is no longer a married woman, Raye can hold her hand. The first reference to the touch was quoted in the Sotheby catalogue, and it is significant that there is a revision to the fair copy of this insertion on the verso of fo. 9 in which the description of how Raye 'put' two fingers inside Edith's glove is changed to 'playfully slipped'. This revision is also noted on the TS., indicating that it was made after the rest of the insertion had been copied to the MS.: Hardy was apparently keen to refine the scene even at such a late stage of composition. Once Hardy had introduced the touch, he then added several more references to it, three of which are marked in pencil in the MS.: Edith is greatly struck 'with the fascination of his touch' (fo. 9) and she wishes that she had married a London man 'who knew the subtleties of love-making as they were [evidently] known to him who had mistakenly caressed her hand' (fo. 11). Later, we learn that he had attracted her 'by his looks & voice – above all by his tender touch' (fo. 19; 'tender' appeared as 'wooing' in *EIM*, though not *HW*, a revision which was probably made at the proof stage to avoid repeating 'tender' later in the same sentence). The serials also include the statement that 'There had been a magic in his wooing touch', but this is not copied on to the MS. (it is either a TS. revision or a proof addition).

Serial versions

The two serial versions of 'On the Western Circuit', *EIM* and *HW*, are not identical; there are 31 sentences which have different substantive readings. However, the differences are rarely more than a word or two, except for the complete, and unique, sentence in *HW* describing Edith's pain when Raye accuses her of having 'ruined' him: 'Her anguish seemed to thrill the very furniture' (p. 948). On balance, *HW* is closer to the MS. than is *EIM;* of all the pairs of variant readings which differentiate the two serial versions, twice as many of the *HW* readings are found in the MS., rather than the *EIM* wording. Thus, *EIM* apparently underwent further proof revision after *HW* had been sent to America.

There are some variants, however, of which neither is to be found in the MS.: these are mainly in those parts of the serial which have been bowdlerized and therefore do not appear in the MS. It is interesting to observe that Hardy felt obliged to prepare two differently bowdlerized versions, one for Britain and another for the United States, and, if anything, *HW* is slightly more toned down than *EIM*. For instance, the British version talks of Raye's 'passion' for Anna and the powerful effect on Edith of his 'wooing touch', but *HW* describes more tamely his 'attachment' to the girl and his 'tender touch', which are both MS. readings. Similarly, where Raye in *EIM* desires 'kisses', in the American version he desires merely 'a kiss' (it is *HW*'s readings in all of these instances which were to be preserved in subsequent editions, making Raye altogether a more lukewarm lover at the beginning). There is a slightly different shape to the progress of Raye's emotions in the two serials: in *EIM*, he starts out quite warmly and then marries Anna because he feels sorry for her, but in *HW*, he is more of a trifler at the start and only later does he become romantically involved. Thus, the British version talks of his initial passion which gives way to a feeling that 'she should not suffer for his sake' and so he marries her out of 'compassionate folly'. These two phrases are given a quite different emphasis in *HW*, where he feels that 'he could not live without her' (the MS. reading) and so marries her out of 'romantic folly' (the MS., though, had talked of him making 'the best of a bad piece of business', fo. 26). Again, it is the American reading which was to be retained in *1894*. A rather bathetic variant illustrates the more emotionally involved and love-sick Raye who is depicted at the start of the British version: in *EIM,* he 'would enter the dim religious nave of the Law Courts because it was something like her cathedral' (he had met Anna in Melchester), but in *HW* we learn merely that he 'would enter the dim religious nave of the Law Courts by the north door' (which is the MS. and *1894* reading).

One significant difference between the two serials occurs in the list of possible consequences when lovers first meet. When Raye and Anna meet at the start of the British serial, they look at each other with that 'unmistakable expression' which leads to such 'passion, heart-ache, union, disunion, devotion, overpopulation, drudgery, *discontent*, resignation, *as none can foretell*' (my italics). The American serial, however, speaks not of 'discontent' but of 'content', which is the MS. reading. The collected editions of 1894 follow *HW*, but the last four words of the serials (also in the MS.) are replaced by 'despair' in *1894*. Incidentally, the list in the MS. uniquely included 'procreation' before 'devotion'.

In *EIM*, Anna speaks occasionally in dialect, but *HW* gives her the same standard English that she had in the MS., so *HW*'s 'it has been' becomes *EIM*'s 'it has b'en', and 'plenty of money' becomes 'plenty o' money'. These two instances of dialect in *EIM* occur when Anna is speaking to Raye, and Hardy preferred the standard *HW* reading for *1894*, no doubt thinking it inappropriate for her not to speak standard English to him when she has been taught to do so by her mistress, thus making it more plausible that Raye should believe her capable of writing such literate letters to him. The collected editions of 1894, however, also introduce some dialect for the first time; when she is speaking to Edith, Anna in *1894* slips back into dialect: in the serial versions, Anna had spoken to Edith of that 'niceness' in her letters which 'I can't make up out of my own head', but in the 1894 editions this reads 'I can't for the life o' me make up out of my own head' (*1894*, p. 110). This distinction between Anna's use of standard English to Raye and some dialect to Edith did not exist before *1894*.

Preparing the galley proofs of *1894*

The first galley proofs of *1894* have survived (they are held in the Dorset County Museum), and the sheets of 'On the Western Circuit' bear the printers' date stamp 12 December 1893. An analysis of the proofs shows that Hardy made the alterations to the serial version at three distinct stages when preparing the story for publication in *1894*. The bulk of the revisions were made when preparing a revised copy of the story which was used to set up the galley proofs. The next stage was Hardy's marginal emendation of these proofs. These emended proofs must have been the basis of at least a second proof, or revises; these have not survived but their existence can be posited because, on a number of occasions, *1894* has a reading which is different from the emended galley proofs and which must have been introduced at a later stage.

The relation of the MS. and the serials to the galley proofs of *1894* is very complicated. The MS. and both serials each contributed unique substantive readings to the galleys. It would appear that Hardy consulted all three when preparing printers' copy.

From the relative contribution of the two serials to the galleys, it is possible to make a conjecture. There are more than 200 variations in accidentals between *EIM* and *HW* but only on 24 occasions does *1894* choose the *HW* variant. Moreover, there are only forty variations in accidentals between *EIM* and *1894*, a remarkably small number. It would seem then that *EIM* is probably the basis for the galleys, and Hardy incorporated into it a number of alternative readings from the MS. and from *HW*, as well as adding a number of new passages, mainly to remove bowdlerized scenes.

One can reconstruct an image of Hardy scrupulously collating the MS. with the serial versions to produce the galley proofs of *1894*: excluding the frequent substitutions of 'husband' for 'uncle', and counting only substantive readings, there are thirteen occasions when Hardy restored a MS. reading which had been in neither of the serials. Many of these restored passages occur in consecutive clusters, as if Hardy kept taking a temporary preference for the MS. version before changing his mind again and choosing to rewrite rather than restore. There are also four partial restorations, and, most interestingly, there are three places where he restored a reading which he had initially deleted in the MS. It would seem, then, that Hardy prepared *1894* by carefully comparing the alternative readings of the MS. and the serials, and if he chose not to restore a

MS. reading, it was a *positive* rejection of it, not simply an oversight. In total, *1894* makes about 150 substantive changes to the serial, including the restored passages but excluding the rewriting of some bowdlerized scenes.

The three readings deleted within the MS. and omitted from the serials but restored to *1894* are all single words, and they show the degree of care which Hardy put into the revision. In the MS., Edith Harnham is described as being 'sensitive - |& mobile-|lipped' (fo. 8), which is what the serials read, but *1894* has 'with sensitive lips' (p. 95).[5] The MS. similarly referred to 'the luxury |pleasure| of writing' (fo. 18) to Raye which Edith enjoyed, and this is what the serials read, but *1894* restores the deleted 'luxury' (p. 107), heightening Edith's sense of indulgence. Another original reference to her 'pleasure' in the next sentence is also altered in *1894* to 'luxury', although it had remained unchanged in both the MS. and the serials. Finally, at the end of the story, Edith in the MS. was said to have 'whispered |murmured|' (fo. 31) to herself that she had forgotten about having a husband; this passage was omitted in the serials for reasons of bowdlerization, but Hardy brought back the deleted 'whispered' (p. 121) when revising for *1894*. It is apparent that Hardy could never desist from revising, and his first deleted thoughts in the MS. could eventually regain favour and become the 'definitive' version of the Wessex edition.

There are three ways in which Hardy altered the serial when removing the bowdlerized passages for the collected editions of 1894: he would either restore the exact MS. reading, or he would partially do so, or he would give an entirely new reading (he chose each of these procedures in roughly equal proportions). Ignoring changes which are simply widow/wife substitutions and the like, there are more than twenty occasions on which Hardy altered the serial to remove bowdlerization, ranging in length from a single word to a passage of four paragraphs; on eight of these occasions, Hardy restored the exact MS. reading, and, significantly, these restorations constitute eight of the last nine alterations he made, as if he decided against any new revision as the story neared its end and simply substituted previous readings instead.[6]

With one exception, these restored MS. readings are rarely more than a phrase in length; for instance, in the serial, Edith had exclaimed about Raye that 'I wish he was mine – I wish he was!' while the 1894 editions have her exclaiming about Anna's forthcoming baby by Raye that 'I wish it was mine – I wish it was!'[7] which is what the MS. read. Similarly, where the serial talks of 'the formalities of the wedding', *1894* describes 'the formalities of the wedding – or rather ratification of a previous union' (p. 116).[8] The four removals of bowdlerized parts in the final section of the story are all achieved by returning to the precise (or even a deleted) MS. reading. The most interesting of these is the deletion which is restored. Edith's penultimate comment that '"Ah – my husband! I forgot I had a husband" she whispered to herself' (p. 121) could not of course have been said in the serial, since she is a widow speaking there to her uncle. As we saw earlier, 'whispered' was in fact deleted in the MS. in favour of 'murmured' but was finally chosen in *1894*. Incidentally, in the MS. Edith's comment about remembering she had a husband occurs three sentences later than in *1894*,[9] so Hardy returned to the MS. wording but placed it slightly earlier when revising the serial.

There are two long revisions which Hardy made to the serial, and they are each about three or four paragraphs in length. On both occasions, Hardy partly restored MS. readings but also added some new material. The first of these is near the end of Section IV of the story, where Anna confesses to Edith that she is pregnant and begs her to write to Raye. In the serials, Anna simply told Edith that she wished to see her lover about 'something' and asked her to write. The serials then read thus:

> This Mrs. Harnham did, although she had written but such a short time previously; and the result was that Raye sent a hasty note to say how much he was won by her sweetness; it made him feel that he must run down for a day to see her as requested.

In *1894*, Hardy replaced this with the following three paragraphs, and the words in italics indicate those which are also present in the original MS. account of this scene:

> There was *a strange anxiety* in her *manner* which did not escape Mrs. Harnham, and *ultimately resolved itself into a flood of tears. Sinking down at Edith's knees, she made confession* that the result of *her relations with her lover* it *would soon* become necessary to *disclose.*
>
> Edith Harnham *was generous enough* to be very far from inclined to cast Anna *adrift* at this conjuncture. *No true woman* ever is so inclined from her own *personal point of view, however prompt she may be* in taking such steps to *safeguard* those *dear to her.* Although she had written to Raye so short a time previously, she instantly penned another Anna-note *hinting* clearly though *delicately the state of affairs.*
>
> Raye replied by a hasty line to say how much he was affected by her news: he felt that he must run down to see her almost immediately.[10]

The second lengthy alteration concerns Raye's reaction to receiving the news that Anna is pregnant at the start of Section V. In the serials this part of the story simply says that 'The damps of winter, aggravated, perhaps, by her secret heart-sickness at her lover's non-appearance, made Anna unwell' (the last word in *HW* reads 'ill'). *1894* replaces this with the following (again, italics indicate those words found also in the MS.):

> The letter *moved Raye considerably when it reached him. The intelligence itself* had affected him less than her unexpected *manner of* treating him in relation to it. The absence of any *word of reproach, the devotion to his interests,* the *self-sacrifice* apparent in every line, all *made up a nobility of character* that he had never dreamt of finding in womankind.
>
> '*God forgive me!*' he said tremulously. '*I have been a wicked wretch. I did not know she was such a treasure as this!*'
>
> He reassured her instantly; declaring *that he would not of course desert her,* that he *would provide a home for her* somewhere. Meanwhile *she was to stay where she was as long as her mistress* would allow her.

> But a *misfortune supervened* in this direction. Whether *an inkling* of Anna's circumstances *reached the knowledge of* Mrs. Harnham's husband or not cannot be said, but the girl was compelled, in spite of Edith's *entreaties, to leave the house*.[11]

It is apparent that here, and in the previous example, Hardy altered the bowdlerized passages by writing out the scene as it was in the MS., but changing the original wording frequently. He performed a similar task when describing Edith's 'strange position' in writing to Raye. In the serial versions, she is shown as corresponding 'with a man not her lover, in terms which were those of a devoted sweetheart', but *1894* reads '*with a man not her husband, in terms which were virtually those of a wife*, concerning a condition that was not Edith's at all' (italics indicate MS. reading).[12] In other words, the first two clauses of this alteration to the serial are to be found in the MS., while the third is new.

Another partial restoration of a passage bowdlerized in the serial is *1894*'s comment that, after seducing Anna, Raye will visit her again: 'He could not desert her now' (p. 101). This sentence is entirely missing from the serial versions, but it has its source in the MS., which reads 'He could not absolutely desert her if he had a ~~sp~~ throb of good feeling left in him' (fo. 12). Other partial restorations of the MS. not connected with removing the serial's bowdlerization confirm Hardy's working methods here. Compare, for instance, the following three descriptions of Raye's intentions towards Anna after seducing her:

MS.	Serials	1894 editions
Conduct of which a week earlier he would not have believed himself capable threw him into a state of the greatest depression.	Thoughts of a frivolous flirtation, on which a week earlier he would not have believed himself capable of wasting his time, threw him into a state of dissatisfaction.	Thoughts of unpremeditated conduct, of which a week earlier he would not have believed himself capable, threw him into a mood of dissatisfied depression.[13]

In producing *1894*, Hardy seems to have collated the MS. with the serials, retaining words unique to each and also adding new readings. In the opening of the *1894* reading in the table above, for instance, 'Thoughts' is the serial reading and 'conduct' is reintroduced from the MS., while 'unpremeditated' is original. Similarly, *1894*'s 'dissatisfied depression' conflates the MS. 'depression' and the serial's 'dissatisfaction'.

The third and final way in which Hardy removed the serial's bowdlerization was to ignore the MS. altogether and instead insert original text into *1894* to replace the serial's wording. For instance, the comment about Edith's husband that 'Mrs. Harnham did not care much about him' (p. 93) is unique to *1894* and fills the place of the serial's description of how her uncle lived with her temporarily. Another addition of new material serves to make the pregnant Anna both more injured and more pathetic than in the serial, where she was merely love-sick: the serial's account of Edith blaming herself for not interfering in 'a flirtation which had so unsettled the pretty little creature' reads in *1894* 'a flirtation which had resulted so seriously for the poor little creature in her charge' (p. 106). There is no trace of this in the MS. Similarly, the serial's remark about Edith's husband that 'He had died, and she had still remained a woman' becomes in *1894* a description of how the fact of Edith's marriage to her wealthy wine-merchant (who is of course still alive in the unbowdlerized version of the tale) had left her unfulfilled: 'That contract had left her still a woman' (p. 108). The addition here of the legal view of marriage as a contract shows Hardy extending the imagery he had used throughout the story: as Kristin Brady has remarked, 'The very title "On the Western Circuit" and the unobtrusive but deliberate use of legal language throughout the narrative invites the reader to analyse events as though in a court room.'[14]

Quite apart from the need to remove bowdlerization, Hardy took the opportunity to make *1894* more sexually explicit even than the MS. had been. It is only in *1894*, for instance, that we learn how the fact that Raye 'had been able to seduce another woman in two days was his crowning though unrecognized fascination for her as the she-animal' (p. 108: this is a very late addition – see the section on galley proof revisions below). The description of Raye's seduction of Anna also becomes more direct in *1894*: the MS. tells us how he had 'won her entirely' (fo. 12) which reads in *EIM* as 'won her heart entirely' and in *HW* as 'won her heart', carefully omitting any sexual implication, but *1894* explicitly states 'won her, body and soul' (p. 101).[15]

Hardy slightly altered the characterization of his central three figures when revising for *1894*. Edith becomes more stimulated by her sense of wrong in being attracted to Raye: whereas in earlier versions she had simply found Raye to be 'very nice', she now thinks of him as 'very wicked and nice' (p. 98). She also feels less guilty about allowing Anna to become involved with Raye: in the MS. and the serials, she had 'blamed herself much', but in *1894* she merely 'blamed herself' (p. 106). Similarly, she no longer feels 'seriously bound to accede' to Anna's request to write to Raye in her name, the adverb being omitted in *1894*. Three changes show Edith being less scrupulous in writing letters for Anna and showing her what she has written. In the MS. and the serials, she at first sends Anna exact copies of her replies to Raye and then continues to send her rough copies, always consulting her about the contents of the letters, but in *1894* she at first sends only rough copies and then fails to send her details of many letters altogether.

The other two central characters are also more sharply defined in *1894* than they were previously. Anna is shallower, being now merely 'in distress' (p. 114) rather than 'in deep distress' as she had previously been, and we also learn for the first time that she writes 'with the ideas of a goose' (p. 118). Raye becomes much more emotional about Edith and his blighted future at the end of the story, and he is much more involved with her than he had been in earlier versions. He describes himself and Edith as 'devoted lovers', tells her that he has married her 'in soul' as well as in spirit and addresses her as 'O my cruel one' (pp. 119–20), all for the first time. The last three words of the story show him reading over the letters with 'dreary resignation' (p. 122), which in the serial versions had been the more stoical 'dry resignation'. (The MS. has neither of these, ending with 'he replied', although a heavily scored out final line seems to add 'in the voice of a hopeless man', fo. 32.) Hardy also made Edith more passionate at the end of *1894*: whereas earlier her face had shown 'her miserable sense' of the end of her dream, we now hear how she 'showed the very stupor of grief, her lips still tingling from the desperate pressure of his kiss' (p. 121). None of these changes has any relation to removing a bowdlerized passage in the serial, for in each case the serials read the same as the MS.; they are original additions to the story in 1894, showing Hardy's increasing frankness in portraying passion.

Revision of the galley proofs of *1894*

Hardy's marginal emendations to the proofs of the story number approximately forty, of which three-quarters are substantive. One of them concerns the honeymoon destination of Raye and Anna. In the serials they were to have honeymooned in Tunbridge Wells, but the galley proof has them going instead to Solentsea. Hardy amended this in the margin to 'Knollsea' (Swanage) which is what eventually appeared in *Life's Little Ironies*. Solentsea therefore only ever appeared in the galley proof of the story and was never in any published version. The wider significance of this revision is discussed above in Chapter 18 on 'An Imaginative Woman'.

The remainder of the marginal insertions show, among other things, Hardy making last-minute alterations to his conception of the relationship between Raye and Anna: he is made a slightly keener lover, and she is made more stupid. He now '*asked for another letter*' (italics indicate inserted words) and promised that he would try to see her again '*on* some *near* day'. Anna, however, is found at the end to be able to write only 'in the characters *and spelling* of a child of eight, *and with the* ~~incapacity~~ ‖*ideas*‖ *of a goose*'. Her apparent education is stressed when Raye's sister remarks that she seems 'fairly *educated*' (removing the earlier 'fairly ladylike') '*thanks to these elementary schools*' (ironically, since Anna has not been to school at all). By a neat inversion, there is now less emphasis on Raye's education, and a description of him as 'qualified' is changed to '*well-bred*'. After the revelation of her illiteracy, Anna is made a more pathetic figure, clasping his waist '*abjectly*' rather than 'passionately', and Raye too is more stricken, speaking to her with a '*wan*' rather than a 'sad' quietude. Finally, a characteristic Hardy touch is that he refines Wessex topography, so that Anna is now said to have grown up on the 'Great *Mid-Wessex* Plain'.

These emended proofs must at this stage have been sent to Harper & Brothers in New York to form the basis of *1894H*, since they are virtually identical in substantives.[16] For the British edition, however, the proofs underwent a further revision, and the following account of these second proofs is therefore an account of the differences between the British and American editions of 1894.

There are ten substantive additions or alterations at this second proof stage. The principal addition is the following sentence: 'That he had been able to seduce another woman in two days was his crowning though unrecognized fascination for her as the she-animal' (*1894*, p. 108). This gives a decidedly frank estimate of the sexual nature of Edith's otherwise imaginative and romantic relationship with Raye. Hardy's increasing freedom from the earlier demands of bowdlerization shows itself in his description of the first letter which Raye receives from Anna, which will, he expects, contain the usual 'passionate retrospect' (p. 103) which such letters normally express (elsewhere it reads 'affectionate retrospect'). The second proof similarly adds a description of Edith travelling back home after Anna's wedding to Raye with 'her lips still tingling from the desperate pressure of his kiss' (p. 121).

Other notable changes at this stage show Hardy removing yet another reference to Anna as 'young'; when preparing the first galley, he had removed three such descriptions of Anna and Edith which had been in the MS. and the serial, making them more mature and responsible. He also took the opportunity to tidy up some plot details. When Anna is living on the Plain, she hopes to find a neighbour to read her letters to her, 'if a trustworthy one could be met with' (p. 111). This replaces the wholly obvious information that such a neighbour would be 'disqualified from replying for her because of the hand'. Another revision concerns the account of the 'patient idlers' outside the court which Raye attends: they had waited to enter since eight in the morning because, 'like him, they belonged to the classes that live on expectation' (p. 102). All previous versions read 'like him, they belonged to the classes that live without working', which, in Raye's case, is obviously untrue.[17]

1912 Macmillan Wessex edition

Finally, there are six substantive changes which Hardy made to *1894* when revising for the 1912 Wessex edition of *Life's Little Ironies*, and since they are all very brief they can be listed in full (*1912* pagination):

	1894	1912
p. 109	the two quiet lives hereafter depicted	the two quiet feminine lives hereunder depicted [i.e., *Hardy is making clear that it is not Edith and her husband who are disturbed but Edith and Anna*]
p. 116	came to her assistance	came to help her alight [*explaining that Raye's help is physical, and he is not helping her out of an awkward situation*]
p. 126	he was affected by her news	he was concerned at her news [*that she is pregnant*]
p. 127	I wish it was mine	I wish his child was mine [*Edith's wish*][18]

p. 128	concerning a condition that was not Edith's at all	concerning a corporeal condition that was not Edith's at all
p. 129	selfish	sensuous [*description of Raye*]¹⁹

In conclusion, it is apparent that Hardy took the opportunity at each stage of publication to revise 'On the Western Circuit' very carefully and alter even quite minor touches of characterization. The major change was between the bowdlerized serial versions and the editions of 1894, which partially restored original MS. readings but also added new material to make the story even more sexually explicit than it had been in its original conception.

Notes

1 The manuscript is in Manchester Central Public Library, MS 823.892.U3.4. Alan Manford (1990), 89–100, has given an extensive account of it.

2 See Purdy, p. 85.

3 Norman Page (1977), p. 128.

4 See *Letters*, I, 243, 251.

5 Page references to 'On the Western Circuit' are to *1894*, unless otherwise stated.

6 The following restorations of MS. substantive readings are not discussed (in each pair, the first is the serial reading and the second is the MS. and *1894* reading): 'had been a rich/was a rich' (p. 93); 'capable of wasting his time/capable' (p. 101); 'Occasionally, when one of these letters/When the letter' (p. 110); 'would bow/bowed' (p. 110); 'weep/wept' (p. 110); 'became/become' (p. 114). Instances of uncle/husband substitutions have been omitted.

7 This is p. 110 of *1894*, but *1912* altered it yet again, as I shall describe later.

8 The MS. reads thus also, except it speaks of 'the ratification'.

9 After 'I hope so, for 'twas time'.

10 *1894*, pp. 108–9; most of the italicized words are to be found on fos. 19–20 of the MS., but the passage about Anna crying and confessing has been moved from an earlier scene on fo. 17.

11 *1894*, pp. 110–11.

12 *1894*, p. 111; *1912* was revised again, talking of Edith's 'corporeal' condition.

13 *1894*, pp. 100–101.

14 Brady, p. 125.

15 *1894* also adds two thoroughly innocuous references to 'bed' (pp. 104, 107) which had not been present in the MS. or the serial.

16 There are in fact two substantive differences between the proofs and *1894H*, but they are probably the result of in-house editing: the American edition has Anna telling Raye that, when he comes in spring, it will be 'time' enough to discuss what to do (all other versions read 'soon'), and Anna later says she is 'very glad' that the wedding is so near (other versions read 'glad'). There are 130 differences in accidentals between the emended proofs and *1894H*.

17 The remaining second proof alterations are as follows (*1894* is given first, followed by the reading of the emended galley proof and *1894H*; pagination is that of *1894*):

'architecture/ecclesiology' (p. 90); 'as herself/as she' (p. 94); 'was there/were there' (p. 103); 'name/shape' (p. 108; 'shape' was a marginal emendation to the galley which either Hardy later reversed in favour of the original 'name' or the compositors overlooked).

18 The serial had read 'I wish he was mine – I wish he was'.

19 For the sake of a complete record, the other revisions to *1894* for the Wessex edition are as follows (*1912* is quoted first, and the pagination is that of *1912*): 'befell/befel' (p. 128); 'said, crying/said crying' (p. 136); 'said, shrugging/said shrugging' (p. 136).

CHAPTER 23

'To Please His Wife'

Thomas Hardy wrote 'To Please His Wife' in late 1890 or early 1891, receiving £50 for it from S.S. McClure, who had founded the first newspaper syndicate in the United States.[1] Hardy sold him the rights to the story on 17 September 1890, although it would seem that he had not yet written it. The published forms of the story which have textual significance are as follows (the manuscript has not survived):

Serial	*Black and White*, 27 June 1891, pp. 678–82, with a small portrait of Hardy and two illustrations by W. Hennessy.
1894	*Life's Little Ironies* (London: Osgood, McIlvaine, 1894), pp. 123–48. Published at 6*s.* in an edition of 2000 copies on 22 February 1894.
1894H	*Life's Little Ironies* (New York: Harper & Brothers, 1894), pp. 107–28. Published in March 1894.
1896	*Life's Little Ironies* (London: Osgood, McIlvaine, 1896), pp. 123–48. Volume XIV in the Wessex Novels, the first uniform and complete edition of Hardy's works. Plates of the first edition were used.
1912	*Life's Little Ironies* (London: Macmillan, 1912), pp. 141–61. Volume VIII of the Wessex edition.

Sources

The surnames of all four characters in the story (Jolliffe, Henning, Phippard and Lester) can be found on monuments in St James's Church in Poole ('Havenpool'), as described in Hutchins's *History of Dorset* (I, 47–9).[2] Of special nautical relevance is Hutchins's earlier account of the exploits of Captain Peter Jolliffe of Poole, who in 1694 captured a French privateer, three times the strength of his own craft, off the Isle of Purbeck and forced it ashore near Lulworth. He was awarded a gold medal and chain by the King (Hutchins, I, 14–15). Hardy's Jolliffe also has heroic qualities in facing danger, and his first name, Shadrach, may have affinities with his biblical counterpart who 'survived the fire because of his faith in God: this latter-day Shadrach is saved "providentially" from death at sea, and has an unquestioning belief in the forces of goodness' (Brady, p. 130).

The serial and the galley proofs of *1894*

Galley proofs of the Osgood, McIlvaine edition of *Life's Little Ironies*, variously dated 1 to 30 December 1893 and showing a number of alterations in Hardy's hand, are in the possession of the Dorset County Museum. The dates on 'To Please His Wife' are 13 and 14 December.

The status of these galleys and their position in the chain of textual transmission are complex. They were clearly set up from the serial, for they are identical to it, except for eighteen occasions where the serial has been altered so that the galleys print the reading which will eventually be found in *1894*. Of these eighteen alterations, all but one are accidentals (e.g., 'business man' becomes 'business-man', and 'sailor's wives' is corrected to 'sailors' wives'); the only substantive change is the addition of 'that' after 'supposed' (p. 135).[3]

Hardy made or approved some eighty changes to the serial when publishing the story in *1894*, of which about twenty-five are substantives. Of the eighty alterations, just over half are marginal revisions which Hardy made in the galleys. The most interesting of these changes concerns the education of the two sons of Shadrach and Joanna. In the revised version of the story, Joanna jealously tells her husband, 'But see how well off Emmy Lester is, who used to be so poor! Her boys will go to College, no doubt; and think of yours – obliged to go to the Parish School!' (p. 137). In the serial and the galley, 'Parish School' had read 'National School' until Hardy altered the galley. This revision serves to increase the educational gap between the two families. Hardy himself at the age of eight had begun attending the new National School in Bockhampton, established by Mrs Julia Martin, and he stayed there for a year, asserting later in life that it was 'far superior to an ordinary village school'.[4] Since Hardy had said earlier in the story that the boys' education was to be 'of the plainest' (p. 134), he obviously did not want them to attend the same kind of school which he had attended and so he altered the serial to read 'Parish School'.

Of the 45 marginal revisions which Hardy made to the galleys, some 25 are substantives. A number of these show that Hardy was keen to increase the sense of social distance between Joanna and Emily; for instance, he adds to a description of a carriage stopping at Emily's house that it was 'a wealthy visitor's' (p. 136), and, when speaking of Emily's boys and their prospects, Hardy adds that 'the University was talked of for them' (p. 144). He also italicizes Joanna's remark to Emily that '*You* are all success, and *I* am all the other way!' (p. 144). To highlight the social difference further, Shadrach's speech is made more non-standard, and he asks at the start of the story, 'Who may them two maids be?' (p. 127) when he first sees Emily and Joanna together, whereas in the serial he had enquired about 'those two maids'.

The galleys cast some light on Hardy's attitude to accidentals. While in general his manuscripts tend to be less heavily pointed than the printed versions, here we see Hardy adding in the margins quite a few extra marks. He adds hyphens to nine pairs of words, for instance, scrupulously hyphenating 'chancel-step' and 'stationery-shop' among others. He also inserted ten exclamation marks, but he was much more conservative in his revision of commas, adding two and deleting two.

The status of the galleys is complicated because, although all of Hardy's marginal revisions are included in *1894*, the latter also has twenty further changes which are not indicated in the galleys and which must therefore have been added at the second proof stage before publication. Approximately half of these additional revisions are substantives, and they include the change of 'arose' to 'rose' on two occasions (p. 126), while the 'mass of guineas' which Shadrach brings back from his first voyage and which his wife finds so inadequate swells to become a 'mass of sovereigns and guineas' (p. 139) in *1894*. Shadrach's comment in the serial and galleys that 'there isn't a more cranky place in the South Seas' than Havenpool places the port in the 'Northern Seas' (p. 141) in *1894*. Other revisions which occurred during this second proof revision include the substitution of 'she had written' for 'she had penned', and 'to post it' later in the same sentence became 'to send it' (p. 129).

1894 Harper

The emended proofs appear to have been sent to Harper & Brothers in New York to form the basis of *1894H*, since they are virtually identical in substantives. The proofs of the British edition, however, then underwent a further revision, and therefore any second proof revisions are missing from *1894H*. For example, none of the substantive revisions described in the previous paragraph is to be found in the Harper edition, and there are in total eight substantive variants in *1894H* which follow the readings of the emended proof before it was further revised. There is one additional substantive variant which seems the result of Harper editing, 'Emmy' being changed uniquely to 'Emily'. There are 100 differences in accidentals between the two collected editions of the story in 1894.

1912 Macmillan Wessex edition

Finally, in preparing the Wessex edition of 1912, Hardy made eight alterations to *1894*, all of them substantives, and these are listed in full below, with brief explanations where appropriate (*1912* pagination).

	1894	*1912*
p. 145	What can make ye afraid?	What can make 'ee afraid?
		[*Shadrach's question to Emily*]
p. 146	why do ye get behind there?	why do you get behind there?
		[*Shadrach's question to Emily*]

1894	1912
p. 147	front door	back door
[Joanna cannot leave Emily's shop from the front door because Emily and Shadrach are there]
p. 148	a grocer's shop	a small grocer's shop
[stressing Shadrach's poor prospects in trade]
p. 150	*[not in 1894]*	The way to wealth was not by this route.
[i.e., through Shadrach's shopkeeping]
p. 156	much trading	much speculative trading
p. 158	By long watching the spot as she worshipped it became as if she saw the three returned ones there kneeling.	By long watching the spot as she worshipped became as if she saw the three returned ones there kneeling
[Hardy's omission of 'it' avoids the ambiguity of seeming to say that Joanna worshipped the spot on the ground]
p. 160	Shadrach and his sons could not return	Shadrach and his sons had gone to the bottom.

Notes

1 See *Letters*, I, 216–7, and Purdy, p. 85. The date at the end of the story, June 1891, was added at the galley stage in December 1893 and indicates the date of serialization rather than composition.

2 See also H.F.V. Johnstone (1971), pp. 84–7.

3 Page references are to *1894*, unless otherwise stated.

4 *Life*, p. 23.

CHAPTER 24

'The Fiddler of the Reels'

An analysis of the revisions which Hardy made to 'The Fiddler of the Reels' in its successive published versions reveals his continuing concern for narrative voice and perspective, while he also took the opportunity to introduce subtle changes in characterization. Car'line, for instance, the girl who is bewitched by Mop Ollamoor's music, becomes increasingly selfish and self-pitying, while her husband Ned acquires a sharper personality, growing more grudging towards Car'line and markedly more paternal towards her daughter. The scene of their reunion in London is especially notable for its expansion in each of the later versions.

The published versions of 'The Fiddler of the Reels' which have textual significance are as follows (the manuscript has not survived):

Serial   *Scribner's Magazine* (New York), 13 (May 1893), 597–609, with one illustration by W. Hatherell.

1894   *Life's Little Ironies* (London: Osgood, McIlvaine, 1894), pp. 177–203. Published at 6*s.* in an edition of 2000 copies on 22 February 1894.

1894H   *Life's Little Ironies* (New York: Harper & Brothers, 1894), pp. 152–74. Published in March 1894.

1896   *Life's Little Ironies* (London: Osgood, McIlvaine, 1896), pp. 177–203. Volume XIV in the Wessex Novels, the first uniform and complete edition of Hardy's works. Plates of the first edition were used.

1912   *Life's Little Ironies* (London: Macmillan, 1912), pp. 165–85. Volume VIII of the Wessex edition.

'The Fiddler of the Reels' was written between late November 1892 and mid-January 1893. Hardy wrote to Charles Scribner's Sons on 20 November 1892 to say that 'I am in receipt of your letter of the 28th ult. asking for a short story for the Exhibition number of the Magazine: & I will during the next week or two ascertain if I can think of such a story, & could get it written in time'.[1] Chapter XXI of the *Life* opens by announcing 'Jan. 13. "The Fiddler of the Reels" (Short Story) posted to Messrs Scribner, New York.'[2] As R.L. Purdy notes, the serial appeared in a special 'Exhibition Number' for the Chicago World's Fair, which accounts for the opening lines of the story and Hardy's use of the Great Exhibition of 1851.[3]

In statistical terms, some eighty sentences in the serial underwent some kind of alteration when being reprinted in *1894*, but only fifty of these contain substantive differences. The serial tends to be more heavily pointed, having, for instance, sixteen commas which are omitted from *1894*, although the latter adds three not found in the serial. In addition, *1894* has seven new exclamation marks, two words set in italics and two new paragraph divisions. It also has five new complete sentences. *1912* contains 22 sentences which differ from *1894*, of which thirteen introduce substantive variants, and there are two new sentences added.[4] (The readings of *1894* are also those of *1912* unless otherwise stated.)

The first galley proofs of *1894* have survived (they are held in the Dorset County Museum), and the sheets of 'The Fiddler of the Reels' bear the printers' date stamps 20 and 23 December 1893. An analysis of the proofs shows that Hardy made the alterations to the serial at three distinct stages when preparing the story for publication in *1894*. The bulk of the revisions (just over fifty, of which slightly over thirty are substantive) were made when preparing a revised copy of the serial which was used to set up the galley proofs. The next stage is Hardy's marginal emendation of these proofs, where he introduces a further twenty alterations (all but three of which are substantive). These emended proofs must have been the basis of a second proof, or revises; these have not survived but their existence can be posited because, on eleven occasions, *1894* has a reading which is different from the emended galley proofs and which must have been introduced at a later stage. (Of these eleven revisions, five are substantive.) In the remainder of this chapter, I shall indicate, where significant, whether the alterations under discussion were introduced at the first galley stage, or were written by Hardy in the margin of the first galley, or were added to the second galley.

A copy of these first emended proofs must have been sent to Harper & Brothers in New York to form the basis of *1894H*, for they are virtually identical in substantives. Since the proofs for the British edition, however, underwent a further revision, any second galley revisions are missing from the American edition of 1894.[5]

In the serial, the narrator occasionally speaks in the first person singular, but such instances are all removed in *1894*; thus 'I am bound' becomes 'one is bound' (p. 186; first galley) and 'these observations led me onward to think' becomes 'these observations led us onward to talk' (p. 180; first galley). He is at pains to stress that he did not know Mop Ollamoor well, if at all, thus producing a distance between himself and his tale which would have been lessened if he had retained the first person singular of the serial. This is an old story which he has only heard about from his seniors, which allows him, as Kristin Brady points out, to combine nostalgia, hindsight and objectivity.[6] The narrator in *1894* thus adds phrases such as 'whom the seniors in our party had known well' and 'he was a woman's man, *they said*' (p. 180; my italics; both are second galley revisions) to stress his reliance on the information of others. Hardy's attention to matters of narrative perspective and consistency is seen in one phrase which he changed again as late as 1912. Mop's violin in *1894* is said to have originated in some 'Italian city' (first galley: the serial read 'Italian spot'). Hardy obviously realized that this causes a slight narrative problem: his narrator does not know where Mop came from, or even whether Mop Ollamoor was his real name, and he does not know whether Mop was really in London when Car'line thought she saw him, so how can he be so definite about the origin of Mop's violin when he is so uncertain about much more important personal details? In *1912*, Hardy introduces the necessary vagueness to his narrative at this point by tracing the violin to some 'Italian or German city' (p. 182).

Characterization changes slightly in the three versions. Mop Ollamoor is made arguably rather less unpleasant; in the serial he is described as 'perhaps not repulsive; merely, in his better moments, tolerable', but *1894* and *1912* read 'perhaps a little repulsive at times' (*1894*, p. 180; first galley). The other three principal characters have more sharply defined identities. Ned, for instance, the rather passive and blank husband of the serial, takes on a sharper edge in his relationship with his wife, Car'line, and is notably more close to her daughter. He is grudging towards his wife when she joins him in London, accompanied by her daughter, and he speaks to her 'gruffly' (*1894*, p. 192; not in serial). He accepts that 'you must bide here to-night, anyhow', with *1894* adding 'I s'pose!' (p. 192). He is also more vocal in his response to learning of Car'line's daughter than he was in the serial: '"What the devil can I do!" Hipcroft groaned' (p. 191; not in serial; all three are first galley revisions).

A harsher and more critical portrait of Car'line progressively emerges. In the serial, when Ned writes to her from London to say that she should come and be his wife, he says that he will marry her because he knows 'what a good little woman she was to the core', but *1894* changes the last three words to 'at the core' (p. 188; second galley): she is now not thoroughly good but only fundamentally good, which leaves much more scope for her weaknesses. She is made to appear increasingly selfish, childish and self-pitying; for instance, here is how she pleads for Ned's forgiveness when she arrives in London, with the daughter he knows nothing about:

Serial	*1894 & 1912*
I hope you'll excuse it, dear Ned, now I have come so many miles!	I hope you'll excuse it this once, dear Ned, and not scold me, now I've come so many, many miles! (*1894*, p. 191)[7]

She reacts like a naughty child in asking him not to scold her, and begs him to forgive her 'this once' for having a child by Mop Ollamoor as if it were a prank. Her selfishness is seen near the end of the tale, where Hardy's emendations serve to increase her self-absorption. Ned, who cares deeply about the disappearance of the girl, cries that Mop Ollamoor is 'torturing her to maintain him!', but she dismisses his concern:

Serial	*1894 & 1912*
To which his wife would answer, plaintively, 'Don't 'ee raft yourself so, Ned; he won't hurt her!' and fall asleep again.	To which his wife would answer peevishly, 'Don't 'ee raft yourself so, Ned! You prevent my getting a bit o' rest! He won't hurt her!' and fall asleep again. (*1894*, p. 202; first galley)

'Peevishly', it would seem, was substituted to stress that she has not changed, and certainly not matured, from the start of the story, where she is introduced as being one 'whose chief defect as a companion with her sex was a tendency to peevishness now and then' (*1894*, p. 182).

Before moving on to look at those changes which are unique to *1912*, there is one other minor but interesting alteration which Hardy made to the serial for *1894*. The Wessex topography in 'The Fiddler of the Reels' is accurate, unlike the similar setting (Bloom's End, the Quiet Woman) in *The Return of the Native*; one indication of Hardy's care with his location in the short story is his alteration of the distance between Lower Mellstock and Moreford (Moreton) which is given as six miles in the serial and, more accurately, as five miles in *1894* (p. 126; second galley).

The principal change in *1912* is the heightening of the relationship between Ned and Car'line's daughter, Carry, who is eventually carried away by Mop Ollamoor, leaving Ned distraught but Car'line unaffected. This sharper outline to the portrayal of Ned and Carry had begun in *1894*, where Carry's 'features' in the serial become her 'tender face' (p. 190; first galley), making her a more appealing child, and from the very start Ned takes to her. Whereas in the serial he had offered her some bread and butter in a tone which had a 'preoccupied hardness of utterance', in *1894* he is only pretending to be gruff and speaks to her with a 'factitious hardness' (p. 192; first galley). This instant rapport between Ned and Carry is strengthened in *1912*; in earlier versions, Carry had simply 'nodded' when Ned asked her how she was, but now she 'nodded beamingly' (p. 177). *1912* is also the first version to italicize Ned's claim at the end of the story that '"she *is* mine, all the same"' (p. 184). Hardy was at pains at the end to give more emphasis in *1912* to Ned's feelings for Carry. His assertion of earlier versions that 'Carry's everything!' is revised to 'Carry's the whole world to me!' (p. 184) and Hardy gives a fuller explanation of Ned's behaviour by adding that he is distracted 'by his passionate paternal love for a child not his own' (p. 184). This greater emphasis on Ned and Carry sets up a structural parallel to Car'line and the Fiddler: Mop Ollamoor's disappearance leaves Car'line lifeless and drained while Carry's disappearance fills Ned with a passionate 'intensity' (p. 185), starkly contrasting Car'line's sexual loss and Ned's paternal loss.

One scene which Hardy revised on each occasion is the reunion in London when Car'line arrives to marry Ned, bringing with her the daughter whom he did not know about. In *1894*, Hardy made the scene more melodramatic than it had been in the serial; Ned gazes at them 'palely' instead of 'steadily' and he now stands back from them 'with a start'. Car'line 'gasped' instead of 'sighed' and she begins to 'sob outright' (p. 191; all first galley revisions). Hardy also felt the need to expand their initial conversation in which Ned asks about the child; the three versions of this interrogation (which is the story's first instance of direct speech between them) are as follows:

Serial	1894	1912
'Who is this – somebody you know?' asked Ned, curiously.	'Who is this – somebody you know?' asked Ned curiously.	'Who is this – somebody you know?' asked Ned curiously.
'Yes, Ned. She's mine'.	'Yes, Ned. She's mine'.	'Yes, Ned. She's mine'.
'Yours?'	'Yours?'	'Yours?'
'Yes – my own!'	'Yes – my own!'	'Yes – my own!'
'Well – upon my –'	'Your own child?'	'Your own child?'
	'Yes!'	'Yes!'
	'Well – as God's in –'	'But who's the father?'
		'The young man I had after you courted me'.
		'Well – as God's in –'
		(p. 175; first galley)

In the serial, Ned is incurious to the point of naive apathy, but at least by *1912* he gets round to asking the obvious question (he was, after all, about to marry her the next day and here she is, arriving with a child of whom he knew nothing). The revisions are in line with the gradually more assertive presence which Hardy gives Ned over the years.

The irony of Car'line describing the demonic Mop Ollamoor as her 'young man' is seen also in the way she describes to Ned the occasion of her seduction:

Serial	1894	1912
'I was so onlucky to be catched'	'I was so onlucky to be catched the first time'	'I was so onlucky to be catched the first time he took advantage o' me' (p. 175; first galley)

Being 'taken advantage' of is Car'line's simplistic attempt to understand the kind of diabolic power which Mop Ollamoor exerts over her, and she takes refuge in a self-pitying notion of herself as an unlucky victim, a poor man's Tess; as Kristin Brady rightly says, her essential characteristic is 'her utter lack of self-knowledge'.[8] In a story so concerned with the nature of change and progress, Hardy's revisions here work to give a ballad-like timelessness to the tale.[9]

Notes

1 *Letters*, I, 289.
2 *Life*, p. 267.
3 See Purdy, p. 83.
4 American spellings in the serial are not noted.
5 *1894H* therefore has none of the five substantive revisions made at the second galley stage of *1894*. The only one not described later in this chapter is a reference to a 'window' where *1894* reads 'casement'. There is one indication of a possible

substantive editorial revision at Harper's: in the British edition, Car'line sobs that she has not deceived Ned 'because – because' (p. 191) he can send her home again, but *1894*H uniquely has only one 'because'. Ignoring US spelling, there are some fifty differences in accidentals between the two editions of 1894.

6 Brady, p. 133.

7 This is mostly a first galley proof revision, except that Hardy added 'and not scold me' in the margin.

8 Brady, p. 136.

9 For the sake of a complete record, the other revisions to *1894* for the Wessex edition are as follows (*1912* is quoted first, and the pagination is that of *1912*): 'further/farther' (p. 168; two more instances on pp. 170 and 179); 'O–O–O/Oh–oh–oh' (p. 170); 'lovemakings/performances' (p. 170); 'point-blank/point blank' (p. 176); 'dare say/daresay' (p. 176); 'send you/send 'ee' (p. 177); 'pride/pleasure' (p. 178); 'Woman/Woman Inn' (p. 178); 'passage in/passage, in' (p. 181); 'whimpered/said' (p. 183); 'visited/revisited' (p. 183); 'and raise a dance/[*not in 1894*]' (p. 183); 'or to/or' (p. 185).

CHAPTER 25

'A Few Crusted Characters'

Thomas Hardy wrote 'A Few Crusted Characters', a sequence of nine linked sketches, in late 1890 and early 1891, at about the same time as the majority of the other short stories which he later collected in *Life's Little Ironies*. Its textual history is unique among Hardy's work in that a rough first draft, which is occasionally in note form, has survived, providing an opportunity to study the story at a very early stage in its conception. Hardy later revised for publication all of the nine sketches on at least three occasions, and most of them were revised yet again when Hardy was preparing the Wessex edition of 1912. Some of the most interesting changes occurred when Hardy was preparing the collected editions of 'Andrey Satchel and the Parson and Clerk', which was made increasingly explicit about Jane's pregnancy.

The published versions of 'A Few Crusted Characters' which have textual significance are as follows:

Serial   As 'Wessex Folk', *Harper's New Monthly Magazine* (American and European editions), March–June 1891, with headpiece of Dorchester High St by Alfred Parsons and seven illustrations by Charles Green. The instalments were divided thus: March, [Introduction], 'Tony Kytes, the Arch-Deceiver' and 'The History of the Hardcomes' (pp. 587–99); April, 'The Superstitious Man's Story', 'Andrey Satchel and the Parson and Clerk' and 'Andrew Satchel's Experience as a Musician' (pp. 698–705); May, 'Absent-Mindedness in a Parish Choir' and 'The Winters and the Palmleys' (pp. 890–97); June, 'Incident in the Life of Mr. George Crookhill' and 'Netty Sargent's Copyhold' (pp. 121–7).

1894   *Life's Little Ironies* (London: Osgood, McIlvaine, 1894), pp. 217–301. Published at 6*s.* in an edition of 2000 copies on 22 February 1894.

1894H   *Life's Little Ironies* (New York: Harper & Brothers, 1894), pp. 187–268. Published in March 1894.

1896   *Life's Little Ironies* (London: Osgood, McIlvaine, 1896), pp. 217–301. Volume XIV in the Wessex Novels, the first uniform and complete edition of Hardy's works. Plates of the first edition were used.

1912   *Life's Little Ironies* (London: Macmillan, 1912), pp. 187–259. Volume VIII of the Wessex edition.

The manuscripts

A manuscript of these sketches, entitled 'Wessex Folk', is located in the Berg Collection of the New York Public Library. Purdy accurately describes it as 'a very rough hurried first draft (in places hardly more than notes) of a kind Hardy almost invariably destroyed' (p. 84), and Gatrell notes that it is 'the most substantial piece of evidence available to anyone trying to piece together Hardy's preliminary working habits' (1984, p. 11). The manuscript consists of 30 leaves (some of which are cut down to varying sizes), foliated 1–31 by Hardy, although five are missing and four are supplementary leaves. Each of the manuscript's sketches will be discussed at the appropriate place below. Hardy gave this draft of 'Wessex Folk' to Edmund Gosse in July 1913, and wrote at the time in red ink at the top of the first leaf, 'First Rough Draft of some of the tales afterwards called "A Group of Noble Dames"'. He noticed the mistake almost straight away and wrote to Gosse a few days later to point it out: 'What a stupid thing I did when sending it. In my hurry I put on it that it was afterwards published as "A Group of Noble Dames" – when I meant "A few Crusted Characters." Please make the correction' (*Letters*, IV, 287; the error was allowed to remain, however).

Revised numbering of the leaves shows that the story which came to be called 'Netty Sargent's Copyhold' and which is now the final one in the sequence was originally to have been the first; the opening leaf of the story, now fo. 28a, was cut off from the bottom of fo. 3, and the deleted foliation on the other surviving leaves runs from 4–6. All of the other stories in the sequence remained in their current order, but all their leaves needed to be renumbered, indicating that Hardy decided to move 'Netty Sargent's Copyhold' after he had completed this manuscript. He may have moved the story to the end because it provides a more appropriate close to the sequence than the inconsequential story about George Crookhill, which would otherwise have been the final one: Netty's experience of death and the comic continuity between generations leads ironically into the epilogue which shows the returning native wandering around the churchyard and its head-stones, feeling dislocated from his community and cut off from his forebears.

On the verso of what became the final surviving leaf of the MS. (which breaks off just before the end of 'Netty Sargent's Copyhold'), Hardy experimented with some 21 different names for the carrier's destination, and these are scattered across the page in no particular order of preference:

> Fiddlington, Liddlington, Joggington, Hide Trent, Trudgington, Trentingdale, Middlehinton, Piddinghide, Middletrenton, Puddle-cum-quack, Fudley-cum-Pipes, Puddle-cum-Ales [with 'slouch' written as an alternative above 'Ales'], Trentpuddle, Longpuddle, Hidehinton, Hidepuddle, Trentington [the only one to be circled], Hintonhide, Hinton, Hintonhyde, Plyntonhide. (fo. 31ᵛ)

There are also three names which Hardy began to write but did not complete: 'Hint', 'Bu' and 'Pie'. Most of these names suggest Piddletrenthide or

Piddlehinton, which are villages in the Piddle or Puddle valley above Puddletown, and some suggest the difficulty of reaching the place or its apparent reputation for smoking, drinking and idleness. For the serial and all later versions of the story, Hardy settled on 'Longpuddle', which is both less picturesque and less identifiable than many of the alternatives. The same kind of uncertainty about placenames is also evident in the 'Introduction' (see below), and 'Longpuddle' must have been a relatively late choice, since it does not appear in the manuscript. It is important to stress that the leaf on which these experimental names were written may now be the final one, but it was originally numbered fo. 6, which means that Hardy began his list of suggested names at an early stage in the story's composition.

Also on this final verso is a list of characters' surnames occupying two lines (curiously, they do not appear to have been discussed before):

> ~~Sargents~~. Kyteses |Sallets| Darths Pawles Privett. |Satchels| Sargents
> The Jickses & the Coxes & the Crosses & the Ropers

The names in the first line are some of those which feature prominently in the stories, and they are listed in the order in which they appear. Hardy's deletion of 'Sargents' at the start of the line and his removal of it to the end, after the period which follows 'Privett', reflects his decision to move 'Netty Sargent's Copyhold' from first to last after he had completed the manuscript, and presumably after he had written this original line of names. Unity Sallet is one of the three girls courted by Tony Kytes, and so her name was inserted immediately after his. The Satchels are not named in the MS., which suggests that Hardy added their name to their stories at a later stage before the serial and then returned to this list and inserted the reference to them in the correct sequence. A notable omission might appear to be the name of the Hardcomes, but the cousins are not given a surname in their story, and Hardy may have forgotten to add their names to the list when he later decided to call them the Hardcomes. The cousins' wives, Emily Darth and Olive Pawle, may have been named on a leaf which is missing from the MS. and which corresponds to the point in the serial where their names are given. The fact that the list is sequential and that the revisions maintain this principle indicates that Hardy returned to it and supplemented it as he wrote and revised the stories: all of the names in the first line were used, and they are not experimental and in random order like the placenames on the same verso. Oddly, all of the surnames except one appear in plural forms, although there is only one character called Sallet, Darth or Pawle in the stories. The reason for this will become apparent if we examine the names in the second line.

These four surnames are not those of characters (although 'Cox' is noted on fo. 7 as a possible alternative name for the Jollivers in 'Tony Kytes, The Arch-Deceiver'). Two of the four surnames, however, feature in the list of families whose head-stones are seen by Lackland in the church-yard at the end of the story:

> Here, besides the Sallets, the Darths, the Pawles, the Privetts, the Sargents,
> and others of whom he had just heard, were names he remembered even
> better than those: the Jickses, and the Crosses, and the Knights, and the

Olds. [serial version]

The ending of the manuscript is missing, so it is impossible to know what Hardy originally wrote, but it is clear from his list on the verso of fo. 31 (the former fo. 6) that he intended from the outset to conclude the story with this roll-call of the dead and, for this purpose, he made a note of some of the names he had used and kept revising their sequence as he composed. The Kyteses and the Satchels are omitted from the original list, perhaps because Hardy did not wish it to appear too comprehensive. The Coxes and the Ropers are similarly missing from the second line of names, and they are replaced by the Olds and the Knights, the latter being the name of a family with whom the Hardys had many connections (see *Life*, pp. 262, 445; Hardy's great-grandfather, John Hardy of Puddletown, had married a Jane Knight). Kay-Robinson says of Hardy's list that 'they are not names in the registers of the real churches' (p. 126).

A later fair copy of a manuscript of 'Wessex Folk' may be extant, but its current location has not been discovered. A page of it was reproduced in facsimile in *Harper's Monthly Magazine* in July 1925 (p. 241), showing the opening of 'Incident in the Life of Mr. George Crookhill' (see below).

Hardy wrote to Florence Henniker on 22 October 1893 that he had 'been hunting up the tales I told you of ('Two Ambitions' being one of them). They are now fastened together to be dispatched to the publisher.'[1] This is clearly a reference to *Life's Little Ironies*, which contained 'A Tragedy of Two Ambitions'. On 23 December, he mentioned to Lena Milman how 'my proofs wander away to Scotland out of pure festivity, it seems, before they come to me from London'[2] (they were being printed by the Edinburgh firm of R. & R. Clark). *Life's Little Ironies* was shortly afterwards published on 22 February 1894.

The galley proofs of *1894*

The first galley proofs of *1894* have survived (they are held in the Dorset County Museum), and the sheets of 'A Few Crusted Characters' bear the printers' date stamps 25, 26, 28 and 30 December 1893 at intervals of two sheets. An analysis of the proofs shows that Hardy made the alterations to the serial at three distinct stages when preparing the story for publication in *1894*. The bulk of the revisions were made when preparing a revised copy of the serial which was used to set up the galley proofs. The next stage was Hardy's marginal emendation of these proofs. These emended proofs must have been the basis of at least a second proof, or revises; these have not survived but their existence can be posited because, on many occasions, *1894* has a reading which is different from the emended galley proofs and which must have been introduced at a later stage. I shall indicate, where significant, whether the alterations under discussion were introduced for the first proof stage, or were written by Hardy in the margin of the first proof, or were added to the second proof.

These emended first proofs must at this stage have been sent to Harper & Brothers in New York to form the basis of *1894H*, since they are identical in substantives.[3] Since the British edition underwent a further revision, however, any description of the second proofs is therefore also a description of most of the differences between the British and American editions of 1894.

In the remainder of this chapter, I shall comment on the sketches individually, where necessary drawing attention to features of Hardy's revisions which have a bearing on 'A Few Crusted Characters' as a whole. Unless specifically stated to the contrary, it should be assumed that alterations in the galleys were made by Hardy when preparing the first proof, that is, the earliest stage of revising the serial for publication in *1894*.

'Introduction'

The 'Introduction', untitled until the Wessex edition of 1912, comprises the opening three leaves of the manuscript, although the final four paragraphs of the printed versions are not present. The first four sentences give a clear demonstration of Hardy's working practices as he jots down a framework, often in note form and with immediate deletions of phrases, and then expands it, setting himself questions to answer and leaving himself alternatives to choose from later (Hardy's vertical lines join uncancelled pairs of words, written one above the other):

> It is a quarter to 4 on Sat^y afternoon |winter or summer?|, & the scene is
> county
> the high street of market |town. As the hour draws near a |large carriers|
> |White
> van standing in front of the |Black Hart inn: no horse in: no sign of the
> carrier. |on the side of the tilt: Burden – Carrier of to Upper Trentrimple/
> Joggingford/ton.| Timed to leave at 4. At half past 3, packages arrive.

Hardy's chief concern appears to have been to add precise local detail, which often has its source in a familiar reality. For instance, he is thinking of the setting here as Dorchester, which can correctly be described as both a market town and a county town, and the inn from which carriers departed from the east of town was indeed the White Hart Inn, although Hardy's first impulse was to give the name a rather transparent disguise (which he later deleted in favour of the actual name). An opposite impulse is apparent in Hardy's choice of name for the carrier: Simon Gatrell reports that 'in 1890, when Hardy was writing the sequence, there was really a carrier called Burden who left from the White Hart every day for Troy Town and Puddletown' (p. 112). However, in all printed versions of the story he has been called Burthen.

A comparison of the MS. with the serial at this point shows the kind of expansion of the four sentences which Hardy undertook after this initial scheme was established (italics indicate words present in the MS., with the exception of *diligences*):

> *It is* a *Saturday afternoon* of blue and yellow autumn-time, *and the scene is the high street of* a well-known *market-town. A large carrier's van* stands *in* the quadrangular fore-court of *the White Hart Inn*, upon *the* sides *of* its

spacious *tilt* being painted, in weather-beaten letters, "Burthen, *Carrier to Longpuddle.*" These vans, so numerous hereabout, are a respectable if somewhat lumbering class of conveyance, much resorted to by decent travellers not overstocked with money, the better among them roughly corresponding to the old French *diligences.*

The present one is *timed to leave* the town *at four* o'clock precisely, and it is now *half past three* by the ancient dial face in the church tower at the top of the street. In a few seconds errand-boys from the shops begin to *arrive* with *packages*, which they deposit in the vehicle, and then they turn away whistling, and care for the packages no more.

Most of the serial version is new, presumably added in a fair-copy manuscript deriving from the MS. Hardy settled the question of winter or summer by deciding on autumn, an appropriately valedictory season for the visitor's final return to Longpuddle. The narrator immediately establishes his credibility by showing his local knowledge: he is familiar with the vans which are 'so numerous hereabout' and which are 'much resorted to' by certain kinds of travellers. Yet he also has more than merely local knowledge, and he can make the comparison with what French carriages used to look like: this is a man with experience of different times and different places. While the vans may be 'respectable' and the travellers 'decent' (an assurance to gladden the heart of a magazine editor), one feels that the narrator would not himself choose to travel by such means. Hardy's expansion of his manuscript works deftly and economically to open up that distance between the urbane narrator and his Wessex Folk which is so characteristic of Hardy.

The bald indications of time and place in the MS. are animated and set in motion. The clock in the church-tower begins to tick, as it were, towards the precise moment of departure, and 'in a few seconds' the errand-boys arrive. The description of the Inn acquires exact architectural dimensions in the reference to its quadrangular forecourt, and the carriage gains a history with its weather-beaten letters. Finally, the narrator performs an action which Simon Gatrell has defined as Hardy's speciality: 'worming his way into the consciousness or subconsciousness of evidently unknown characters by intuitive imagination – here the object is the collective unconscious of the errand-boys' (p. 113).

The main uncertainty in the opening of the MS. concerns the choice of destination for the carrier: Upper Joggingford, as it finally became at the end of the second sentence in the MS., later appeared in the 'Introduction' as '|Upper| Joggington|ham|' (fo. 2) and then as the non-committal 'J.' (fo. 3), as if Hardy were postponing the need to choose. Another decision concerns the age of the curate: he is described in successive lines as 'that young |old| man' and as an 'old |young| man' (fo. 1; in the latter, the adjectives are written one above the other, and neither is cancelled). On the next leaf Hardy inserted a reference to his '|white|' beard to settle the matter. Some surnames are tentatively given: the parish clerk, for instance' is called 'Mr —' originally, and then Hardy inserted some possible names, '|Tone, Mexton, Toneall|' (fo. 1) but the serial settles on 'Maxton'. The name of the schoolmaster, Mr Profitt, was interlined in the MS., but the master-thatcher was not identified as Christopher Twink until the serial.

The surname of John Lackland, the returning stranger, is given as 'Trent' and 'Trantwell' in the 'Introduction' (fo. 3; both uncancelled), but in the margin of 'Tony Kytes, The Arch-Deceiver', Hardy wrote 'Trentide' (fo. 3a), although it has no relation to anything at that point in the story. 'Trentide' may be an experimental suggestion either for the name of the stranger or his destination; certainly, the first name given, 'Trent', calls to mind Piddletrenthide, so that we have another example of Hardy's custom of allowing the name of a fictional character to hint at the name of the story's real location (as in Jude Fawley and Grace Melbury). Incidentally, the stranger and his family were said in the MS. to have emigrated to New York, but in all printed versions their destination is left unspecified: because the story was being published in an American serial, Hardy might have felt that a statement such as 'Even in America, you know, there are failures' (fo. 3) might have sounded either offensive or naive (the serial replaced 'America' with 'new countries'). With regard to the stranger's age, Hardy originally wrote that he emigrated 31 years ago at the age of nine, but he deleted 'nine' and substituted 'eleven' (fo. 3), making him a couple of years older.

On the first two leaves, Hardy kept a running count in the margin of the number of passengers who were in the van: there were originally to have been fourteen plus the carrier, but Hardy reduced the load in the serial by deleting the cider maker's wife. (The passengers were at one time to have included the master-thatcher's wife, but she was deleted in the manuscript.) Uniquely, the manuscript gives the length of their journey as 'seven miles' (fo. 1), where published versions do not specify the distance.

In preparing *1894*, the most interesting change which Hardy made to the serial version of the six-page 'Introduction' is his alteration of the position of the clock which tells us that it is now half-past three in the afternoon. In the serial, the time is told by 'the ancient dial face in the church tower', but in *1894* this becomes 'the clock in the turret' (p. 219).[4] Simon Gatrell correctly speculates that this revision 'may well have been a response to Alfred Parsons' headpiece-illustration in *Harper's*, which showed High East Street in Dorchester, with carriers' vans parked along the side of the road. It also showed quite clearly that the clock visible from that point is in the thin-spired tower of the town hall and not the solid, square church-tower of St Peter's.'[5] The large, half-page illustration which began the serial therefore directly contradicted Hardy's description of the same scene eighteen lines below it on the same page. Hardy did not, of course, alter his description solely for this reason, since *1894* did not reproduce the illustration; rather, he was motivated by what Gatrell calls his 'anxiety to secure accuracy of topographical description wherever possible'.[6] Gatrell's hypothesis that the illustration led Hardy to introduce this change is strengthened by the fact that Hardy made this alteration for the first proof, when he was preparing a revised copy of the serial and presumably had the illustration immediately in front of him.

Hardy also took the opportunity to heighten the dialect and non-standard speech of the local occupants of the van who are going to Longpuddle, a process which he would continue throughout the sequence (the serial was published in America, and Hardy possibly felt reluctant to use very much dialect originally).

For instance, the serial's 'I said' becomes 'I said to 'en' (p. 221).

The 'Introduction' also anticipated another change which Hardy would make later in 'A Few Crusted Characters', namely the slightly less respectful portrayal of the clergy, as we shall see in 'Andrey Satchel and the Parson and Clerk'. Here, the curate who is late for joining the van is described in the serial as 'a reverent old church minister' but in *1894* he becomes merely 'a serious old church-minister' (p. 221). The clerk's name, incidentally, was changed from Maxton to Flaxton at this time.

'Tony Kytes, The Arch-Deceiver'

This sketch describes how Tony, on his way home from market in a cart, gives a lift to three girls who each want to marry him. He tries to decide which of them to choose as first Unity and then Milly hide in the waggon when the next girl climbs aboard.

The manuscript of the story is 5½ leaves in length (fos. 3a–8), and the opening leaf gives the title as 'Tobias |Tony| Kytes, the arch deceiver'. This change of name must have been made relatively late, since Tony is described as 'Tobe' or simply 'T.' throughout the MS. Milly Richards, as she became in the serial, is Milly Roberts in the MS., and Anna (known as Hannah in collected editions) is referred to as a Jolliver when she is first introduced, but when her father arrives on the scene Hardy made a note to himself that he was to be '(registrar (Mr Cox))' (fo. 7). Although he did not cancel the earlier reference to Jolliver, Hardy seems to have decided on this change to Cox, and also a further one to Anna's forename, because he made a reminder to himself in the margin that now 'she is Betsy C[ox].' (Hardy did not eventually alter her name in this way, but he later used 'Betsy' for Mrs Privett's forename in the manuscript version of 'The Superstitious Man's Story'.) Another indication that Hardy had decided on Cox is that, at the end of the story, we learn that Unity married 'Jolliver, the farmer' (fo. 8), so Hardy retained the surname for a different character. In the serial, though, Anna and her father remain Jollivers, and there is no mention of Unity marrying her farmer of that name. One placename is unique to the MS.: the horse overturns the waggon when trying to turn the corner to 'Lewgate' (fo. 7), which is Hardy's name for the upper end of Higher Bockhampton, but all printed versions read 'Lower Longpuddle'.

The second half of the opening paragraph is in Emma Hardy's hand (and identified as such, but not, apparently, by Hardy or Emma); there are no alterations in the four lines, which suggests that they might have been written from dictation. The rest of the MS. is heavily revised but is not in note form: there are only two outlines awaiting later expansion, the first being the phrase 'Talked very lovingly....', which Hardy worked up into four lines of serial text (the other outline will be discussed shortly), and there are only three pairs of uncancelled alternative readings, one above the other; for instance, in the second line of the story, Hardy could not decide whether Tony had smallpox 'after you left' or 'when he was a boy' (fo. 3a; Hardy eventually settled on the latter).

The other outline and unresolved alternatives occur in the only scene where Hardy betrays any indecision: when Tony nears home, should it be his own father or Anna's father whom he sees and speaks to in the field? Originally, Hardy wrote that it was 'his father', but added 'Anna's' (fo. 6) above the phrase, and added the following marginal note alongside: 'Anna's father for sake of sequel'. This sequel is the arrival of Anna's father just as Tony is announcing that he has proposed to Anna and she is willing to marry him. Originally, it had been Anna herself who replied, 'She is not willing, sir' (fo. 7), and went on to say that she would 'sooner marry a scarecrow |Mormon|' (referring to Tony's apparently polygamous instincts; neither of the alternatives was eventually used), but Hardy then made a marginal note: 'Modify to A's f[athe]r takes him [sic] away. She w^d have accepted him.' Hardy later added an outline to the start of the scene to take account of this revision: 'Now T. hadn't seen that A's father come up behind .. hated T...' (not 'hated T...'s father', as one critic reads it). In the serial version, Tony speaks first to his own father in the field, and then Anna's father declares that she is not willing to marry him, but Hardy did not make any mention of her father hating Tony.

While the manuscript is not in note form, it is little more than a bare outline of the story, which Hardy later supplemented for the serial. The principal aim of this revision was to give individuality to each of the three girls whom Tony meets, for they are hardly characterized in the manuscript. The first girl he encounters is Unity Sallet, and her conversation with Tony is represented in the manuscript thus: 'T: she s^d. Why did you desert me for that other one. I sh^d. have made you a more loving wife than she..... |You deceived me T. &c| Well they talked on' (fo. 3a). The ellipsis and the '&c' indicate that the dialogue was to be added later, and in the serial their conversation at this point is 23 lines long. Hardy did not, in fact, develop the note that Tony had 'deceived' Unity, despite its relevance to the story's title. Instead, Unity reminds him of their long acquaintance since childhood and then tries to seduce him with the rather forward question, 'And – can you say I'm not pretty, Tony? Now look at me!' Instead of the harangue from Unity which the manuscript seems to threaten ('You deceived me T.'), she instead coaxes him with some favourable comparisons between herself and Milly ('In what is she better than I?', 'Prettier than she?'). While Unity may be taking the lead in the flirtation on this occasion, she reminds him that she has not done so before: ''Tisn't girls that are so easily won at first that are the best.'

The next girl he meets on the road is Milly, who mentions almost in passing in the manuscript that she has walked out to meet him because 'you asked me'. The serial, however, makes this detail much more prominent, and she repeats it later: 'you asked me, and I promised. But I shouldn't have come else, Mr Tony!' While all three girls in the manuscript are quite forward and bold, the serial is careful to show that this is not their normal behaviour or, in the case of Milly, that Tony invited it. As Gatrell remarks, 'it is not clear whether this is a generalization about the nature of girls when faced by the exigencies of securing a husband, or whether some editorial hand, perhaps at Harper's, or perhaps Hardy pre-empting such interference, decided that such a coming-on disposition in three girls had somehow to be qualified' (pp. 115–16).

The kinds of revision which Hardy made to the manuscript when preparing the serial are best exemplified in Tony's encounter with the third woman, Anna. In the manuscript, Tony meets all three girls at the roadside, but the serial adds some variation by having Anna hail him from an upper window of her aunt's house. Hardy sought in the serial to capture the nuances of Anna's delicate evasions, hints and advances which culminate in her unequivocal exultation when she thinks she has captured Tony and, just as importantly, defeated Milly. The scene in the manuscript, by comparison, lacks this sense of dramatic development and interplay between the characters. Tony's sense of panic and confusion about talking to Anna while he has two other women hiding in the waggon is also largely absent from the manuscript, and for the serial Hardy added the description of him speaking to her 'in a flutter' and 'feeling a dim sort of sweat rising up inside his clothes'. He then speaks to her in such a low voice when he denies that he has arranged to marry Milly, to prevent being overheard by her, that Anna has to ask him to repeat himself, and he comically apologizes for the hoarseness of voice from which he pretends to be suffering. Their growing intimacy is stressed in the description of them sitting with 'their feet upon the foot-board and their shoulders touching', and Tony eventually calls her 'dear Anna' and takes her hand. She then coyly broaches the question of marriage by saying that 'I wouldn't say no if you asked me – you know what' (the last three words are not in the manuscript, making her remark much more forward). Tony continues the serial's evasive tone by replying that he thinks he can escape any engagement with Milly and 'ask you that question' (the manuscript reads 'marry you'), at which point Anna triumphantly proclaims, 'Throw over Milly? – all to marry me!', which is now the first direct reference to marriage, cutting through all the demure hints and circumlocutions with which the pair have approached this moment. The manuscript then explains how 'T. was so won over by her pretty way (A. had a pretty way with her, if you can mind)' (fo. 5), but the serial, in keeping with the depiction of the other girls, alters this to emphasize that such forward behaviour is out of character for Anna: 'Tony was so won over by this pretty offering mood of a girl who had been quite the reverse (Anna had a backward way with her at times, if you can mind).'

After the accident, in which the three girls are thrown out of the waggon, the manuscript says that Tony kissed them all 'las fair as a man couldl' (fo. 7), but the serial says, perhaps more realistically, that he *would* have kissed them, but 'they were in too much of a taking to let him'. Anna's rejection of Tony in the manuscript is quickly effected: 'I'd sooner marry a scarecrow lMormonl. lAnd away she walked with her head in the cloudsl', but the serial replaces this with a passage which captures her conflicting emotions and secret hopes:

> 'Never – I would sooner marry no–nobody at all!' she gasped out, though with her heart in her throat, for she would not have refused Tony if he had asked her quietly, and her father had not been there, and her face had not been scratched by the bramble. And having said that, away she walked, upon her father's arm, thinking and hoping he would ask her again.

Tony is next rejected by Unity, who scornfully walks away too, but the serial adds that 'she looked back when she'd gone some way, to see if he was following her'. These serial additions, Gatrell suggests, show that Hardy came to feel that girls in such a situation 'would be incapable of sustaining the proud and dismissive reactions of the manuscript' (p. 117).

Tony then turns to Milly, the only one of the three who remains, and says fatalistically, 'What must be must be, I suppose.' Milly in the manuscript makes no reply, but she apparently consents because we learn that the banns are put up the next Sunday. Her silence is replaced in the serial, however, with a brief exchange between the two:

> 'If you like, Tony. You didn't really mean what you said to them?'
> 'Not a word of it,' declares Tony, bringing down his fist upon his palm.

Milly's mute assent in the manuscript seems rather improbable, while Tony's reassurance defines him as the 'deceiver' of the story's title. Incidentally, Tony's deception was originally to have been more heinous in the manuscript, where we learn near the beginning that he 'was going to put up the banns of marriage' with Milly on the next Sunday, but in the serial he is less committed to any one of the three girls and he is merely 'thinking of putting the question' to Milly about the banns. Indeed a cancelled phrase in the MS. says that Tony had also 'promised secretly to marry' Anna (fo. 4), but Hardy immediately deleted this (perhaps because it made him too devious and duplicitous for a comic tale) and replaced it with the comment that Tony had simply 'always wished' that he had arranged to marry Anna. In the published versions, Tony's deceptions all occur within the story and not prior to it.

In preparing *1894*, Hardy makes the story increasingly explicit. The key scene in this respect is the confrontation near the end between Tony and all three girls. He announces that he has chosen Hannah to be his wife, but her father joins the group and tells her in the serial to refuse him. The first galley proof, however, here has the father adding a warning that she should do so only

> 'if yer virtue is left to 'ee and you run no risk'.
> 'She's as sound as a bell for me, that I'll swear!' says Tony, flaring up.
> 'And so's the others, come to that'. (p. 235)

In the margin of the first proof, Hardy makes Tony continue by saying, 'though you may think it an onusual thing ~~for me to say~~'. The revises add to this rather ambiguous remark yet again, with Tony now saying, 'though you may think it an onusual thing *in me*' (my italics). The last two words make Tony rather more chivalrous, for he is now saying that the father may think it unusual *in him*, not the girls, to have been chaste. Hardy took the opportunity in revising to make the story more realistic by adding the father's pragmatic recognition that Hannah could be pregnant. We can here see each of the three layers of proof revision between serial and *1894* as Hardy first augments and then refines the scene.

In the version of the story which we read now, we learn how Tony used to sing what sounds like a rather improper song called 'The Tailor's Breeches', one line of which we hear: 'O the petticoats went off, and the breeches they went on!' (p. 225). The song in the serial, however, was much more respectable and conventional, which is no doubt why five lines of it were quoted (the same five lines were sung in *Far from the Madding Crowd*, chapter 23):

> 'I've lost my love, and I care not–
> I've lost my love, and I care not!
>   I shall soon have another
>   That's better than t'other
> I've lost my love, and I care not!'

The serial version of the song, in fact, has more direct relevance to the characterization of Tony as fickle in love, but the line from 'The Tailor's Breeches' which Hardy came to prefer allowed him to add, after quoting the line, the information that Tony used to sing songs like this and 'all the rest of the scandalous stuff. He was quite the women's favourite [...]' (p. 225; the latter sentence was in the serial). The addition of Tony's liking for the 'scandalous stuff' permits Hardy to imply a mischievously causal link between it and his status as the women's favourite.

Hardy made the confrontation between the three women when they discovered each other's presence rather more melodramatic and downright noisy than it had been in the serial. In *1894*, for instance, they 'screeched and sobbed till they was quite spent' and Tony can speak only 'as soon as he could get heard' (p. 234). Hannah then saw her father, and ran to him, 'crying worse than ever' (p. 235). All of these additions were introduced in preparing the first proof.

Two of Hardy's marginal emendations to the first proof are worthy of note. The first is the decision, for no apparent reason, to rename one of the girls Hannah (she had been Anna in the serial and first proof). This decision necessitated some thirty alterations. The second concerns a seemingly minor accidental but it shows Hardy's concern for the subtlest psychological nuance. In the serial, Tony had asked his father which of the three girls he ought to marry, and his father had replied, 'Whichever of 'em did *not* ask to ride with thee?' In revising the first proof, Hardy simply deleted the question mark, so that the father now *tells* Tony to marry Milly, rather than, as in the serial, merely suggesting it tentatively as a solution. This emended version better motivates Tony's later contrary feeling that 'of all things that could have happened to wean him from Milly there was nothing so powerful as his father's recommending her. No; it could not be Milly, after all' (p. 233).

The main change in the revises creates an improvement in plotting. In the serial, Milly (the second girl in the waggon) hides under the tarpaulin at the front when Tony sees Hannah. The first girl, Unity, is also under the tarpaulin, but at the back. This causes a slight narrative problem in the serial when Hannah hears 'a little screaming squeak under that tar-cloth': is it Unity or Milly who is protesting about Tony making love to Hannah? We cannot tell, since both are under the tarpaulin. In *1894*, Hardy changed Milly's hiding place to the empty sacks, making it clear that the squeal comes from there. This required Hardy to make a total of seven alterations in details of plot throughout the story.

Hardy made nine changes when preparing *1912*, of which six are substantive, involving the addition of some twenty words. When Hannah comes out to the waggon, Tony in *1912* helps her up beside him, 'her feet outside' (*1912*, p. 198). We also learn for the first time that Tony realizes he could not marry all three girls 'as he longed to do' (*1912*, p. 201), his polygamous desires no doubt having been judged too shocking for earlier versions of the sketch.

Two final changes show Hardy with a keen eye for the details of his plot and characterization some twenty years after first writing the story. The first of these draws attention to a bizarre omission in the serial and *1894*; in these previous versions, the girls are eventually thrown from the waggon when the horse speeds off, yet a couple of pages later Tony and his bride-to-be, Milly, are able to climb up into the waggon. How had they got the horse back? *1912* adds the necessary information, explaining how 'the horse looked round and stood still' (p. 202) after throwing out the girls. Finally, in the preceding versions of the sketch, Hannah is in a 'tantrum' at the end, partly because of the scratch on her face which she had received from a hedge when being catapulted from the waggon. Hardy must have felt that a scratch was hardly motive enough to justify a tantrum, and so in *1912* he makes her anxious instead about 'the scar that might be left on her face' (p. 203).

'The History of the Hardcomes'

This tragic sketch tells how two cousins, James and Steve, were so carried away when dancing with each other's fiancée at Tony Kytes's wedding that they decided to swap partners and marry them. Some years later, Steve went on a rowing trip with his original fiancée and they fell into a tender reverie, going far out to sea and being found the next day, drowned in each other's arms.

The MS. is on six leaves, fos. 8–14, and fo. 10 is missing. The title is given as 'Incident at the wedding party', and James is called 'Jose' or 'Josey' throughout. In the preamble to the story, the wedding party was not Tony Kytes's but that of Unity Sallet, who married a farmer called Jolliver. Later in the MS., however, Emily recalls 'our changing partners at T. K's wedding' (fo. 12), so Hardy had obviously decided to create this structural link to the previous story in the sequence in the course of composition. There is no indication that the cousins are called Hardcome, although the preamble to the next tale states that Betty Privett used to do the washing for Mr and Mrs Hardcome, so Hardy appears to have settled on their surname by the time he finished the story. The parish clerk narrates the entire episode in the MS., and the curate does not replace him half-way through, as he does in the serial. The MS. originally ended with a description of the marriage of James and Emily proving to be in every respect a happy one. Hardy then wrote the title of the next story but immediately deleted it and continued with the visitor asking whether the Hardcomes were still alive. Hardy was apparently unsure of the narrator's reply, for he brackets two possible answers, to the effect that they are indeed dead or that the narrator does not know because they emigrated to Australia (the latter was rejected for the serial).

Hardy added three distinct features to the story when revising the manuscript for the serial version. The first concerns the explanation at the end of the story of how the tragedy might have happened:

> Conjecture pictured that they might have fallen into tender reverie while gazing each into a pair of eyes that had formerly flashed for him and her alone, and, unwilling to avow what their mutual sentiments were, they had continued thus, oblivious of time and space, till darkness suddenly overtook them far from land. But nothing was truly known.

The first half of this (up to 'avow') is present only in note form in the manuscript, squeezed between paragraphs as an after-thought, and Hardy supplemented it for the serial. After he had shown the lovers 'gazing each into a pair of eyes', he must have decided to make this reverie the key element in their deaths and he added three earlier references to them facing each other in the boat, none of which is in the manuscript.

The second feature of Hardy's revision of the manuscript shows his keenness to justify his narrators, who explain how they came to know details of the story in four new passages. Indeed, the decision to introduce the curate as narrator in the middle of the story was probably intended to provide a more credible witness than the clerk, for the curate had heard the facts 'from their own lips' and 'almost word for word as I have told it to you' when James came to give him notice of the proposed wedding.

The third feature of the manuscript revision is Hardy's increased emphasis on the 'mismating' of the two couples: James is said in the serial to be 'a quiet, fireside, perusing man' and he 'felt at times a wide gap between himself and Olive', while Steve, who was 'always knocking about hither and thither', had a wife who 'worked samplers and made hearth-rugs [...] and only drove out with him to please him'. The incompatibility of the two couples is later seen when James tells Emily that he merely pretends to be a horseman on Olive's account, and we learn that they ought to have married as had been planned 'by nature'.

A note which Hardy made in the manuscript reads simply 'He often comes...' (fo. 12), and the serial expands this to give a credible reason for Steve's impressive prowess at rowing: 'He often comes here on business, and generally has a pull round the bay.' The brevity of the note suggests that Hardy was intending to revise the manuscript soon after it was completed and would need only a cue to prompt him. Another revision for the serial concerns the depiction of James and Emily at the end of the story: in the MS., they are rather dismissively described as 'the other two less romantic ones' (fo. 14), but this became in the serial 'the remaining two [...] were a more thoughtful and far-seeing, though less romantic couple than the first', and they are able to fulfil their original 'and calmly formed' intention to marry. These revisions give a much more positive depiction of their relatively sober love compared to the heady intoxication of the drowned couple.

The most significant revision to the serial is *1894*'s presentation of the discovery of the drowned couple washed up on the shore: 'It was said that they had been found tightly locked in each other's arms, *his lips upon hers*' (p. 248; my italics), the last four words having been added to the serial version of the scene. This is in keeping with the franker and more explicit portrayal of passion in the volume as a whole.

After they had been married for a year or two, the cousins began to wonder 'what had made 'em so mad at the last moment to marry crosswise as they did, when they might have married straight, as was planned by nature, and as they had fallen in love' (p. 240). This final phrase read in the serial, 'as they had *first* fallen in love' (my italics), implying that the cousins really had fallen in love for a second time at Tony Kytes's wedding; *1894*, however, denies this possibility, making the dance seem instead a moment of mad infatuation, such as we had seen earlier in *Life's Little Ironies* in the depiction of Mop Ollamoor, the bewitching musician in 'The Fiddler of the Reels'.

The first narrator of 'The History of the Hardcomes' is a church-officer and his presentation changes subtly. In the serial, he explains how he was one of the first to leave Tony Kytes's wedding party because of his 'serious calling', but in *1894* he ascribes his early departure simply to 'my morning's business' (p. 239), making him seem much less stuffy and pompous. Other changes show that Hardy repeatedly had difficulty in deciding how to refer to the married couples: in the serial and first proof, James and Emily are the 'friends' of the dead couple, which Hardy emended in the margin to 'consorts', while *1894* finally read 'spouses' (p. 247). This last revision serves to reinforce the opposition in the sketch between lovers and marriage partners, Steve loving Olive but being the 'spouse' of Emily, for instance. Another late addition which must have been similarly made at the second proof stage is the description of how Emily and James caught the Budmouth train, 'the line being just opened' (p. 248). This places the story in 1857 or shortly afterwards, and shows Hardy's increasingly realistic portrayal of an ever more thinly disguised Wessex.

1912 shows Hardy continuing to refine the mystery of what occurred between Steve and Emily in the boat which made them drift off to sea, oblivious of their surroundings. In *1894*, the narrator had stressed that 'underhand behaviour was foreign to the nature of either' (p. 249), but *1912* talks rather of 'underhand behaviour *at starting*' (p. 214; my italics). Hardy stresses that Steve and Emily did not *begin* the boating trip with any romantic intent, but he must have come to feel that if underhand behaviour was *always* unknown to them, they would not have been found in the previous paragraph tightly locked in each other's arms, his lips upon hers. Hardy does emphasize, however, that the boat trip was relatively innocent until the passionate embrace of drowning; conjecture pictured them gazing into each other's eyes in a romantic reverie, but 'they had done no more than continue thus' (*1912*, p. 214). This is even more emphatically stating the couple's innocence than *1894*'s 'they had continued thus' (p. 249). Hardy may make the discovery of the bodies a more passionate spectacle than it was in the serial but he does not ruin the sketch by allowing any hint that the two lovers drifted out to their deaths because of some moment of sexual rather than emotional distraction.[7]

'The Superstitious Man's Story'

Hardy gave some background information about this story in a letter to E.B. Poulton on 20 May 1924:

> The incident of the "miller moth" flying out of a man's mouth at the moment of his death – supposed to be his soul – is or was a belief of this county.
>
> The spot whereon the particular instance of it that I had in mind is assumed to have occurred was a place called "Buttock's Spring" in the parish of Melbury Osmund.
>
> How old the superstition may be I do not know. The old lady who told it to me said it happened in her childhood, & that would have been about 1820.
>
> The common white moth is still called a "miller's soul" by the peasantry, for obvious reasons. (*Letters*, VI, 251–2; the editors note that Hardy originally wrote 'supposed' for 'assumed')

Similarly, he had told Edward Clodd in 1894 that 'all that about the "miller's-soul" is, or was till lately, an actual belief down here. It was told me years ago by an old woman' (II, 54). This old woman is likely to be Hardy's mother, Jemima, who was born in 1813 and spent her childhood in Melbury Osmund. In the MS., 'Buttocks Spring' is said to be the name not of the site where William died but of the spring, two miles away, where his spirit was later seen: that is, Hardy moved the spot where the 'miller's-soul' appeared but retained the actual place-name for another incident. (In the MS., incidentally, 'Buttocks Spring' is one of two alternative names for the site, the other being the more decorous 'Arm Spring'; all printed versions read 'Longpuddle Spring'.)

This very brief sketch about a man's death and the supernatural incidents accompanying it was little revised after it was first composed. The MS. consists of three leaves (fos. 14–15, 15a). The melancholy man who narrates the story is the master-thatcher, not the seedsman's father, as it is in all printed versions. There were also some changes to the names of minor characters: the man who is present when William dies was originally called 'Chandler', but this was deleted and replaced by 'Chawles' (all printed versions read 'Chiles'), while Philip Hookhorn, who sees William's spirit, was called 'Henry Crookhorn' in the MS. Longpuddle was Lewgate in the manuscript. A lengthy addition on the verso of fo. 14 shows the whole of the meeting between Betty Privett and Nancy Weedle, who describes how she saw William's shape enter the church on Old Midsummer Eve.

The main additions to the manuscript for the serial seek to heighten Betty's apprehension about her husband's behaviour. For instance, where the MS. merely talks of her 'surprise' at finding his boots at the foot of the stairs when she believed that he had gone outside, the serial refers to her 'great surprise, and I might say alarm'. The serial also describes how, the next morning, 'she waited his return to breakfast wi' much anxiety for an explanation, for thinking over the matter by daylight made it seem only the more startling', and she is said to be 'too' disturbed to argue with him. The only other significant additions to the manuscript are a couple which characterize William more fully at the start of the story: in the serial, we learn that one could sense when he was 'anywhere behind your back', making Betty's certainty that he really had left the house more plausible, and the incident is said to occur 'at a time that William was in very good health to all appearance', so that the premonitions of his death cannot readily be explained away as mere anticipations of a likely event.

The majority of Hardy's alterations for *1894* were made in the margins of the first proof and chiefly they increase the dialect content of the tale ('wi'', 'them words', 'nunch' and 'pa'son', for instance). The principal change in *1912* concerns the church bell which the sexton is tolling on the Sunday before William Privett's death. In *1894*, the sexton explained how he had 'not known the bell go so heavy in his hand for years – it was just as if the gudgeons wanted oiling' (p. 250). This rational explanation of the event rather takes away its purpose in the story, which is to serve as one more omen of William's death, and in *1912* Hardy replaces the earlier explanation with the sexton's comment, 'and he feared it meant a death in the parish' (p. 216), which also helps to establish the narrator as the 'superstitious man' of the story's title.

'Andrey Satchel and the Parson and Clerk'

This sketch, in the collected version which we now read, tells how a young woman called Jane is in urgent need of getting married, since she is about to give birth at any moment. She manages to get an inebriated Andrey to the church but the parson refuses to marry them until he is sober. Locking them both in the church at Jane's request, the parson leaves and is later caught up in the excitement of a hunt, forgetting about Jane and Andrey until the next day. The parson and his clerk rush round to the church and find, most importantly, that Jane has not yet given birth. The sketch ends happily with their timely marriage.

An entry in Hardy's 'Memoranda I' notebook, dated November 1878, may have provided a source for one of the story's details:

> The honest Earl. Earl is accidentally shut up in a tower – the Hardy monument, say – with a blacksmith's daughter. Goes to parson next day & says he feels it his duty to marry her. Does so. Finds her not so good as she seemed, &... (Taylor, p. 19)

The fate of the fox which the parson and clerk are chasing has its origin in an anecdote which Hardy heard in October 1886: '"Lord Portsmouth made his whipper-in tell Emma the story of the hunted fox that ran up the old woman's clock-case, adding corroborative words with much gravity as the story proceeded, and enjoying it more than she did, though he had heard it 100 times"' (*Life*, p. 190).

The MS. of the story comprises three leaves (fos. 16–18); the ending is missing (fo. [19]), and the MS. breaks off with the return of the parson and clerk from the hunt. The title is given as 'The story of the parson & clerk' and was interlined. There is not the slightest hint in this MS. version that Jane could have been pregnant, so the couple of indications in the serial (discussed below) must have been late additions. The surname 'Satchel' does not appear in the MS., and the first reference to Andrey and Jane appears to read 'W^m.|Joey Andrew| & Jane Vallens' (fo. 16). 'William' might have been rejected because that is the name of the Superstitious Man of the previous story. The decision to call him 'Andrew' must have been made almost immediately (there is another deleted 'W^m.' three lines below the first one), because the name is used thus in what is now the story's opening sentence (and he is 'Andrey' in the next one). Andrew is described as '|the son of the V.| that you knew' (fo. 16), indicating that Hardy originally intended his surname to be Vallens; after the alteration to Satchel for the serial, Hardy retained Vallens for Jane's maiden name. The parson's name is given variously in the MS. as 'Mr Matthews' and 'Mr Millhead', but in the serial he is called ironically 'Billy Toogood'. The MS. is the only version of the story to give the clerk a name, where he is called Simeon on one occasion.

The only reference to the narrator in the manuscript is at the very beginning of the story: 'Well, I can soon tell it. |s[ai]^d the C.W. master-thatcher|' (fo. 16). The narrator, then, was originally intended to be this deleted 'C.W.', which might be a reference to the cider maker's wife, who is listed on the first leaf as one of the occupants of the van (though she never appeared in any published versions). If so, perhaps Hardy later decided that this story of drunkenness and pregnancy was rather too indelicate to be told by a female narrator. In preparing the serial, Hardy went on to add quite a lot of characterization to the master-thatcher, none of which is found in the manuscript. For instance, he is described in the serial as 'a man with a spark of subdued liveliness in his eye, who had hitherto kept his attention mainly upon small objects a long way ahead, as he sat in front of the van with his feet outside', and the carrier warns Lackland 'that Christopher's stories will bear pruning'.

Most of Hardy's main revisions to the story, both within the manuscript and at a later stage of preparing the serial, are intended to make it plausible that Andrey and Jane could stay locked up in the church tower all night without being discovered. Firstly, Hardy needed to dispose of the witnesses to the wedding, so that they would not be in the vicinity to raise the alarm: he achieved this by adding the following insertion on a verso, marked for insertion:

> The witnesses A's brother & brother's wife, neither of whom wished cared about Andrey marrying Jane, & had come |rather| against their will, said they couldn't wait & wished to get home before dinner time to where they lived, some miles away. (fo. 16^v)

Earlier in the manuscript, the witnesses had been said to be *Jane's* brother and sister-in-law, who would presumably have been keen to stay and see Jane married, especially when, in the serial, she is pregnant. By changing the witnesses to Andrey's relatives, Hardy can give them a plausible motive for not staying. A consequence of this alteration is that he also needed to move the venue of the christening which Andrey had attended the previous night: in the MS., it was said to be his brother's child who was being christened, but this would now mean that one of the witnesses would probably be as drunk as Andrey, so in the serial Andrey attends the christening of a neighbour's child.

Another addition on the same verso shows Jane asking to be locked up in the church tower: 'lIf we bide in the churchl Folk may see us through the winders, & 'twould be such a scandal, & perhaps Andrey too ~~wou~~ may try to get out.' This addition has the double advantage of making them securely locked in and also completely invisible. Later in the MS., Hardy started to describe the parson scrambling into his hunting clothes, but he crossed it out after writing five lines and showed instead the clerk's excitement about the hunt and his pleading to be allowed to exercise the horses. Hardy must have realized that he needed to get the clerk involved in the hunt and away from the church all night to ensure that Andrey and Jane would not be rescued.

Even after he had completed the manuscript, Hardy made other alterations for the serial which would explain more reasonably how Andrey and Jane were not discovered. For instance, we learn that keeping the matter a secret 'was not a very hard thing to do, the place being so lonely, and the hour so early': this addition ensures that no one else knew they were locked up, and no one would be able to hear their cries for help during the night. Similarly, a reference in the MS. to the clerk's wife was deleted from the serial, so that there is no one left in the village who might conceivably know that the pair are imprisoned.

The characterization of the parson is subtly changed in the MS. by two lengthy additions made on the verso of fo. 17. These show the conversation of the parson and clerk as they ride with the hunt. The clerk utters an oath, 'dammy', and the parson rebukes him and begs him to 'remember our calling', which is ironic in that he has not remembered about Andrey and Jane in the excitement of the hunt. Later, the clerk says that the chase is 'better than crying "Amen" to your ~~world wi~~ "ever & ever"' (in printed versions, the addition of 'on a winter's morning' to the end of the clerk's sentence makes the statement slightly less impious). The parson replies:

> Yes indeed clerk. To everything there's a season, says Mr M. lquite pat,l
> for he was a lwelll learned ~~pious~~ lworthyl lldevoutll Xtianl man & lalwaysl had
> his chapter & verse at his tongue's end as a pa'son should.

Hardy can be seen striving here to capture the precise note of complacent hypocrisy in the parson: 'pious' and 'worthy' may have struck him as too obviously ironic, while 'devout' is a more tellingly inappropriate description of this negligent cleric. Hardy revised this addition again for the serial: he omitted 'well' in 'well learned', perhaps feeling that it was not particularly remarkable for a parson to be able to quote from Ecclesiastes, and he added 'when he liked' after the description of him as a learned and devout Christian man ('and devout' was to be omitted in *1894*).

A few minor details are different in the MS.: after their wedding, Andrey and Jane were originally going to walk 'to C[asterbridge]. & go on to ~~some~~ B[udmouth].' (fo. 16), but in the serial they drive instead to Port Bredy. In the MS., Jane lives with her father, which raises the question why he was not at the wedding, and so in the serial she is said to live with a 'distant relation'. The time of year in the MS. is given as '~~January~~ |December|' (fo. 16), but this was changed again to November in the serial, perhaps to make better sense of the clerk's later comment that 'it may be frosty in a day or two' (fo. 18), which would prevent them exercising their horses 'for weeks'. The route which the hunt takes is different in the MS., where they cross the fallow ground between Yalbury Wood and Green's Wood (Lippet Wood and Green's Copse in the serial, respectively) and then continue 'lup hill & down dalel' (fo. 18), a vague phrase which is preceded in the serial by a specific and lengthy itinerary which explains why the parson and clerk are so late in returning home: 'into Green's Copse, then across to Higher Jirton; then on across this very turnpike-road to Climmerston Ridge, then away towards Yalbury Wood'.

The *1894* revisions to 'Andrey Satchel and the Parson and Clerk' are the most interesting and most substantial in the whole of 'A Few Crusted Characters'. In addition to numerous individual words, Hardy inserted three passages totalling thirty lines in length (all of which are present in the first proof). Much of the humour of the sketch arises from the urgency of Jane's need to get married and the parson's anxiety to rescue her from the church before she gives birth, but in the serial it is only hinted at in the most discreet way that she is even pregnant. We learn, for instance, how she implored the parson to continue with the ceremony 'which, poor soul, she had very good reason to hasten'. The only other reference to her condition is in the final sentence of the sketch where we are told that she 'saved her name'; apart from these two allusions, one could easily think that her wish to marry quickly is because she is getting on in years and is somewhat older than Andrey.

Hardy sought in *1894* and *1912* to make the sketch much more explicit and, consequently, much more comic. The serial began by explaining how Jane's age, 'coupled with other circumstances, made her very anxious' to get married. The first proof of *1894* emended this to

> coupled with other circumstances–'
> ('Ah, poor thing!' sighed the women.)
> '– made her very anxious [...]

Hardy altered this further by adding 'bodily' to 'circumstances' (p. 256) in the margin of the proof, while in *1912* he revised the phrase yet again to its present reading: 'coupled with other bodily circumstances owing to that young man' (p. 220). *1912* also has the parson telling Jane that he is sorry for her, 'seeing the condition you are in' (p. 222). One cannot now avoid realizing that Jane is pregnant.

Two of the three substantial inserts serve to foreground the impending birth and the urgency of the parson getting back to the church as quickly as possible. An eleven-line addition ('It is, sir; very. [...] like plain honest men', pp. 263–4) shows the clerk's anxiety lest 'we've ruined the 'ooman!' and his fear of the consequences if 'anything has happened to her up in that there tower, and no doctor or nuss –'. A later insertion occurs when the parson and clerk reach the church and the former asks, 'Does she look as if anything premature had took place?' (p. 265).[8] Jane shortly emerges 'pale and cold, but otherwise as usual' (i.e., still pregnant, the last four words being an addition to the serial). The final addition to the serial which makes it more explicit concerns the reason for Andrey's drunken state on the morning of the wedding. In the serial, he explains how he had been godfather to a neighbour's child on the day before and they had stayed up all night to celebrate the christening: 'Not if I live to be a thousand shall I again be made a godfather one day and a husband the next', and Hardy adds in the margin of the first proof, 'and perhaps a father ~~soon after~~ [?] the next' (p. 257).

The characterization of Parson Toogood undergoes much improvement in the course of revisions, making him more individual and human. The serial describes him as 'a very worthy, strict man', but the first proof of *1894* omits 'worthy' (p. 257). This is in line with the tendency of the revisions to make him much less ecclesiastical and divine, and rather more an ordinary mortal with venial weaknesses, keener on the hunt than the church. For instance, the serial's reference to him as 'a learned and devout Christian' reads simply 'a learned Christian' (p. 262) in *1894*. Similarly, his 'holy white surplice' of the serial becomes just a 'clane white surplice' (p. 258) in the first proof. The first of the three lengthy inserts, indeed, is devoted to making the parson a very idiosyncratic character:

> And – being a bachelor man – every time he went to bed in summer he used
> to open the bed at bottom and crawl up head foremost, to mind en of the
> coming winter and the good sport he'd have, and the foxes going to earth.
> (pp. 259–60)[9]

This insert also tells us how the parson would celebrate a child's christening with a bottle of port wine, thus making his refusal to marry Andrey for being drunk after a christening rather hypocritical. Similarly, later in the sketch, one of the other inserts has him swearing in his anger at forgetting about Jane and Andrey: '"Why the hell didn't I marry 'em, drunk or sober!" (Pa'sons used to cuss in them days like plain honest men)' (p. 264). This is only a couple of pages after he had rebuked his clerk for saying 'dammy': 'Don't let me hear that word again! Remember our calling' (p. 262). Hardy's revisions in his characterization, then, serve to make Parson Toogood an increasingly ironic name.

The first proof shows Hardy making the sketch much more 'Wessex' by the introduction of frequent dialect words, which he had possibly felt would have been out of place in the American serial. Thus we have 'sojers', 'wambling', 'clane', 'oncontrollable', 'knowed', 'hosses', 'theirselves', 'half-chawed', 'sparrer', 'they seed', 'winder' (*window*), ''twould gie me', 'jineral' and 'a' onion', all of which are printed in the first proof, with the exception of the last two which Hardy altered in the margin. He also evidently grew increasingly attached to the reading of 'parson' as 'pa'son', making thirteen changes to the serial in the first proof, adding an equal number in the margins and yet two more in the second proof.

The *1912* revision of this sketch was also the most substantial of any of those in 'A Few Crusted Characters', adding some 24 words not found in *1894*. Apart from the increasingly explicit presentation of Jane's condition which has been discussed earlier, Hardy's main alteration was to reduce slightly the number of dialect forms or indications of local pronunciation, quite the opposite of his tendency when preparing the earlier volume. Thus, 'winders' became 'windows' (p. 223), although he allowed two later instances of 'winders' to remain, and 'jineral manager' reverted to its original serial reading of 'general manager' (p. 224). He altered ''scaped' to 'escaped' and 'a sparrer's feather' to 'a sparrow's feather' (p. 228). Hardy also added a better reason why the parson may not be able to take the horses out for several weeks: it may be frosty 'and slippery' (p. 225).

'Old Andrey's Experience as a Musician'

There is no evidence of this story in the manuscript, although there may have been some on the missing fo. 19, which would be the appropriate place in the sequence. The serial version of the sketch was called 'Andrew Satchel's Experience as a Musician', and the change in *1894* stresses that the Andrew of this story is the father of the Andrew Satchel in the previous one. In this brief sketch, Andrey pretends to be a member of the local choir in order to attend the squire's Christmas party, but he is discovered to be unable to play his instrument, much to his embarrassment and the fury of the squire.

The most significant of Hardy's few revisions to this sketch were the marginal emendations which he made to the first proof. It is at this stage, for instance, that he heightened the grandeur of the squire's guests who listen to the choir, thus increasing Andrey's social discomfiture. We learn how 'the archdeacon, Lord and Lady Baxby, and I don't know who' (p. 267) are present, and that it is 'no other than the archdeacon' (p. 269) who discovers that Andrey is holding his fiddle upside down. The only other revision of any interest, again a marginal emendation, is the description of the master-thatcher who is about to begin narrating the next sketch. In the serial he 'cleared his throat at the bottom, and then at the top, and went on', but in *1894* we read that 'the master-thatcher attentively regarded past times as if they lay about a mile off, and went on' (p. 270).

The four revisions for *1912* comprise two substitutions of 'O' for 'Oh' and two more of 'quire' for 'choir'.

'Absent-Mindedness in a Parish Choir'

This sketch describes the demise of the Longpuddle choir after they consumed alcohol in church one Christmas to keep themselves warm: waking from their nap in the gallery, they mistakenly thought they were at a party they had attended the night before and started playing a profane tune. The squire banished the disgraced choir and replaced them with an organ.

The MS. of this story is complete (fos. 20–21) but it is untitled, suggesting that it may have been originally conceived as the concluding part of the previous story, giving another incident in the life of the old choir. Perhaps Hardy was obliged to give 'Absent-Mindedness' a separate title because it appeared in a later instalment of the serial. This conjecture that the story was at one time part of 'Old Andrey's Experience as a Musician' might also explain why there is no indication of the identity of the narrator in the MS., since it would presumably have been told by the schoolmaster who recalled Old Andrey. If this hypothesis is plausible, the previous story, which is missing from the manuscript, might originally have had a title which encompassed the two incidents concerning the choir.

Several names are different in the manuscript: Dan'l Hornhead is called 'Dan'l Muggeridge', and at the end of the story Hardy made a list of alternative surnames for him, with the last one being the closest to his eventual name: 'Lornridge Dugridge Luggridge Lornhead' (fo. 20). Levi Limpet, the boy who sits in the gallery, is called Levi Drummell in the manuscript and he misleads Timothy and Nicholas by mischievously nudging them and saying, 'Another |reel hornpipe| dance. ~~They~~ |Quick – the couples| be waiting' (fo. 21). In published versions, he merely tells them to begin playing, and Nicholas is solely responsible for his mistake. Mr Nicks, who plays the oboe, is not mentioned in the manuscript: his name is included in the list of choir members at the start of the story in all published versions, although Hardy omitted to add it to the roll-call of disgraced musicians who creep out of the church at the end (the serial's illustration depicts six players in church, but only five are said to leave, as in the manuscript).

In the MS., the choir was originally said to have been replaced by a young woman playing a harmonium, but this was deleted in favour of a young man with a seraphina (he plays an organ in published versions). In preparing the serial, Hardy added some details to the manuscript to stress the low temperature in the church and justify the choir's drinking: it is 'mortal' cold and the congregation had a stove 'to keep off the frost'. Nicholas says that they need something 'in our insides' to 'make us warm, if it cost a king's ransom' (replacing the MS. 'keep us warm'), so he later brings 'hot' brandy and beer, which they sip in thimblefuls throughout the service (so that they do not notice its creeping effect), rather than consuming it all at the beginning of the sermon, which is the MS. reading. The length of the sermon ('most unfortunately for 'em it was a long one that afternoon') is a new detail in the serial which similarly works to mitigate their offence of falling asleep.

The volume of noise which the tune makes is increased in the serial: the MS. described how it 'shook the church winders', but this became 'made the cobwebs in the roof shiver like ghosts', and the sound is said to be 'raging through the church'. The squire in the manuscript is said to be a 'wicked profane man' but he is merely 'wickedish' in the serial, which perhaps explains why he remembers to include 'God Almighty' in his list of those insulted by the choir's music, a detail missing in the draft.

The only revisions of interest to the serial are the half-dozen occasions on which Hardy altered or added a word to increase the extent of dialect or colloquial usage, with the result that *1894* came to contain 'o' the', 'spaking' (*speaking*), 'gie'd' (*gave*), 'pa'son' and 'sinful inclined' (for the serial's 'badly inclined'). All of these were marginal emendations to the first proof, with the exception of the last one (printed in first proof).

When preparing *1912*, Hardy twice altered 'choir' to 'quire', as in the previous sketch. He also added one more individual, the parson, to the number of people offended by the choir's drunken playing of secular tunes in church. The squire tells the choir that they will never play in church again 'for the insult to me, and my family, and my visitors, and the parson, and God Almighty' (pp. 235–6). Hardy's addition of the parson serves to heighten the sense in which this list turns into a hierarchy of godliness, and the squire has unwittingly put himself first, and presumably lowest, thereby ironically confirming the narrator's comment earlier in the paragraph that 'he was a wickedish man, the squire was, though now for once he happened to be on the Lord's side'.

'The Winters and the Palmleys'

This sketch portrays the hatred of Mrs Palmley for Mrs Winter, whom she blames for taking her lover and for the death of her son. Many years later, Mrs Winter's child, Jack, tries to court Mrs Palmley's niece, Harriet, but she scorns him for his illiterate letters, which she keeps in her workbox. Jack is so ashamed of his letters that he steals the box, which, unknown to him, also contains money. He is tried for burglary, and Mrs Palmley refuses to allow her niece to tell the true circumstances of the theft. Jack is found guilty and his execution is Mrs Palmley's revenge on his mother.

This is the story which underwent most revision between the manuscript and the serial publication. In the MS., there are only the final three leaves extant (fos. 23a–25), and the fragment begins with Jack breaking in to steal Harriet's workbox. There is no mention of the mothers, Mrs Winter and Mrs Palmley, and Hardy seems to have conceived of their bitter feud only after he had composed this manuscript version. The text of the sermon at Jack's funeral is said in the MS. to be '"He was the only son of his mother, & she was a widow"', as in published versions, and it might have been this biblical reference which later prompted Hardy to conceive of giving Mrs Winter a central role. In the story that came to be published, the returning migrant asked about an old gaunt woman whom he remembered, and this turns out to be Jack's mother, but in the manuscript she is revealed to be Harriet, the hanged man's former lover. Harriet as a young woman lived not with her aunt, Mrs Palmley, but with her father (called Palmer). In the MS., Harriet refuses to corroborate Jack's statement that he had intended to steal only the letters and not the money because she is acting under 'the influence of her |father, & her| new lover' (fo. 24). Originally, then, Hardy seems to have conceived the story as showing the tragic outcome of a romantic triangle. In the MS., Harriet's father refuses to appeal for mercy at the trial simply because Jack 'was no favourite of his', and he is duly hanged.

There is an indication that Hardy originally intended this story to be the first in the sequence after the 'Introduction': at the top of leaf 28a (originally part of fo. 3), there is a deleted title which reads 'II. [/] The history of Jack Winter'. Hardy cancelled this and began below it the story which became 'Netty Sargent's Copyhold' (this in turn was later moved to the end of the sequence, as described above). The deleted title makes no reference to the feud between the two families and again suggests that it was a late addition to the story.

The story in the MS. is set in 'G^t. |Kings| Hintock' (fo. 25), not Longpuddle, and Harriet and her husband moved to Lewgate after the trial (the serial says that they moved to an unspecified 'distant town'). Jack's coffin was brought from Casterbridge to King's Hintock along Holway lane, another name for Long Ash Lane. In later versions the story is narrated by the groceress, but it is clear that Hardy had not yet decided on the identity of the narrator when he was making this manuscript version, because there is a note at the very end of the fragment which reads '[N.B. the person who tells this must be an old inhabitant]' (fo. 25). The cancelled title on fo. 28a is preceded by another deleted line which indicates that the narrator at that stage of composition was to have been the schoolmaster, but perhaps Hardy came to feel that he would not be old enough, so he transferred the narration to the 'aged groceress', as she is described on the opening leaf.

In the MS., Jack opened the stolen workbox immediately on returning home, and a deleted passage shows him burning the letters before he goes to bed. This meant that he would have found the money hidden beneath the letters at that time and been able to return the box before Harriet had noticed it was missing, so Hardy postponed the burning of the letters in the serial until the next morning, when Jack could be caught red-handed by the constables.

A detail in the description of Jack's execution is not found in the MS. and was therefore a later addition which typifies Hardy's historical imagination: the weighting of Jack's feet to ensure a swift death recalls Hardy's father's account of an incident in the 1830s. As Hardy told Newman Flower, 'my father saw four men hung for *being with* some others who had set fire to a rick. Among them was a stripling of a boy of eighteen. Skinny. Half-starved. So frail, so underfed, that they had to put weights on his feet to break his neck.'[10] Jack is similarly described as being 'so boyish and slim' in the serial. Four years earlier, Hardy had used his father's recollection of weighting the boy's feet in his description of the hanging of Rhoda's son in 'The Withered Arm'.

In the published versions of the story, the deadly feud between Mrs Winter and Mrs Palmley has two causes: romantic rivalry, when Mrs Winter tempted away the other's lover, and the death of Mrs Palmley's son, for which the mother holds Mrs Winter responsible. Mrs Winter had sent the little boy with a message to the next village and, passing through a wood, something had come out from behind a tree and frightened him into fits. The boy 'became quite a drivelling idiot, and soon afterward died' (p. 275). In the serial, we learn how 'the thriving woman, Mrs Winter, sent the little boy with a message to the next village one winter day, much against his will. It was getting dark [...].' In *1894*, however, Hardy has altered 'winter day' to 'December day' (p. 275). There are two possible reasons for this; either Hardy wanted to place the story at the darkest time of the year, since the darkness is what causes the boy's fear, or else he simply wanted to avoid the repetition of 'Winter [...] winter' in the same sentence. (This revision is a marginal emendation to the first proof.)

Mrs Winter's son, Jack, whose illiteracy causes him such tragic misfortune in his attempt to woo Mrs Palmley's niece, is said in the serial to have 'limited abilities' for 'grappling with the world'. This is ambiguous in that it implies either that Jack is not very bright or that his opportunities are restricted, and Hardy resolved this confusion by altering the phrase to read 'narrow abilities' (p. 279; marginal emendation) in *1894*. There is a further, purely stylistic change regarding Jack. A sentence which now begins 'By forcing' (p. 282) had originally read in the serial 'Jack, by forcing'; Hardy probably made the alteration because otherwise it would have been the third consecutive sentence beginning with 'Jack', as it had been in the serial (this is again a marginal revision to the first proof).

One final alteration shows Hardy taking pains to make his story consistent and to motivate the characters' actions as fully as he can. Here is how the serial and *1894* present the sentence describing Mrs Palmley's motive for seeking revenge by allowing Jack to be executed:

Serial	*1894*
Here was her revenge upon the household which had ruined and deprived her of her one heart's treasure – her little son	Here was her revenge upon the woman who had first won away her lover, and next ruined and deprived her of her heart's treasure – her little son (p. 284; marginal emendation)

Not only does *1894* remember to mention the first cause of the rivalry between them – the stolen lover – but it also better portrays Mrs Palmley's vindictiveness: her revenge is not now directed at the Winter 'household' (Mrs Winter and her son, Jack), as it was mistakenly said to be in the serial, but solely against Mrs Winter. Jack is hanged because he is the quite innocent pawn in Mrs Palmley's plan of revenge, and she has no grievance against him. *1894* therefore better depicts his status as tragic victim.

Hardy made no revisions to this sketch when he was preparing the Wessex edition in 1912.

'Incident in the Life of Mr. George Crookhill'

The germ of this story was a report in the *Dorset County Chronicle* of 2 April 1829, which Hardy summarized in his 'Facts' notebook:

> Gent[n] comes from Inn in Oxford St, intoxicated – falls down – is seen by the landl[d]. to be picked up by a soldier, & assisted on his way. Gent[n]. reaches his house, in company of soldier, who talks familiarly to half-senseless gent[n] before latter's family. A bed is made up downstairs for the gent[n] & another in same room for soldier. The ladies of the house then retire. Next morning the gent[n] is found dead, and his clothes &c gone. Soldier taken into custody

as a deserter the same day, having on the clothes of Mr Neale (the gent[n].) [p. 97]

Only the latter half of the story is extant in the first draft (fos. 27–8). A note on the verso of fo. 21 reads 'Georgy might change clothes with his fellow traveller from motives not purely of robbery' and might indicate that at one stage Hardy was thinking of putting the story immediately after 'Absent-Mindedness in a Parish Choir'.

At the foot of the final leaf of the story, Hardy made a note to himself describing an alternative plot which he did not use:

A better arrangement might be:
Georgy meets with young farmer: sleep together: |young farmer| says he is rich, life spent in acts of benevolence: grows his corn to give away to the poor, &c. Always does his good by stealth, & wishes it never mentioned. Next morning when G. gets up finds benev[t]. man gone in his |old| clothes, ~~hi~~ & on his old horse, having left his own new clothes ~~& horse~~ & young horse, the former labelled, done in charity. Georgy leaves. When he is gone there arrive at the inn a party of soldiers: have come in search of a deserter – a bad case – who has changed clothes with a young farmer, & ridden off upon his horse. The landlord directs them the way Georgy went, &c. (fo. 28)

The only evidence in the MS. of this story-line is an insertion, later deleted, in which Georgy declares to the constables that the man they are seeking is '|The benevolent gentleman/traveller|' (fo. 28). In general, the MS. is close to the published versions of the story, the only noteworthy variant being that in the MS. the soldier is said to have deserted from 'the D[ragoon]. G[uards]. at Budmouth' (fo. 27; Hardy wrote '151st' above 'D.G.' as an uncancelled alternative), but in the serial he deserted from 'the Dragoons at Cheltenham'.

The leaf from the later fair-copy manuscript of 'Wessex Folk' which was reproduced in facsimile in *Harper's Monthly Magazine* in July 1925 (p. 241) shows the opening of 'Incident in the Life of Mr. George Crookhill'. It is essentially identical to the serial, but it is unfortunately not possible to compare it with the earlier manuscript because the corresponding leaf in the first draft, fo. 26, is missing. Deletions within the fair-copy facsimile show that Georgy began the story by riding out of 'Shottsford' ('Melchester' was quickly substituted, because it is used lower down the leaf in an unrevised form), and he originally met the farmer when he was going up 'Raceground Hill', before Hardy changed it to 'Bissett Hill'.

This sketch is only lightly revised after its serial publication. The 'young farmer' whom Georgy met in the serial becomes the 'tall young farmer' (p. 287; marginal emendation to first proof) in *1894*, anticipating four later descriptions of him as tall. His evident height is important in distinguishing the farmer, who is really a deserter in disguise, from Georgy, and Hardy perhaps wanted to stress that there was no likelihood of the two men being mistaken for each other for very long. Thus, when Georgy is later arrested on suspicion of being the deserter, we are assured that the mistaken identity will have no serious consequences and Hardy can maintain the comic tone of the sketch. Indeed, he can even add 'Georgy groaning: "I shall be shot, I shall be shot!"' (p. 290; another marginal emendation) to increase the apparent seriousness of Georgy's predicament.

In the serial (and the fair-copy manuscript), Georgy and the farmer spend the night in the village of 'Tranton', but this became 'Trantridge' in later versions. Kay-Robinson identifies 'Trantridge' as Pentridge, which did not, however, have an inn, while 'Tranton' is 'surely derived from Tarrant Hinton, a village in the right situation for the story and boasting an inn. I think the explanation is that Hardy used the same name ['Trantridge'] for two different places' (p. 91).

The two constables who mistakenly arrest Georgy are acting in the serial 'in the name of the Royal Crown'. This curious expression was perhaps meant to make clear the source of their authority for the benefit of the serial's American audience, and Hardy took the opportunity to revise it in preparing *1894* to read 'in the name of the Crown' (p. 289; marginal emendation). These 'servants of the crown', as they are described in the serial, become 'the two officers of justice' (p. 291; second proof) in *1894*, which seems a more colloquial and realistic way for Georgy to describe them in his own words.

There were no alterations to the sketch in *1912*.

'Netty Sargent's Copyhold'

In this sketch, Netty Sargent wishes to marry, but her future husband will not agree unless she first secures possession of her uncle's house. Her aged uncle suddenly dies as he is waiting for the squire's agent to call and witness his signature of the copyhold which will transfer the property to Netty, but she props him up, holds his hand and fools the agent into believing that he is still alive.

In the MS., the story occupies four leaves, fos. 28a–31, and is virtually complete, breaking off a couple of sentences before the end. The title is given as 'The history of ~~Sus~~ Lucy Serjeant', with 'strange trick' written as an uncancelled alternative above 'history'. Netty is first called 'Susan', then 'Lucy' and finally 'Netty'. Her future husband is called 'James/Jimmy Cliffe' throughout, not 'Jasper Cliff' as he is in published versions. At the start, Netty is said to live with her father, but Hardy later describes her 'uncle's' selfish negligence at the point when Netty first conceives her plan to rescue the copyhold. Hardy's underlining was obviously meant to remind him of this change in relationship, but eleven lines later he refers again to her 'father', and at the end of the story he describes Netty's relative as her 'lg'.l uncle'. The narrator of the story in the MS. is Robert, the parish clerk, not Mr Day, the painter, as it later became.

The MS. lacks several of the legal explanations about copyholds which are present in the serial: for instance, in published versions we learn that Netty's uncle should have seen to the renewal in time, 'owing to the peculiar custom of forfeiture by the dropping of the last life before the new fine was paid', and eventually the documents were prepared, 'for on this manor the copyholders had writings with their holdings, though on some manors they had none'. Several legal terms are unique to the MS.: for example, 'renewal of lives' and 'lease' (fo.

29) were given in the serial as 'admittance of new lives' and 'deed o' grant' respectively. The house was said in the MS. to have been built by Netty's 'grandfather' (fo. 29), but this became 'great-great-grandfather' in the serial, no doubt to make sense of the information later in the same sentence that the copyhold had been held for generations. In the MS., Netty's relative delayed the renewal simply because of his 'dilatoriness' (fo. 29), but the serial gives a more credible motive: her uncle 'didn't very well like Jasper Cliff' and was determined 'to spite the selfish young lover'. Incidentally, in the manuscript the copyhold related to a house and farm, but in the serial it covered a house, a field and a garden.

Several details of Netty's 'trick' are different in the MS.: she is said to have dragged her uncle's corpse from the chair in which he died and propped it up in a higher one beside the table, whereas in the serial her uncle's chair has castors (clearly shown in an illustration) so she can, more realistically, wheel him in the same chair to the table. The MS. also lacks the description of Netty putting her uncle's forefinger on the page so that he appeared to be reading the Bible. Similarly, it is not until the serial that Netty assures the steward that 'I think he's nodding over it just at this moment. However, that's natural in an old man, and unwell.' In the MS., it is the steward's idea for Netty to hold her uncle's hand and guide the pen when he signs, but in published versions it is her own suggestion. Two additions to the MS. stress the uncle's great age and decrepit physical condition, so that the steward might plausibly be fooled by his apparent resemblance to a corpse: the uncle is said to be a 'shrinking, shivering' old man, and Netty describes how his 'poor three' teeth chattered when he heard the steward was coming. The agent also says in the serial that 'I'm sorry for him', which explains why he is willing to comply with all of Netty's suggestions. These alterations to the manuscript serve to make her trick either more credible or more ingenious.

All of the other major revisions to this sketch were made after Hardy had prepared the first proof of *1894*. Two marginal additions to the proof both seek to make Netty's deception of the agent more realistic. We now read how 'she *opened his eyelids a bit, and* put on him his spectacles' (p. 296; italics indicate Hardy's addition), since a dead uncle with his eyes shut tight would not fool anyone. Also, she arranges him so that the agent can see 'the back *and side* of the old man's head' (p. 298); the serial reading hardly allows the agent to identify the uncle if he can only see the back of his head. Another marginal emendation is stylistic, Hardy replacing the serial's 'really I've feared it would really drive him out of his mind' with 'really I've feared it would verily drive him out of his mind' (p. 297), thus allowing Hardy to avoid the awkward repetition of 'really'.

The most substantial and interesting of the revisions occurs, however, in the second proof. It is a six-line insertion describing the consequences of her marriage:

> Every virtue has its rewards, they say. Netty had hers for her ingenious
> contrivance to gain Jasper. Two years after they were married he took to
> beating her – not hard, you know; just a smack or two, enough to set her in

a temper, and let out to the neighbours what she had done to win him, and how she repented of her pains. (p. 299)

This gives an ironic touch of poetic justice to her contrivance to gain the copyhold and secure herself a husband, while also credibly explaining how the tale came to be known about. In the serial, we simply learnt that 'what Netty had done began to be whispered about, for she had told a friend or two', for no apparent reason; Hardy's second proof revision alters this to 'this confession of hers began to be whispered about'.

Conclusion

In total, there were more than five hundred alterations made to 'A Few Crusted Characters' between the serial and *1894*, of which slightly over half were substantive. Three hundred of these alterations occurred when preparing the first proof; Hardy then made a further one hundred and fifty marginal emendations, and another forty changes were made in the revises. There is a clear and understandable pattern here of Hardy beginning by making a large number of revisions to the serial and then altering his text less and less in the later stages of production as it settled into an increasingly refined and satisfactory form. There are a couple of other patterns which one can draw from the figures, however. For instance, if one considers the number of substantive revisions, the first and second proofs show that slightly under half of the total revisions at each stage were substantive, but more than two-thirds of Hardy's marginal emendations to the first proof were substantive, suggesting that, proportionately at least, his concern at this intermediate stage of the proof preparation was more for matters of wording than matters of pointing. Another pattern which can be detected is Hardy's declining intervention in his text: of the five hundred alterations between the serial and *1894*, 60 per cent occurred when Hardy was preparing the first half of the first proof (that is, the Introduction and the first four sketches). This pattern, which suggests nothing more significant perhaps than authorial fatigue, is even more clearly seen in the revisions which Hardy made for *1912*, when he was over seventy years of age. Of the 38 alterations which he made to *1894* when revising it, 27 are in the first half. Indeed, in the last three sketches, Hardy made only two revisions, both in the final one, 'Netty Sargent's Copyhold' (both are very minor: 'Oh' became 'O' and 'a doctor' was replaced by 'the doctor'). One final characteristic of Hardy's revising practice which the statistics do not reveal is his extraordinary capacity for supplementing and reworking his text; there are more than two hundred and seventy substantive changes between the serial and *1894*, but there are only ten occasions on which he simply deleted a wording from the serial without replacing it, and nearly all of these are single words of minor importance ('getting', 'that', 'then', 'Ah!'). Eight of these ten deletions occurred before the story was set up in the first proof; it would certainly seem, therefore, that Hardy was very reluctant simply to delete a word once it was set in print.[11]

Notes

1 *Letters*, II, 38.

2 *Letters*, II, 45.

3 *1894H* has a handful of substantive differences from *1894* which are probably the result of compositorial error: it omits the article in 'a prettier' (p. 196) and 'and' in 'and [I might say]' (p. 219). It also prints 'they ever' (p. 238) instead of 'ever they'. *1894H* spells out 'damn' (p. 224).

4 All page references are to *1894*, unless otherwise stated.

5 Gatrell (1988), p. 114. Gatrell gives a detailed analysis of two of the surviving manuscript sections of 'A Few Crusted Characters' both here and in 'The Early Stages of Hardy's Fiction', *Thomas Hardy Annual No. 2*, ed. Norman Page (London: Macmillan, 1984), pp. 3–29.

6 Gatrell (1988), p. 114.

7 Those interested in the evolution of Wessex topography may like to know that Hardy's only other revision when preparing *1912* was to change 'Lullstead Bay' to 'Lullwind Bay', the emblematic name perhaps stressing that the two lovers had not simply been swept out to sea by bad weather offshore. Three more changes to place names occur later: in 'The Winters and the Palmleys', Exonbury was called Exbury in the serial (p. 276), and in 'Incident in the Life of Mr. George Crookhill', Trantridge was formerly Tranton (p. 287). Both of these are marginal emendations to the first proof of *1894*. For Waterston Ridge, see note 10 below.

8 The five-line insertion runs from 'Does she look' to 'we must know the worst!' (p. 265).

9 The insertion is the whole paragraph, 'In short, except o' Sundays [...] a bottle of port wine' (pp. 259–60).

10 Flower (1950), p. 92. See also Hardy's letter to William Rothenstein in March 1912 (*Letters*, IV, 206).

11 For the sake of a complete record, the other revisions to *1894* for the Wessex edition are as follows (*1912* is quoted first, and the pagination is that of *1912*): 'INTRODUCTION/[*not in 1894*]' (p. 189); 'Longpuddle,/Longpuddle' (p. 192); ''ee/ye' (p. 196); 'a-looking/alooking' (p. 197); 'O/Oh' (p. 199); ''ee/ye' (p. 199); 'nunnywatch/nunny-watch' (p. 200); 'and supposing/but supposing' (p. 216); 'from where she lived/from the houses' (p. 221); 'Waterston Ridge/Climmerston Ridge' (p. 225); 'tower/tower,' (p. 228); 'courage to do it/courage' (p. 229); 'Then the squire/And the squire, too,' (p. 235); 'villainous/villanous' (p. 235); 'the doctor/a doctor' (p. 254); 'O/Oh' (p. 258). The Contents page of the story in *1912* has a misprint referring to 'Andrew Satchel' instead of 'Andrey Satchel' (p. 187).

PART FOUR

A Changed Man and Other Tales

1

INTRODUCTION

A Changed Man and Other Tales

As early as April 1898, Thomas Hardy was thinking of producing an edition of his uncollected stories, and he told Clement Shorter that 'I am trying this summer to get together some short pieces for a volume which have never appeared [except] in periodicals' (*Letters*, II, 191). By July of that year, however, he appeared to have abandoned the project, remarking to Florence Henniker that 'I do not take kindly to publishing my stray short stories. They don't seem to me to be worth reprinting' (II, 197). Hardy must have had second thoughts, because on 3 October 1899 he made a disparaging reference to some '"creative work"' which he was undertaking in a letter to Edmund Gosse, 'the work consisting in hunting up old things & other drudgery under a 4 line whip from the publishers' (II, 231). Purdy and Millgate note that, 'according to a letter of 20 Sept 99 (copy Colby) from the London office to the New York office of Harper & Brothers, TH had agreed to deliver in time for publication in early spring of 1900 the copy for "another book of short stories, of which he has a number which have never appeared in book form"'. However, no such volume was published at that date, and the proposal must have been allowed to lapse, no doubt because of Hardy's lack of enthusiasm for it.

It was more than a dozen years later when Hardy next mentioned his plan to publish what became *A Changed Man*. On 19 January 1912, he told Clarence McIlvaine that he wanted to issue 'The Romantic Adventures of a Milkmaid' in volume form: 'the romance has been popular in America in unauthorized editions, as you may remember, & owing to the constant inquiries for it here I am intending to include it in the uniform series of novels. [...] We did not, you may recollect, put it into our set, because it would not quite fill a volume' (IV, 199). The 'set' to which Hardy refers here is the Osgood, McIlvaine 'Wessex Novels' edition of 1895–96, and it seems likely that the half-novel length of 'The Romantic Adventures' allowed Hardy to complete a volume in 1913 by adding eleven other previously uncollected stories to form *A Changed Man*, published by Macmillan.

Hardy's next reference to the volume which would become *A Changed Man* was in a letter to F.A. Duneka, general manager of Harper & Brothers, dated 20 January 1913: 'as to the possible volume of short stories, I have long thought of bringing out such a volume; but it will require some consideration on what it shall contain. I fear I may not be able to have the material ready in time for the coming autumn, last year having been one of exceptional strain, owing to the Wessex edition, and other matters' (IV, 254; Hardy was writing just a couple of months after Emma's death). To the same correspondent, Hardy lamented in April that 'alas – the volume of short stories is still *in nubibus*' (IV, 265; 'in the clouds'), but later that summer he began to assemble the stories which he might include; for instance, in August he obtained a typed copy of 'What the Shepherd

Saw' which he had lost and which was reproduced for him from Clement Shorter's copy of the Christmas 1881 number of the *Illustrated London News* in which the story had first appeared. On 6 August 1913, he acknowledged receipt of the copy from Maurice Macmillan and added that 'if I reprint the old short stories we talked of it will help to fill the volume. I am not sure about having them ready for the autumn, as I have to find them first & judge them, for some are pretty bad I think' (IV, 293). Hardy must then have rapidly progressed with the work on the volume, because only two weeks later, on 19 August, he announced to Sir Frederick Macmillan that

> I am sending by parcel post a rather formidable bundle of copy, it being the short stories we have talked about collecting, which you suggested in your last letter should be published before the poetry volume. The nature of the tales brings them naturally, I think, into the third division of the novels, so that the book will make No.18 of the prose series.
>
> I have written what I fancy may be the best title for the book, but have an open mind on the point for any other you may suggest. "A Changed Man" is used, as being the first, & I think the best, of the tales; but if the second, "The Waiting Supper", seems more attractive as a title, that can be placed first instead. (IV, 297)

This letter raises two issues, the title of the volume and its numbering, which will be discussed later.

Two days later, Hardy wrote again to Macmillan, noting that 'I thought it would save trouble to the printers if I read the copy through, so that (so far as I can foresee) there will not be many corrections in the proofs, and the book may as well be set up in pages at once' (IV, 298). This would indicate that most of the revisions to the stories were made before Hardy first submitted them to Macmillan. Later in the same letter, Hardy listed the six stories which were already copyrighted in the United States ('A Changed Man', 'The Grave by the Handpost', 'Enter a Dragoon', 'A Committee-Man of "The Terror"', 'Master John Horseleigh, Knight' and 'The Duke's Reappearance'), and he explained why he referred to their legal status: 'I mention this in case the Harpers should wish to print these only, and use the English plates for the other six. Though probably for uniformity of type they will like to print them all' (the Harper & Brothers first American edition of *A Changed Man* was wholly reset). The other six stories had appeared before the introduction in 1891 of the International Copyright Law and therefore were not protected from unauthorized reprinting, a point which, as we shall see, Hardy was to mention to several correspondents as a principal reason for publishing the volume.

Proofs started to arrive within days, as Hardy described to Sir George Douglas:

> just at present the printers have begun sending proofs of a forthcoming volume of short stories of mine – mostly bad – published in periodicals 20 years & more ago, which I am unhappily obliged to include in my set of books because pirated editions of some, vilely printed, are in circulation in America, & imported into England by the curious. I heartily wish I could

snuff out several of them, but my hand is forced, & I shall have the pleasure
of listening to reviewers lamenting the feebleness to which I have declined
(for they always assume everything published to have been written the
preceding month.) (IV, 300)

Hardy wrote to Sir Frederick Macmillan on 6 September that 'I am sending back
the proofs of "A Changed Man" straight to the printers – thinking it will save
time – the corrections being of an ordinary kind' (IV, 302).

In the same letter, Hardy mentioned that he would commission Hermann Lea
to photograph Maiden Castle, which features in 'A Tryst at an Ancient
Earthwork', for use as a frontispiece. Acknowledging receipt of Lea's sample
photographs on 17 September, Hardy expressed his preference for one which
'gives the best idea of a castle artificially constructed. [...] Height and darkness
are the effects required' (IV, 304). In a postcard of the same day to Lea, Hardy
added that 'What is required is that the Castle shd stand high up in the picture, so
that there may be not much sky.' Lea's photograph was used as the frontispiece
for both the first edition and the Wessex edition and it was captioned 'The Castle
of Mai-Dun'.

A sentence from Hardy's original Prefatory Note to the volume was printed in
the *Times Literary Supplement* on 25 September 1913, in which Hardy wrote
that the stories 'would probably have never been collected by me at this time of
day if frequent reprints of some of them in America and elsewhere had not set
many readers inquiring for them in a volume' (p. 402; see Purdy, pp. 155–6, who
suggests that this version of the Prefatory Note was supplied by the publishers
from proof). However, Hardy subsequently revised this Note and he sent the
revised copy to Macmillan on 12 September 1913, commenting that 'it is better
now than as it first stood, which rather gave away the stories' (IV, 303: in the
absence of the full text of the original, we cannot tell how it 'gave away the
stories'). It is this revised Prefatory Note which was published in *A Changed
Man*, where it is dated August 1913.

A Changed Man was published by Macmillan on 24 October 1913 at 6s. in an
edition of 10,000 copies. The complete format is uniform with the Osgood,
McIlvaine edition of the Wessex Novels (1895–96), and 'The Wessex Novels
Volume XVIII' appears on the half-title (Purdy, pp. 152, 154). The full title of
the volume is given as *A Changed Man, The Waiting Supper, and Other Tales,
Concluding with The Romantic Adventures of a Milkmaid*. Kristin Brady
comments that the title 'reveals not only Hardy's three presumable favourites
among the twelve stories but also, by the absence of any thematic concept, his
admission that the book has no coherent unifying principle' (p. 157), unlike his
other three collected volumes of stories.

Hardy's reaction to the publication of *A Changed Man* was rather defensive
and dismissive, since he did not wish to be judged by his work of twenty years
ago. Thus, in the week after the volume appeared, he referred to the tales as
'merely old, very old stories' and as 'only very old ones, some of them
indifferently good' (IV, 313, 315). On 2 November, he told Florence Henniker
that 'I was glad to receive your letter telling me that you like to have the book,
but you must not expect much from it: most of the stories were written so very
long ago, as mere stop-gaps, that I did not particularly care to reprint them.

Readers seem to be pleased with them, however' (IV, 316). Hardy remarked to Arthur Benson in Cambridge on the same day that 'he was ashamed of his little book of republished stories and surprised at its good reception' (Benson, p. 260). Three weeks later, he explained to Lady Ilchester that 'you will realize that all the stories were written many years ago, & that I have republished them rather by compulsion than choice (some having been pirated in America). So you will find them *younger* in method & sentiment than I could make them if I were to write them now. Some of them however are pleasantly creepy for reading these dark evenings' (IV, 323). In March of the following year, he was even more dismissive of the volume, writing that he had been 'compelled by pirates to reprint some old tales that I would have willingly let die' (IV, 22); this is, of course, an exaggeration, since only half of the stories lacked the protection of copyright, but Hardy was replying to a literary agent inquiring about the possibility of him writing new stories in the future and he needed to prevent any misunderstanding which the appearance of *A Changed Man* could have caused. In the event, Hardy's anxiety about the publication of his first volume of prose in nearly twenty years proved unnecessary, for the reception was generous and welcoming; Edmund Gosse, for instance, wrote on 7 November to tell Hardy that *A Changed Man* was 'a cluster of asteroids, which take their proper place in your planetary system, and differ from your novels only in the matter of size. They are uniformly and wonderfully worthy of you, and are wholly precious' (quoted in Millgate, p. 493).

While Hardy was preparing for Macmillan to publish *A Changed Man*, he was also arranging an American edition with Harper & Brothers. He informed them on 24 August 1913 that copy was now ready for the printer (IV, 299). On 17 September 1913, he sent them details of the original serial publications of the stories, which they needed for copyright purposes (Letters, IV, 304),[1] and two weeks later he submitted his contract with Harpers to Sir Frederick Macmillan for approval (IV, 306), returning it to the New York publishers on 9 October (IV, 308). The American edition was published simultaneously with the Macmillan edition, with one of Reinhart's illustrations for 'The Romantic Adventures of a Milkmaid' replacing the photogravure of Maiden Castle as frontispiece (Purdy, pp. 156–7).

A Changed Man was reprinted in Macmillan's Wessex edition in 1914. On 14 December of the previous year, Hardy had written to Sir Frederick Macmillan with some suggestions about the Wessex edition:

> On looking at the stories in "A Changed Man" I think the best way of getting over the difficulty in the numbering is to number the volume XVIII as the printers have done – and to start a new group of novels with it, thus,
>
> IV. – MIXED NOVELS.
>
> 18. A Changed Man and other Tales.
>
> This will not only remove the difficulty as to numbering, but will be a truer description, the volume being really made up of specimens of every class. The new heading would also cover any volume of future sweepings from magazines.
>
> I have marked this arrangement on the proof returned herewith, in case

you should see no objection to it.

I also enclose a few trifling corrections which, though not imperative, it would be as well to make in the Wessex edition, or in any future edition. There is no over-running.

Whenever the map at the end is reprinted I should like to insert two or three extra place-names on the plate. These too, are not imperative, but advisable, in view of letters I get from readers. (IV, 329)

In his letter of 19 August 1913 to Macmillan, quoted above, Hardy suggested making the volume number 18, the last in the prose series, which would have placed it in the 'Novels of Ingenuity' category of his work, together with *Desperate Remedies, The Hand of Ethelberta* and *A Laodicean*. Macmillan must have thought that this would be inappropriate, because, as Purdy and Millgate note, he had written on 12 December to suggest that, if Hardy wanted to put *A Changed Man* into the 'Romances and Fantasies' section of the Wessex edition instead, it would have to be numbered XIV* or XIVa and placed between *A Group of Noble Dames* and *Desperate Remedies*. Hardy's solution, to create a new category of 'Mixed Novels', overlooks the further difficulty that the first three volumes of verse in the Wessex edition had already been published with the numbers XVIII–XX on their spines. Other points to note about the 14 December letter are that the corrections which Hardy enclosed were to *A Changed Man* only, and by 'no over-running' he meant that the resetting of whole pages would not be necessary. Finally, the extra placenames on the map are discussed in the chapter on 'The Romantic Adventures of a Milkmaid' below.

On 5 November 1913, Hardy told Macmillan that Baron Tauchnitz had expressed interest in buying the right to include *A Changed Man* in his 'Collection of British and American Authors' (*Letters*, IV, 317), and he wrote again on 19 November to say that 'I do not myself see any objection to Baron Tauchnitz dividing "A Changed Man" into two books, and giving the second one a new title. I would suggest that the division be at the end of "What the Shepherd Saw" and that "The Romantic Adventures of a Milkmaid" be placed at the beginning of the second volume, so that this well-known story may give its name to the second volume' (IV, 321). Tauchnitz followed Hardy's advice and published *A Changed Man* as vol. 4458 in his series, with *The Romantic Adventures of a Milkmaid* as vol. 4461. Hardy gave permission for some minor alterations to the Prefatory Note (see IV, 325–6). In the same letter, Hardy authorized the Incorporated National Lending Library for the Blind to transcribe *A Changed Man* into Braille. In April of the next year, Hardy gave permission to Mlle Magdelaine de Lansade of Paris to produce a French translation for 100 francs per story. Later that month, she requested a decrease in the fees because she had been unable to find an editor who was willing to pay 100 francs for her translations of 'The Committee-Man of "The Terror"' and 'What the Shepherd Saw'. A fee of two francs per printed page of the English texts was eventually asked, but the fate of the translations remains unknown (V, 24, 33).

Note

1   Three leaves in Hardy's hand, showing lists of contents for the volume, together with details of serial publication, are in the Dorset County Museum. One of the lists gives 'Destiny & a blue Cloak' as the penultimate story, but this title is circled and marked 'not included'.

CHAPTER 26

'A Changed Man'

'A Changed Man' is the last short story which Hardy wrote. The earliest surviving reference to the as yet unwritten work is in a letter from Hardy to Clement Shorter, dated 1 December 1899: 'It is true that I am not writing much now, but I shall have pleasure in sending you a short story if I am not bound to make it reach 4000 words, shd that length be inconvenient' (*Letters*, II, 239). A week or two later, he told Shorter that 'I am bearing in mind yr wish for story also: when *that* will be done I cannot say!' (II, 240). On Boxing Day, he promised Shorter that 'On New Years day I am going to begin shaping the story' (VII, 132), and he mentioned to Florence Henniker on 26 January 1900 that he had finished it (II, 246). He sent the completed tale to Shorter on 29 January for publication in the *Sphere*, a new weekly journal launched by Shorter just two days earlier:

> Herewith I send the story. Unfortunately it measures between 2 & 3 thousand words over 4,000, & therefore may be disqualified, in which case please return it. You may, however, like to divide it into two parts. Anyhow the price is not lengthened: £100, all serial rights. (II, 246).

'A Changed Man' appeared in two parts, on 21 and 28 April 1900. It was Hardy's favourite story among those which appeared in the collected edition bearing its name, as he explained to Sir Frederick Macmillan in August 1913: 'I have written what I fancy may be the best title for the book, but have an open mind on the point for any other you may suggest. "A Changed Man" is used, as being the first, & I think the best, of the tales' (IV, 297).

Hardy's preference for the story may have been because of its personal associations. The subject of 'A Changed Man' is based on the Rev. Henry Moule (1801–80), vicar of Fordington from 1829 until his death, who became celebrated for his heroic efforts to control the cholera epidemic in his parish in 1854.[1] Moule was the father of Hardy's very close friend Horace, and it is in a letter of 1919 to another of his sons, Handley, then Bishop of Durham, that Hardy recalls his memories of the Reverend Moule at that period:

> You may agree with me in thinking it a curious coincidence that the evening before your letter arrived, & when it probably was just posted, we were reading a chapter in Job, & on coming to the verse: "All the days of my appointed time will I wait, till my change come," I interrupted & said: "that was the text of the Vicar of Fordington one Sunday evening about 1860." And I can hear his voice repeating the text as the sermon went on – in the way they used to repeat it in those days – just as if it were but yesterday. [...]

> The study of your father's life (too short, really) has interested me much. I well remember the cholera years in Fordington: you might have added many details. For instance, every morning a man used to wheel the clothing & bed linen of those who had died in the night out into the mead, where the Vicar had had a large copper set. Some was boiled there, & some burnt. He also had large fires kindled in Mill Street to carry off the infection. An excellent plan I should think.[2]

The association in Hardy's memory of Moule's 'cholera years' and his sermon about 'change' seems to provide Hardy with both the subject for 'A Changed Man' and a perspective on it. The verse in the Book of Job which immediately follows Hardy's quotation could serve as an epigraph to the story: 'Thou shalt call, and I will answer thee: thou wilt have a desire to the work of thine hands' (XIV.15). The other main influence on the story would seem to be Hardy's reading of Jane Austen, with Laura as the poor man's Maria Crawford, too worldly to be the wife of a curate and revelling in the amorous intrigue of amateur dramatics.

The versions of 'A Changed Man' which have textual significance are as follows:

Sphere   *The Sphere*, 21 April 1900, pp. 419–21, and 28 April 1900, pp. 451–2. The division occurred at the end of section IV. Each instalment had a half-page illustration by A.S. Hartrick.

Cosmo   *The Cosmopolitan*, May 1900, pp. 35–43.

1913   *A Changed Man and Other Tales* (London: Macmillan, 1913), pp. 1–24. Published at 6*s*. in an edition of 10,000 copies on 24 October 1913.

1913H   *A Changed Man and Other Tales* (New York: Harper & Brothers, 1913), pp. 1–23.

1914   *A Changed Man and Other Tales* (London: Macmillan, 1914), pp. 1–23. Volume XVIII of the Wessex edition.

A bound manuscript of 'A Changed Man' is currently located in the Berg Collection of the New York Public Library. It would seem to be a printers' copy which Hardy sent to Shorter. Proofs of the *Sphere* publication were composed from it, a copy of which was sent to America and became the version of the story which appeared in the *Cosmopolitan*. However, Hardy must have further revised the proofs after sending off the American version, because the *Sphere* has a number of substantive differences from the *Cosmopolitan*, and it is the *Sphere* version which forms the basis for the story's first collected edition in 1913.

The manuscript and the *Cosmopolitan*

The manuscript of 'A Changed Man' is written on 27 leaves of ruled paper, with some minor alterations on every page. A couple of legible deletions show Hardy's changing conception of the relationship between Laura and Vannicock, the lover with whom she is planning to elope. When he is first introduced into the story, Vannicock is described as 'a gentleman a year or two younger than herself', but this is deleted and six lines later Hardy wrote that Laura's age was a year or two 'younger than' his own. This too is deleted and replaced by 'above' (fo. 18), making Laura once again older than her lover and showing her to be, arguably, more culpable in her decision to leave her husband. Another deletion shows that she originally hesitated for a 'fortnight' before agreeing to elope with Vannicock, but this was shortened to a 'week' (fo. 21).

The MS. has five undeleted variants which never appeared in any printed edition of the story. One is a short phrase, 'If you do' (fo. 20), and the others are individual words, the most interesting of which is Hardy's attempt to represent a dialect pronunciation by inserting a hyphen in 'Sure-ly' (fo. 15), the first word of the verdict on Maumbry's performance as a parson delivered by the bar-room judges of the White Hart. Hardy may have deleted the five variants at the proof stage before sending the proofs to the *Cosmopolitan*, or there may have been compositorial error which Hardy overlooked when checking the proofs.

Cosmopolitan is nearer to the MS. than the *Sphere*, whose proofs underwent a further layer of revision. The American publication was completely reset and there are some sixty differences in matters of spelling and punctuation from the English version, no doubt the result of house styling; for instance, *Cosmopolitan* has a greater number of commas and an aversion to semi-colons. There are also sixteen substantive variants (all individual words except for a phrase of two words), not found in either the MS. or the *Sphere*, and these are probably editorial in origin. There is no evidence that Hardy revised the proofs before sending them to America and it is unlikely he would alter one set of proofs and not mark the same revisions on to the *Sphere* copy.

Sphere

The proofs of the *Sphere* appear to have been further revised after a copy had been despatched to America to form the basis of the *Cosmopolitan* version. This might account for some of the *Sphere*'s fifty instances of spelling and punctuation not found in either the American publication or the MS. Hardy also introduced at this stage some 33 substantive revisions, none of which is therefore to be found in the MS. or *Cosmopolitan*. The longest is the sardonic reflection on Maumbry and his wife before his conversion, who went to church for the sake of respectability: 'None so orthodox as your unmitigated worldling.' Some of the revisions are topographical, establishing the story more firmly in a familiar Wessex setting: thus, for the first time in the story we meet references to Grey's Bridge, Budmouth and the 'Roman' amphitheatre in Casterbridge. The theological college which Maumbry attended is revealed to be the one at Fountall (Wells in Somerset), the same one which the brothers in 'A Tragedy of Two Ambitions' had attended. Perhaps Hardy had in mind an ironic contrast between their cynicism and Maumbry's noble self-sacrifice.

Sphere increases the widespread amorous impact which the regiment had, causing bitter tears to several young women 'of the town and country'. After Maumbry's conversion, his loss to the regiment is more lamentable because he had been such a 'dashing' and 'popular' soldier (previously, he had merely been described as a 'fine' and 'spirited' one). Laura's reaction to the news that her husband is to leave the army and join the Church is made more emotional: previously, Maumbry had found her 'weeping quietly', but *Sphere* drops the moderating adverb. When her affair with Vannicock becomes the subject of gossip, in the MS. and *Cosmopolitan* we learn that 'Nobody considered Laura' because of the tragic cholera epidemic which preoccupied the people of Casterbridge. Perhaps Hardy thought it unlikely that her affair would be entirely ignored, and in the *Sphere* he adds the qualification that nobody 'long' considered her.

Some small details are added to the *Sphere*'s description of the cholera-stricken parish and Maumbry's work there. The copper in which Maumbry boils and disinfects linen is now said to be 'vast', both to emphasize the scale of the epidemic and perhaps to give a more accurate reminiscence of the work of the Reverend Moule (Hardy's letter to his son, quoted above, mentioned his large copper set). Maumbry in the *Sphere* toils 'amid this squalid and reeking scene', and the furnace where he burns the bedding is now said to be 'ghastly'. All of these substantive changes to the *Sphere* were retained in the subsequent collected editions.

1913 Macmillan

There are 23 substantive variants in the story's first collected edition in 1913. Hardy took the opportunity to make the location more accurate and detailed. The invalid in the oriel window, for instance, is said to live 'just below "Top o' Town"', whereas previously he had been said merely to live 'near' it. The road to London plunges into 'rustic windings, shy shades' once it is beyond Grey's Bridge (replacing 'straits, windings'). In earlier versions, Laura had been said to live 'at the corner of the town' but now we learn that she lives at the corner of West Street. The way from Durnover Cross to Mellstock Hill is said to be 'across the moor'. Some of the infected bedding and clothes are taken into the 'moor' behind the eloping Laura and Vannicock (replacing 'mead'). The driver of the fly who is to meet the lovers specifies that he has been waiting on Mellstock Hill.

A sprinkling of minor revisions shows Hardy's typical attention to detail. The height of the 'ghost' which the soldiers concoct is reported to be ten feet (one man sitting on another's shoulders, presumably) rather than the earlier unrealistic twelve feet. Maumbry's romantic exploits are enhanced when we learn for the first time that he was one of the Hussars who caused bitter tears among some neighbouring women. Sainway, the preacher who converts Maumbry, is described as the gently 'if narrow-minded' curate, adding a slightly anti-clerical tone to his portrayal. When Laura calls Vannicock over to where she is standing with her husband, he came forward 'reluctantly', which is not surprising since he was supposed to be eloping with her, although it is the first hint that Hardy gives of any unease in the awkward situation. Laura's bag which she had packed for the journey now contains also a 'night-dress' (perhaps in 1900 Hardy had thought this a rather *risqué* item to mention). Finally, the regiment to which Vannicock belongs is altered from the '–th Foot' to the '–st Foot', no doubt to distinguish it more clearly from Maumbry's old regiment, the '–th Hussars'.

1913 Harper

The American collected edition shows five substantive variants from Macmillan 1913, all of which seem to be the result of house styling ('it is' replacing 'it's', for instance) or compositorial misreadings ('lolling upon' for 'rolling upon'). There are sixteen differences in accidentals (mostly in the use of hyphens and commas).

1914 Macmillan Wessex edition

The Wessex edition of the story is identical to the Macmillan edition of 1913. In his study copy of the volume, now in the Dorset County Museum, Hardy has inserted in his own writing the word 'published' before the date '1900' at the end of the story.

Notes

1 The evidence that Hardy had in mind the 1854 epidemic and not the earlier one of 1849 is that, we learn, the Bristol railway was open to Ivell: the Bristol to Yeovil railway was constructed in 1853. See F.P. Pitfield, p. 93.
2 *Letters*, V, 315. The letter is also printed in the *Life*, p. 423.

CHAPTER 27

'The Waiting Supper'

'The Waiting Supper' was first collected in *A Changed Man and Other Tales* (1913), a volume of a dozen short stories which had been published in newspapers and periodicals between 1881 and 1900 and which Hardy was 'unhappily obliged to include in my set of books because pirated editions of some, vilely printed, are in circulation in America, & imported into England by the curious'.[1] 'The Waiting Supper' was one of the six stories in the volume which had first been published before 1891 and therefore did not enjoy the protection of the International Copyright Law. 'The Waiting Supper' should be seen as being exempt from Hardy's begrudging dismissal of most of the stories in *A Changed Man*, for two reasons. Firstly, while it is generally true that they are '*younger* in method & sentiment than I could make them if I were to write them now' (*Letters*, IV, 323), this is to ignore the fact that Hardy made a quite major and thorough revision to the periodical version of 'The Waiting Supper' when he was preparing it for collection in 1913; indeed, it is the most extensively altered of any of the stories in the volume, making it in some ways a newer story more reflective of his outlook in 1913 and suggesting his regard for it at that time. Secondly, Hardy would have been happy for it to be placed first and the volume called after it, showing his willingness to allow the story to feature prominently: as he wrote to Sir Frederick Macmillan in August 1913 when submitting the copy for the volume, 'I have written what I fancy may be the best title for the book, but have an open mind on the point for any other you may suggest. "A Changed Man" is used, as being the first, & I think the best, of the tales; but if the second, "The Waiting Supper", seems more attractive as a title, that can be placed first instead' (*Letters*, IV, 297). Probably as a result of Hardy's comments, the title page of the volume announces *A Changed Man, The Waiting Supper and Other Tales*.

The manuscript of the story has not survived, and the published versions of 'The Waiting Supper' which have textual significance are as follows:

M	*Murray's Magazine* (January 1888), pp. 42–67, and (February 1888), pp. 199–218. The division occurred after episode V.
HW	*Harper's Weekly* (31 December 1887), pp. 965–7, and (7 January 1888), pp. 17–19. The division was the same as above.
1913	*A Changed Man and Other Tales* (London: Macmillan, 1913), pp. 27–85. Published at 6*s.* in an edition of 10,000 copies on 24 October 1913.
1913H	*A Changed Man and Other Tales* (New York: Harper &

Bros, 1913), pp. 25–83.

1914   A Changed Man and Other Tales (London: Macmillan,
        1914), pp. 27–83. Volume XVIII of the Wessex edition.

In addition to these, Purdy notes that 'a condensation of the closing episodes of
the story (the end of VI, and VII and VIII) was published, with no indication of
its earlier existence, as "The Intruder, A Legend of the 'Chronicle' Office" in the
Dorset County Chronicle (Dorchester), 25 December 1890'.[2]

The chronology of the story's composition and revisions can be
approximately sketched out. In *1913*, Hardy added the date 'Autumn, 1887' to
indicate its composition, making it probably one of those stories which he told
Sir George Douglas in July 1887 he would be writing till the end of the year,
staying at home and 'clearing off some minor sketches which I have long
promised to some of the magazines' (*Letters*, I, 166).

Serials

The two serial versions of 'The Waiting Supper', *HW* and *M*, have a dozen
minor substantive differences, and in all but two of these readings *M* is the one
which *1913* retains. These ten readings may have a variety of explanations, and
one cannot be certain that Hardy is responsible for them. For instance, *M* twice
has a more non-standard or dialect form of dialogue, allowing a character to say
'three year' (p. 45) and 'he don't' (p. 54), where *HW* uses the standard form
more comprehensible to its US readers. This could be the work of a Harper
editor, as could an amusing bowdlerization: the animals on Elsenford farm emit
the sound of 'breathings and snortings' (p. 965) in *HW*, but in *M* we hear their
'breathings, belchings, and snortings' (p. 49).[3]

The two instances where it is *HW*'s reading rather than *M*'s which is retained
in *1913* are important because they give a clue to the transmission of the text and
the relation of the serial versions to the collected edition. The two occasions are
as follows: *HW* talks of 'ailments incidental thereto' (p. 17) where *M* describes
'ailments contracted therein' (p. 199), and in *HW* the piles which keep the dead
husband under the descending currents are said to be 'wedging' (p. 18) him,
while *M* talks of them 'holding' him (p. 217). Generally, *M* is much closer to
1913 than *HW* is; for instance, there are only about forty differences in
accidentals between *M* and *1913*, whereas *H* has five times that number
(ignoring US spelling). However, since *HW* has those two readings in common
with *1913* which are not in *M*, then the latter was not the basis for *1913*. A
possible surmise is that the printers' copies for both serial versions were
differently revised forms of a common source (the manuscript, perhaps), and it
was this common source which Hardy retained and revised when preparing *1913*
25 years later. Indeed, it is perfectly possible that many of the revisions in *1913*
outlined later in this article are not revisions at all but are *reversions* to earlier
readings of the story already present in this 'manuscript' which Hardy had
altered for the serial versions but which he restored for *1913*.

1913 Macmillan

The most interesting and substantial alteration which Hardy made when revising 'The Waiting Supper' for *1913* concerns the arrival of Bellston. In the version of the story which readers now know, the long-vanished husband arrives at Casterbridge on the eve of Christine's wedding to Nicholas and sends a porter to the house with his portmanteau and great-coat. This is the only contact he has with his wife before he is drowned on his way to call upon her, but in the serial he does in fact call on her and is drowned when he goes out for an hour to give her a chance to explain his return to Nicholas.

The Bellston who returns in the serial after nine years does not seem at all like the one who, we learn, had not been 'a good husband to the young lady by any means' (*M*, p. 205) and whose 'terrible temper' (p. 207) had led him to hit Christine and leave a scar on her forehead. Indeed, he seems very much a reformed character, blaming himself for his long absence, apologizing for leaving his arrival so near the time of the wedding because of bad weather, saying that Nicholas must be told of his return 'in common civility' (p. 210) and conveying his apologies to him before tactfully leaving Christine alone to have a private conversation with the man she was to marry the next day. Why did Hardy omit Bellston's reappearance in *1913*? The later version is certainly more consistent and plausible; in the serial, Bellston arrives and says nothing to suggest that he has done so only to be vindictive and spoil Christine's happiness by showing her he is still alive. Indeed, Christine even acknowledges that 'perhaps, Nicholas, he is a changed man' (p. 211), so why do Christine and Nicholas nevertheless act later on the assumption that he must have come out of malice and vanished when he left the house, always threatening to return if they ever try to marry? In *1913*, not having seen him, Christine reasonably assumes that he is the same as ever and that he sent his portmanteau and coat as a taunting proof of his existence.

That conjecture in the serial that Bellston may be 'a changed man' is another possible reason why Hardy decided not to let him reappear in the collected version. Hardy clearly wanted to avoid the possibility of readers comparing 'The Waiting Supper' to the preceding story in the volume, 'A Changed Man', and in *1913* he even revised Christine's conjecture about her husband so that she asks if he may be 'an altered man' (p. 75). By removing any similarities between the first two stories in *A Changed Man,* Hardy does not permit a reader to gain the mistaken impression that the volume will have a coherent unifying principle (a series of variations on the theme of reformed characters, say), as was the case with Hardy's first three volumes of tales.

There are a number of other less significant changes in *1913*, some of which are characteristic of Hardy at this time as he was preparing the Wessex editions of all his other prose fiction. In 'The Waiting Supper', he alters the serial's placenames so that they become consistent with the Wessex topography he was establishing in many of his other works, and he also seeks to give a greater amount of detail and accuracy to the story's setting. So the serial's River Swenn becomes the familiar Froom, and Swenn-Everard House, where Christine lives, becomes Froom-Everard House, making it more identifiable as Stafford House, below Lower Bockhampton, which had formerly been known as Frome Everard, according to Hutchins's *History of Dorset*.[4] Similarly, Eldhampton Hall is called in *1913* Athelhall, recognizable as Athelhampton Hall, east of Puddletown. The serial's reference to Salisbury is altered to its Wessex name of Melchester, while Troyton becomes Roy-Town, as Hardy had called it in *Far from the Madding Crowd* (the name of the Buck's Head Inn, where Joseph Poorgrass stops to drink when taking Fanny's coffin to Weatherbury, is also introduced into *1913*). Those interested in Hardy's continuing refinement and accurate presentation of Wessex might like to know that the serial's reference to 'the well-watered meads on the right hand' (*M*, p. 206) which Nic sees as he walks from Casterbridge along the Froom valley becomes 'the well-watered meads on the left hand' (p. 69) in *1913*.[5] Another change of name occurs when Nic's farm, known as Homeston in the serial, becomes Elsenford in *1913*, the possible echo of Elsinore perhaps underlining his role as indecisive lover.[6] Finally, an alteration which does not appear to have any significance is that Mr Bealand, the rector who refuses to marry Christine and Nicholas, was called Mr Eastman in the serial.

Characterization is subtly changed in *1913*, notably that of Nicholas, who is made slightly less of a Dick Dewy in his devotion to Christine. If we think that his ten-mile hike to dance with Christine is rather excessive, in the serial he walked 22 miles. After the return of Bellston in the serial, Nic is positively suicidal: 'he was more than once tempted to descend into the meads instead of keeping along their edge' (*M*, p. 212) but in *1913* Hardy revises this so that 'if he had been younger' he might have felt tempted to drown himself, 'but he was too old to put an end to himself for such a reason as love' (p. 76). Nic's social relation to Christine is made more independent in *1913* by moving his farm out of her father the Squire's parish and into a neighbouring one. This removes those undertones in the serial of the Poor Man and the Lady theme, and any obstacles to their union in *1913* are caused solely by the temperaments of the two lovers; as Kristin Brady puts it, 'the differences between Christine and Nic exist more in their own expectations about each other than in their actual circumstances'.[7] While the social difference between them is reduced, the distance between their two houses at the end is increased from 200 yards to 500 yards, perhaps to indicate the continued distance between them after all these years.

1913 seems generally to be more concise, avoiding Latinate or grandiloquent expressions; for instance, where the serials describe how Christine was 'even cognisant of the presence of him' (*M*, p. 43), *1913* says simply that she was 'quite conscious of his presence' (p. 28). Christine speaks more naturally and less like an Arthurian maiden in the later version, no longer using expressions like 'your plighted one' and 'my favour' (*M*, p. 45) when speaking to Nic.

Some of Hardy's later revisions work to make the motivation of the plot more plausible. For instance, during the scene in which Christine's father changes his mind about her marrying Nic, Hardy adds in *1913* the following remark by him: 'Christine, here's a paragraph in the paper hinting at a secret wedding, and I'm blazed if it don't point to you' (p. 54). This makes sense of his sudden change of mind in the last fifteen minutes, for he now has reason for 'an entirely different view of circumstances' (p. 54), and his wish for Christine and Nic to marry has been brought about by reading his paper and wishing to avoid scandal. In the serial he seems to move too quickly and for no obvious reason from calling Nic a scoundrel to accepting him as a son-in-law. Nic then, rather perversely it seems in the serial, refuses the Squire's offer to marry his daughter, but *1913* gives more insight into Nic's view of the proposal and helps us to understand why he spurns it by adding 'obviously it was hotly made in his first bitterness at what he had heard' (p. 58).

1913 Harper

The 1913 New York edition of 'The Waiting Supper' is virtually identical to the Macmillan edition of that year. There are some thirty variations in accidentals, half of which are matters of hyphenation, and nine substantive differences in individual words, none of which is at all significant (e.g., a/the, inspiring/inspiriting, he/they). All of them can be explained as either compositorial error or mild editorial intervention at the Harper office. In other words, it does not look at all as if Hardy himself was responsible for these variations between the British and New York editions, as he was for many of the variants in, for instance, the Harper's edition of *Life's Little Ironies*, when he further revised the first proofs for the Macmillan edition after they had already been sent to New York.

'The Intruder'

A greatly shortened version of 'The Waiting Supper' was published as 'The Intruder: A Legend of the "Chronicle" Office' in the *Dorset County Chronicle* on Christmas Day, 1890.[8] Nothing is known about the date or purpose of its composition. 'The Intruder' gives in very truncated form the arrival of the husband and its aftermath. Hardy gives a spurious topicality to the story by having Christine (now called Cecilia Belland) living in the building in High West Street, Dorchester, which in 1890 housed the offices of the *Dorset County Chronicle*. Another attempt to make 'The Intruder' topical led to an amusing error on Hardy's part: as in the serial, Cecilia goes to bed on 23 December, but she wakes up on Christmas Day, no doubt to create a festive coincidence with the day on which the story appeared in the paper. This case of the missing day clearly indicates that Hardy took no great pains with 'The Intruder'.

The names of the characters are changed from 'The Waiting Supper', so that now we encounter Cecilia and James Belland, Nathaniel Arden (the new name for Nic) and Mrs Waye (Wake). As in the serial, Belland does arrive in person and leave the house, but no skeleton is found at the end; instead, we are simply told that 'the severed pair waited for the whole remainder of their lives; but Belland never re-appeared'. Kristin Brady shrewdly suggests that this is 'to remove the similarity in plot to "A Tragedy of Two Ambitions"' which had been published two years previously.[9] Small changes in characterization are made; for instance, Belland is not now an explorer but a roving actor who, 'arriving at the local theatre over the way (now used as a china-shop) had wooed and married her'. This alteration was no doubt made to allow Hardy to introduce a little more local colour. The building in High West Street, Dorchester, which was then occupied by Mr J.T. Godwin's china-shop, still retained many features of the theatre which it had formerly been and where Edmund Kean had acted in 1813.[10]

In 'The Intruder', the clock does not ominously fall before the husband's return, and Nathaniel does not go away and contemplate suicide (not suitable Christmas reading, perhaps), but otherwise it gives a condensed, often verbatim version of the last two sections of the serial. However, by omitting the earlier history of the lovers, the dinner scene loses its greater sense of irony that this is but one more episode in a long series of postponements and frustrations.

1914 Macmillan Wessex edition

The Wessex edition of 1914 contains fourteen alterations to Macmillan's collected edition of the previous year, most of which are matters of hyphenation, and there is no substantive variation of any significance. A complete list of all such alterations is given below.[11]

Finally, 'The Waiting Supper' provides a cautionary tale for textual editors, who had all missed an amusing discrepancy until it was first spotted by Desmond Hawkins in 1989.[12] This concerns the curious 'sex-change' in Section 3 of the story, where a cousin of Nicholas Long's appears at the dance 'with her husband and children', only for her on the next page to have acquired a wife! Not even Hardy, for all his meticulousness, could spot every solecism.

Notes

1 *Letters*, IV, 300. Later quotations from the letters are included in the text. Hardy makes similar comments about his wish to avoid pirating elsewhere: see, e.g., *Letters*, IV, 299, 302 and V, 22.

2 See Purdy, p. 152.

3 For the sake of a complete record, the substantive differences between *M* and *HW* not otherwise recorded in this chapter are as follows (*M* is given first, and the pagination is *M*'s): 'whilst/while' (p. 48); 'tragi-comedies/tragic-comedies' (p. 53); 'amongst/among' (p. 54); 'there's/there is' (p. 58); 'more in/more' (p. 64); 'the distant/a distant' (p. 199); 'open to it/open it' (p. 209). All of *M*'s readings are in *1913*.

4 See *Life's Little Ironies [and] A Changed Man*, New Wessex edition, ed. Pinion (1977), p. 495.

5 Was the serial reading an attempt by Hardy to disguise the real place? Compare Gatrell's comment on *Far from the Madding Crowd*: 'Hardy was well aware that Joseph Poorgrass, returning from Casterbridge to Weatherbury with the coffin of

Fanny Robin, would have had the sea on his right hand were he in fact driving from Dorchester to Puddletown. The first edition, though, has "left", which was emended to "right" in the Osgood edition; it is possible to show Hardy consciously at work on the disguise of the landscape detail here, because the manuscript at this point originally read "right", and he altered it above the line to "left"' (pp. 120–21).

6 See Brady, p. 215, n.57.

7 Brady, p. 177.

8 *Dorset County Chronicle* (Dorchester), 25 December 1890, p. 10.

9 Brady, p. 176.

10 See *Life*, p. 340, and *Letters*, VI, 248.

11 For the sake of a complete record, the other revisions to *1913* for the Wessex edition are as follows (*1914* is quoted first, and the pagination is that of *1914*): 'had ever been danced/had been ever danced' (p. 44); 'sobbed:/sobbed;' (p. 53); 'Well, this is/Now, this is' (p. 54); 'well-founded/well founded' (p. 58); 'half-an-inch/half an inch' (p. 69); 'open it/open to it' (p. 71); 'greatcoat/great-coat' (p. 71. There are three more instances of this alteration); 'will be here/well be here' (p. 71 – a misprint in *1913*); 'half an hour/half-an-hour' (p. 71); 'upstairs,/upstairs' (p. 76); 'burned/burnt' (p. 76).

12 See Hawkins (1989), p. 93.

CHAPTER 28

'Alicia's Diary'

'Alicia's Diary', Hardy's only attempt at this form of narrative, was first collected in *A Changed Man* as one of the six stories in the volume which had first been published before 1891 and therefore did not enjoy the protection of the International Copyright Law.

The published versions of 'Alicia's Diary' which have textual significance are as follows:

Serial   *Manchester Weekly Times* (Supplement), 15 October 1887, pp. 2–3, and 22 October 1887, pp. 2–3. The division occurs at the end of section 5. Purdy notes that 'the story was sold to Tillotson & Son for their syndicated fiction business [...] and was widely printed, especially in provincial papers. American rights they sold to S. S. McClure for his similar syndicate in November 1887' (p. 152).

1913   *A Changed Man and Other Tales* (London: Macmillan, 1913), pp. 87–128. Published at 6s. in an edition of 10,000 copies on 24 October 1913.

1913H   *A Changed Man and Other Tales* (New York: Harper & Brothers, 1913), pp. 85–126.

1914   *A Changed Man and Other Tales* (London: Macmillan, 1914), pp. 85–125. Volume XVIII of the Wessex edition.

In 1923, Hardy twice stated in his 'Memoranda, II' notebook that the manuscript of 'Alicia's Diary' was 'not in existence'.[1]

Hardy's first reference to 'Alicia's Diary' is in a letter to Tillotson & Son, dated 12 March 1887. Hardy sold the story to Tillotson's Newspaper Fiction Bureau, which 'ran a very active syndicated fiction business at this period, purchasing serial rights from authors and then selling the stories to magazines and, especially, provincial newspapers both at home and abroad'.[2] Through their agency, the story was to be widely reprinted in later years, especially in provincial newspapers. 'Alicia's Diary' was the third of four short stories and a novel which Hardy was to sell to them between 1881 and 1892.[3]

In his letter of March 1887, Hardy noted that

> I am not quite sure as to the date at which I can deliver the promised story. Having now just finished The Woodlanders I propose leaving England for a month or two. It shall be the first work I take in hand on my return; – & I think you may calculate on receiving the MS. some time during the summer. (*Letters*, I, 163)

His destination was Italy, and the story's scenes in Venice and Milan owe much to his recent holiday experience. Hardy and Emma set off from London on 15 March 1887 (the day *The Woodlanders* was published), and they entered Venice on 13 April, staying until 22 April before going to Milan for a day and then reaching England five days after leaving Venice, which is the same itinerary and in the same month as Alicia and her family in the story (indeed, the timescale of the journey from Venice to England appears identical). The Hardys stayed in a hotel on the Riva degli Schiavoni in Venice, which is where M. de la Feste stays, and Hardy's *Life* mentions Milan's Gallery of Victor Emmanuel (p. 203) which Alicia visits. Emma Hardy's diary which she kept during the trip mentions other sites referred to in the story, such as the Grand Canal, the Rialto, the Bridge of Sighs, the Church of the Frari and Milan's Galleria Vittorio Emanuele.[4] (Incidentally, Emma's diary may have given Hardy the idea for the form of his story.) The Hardys returned to London at the end of April but did not go home to Max Gate until the end of July, so, assuming that Hardy kept his promise to Tillotson to give the story priority, the composition of 'Alicia's Diary' can be approximately assigned to August 1887.

A diary entry which Hardy quotes in his *Life* observes, "'Venice is composed of blue and sunlight. Hence I incline, after all, to 'sun-girt' rather than 'sea-girt', which I once upheld'" (p. 201). The reference is to Shelley's 'Lines written among the Euganean Hills' where Venice is addressed as 'Sun-girt City' (l. 115). In the first collected edition of 'Alicia's Diary', Hardy described the city's 'sea-girt' (p. 117) buildings, and the self-consciously Shelleyan echo makes it almost certain that the serial's 'sea-skirt' is a misprint.

Manchester Weekly Times

In the serial, the Scripture reader who eventually marries Caroline was called Highman, but Hardy changed his name to Higham in later editions, perhaps because he felt the original name was too obviously meant to associate him with High Anglican views. However, Hardy overlooked Higham's first appearance in the story, where he is called Highman even in the Wessex edition (p. 93). Highman is described as a 'virtuous' young man in the serial, but this is altered to 'thoughtful' in subsequent editions, presumably because a wholly virtuous young man would not have been willing to conduct the bogus marriage ceremony between Caroline and M. de la Feste (who, incidentally, is called M. de la Heste in the serial).

There are two mis-spelt words in the serial, only one of which has ever been corrected. 'Gallerio' was altered to 'Galleria' in *1913*, but all printed versions have referred to Milan's 'Via Allesandro Manzoni' instead of 'Via Alessandro Manzoni' (*1914*, p. 122).

Caroline is said at one point to tell Alicia 'plainly' that Charles would forgive her if he knew how she thinks of him all the time, but the context makes it clear that the later editions are correct to say that she spoke 'plaintively' (*1913*, p. 115).

1913 Macmillan

1913 omits a sentence from the serial: when her father finally catches up with Caroline in Venice, she asks him, 'And were *you*, papa, party to this strange deed of kindness?' (p. 120). In the serial, however, immediately before this the story had read 'She raised her face and asked him abruptly'. These eight words are missing from *1913* and they occupy a complete line of print in the serial. Their omission might indicate that a copy of the serial was used to establish *1913*, and the compositor's eye skipped a line at this point in the story.

The only significant addition for *1913* was an extra sentence describing the Church of the Frari: 'A sickly-sweet smell pervaded the aisles' (p. 122). If an emended version of the serial was copy-text, it might be relevant that this sentence is inserted at a place in the story which is very close to the top of one of the serial's tightly-packed columns, so that Hardy would have had space to add the sentence in the header. (Of course, it might have been added to the proofs.)

Other minor alterations to the serial in *1913* include changing Budmouth to Budmouth Regis and the addition of the date of first publication, 1887, at the end of the story.

1913 Harper

The New York edition has a couple of dozen variants, including four substantive ones involving individual words which were no doubt editorial. It corrects the 'Highman' misprint discussed above.

1914 Macmillan Wessex edition

There are only eight differences between *1914* and *1913*, and they are all very minor.[5]

Notes

1 See Taylor, pp. 65, 68.
2 Purdy, pp. 340–41.
3 As Purdy notes, the others were 'Benighted Travellers' ('The Honourable Laura'; 1881), 'A Mere Interlude' (1885), 'The Melancholy Hussar' (1890) and *The Pursuit of the Well-Beloved* (1892). Tillotson's contract with Hardy for *Tess of the d'Urbervilles* was subsequently cancelled: see Purdy, pp. 71-3.
4 See *Emma Hardy Diaries*, ed. Richard H. Taylor (Ashington, Northumberland: Mid Northumberland Arts Group and Carcanet New Press, 1985), pp. 168, 173, 175, 177, 179 and 191.
5 The following is a complete list of the differences between *1913* and *1914* (the reading in *1914* is given first, and the pagination is that of *1914*): 'scrutinize/scrutinise' (p. 92); 'for, as/for as (p. 93); 'for this;/for this:' (p. 95);

'promised/promised,' (p. 96); 'lover's/lovers'' (p. 99); 'step? Besides/step; besides' (p. 104); 'said I/said I,' (p. 119); 'said she shyly/said she, shyly' (p. 122).

CHAPTER 29

'The Grave by the Handpost'

'The Grave by the Handpost' was first collected in *A Changed Man* as one of the six stories in the volume which had first been published after 1891 and therefore already enjoyed the protection of the International Copyright Law. Hardy's begrudging dismissal of most of the stories in the volume disguises the fact that he made a quite careful revision to the periodical version of 'The Grave by the Handpost' when he was preparing it for collection in 1913, and again in the following year for the Wessex edition, so he must have thought it worth the trouble.

The manuscript of the story has not been located since R.L. Purdy noted that it was owned by a Mr Halsted B. VanderPoel, and the *Index of English Literary Manuscripts* gives no further information.[1] The published versions of 'The Grave by the Handpost' which have textual significance are as follows:

S	*St James's Budget*, Christmas Number (pub. 30 November) 1897, pp. 8–11, with four illustrations by George M. Patterson.
HW	As 'The Grave by the Handpost: A Christmas Reminiscence', *Harper's Weekly*, 4 December 1897, pp. 1203–6, with three of Patterson's illustrations (unsigned).
1913	*A Changed Man and Other Tales* (London: Macmillan, 1913), pp. 129–44. Published at 6*s*. in an edition of 10,000 copies on 24 October 1913.
1913H	*A Changed Man and Other Tales* (New York: Harper & Brothers, 1913), pp. 127–42.
1914	*A Changed Man and Other Tales* (London: Macmillan, 1914), pp. 127–41. Volume XVIII of the Wessex edition.

The story appears to have been written in the middle of 1897; in a letter to J. Penderel-Brodhurst, the editor of the *St James's Budget*, dated 9 July of that year, Hardy mentioned that 'the rough draft of the story is finished, but it has to be rewritten. Would the 26th of this month be soon enough?' (*Letters*, II, 171). Hardy had made a note of the practice on which the story is based in May 1882, as he had seen it reported in the *Times*: 'Burial of suicides at cross roads abolished c 1830. (Stake driven through it: between 9 & 12.)'[2] Also, as Kristin Brady reports, Hardy's 'Facts' notebook records the interment of a 'Girl who committed suicide' which reminded him of a 'similar burial on Hendford Hill'.[3]

St James's Budget is the basis for *1913*, since it contains five variant readings not found in *Harper's Weekly* but which are present in *1913* (there are six variant readings if one includes *Harper's Weekly*'s sub-title, 'A Christmas Reminiscence' which is not found elsewhere). It would appear that *Harper's*

Weekly is an earlier version of the story which Hardy slightly revised for *St James's Budget*.

The five variant readings are as follows (*St James's Budget* is the pagination here):

(i, ii) *St James's Budget* adds 'as has been stated' (p. 8) to the comment that the road between the two villages crosses at right angles the old road known as Long Ash Lane, of which Hardy also adds in *St James's Budget* 'and has often been mentioned in these narratives'. These additions to *St James's Budget* are retained in *1913*. Hardy gives the lane increased prominence and importance, as he was again to do in *1914*.

(iii) In *St James's Budget*, the grave-diggers 'prepared to depart' (p. 8) but in *Harper's Weekly* they 'prepared to take their departure'.

(iv) In *St James's Budget*, after Luke has asked the choir whether they will help him move his father's body, 'Lot asked Ezra Cattstock what he thought of it' (p. 10), but in *Harper's Weekly* we read that 'Lot then asked Ezra Cattstock and the others what they thought of it'.

(v) The tombstone for Luke's father gives the date as 'DECEMBER THE 20TH' (p. 10) in *St James's Budget*, but in *Harper's Weekly* it reads 'DECEMBER 20TH'.

St James's Budget contains the three illustrations which are in *Harper's Weekly* but adds a fourth entitled 'Sat down on the bank by the wayside' showing a disconsolate Samuel Holway after reading his son's letter. Finally, there are some 80 differences in accidentals between *St James's Budget* and *Harper's Weekly*, but only seven between *St James's Budget* and *1913*, again showing that *St James's Budget* was the basis for the latter.

1913 Macmillan

1913 again sees Hardy augmenting the information we receive about Long Ash Lane, part of the Dorchester–Yeovil road where the grave and handpost of the story's title are situated. We learn that the Lane stood 'on the foundation of a Roman road' (p. 132), a feature which the antiquarian Hardy had noted when mentioning the Lane in 'The First Countess of Wessex' and *Tess* (xliv). In *1913*, Hardy also made the son's letter lamenting his choice of the army as a career, which drove his father to suicide, much crueller than before. Now we read of the 'sarcastic stings' (p. 135) which he wrote, rather than of the mere 'reproaches' which he had penned in the earlier serial versions and which hardly seem enough to lead his father to kill himself in his guilt for having encouraged him to join the army.

Three other changes in *1913* can be briefly described. Ezra Cattstock refers to his parson as simply 'Mr. Oldham' (p. 139), rather than as 'Mr. Stephen Oldham' as he had done in the serials. Perhaps Hardy felt it would be disrespectful and unlikely of Ezra to refer to the parson by his first name, particularly as he was also the brother of Lord Wessex. In *1913*, Luke the son mentions the war in Spain where he will go to fight, adding that it is 'another chance for me to be worthy of father' (p. 139), the last five words being an addition to the serials and emphasizing yet again that his motive is to atone for his father's death, rather than, say, to win worldly advancement. Finally, *1913* has much less use of dialect than the serials, so that 'wi'', 'mid' 'upon's', 'martel's', 'afore', and 'haint' become instead 'with', 'may' or 'might', 'upon his', 'mortal's', 'before' and 'haven't' respectively.

1913 Harper

The 1913 New York Harper's edition of 'The Grave by the Handpost' is virtually identical to the Macmillan edition of that year. There are only some fifteen variations in accidentals, all but three of which are matters of hyphenation. All of them can be explained as either house styling or mild editorial intervention at the Harper office. In other words, Hardy himself is not responsible for these variations between the British and New York editions.

1914 Macmillan Wessex edition

The Wessex edition of 1914 was published only the year after the previous Macmillan edition, but Hardy took the opportunity to make three substantive alterations. In the serials and *1913*, Ezra Cattstock had made 'inquiration o' the Sidlinch men that buried 'en' whether Samuel Holway had been buried with a stake through his heart. *1914* however has him telling the parson that he had made 'inquiry of a Sidlinch woman as to his burial' (p. 138). Since Ezra is supposed to be secretive about their plan to remove the body, it would hardly be very discreet of him to consult all the men who had buried Samuel Holway, so *1914* makes much more sense. This alteration necessitates a further one: Ezra now says that his belief that Samuel had been buried with a stake through his heart 'seems true' (p. 138). In earlier versions, he had said it 'is true', but in *1914* he has not consulted the men who had done it, so he cannot be so certain as he was before. Finally, Ezra adds for the first time in *1914* that the men who put the stake through Samuel's heart 'won't own to it now' (p. 138), which seems more credible than their earlier happy admission of such a barbarous and superstitious act.[4]

Notes

1 See Purdy, p. 154.
2 Taylor (1978), p. 24.
3 Brady, p. 216, n102.

4 There are only two other variations between *1913* and the Wessex edition (*1914* is quoted first, and the pagination is that of *1914*): 'handpost/hand-post' (p. 135); 'midn't/mid'nt' (p. 137).

CHAPTER 30

'Enter a Dragoon'

'Enter a Dragoon' was completed in early 1900 at about the same time as 'A Changed Man', and they were the last two stories which Hardy wrote. It was now five years since the appearance of his final novel, *Jude*, and the stories were written in fulfilment of earlier promises at a time when he was dedicated to poetry. As Michael Millgate says of Hardy in 1899, 'it was significant of the profound change in Hardy's habits of thinking and writing that the verses should now come so swiftly and, on the whole, so richly, even while he found some difficulty, that November and December, in finishing the last two prose narratives he was ever to write' (p. 402). For instance, he wrote to Florence Henniker on 24 November 1899 that 'I am trying to write a little story long promised to Harper's Magazine; but I have not been able to get on with it much owing to a distressing nausea & headache which lasted nearly all last week' (II, 238). He mentioned to her on 26 January 1900 that he had finished 'Enter a Dragoon' (II, 246).

The versions of the story which have textual significance are as follows:

Harper's	*Harper's Monthly Magazine* (New York), December 1900, pp. 25–35, with a full-page engraving by A. Hayman.
1913	*A Changed Man and Other Tales* (London: Macmillan, 1913), pp. 145–70. Published at 6*s.* in an edition of 10,000 copies on 24 October 1913.
1913H	*A Changed Man and Other Tales* (New York: Harper & Brothers, 1913), pp. 143–67.
1914	*A Changed Man and Other Tales* (London: Macmillan, 1914), pp. 143–67. Volume XVIII of the Wessex edition.

No manuscript of the story is known to have survived.

Harper's Monthly Magazine and *1913* Macmillan

In the serial, each of the story's six numbered sections begins with an epigraph, but these were omitted from *1913*.

I   My old Love came and walked therein,
                    And laid the garden waste.
                        – O'SHAUGHNESSY

This epigraph is from Arthur O'Shaughnessy's 'Song' whose first lines are 'I made another garden, yea, / For my new love',[1] but this opening stanza ends with the lines which Hardy quotes. The failure of the new love to thrive because of the blighting return of the old parallels Selina calling off her marriage to Miller on the dragoon's return.

II The second epigraph is not identified by Hardy, and was not noted by Purdy:

> And shall I see his face again
> And shall I hear him speak?

This is a quotation from 'The Sailor's Wife' by William Julius Mickle (1735–88), 'that neglected Scotch poet', as Hardy described him in 1924, who 'was not great, but I used to be much interested in him when I was a boy' (*Letters*, VI, 266).[2] Hardy's estimation of Mickle may have meant that he did not wish to identify him in the company of other epigraphs by, for instance, Shakespeare and Jonson. 'The Sailor's Wife' would have been familiar at the time, having been reprinted in Palgrave's *Golden Treasury*. The poem tells of a wife rejoicing at the news of her husband's safe return from sea, and such a context is ironic here, in that the returning dragoon is *not* Selina's husband.

III
> Yet went we not still on in constancy?
> – DONNE

This quotation comes from Donne's 'Elegy 12', which is entitled 'His Parting from Her'. The line anticipates the renewal of love between Selina and the dragoon in the section which follows, but the title foreshadows his imminent death.

IV
> "And their souls wer a-smote wi' a stroke,
> As the lightnen do vall on the oak,
> And the things that were bright all around 'em
> Seem'd dim...." – W. BARNES.

The quotation from the first stanza of William Barnes's 'Bad News' gives a note of foreboding at the start of the section in which John Clark dies. Again, however, the context is ironic, since Barnes's poem ends with laughter when the unspecified 'bad news' turns out to be untrue. There is no such reprieve for Selina.

'Bad News' was published in Barnes's *Poems of Rural Life in the Dorset Dialect* in 1879, but Hardy did not mention it in his review of the volume, nor did he include it in his *Select Poems of William Barnes* which he edited in 1908.[3] Hardy's spelling differs from that of Barnes, who consistently prints *And*, *were*, *oak* and *'em* as *An'*, *wer*, *woak* and *em* in the quotation, while it is possible that the serial's compositors were not able to reproduce Barnes's stress in *lightnèn*.

V
> For Love's sake kiss me once again!
> I long, and should not beg in vain. – BEN JONSON

The quotation, from 'A Celebration of Charis', anticipates Miller's renewed courtship of Selina.

VI   Men are as the time is. – KING LEAR

The quotation continues: 'to be tender-minded / Does not become a sword' (V.iii.31–3). In this section, the dragoon is revealed to have been intending to marry Selina as a bigamist.

There are some seventy substantive differences between the serial and *1913*. The name of the inn where the dragoon purchased his cask of ale was changed from the 'Three-Mariners' to the 'Phoenix'; both were the real names of inns which stood opposite each other in High East Street, Dorchester, at the time of the story, and Hermann Lea noted that the 'Phoenix' 'has always been favoured by the soldiery at the barracks'.[4] It is in *1913* that Hardy specifies the churchyard in Durnover (Fordington St George) as the dragoon's burial place, and after the funeral Selina returns home over Swan Bridge, which is named for the first time. Hardy is more willing to identify what have become familiar Casterbridge landmarks in his other works.

The longest addition to *1913* is the entire new paragraph in which Bartholomew Miller explains to Selina that he wishes to marry soon because his mother is growing old and he wants to have someone to be with her. This insertion allows the later reflection that, 'however, Selina would not consent to be the useful third person in his comfortable home – at any rate just then' (p. 168). Hardy probably explained Miller's motive here so that the news which we receive three paragraphs later (and which is in the serial) that he has married someone to obtain a companion for his mother is consistent with his proposal to Selina: presumably he would have mentioned it to her if it was such a pressing reason to marry.

After the dragoon's death, Selina opened a shop and painted the name 'Mrs. John Clark' on her signboard, 'no man forbidding her' (p. 166). This last phrase is an addition in *1913* and is a biblical allusion to the closing words of Acts, where Paul's freedom to preach is described:

> Preaching the kingdom of God, and teaching those things which concern
> the Lord Jesus Christ, with all confidence, no man forbidding him.
> (XXVIII.31)

The allusion ironically shows Selina asserting her assumed name as if it had the truth of holy writ.

Some new details are added in *1913* to the encounter between Selina and the dragoon's widow. In the serial, the widow brings with her 'a little boy' but this became 'a tiny boy' (p. 169) in *1913*, stressing just how recently Clark had been someone else's legal husband and making Selina's assumption of widowhood more ironic and unjustified. Similarly, Selina tells the real widow that she and the dragoon 'were going to be married in a few days – twice over'. This is misleading, since they had not previously been married, whatever Selina might think, and *1913* has her saying more accurately instead that Clark was 'as good as my husband, for he was just going to be' (p. 169). In her closing speech, the widow does not refer to the dragoon as a 'poor man', as she had done in the serial, where her pity for the husband who deserted her seems misplaced, and she explains that Clark had vowed to emigrate and not return 'to me', the addition of the two words stressing that Clark was specifically renouncing his wife, and not his country.

In *1913*, the opening sentence's parenthesis about 'the gentleman who is answerable for the truth of this story' is new, and was perhaps intended to prevent the first-person narrator being mistaken for an authorial voice. *1913* also has less dialect, with the serial's 'he have', 'a-coming' and 'coortship', for instance, being replaced by standard forms. The dragoon gives Selina a more realistic view in *1913* of their prospects if they emigrate to New Zealand, the serial's 'large' income becoming merely a 'larger' (p. 160) one. A more detailed cause of the dragoon's sudden death is given in *1913* by the insertion of a reference to his heart's 'fatty degeneration' (p. 164).

The date, 'December 1899', which Hardy added at the end of *1913*, indicates the period of composition.

1913 Harper

There are five differences in accidentals between *1913* and the American edition, and two misprints (*1913H* omits an article and has 'nearly' instead of 'really').

1914 Macmillan Wessex edition

There are only nine differences in accidentals between *1913* and the Wessex edition, and no substantive ones.[5]

Notes

1 *Music and Moonlight* (New York: Garland, 1977), p. 39.
2 I am indebted to my colleague, Mr J. Derrick McClure, for identifying this poem's title.
3 *Poems of Rural Life in the Dorset Dialect* (London: C. Kegan Paul, 1879), pp. 448–9. Hardy's review, the only one he ever wrote, was published in the *New Quarterly Magazine* in October 1879.
4 Lea (1966), p. 264.
5 For the sake of a complete record, the revisions to *1913* for the Wessex edition are as follows (*1914* is quoted first, and the pagination is that of *1914*): 'Why,/Why' (p. 151); 'matter?/matter,' (p. 151); 'sweetheart/sweetheart,' (p. 155); 'Church's/ church's' (p. 156); 'replied/replied,' (p. 158); '"topper"?/ "topper,"' (158); 'I, away/ I – away' (p. 159); 'fiddler?/fiddler.' (p. 160); 'Owlett's/Owlett's,' (p. 160).

CHAPTER 31

'A Tryst at an Ancient Earthwork'

'A Tryst' is one of Hardy's least successful short stories. One feels that he wanted to write a moody, evocative sketch about Maiden Castle, but then felt obliged to tack on some narrative stage business at the end to justify it. In its earliest publication in America, 'A Tryst' has a plot and characterization which are more perfunctory even than in the version which we read now. It is one of Hardy's very few sustained first-person narratives, and, as 'Alicia's Diary' also shows, this was not a form which was at all congenial to him.

The versions of the story which have textual significance are as follows:

DP	'Ancient Earthworks and What Two Enthusiastic Scientists Found Therein', *Detroit Post*, 15 March 1885.
EIM	'Ancient Earthworks at Casterbridge', *English Illustrated Magazine*, December 1893, pp. 281–8, with four photographs of Mai-Dun by W. Pouncy of Dorchester.
1913	'A Tryst at an Ancient Earthwork', *A Changed Man and Other Tales* (London: Macmillan, 1913), pp. 171–86. Published at 6*s.* in an edition of 10,000 copies on 24 October 1913.
1913H	'A Tryst at an Ancient Earthwork', *A Changed Man and Other Tales* (New York: Harper & Brothers, 1913), pp. 169–84.
1914	'A Tryst at an Ancient Earthwork', *A Changed Man and Other Tales* (London: Macmillan, 1914), pp. 169–83. Volume XVIII of the Wessex edition.

A manuscript of the story has survived, and will be discussed in detail later. It is currently located in the Harry Ransom Humanities Research Center at the University of Texas at Austin. It is not the manuscript of the *Detroit Post* story but was used to prepare proofs of the English publication in 1893.

The story first appeared in March 1885, and its subject reveals the kind of antiquarian and archaeological interests which are seen in *The Mayor of Casterbridge*, completed in the following month, and in the paper which Hardy had read to the Dorset Natural History and Antiquarian Field Club the previous May, entitled 'Some Romano-British Relics Found at Max Gate, Dorchester', in which he described the urns and skeletons which were discovered while excavating the foundations of his new house.

The earliest surviving reference to 'A Tryst' is on a postcard dated 3 February 1885 which Hardy sent to T.H.S. Escott, informing him that 'MS. is in preparation. / Will send it in a day or two'. Hardy received payment for the story within a fortnight but had to return the cheque to Escott on 19 February because he had omitted to sign it (*Letters*, I, 130). Escott, the editor of the *Fortnightly Review*, must have been an intermediary in arranging for the story's appearance in the *Detroit Post* the following month. Hardy probably chose a distant American journal for the story's first publication because the unscrupulous archaeologist whom he described in it was based on a recognizable local character named Edward Cunnington (1825–1916), a prominent Dorchester antiquary. Michael Millgate gives a telling account of how Cunnington was viewed at this time:

> Hardy seems to have found himself at cross-purposes with Edward Cunnington, a local antiquary of what Hardy evidently took to be rather rapacious habits: Henry J. Moule [Curator of the Dorset County Museum], writing on the last day of 1883, reports that he has told Mr Cunnington about some arrow points Hardy had found on the heath, 'carefully concealing name of person & *places*. He was much moved.' Cunnington made a number of significant archaeological 'finds' near Dorchester in the early 1880s – including, according to a recent authority, 'an amber cup, allegedly complete till Cunnington trod on it' – and his excavation of a Romano-Celtic temple at the eastern end of the great Iron Age hill fort known as Maiden Castle was made – almost libellously, one would think – the subject of Hardy's story 'A Tryst at an Ancient Earthwork', published in the *Detroit Post* in March 1885 but not printed in England until December 1893. (p. 244)

In his paper on 'Some Romano-British Relics', Hardy had made an ironic reference to Cunnington as 'our local Schliemann',[1] an allusion to Heinrich Schliemann (1822–90), the German archaeologist who had excavated Troy. Although Hardy probably no longer cared if he offended Cunnington when he decided to publish the story in England in 1893, he nevertheless chose to lessen the implication that Cunnington was motivated by personal gain in his digging by changing the description of the statuette of Mercury which the archaeologist stole: in the earlier American version, the statuette had been made of gold but in the 1893 publication it is probably just bronze-gilt.

The next reference to the story occurs in a passage in the *Life* which Hardy himself clearly deleted from the typescripts. A few lines after describing how Clement King Shorter, editor at this time of both the *Illustrated London News* and the *English Illustrated Magazine*, had been to lunch in September 1892 and asked for a story or an article, Hardy wrote: 'Sept. 11. Article on "An Ancient Earthwork", originally printed in an American paper, revised and sent to Mr Shorter, for him to consider if he will reprint it in the I.L.N., as I have nothing else.'[2] It seems possible that this reference to the story in the *Life*, and also the account of Shorter's visit, are wrongly dated and should be assigned to September 1893, not 1892. They would then form a sequence of events leading up to Hardy's letter to Shorter of 18 September 1893, where he writes that

> I will re-write the article, & let you have the use of it in the English

Illustrated for £20 – improved and expanded.

But it ought to be accompanied by photographs of the place (wh. you have seen). Curiously enough it has, I think, escaped the illustrated papers hitherto. (*Letters*, II, 34)

If my surmise about the misdated entry or entries in the *Life* is correct, then the sequence of events would appear to be thus: Shorter called for lunch in September 1893 and asked for an article or story, which Hardy submitted on 11 September, to be considered for publication in the *Illustrated London News*. Shorter replied, presumably, suggesting that it appear instead in his other journal, the *English Illustrated Magazine*, and Hardy wrote on 18 September to accept this offer and agreeing to revise the story, perhaps in response to Shorter's comments on it.

On 23 September 1893, Hardy submitted the revised version to Shorter: 'By Parcel Post to-day is sent you the article "An Ancient Earthwork". Also 3 photographs of Maiden Castle – the best I could get' (*Letters*, II, 35; in fact, four photographs were used to illustrate the story). When the story was published, he wrote to Florence Henniker on 1 December 1893:

An article I wrote on some earthworks near here appears in this month's English Illustrated Magazine: & I am intending to send that too. The editor has taken it upon himself to identify the spot with Dorchester, which I did not wish him to do, since it is just possible that a character who appears in the narrative may be said to be drawn from a local man, still living, though it is really meant for nobody in particular. (*Letters*, II, 43)

It seems disingenuous for Hardy to complain that Shorter has identified the spot with Dorchester. It is true that Hardy's chosen title in the manuscript of the story reads 'An Ancient Earthwork', which Shorter must presumably have altered, even after Hardy had corrected the proofs, to 'Ancient Earthworks at Casterbridge', but Hardy himself had identified Casterbridge Museum in the final two words of the story (this is in the manuscript, but not in the earlier *Detroit Post* version, where Hardy refers simply to 'the — Museum'). Furthermore, it was Hardy who suggested illustrating the story with photographs which are clearly identifiable, and their captions simply repeat the information that Hardy himself gives in the story, that the place is Mai-Dun. If he was concerned about the local antiquary being identified, then why did he give (as we shall see) a much more prominent and critical portrait of him in the revised version? While Shorter may have been responsible for highlighting Casterbridge in the title, he was not giving away any information which Hardy's text and choice of photographs do not make fully explicit. Hardy's apprehension that the model for his archaeologist would be recognized was eventually proved to be unnecessary, since there do not appear to have been any repercussions following the English publication.

Detroit Post

The unique features of the earliest version of the story are perhaps best defined by comparing the American publication with the version of the story which Hardy prepared for the first English publication in 1893 and which is virtually the same as the 'definitive' version which we now read.

The principal changes give a greater presence to the narrator and the shady antiquary, substantially increasing their prominence in the closing part of the tale and turning a rather static sketch about Mai-Dun into more of a dramatized work of fiction. More than fifty lines are added for the English serial when the two men meet near the end. Hardy also seems to find a clearer thematic perspective on his material in the later version, introducing a stark contrast between the technological foresight and ingenuity of those who built the earthwork and the myopic self-interest of the 'scientist' who scrapes about and digs in the dark. The pioneering brilliance of the ancient engineers has been replaced by the grubby and furtive work of the modern archaeologist, who can merely scratch at the surface of their world and plunder their valuables. Finally, in the eight years between the American and English publications of the story, Hardy seems to have changed his mind entirely about the identity of the earthwork's earliest inhabitants.

The enhanced prominence of the first-person narrator and his relationship to the scene which he describes is indicated by a change at the end of the opening paragraph. In *DP*, Mai-Dun is a so-called immutable 'object' but in *EIM* this becomes a 'spectacle'. Mai-Dun is now something to be *seen*, the product of perception, and there is a much greater emphasis in *EIM* on the narrator as perceiver, his point of view, and the angles and directions from which he observes the scene. The changes for *EIM* give an impressionistic quality to the narration: this is how the scene strikes the perceiving eye under particular aspects of light and weather. The opening of the story, especially, is altered to give a clear sense of the direction of the narrator's gaze. In *DP*, the birds merely rise from 'the other side' of Mai-Dun, but in *EIM* we learn that they ascend 'from the invisible marine region on the other side'. Since the earthwork is a couple of miles south-west of Dorchester, and the sea is invisible to the narrator, he is approaching Mai-Dun from the north; i.e., the point of view in the story is that of someone looking out to the earthwork from the direction of Dorchester. This clear sense of location and direction in *EIM* is added right from the first sentence, where we learn that the ruin rises against the 'south' sky, a detail lacking in *DP*, and similarly the start of the third paragraph gives us the 'eastward' view of the stronghold's profile. The American publication lacks this firm focalization through a specific observer in a specific location.

The play of light in *DP*'s opening paragraph is ambiguous, since we are told that 'wan' light is replaced by 'sombre melancholy', although it sounds quite melancholic already, and wan light would not explain why the bluffs are 'luminous'. *EIM* gives a much stronger contrast, 'broad lights' giving way to 'melancholy gray'. Another change to the opening paragraph involves the personification of Mai-Dun; in *DP* it has a 'Titanic personality' but in *EIM* it has an 'obtrusive personality' and a 'high-shouldered' presence. Hardy seems to have been particularly concerned to animate the whole scene when preparing *EIM*; for instance, the fort is said to have an 'animal' aspect, and to loom out of the dark 'like a thing waking up and asking what I want there'. Similarly, the clouds which seem to stroke the birds with their 'bagging bosoms' in *EIM* were not personified in *DP*, and the whole atmosphere before the storm heaves 'like the sigh of a weary strong man on turning to re-commence unusual exertion'.

A new detail about the narrator in *EIM* is that, he tells us, 'I am ensconced in a cottage', a mile away from the fort. In *DP*, he had just been looking at the ruins from this outdoor spot where 'I still linger on', but one wonders why he has lingered on at the same site for so many hours until the night is far advanced and the time for his tryst with the archaeologist arrives. In *EIM*, he is waiting at home. This strange request for a meeting late at night curiously elicits no response from the narrator in *DP*, and he simply sets off to the earthwork without any comment, but at least in *EIM* we learn that the archaeologist's request 'concerns an appointment, which I rather regret my decision to keep now that night is come'. On his way to the tryst, we see him in *EIM* plodding 'stumblingly' across the fields, rather than 'laboriously' in *DP*, and this revision serves both to increase the narrator's physical presence in the story and to avoid a repetition of 'laboriously' in the next paragraph. Later in *EIM*, he has to 'clamber up' the fort's slope, which replaces *DP*'s mundane 'walk up'.

The contrast between technology and science then and now is foregrounded through two changes to *DP*. The narrator in *EIM*, reflecting on the identity of the man who decided to site the earthwork here, considers whether it was 'the travelling engineer of Britain's united tribes' who chose the spot with his 'prospective reasoning', his foresight contrasting with the shabby, skulking science of today, as represented by the archaeologist. 'Prospective reasoning', which replaces *DP*'s 'subtle reasoning', sets up a further opposition between the ancient Britons, who needed to look forward to anticipate a deadly attack, and the narrator and archaeologist, who seem able only to look back and who face merely the danger of legal prosecution.

A further introduction of the theme of science in *EIM* occurs during the simile which likens the lightning to 'a presiding exhibitor who *unrolls the maps, uncurtains the pictures*, unlocks the cabinets, and effects a transformation by merely *exposing the* materials *of his science*, unintelligibly cloaked till then' (italics indicate words which are new to *EIM*, and they are all interlineations in the MS.). The good scientist is like the lightning, illuminating and exposing the truth, unlike the archaeologist who must conceal any trace of his excavations in the dark and who removes his evidence.

Who built Mai-Dun? The conjecture about the travelling engineer of the British tribes replaces *DP*'s suggestion that it might have been the work of the Anglo-Romans (this is a late change, since 'Anglo-Romans' is deleted in the MS. for *EIM*). In the American publication, Hardy is non-committal about the identity of Mai-Dun's earliest inhabitants, although his archaeologist is adamant that they were Roman, but in *EIM* he suggests that Mai-Dun is at least partly the work of the British tribes. Thus, in the earlier version, the archaeologist exclaims on finding the mosaic that 'it is a Roman fort and not British at all', but he carefully qualifies this in *EIM*, where the manuscript reads as follows: 'it is a~~Roman~~ |not a Celtic| stronghold ~~essentially, rather than a British Celtic,~~ |exclusively, if at all; but a Roman;| the former people having |probably| contributed little more than the original framework, which the latter took & adapted till it became the present imposing structure' (fo. 13). Again, this is a late alteration in the MS. of *EIM*, where Hardy began by following the *DP* reading that 'it is a Roman' fort, before deleting it and qualifying the assertion, and it seems clear that Hardy changed his mind about the origins of Mai-Dun when he had nearly completed the MS. Another alteration which bears this out occurs during the narrator's ruminations about the warriors who went out of the fort's gates in the morning to do battle: in *DP*, there is no indication whether these warriors are British or Roman, but an interlineation in the MS. of *EIM* asserts that they went to battle '|with the Roman legions under Vespasian|' (fo. 7). The narrator is obviously thinking of the Durotriges leaving the camp to do battle with the Romans, but before the revision he could just as easily have been thinking of the Romans departing to fight the local tribes. Similarly, the narrator in *DP* later envisages the 'king or leader' looking out of the camp 'for legions approaching either to succor or to attack'. Hardy here leaves it deliberately unclear whether the legions of, presumably, Roman soldiers are friendly or hostile to the inhabitants of Mai-Dun; in *EIM*, however, he eventually decided that the inhabitants were British, so 'legions' was deleted in the MS. and replaced by '|armed companies|' (fo. 10), since legions of Romans would not now be approaching to give succour.

The most substantial new material for *EIM* involves the dozen or so additions which give personal and invariably critical information about the archaeologist. In *DP*, he is little more than a cipher, presented with barely any characterization, but the risk of the local antiquary being identified in the English publication certainly did not deter Hardy from giving him a much more prominent and satirical presence in *EIM*. The longest entirely new addition shows the archaeologist's fevered mania in his pursuit of his hobby:

> He is a man about sixty, small in figure, with gray old-fashioned whiskers cut to the shape of a pair of crumb-brushes. He is entirely in black broadcloth – or rather, at present, black and brown, for he is bespattered with mud from his heels to the crown of his low hat. He has no consciousness of this – no sense of anything but his purpose, his ardour for which causes his eyes to shine like those of a lynx, and gives his motions all the elasticity of an athlete's.
>
> 'Nobody to interrupt us at this time of night!' he chuckles with fierce enjoyment.

A little later, 'he chuckles fiercely again with suppressed delight' and says, in reply to the narrator's query why he did not obtain permission to dig, '"Because they wouldn't have given it!"' In *DP*, there is no direct speech at all in the story, so Hardy's revisions serve to dramatize the tryst a little. The archaeologist's undignified appearance and gleeful delight in his crime are in ironic contrast to his status as 'a professed and well-known antiquary with capital letters at the tail of his name' (this is also new for the 1893 English publication, and one begins to wonder why Hardy bothered to omit Cunnington's name. Michael Millgate is certainly correct when he says that Hardy was in a 'publish and be damned' mood by this time[3]). A similar contradiction appears in *EIM* when he is seen flourishing his tools 'with the skill of a navvy, this venerable scholar with letters after his name'.

In *EIM*, the archaeologist insists that he has a 'justifiable' intention in his digging and that it is 'no such monstrous sin'; in *DP*, though, he had been adamant that it was 'no sin' whatsoever. On discovering the Roman origins of the fort, he exclaims that it proves all the world except him to be wrong 'in this great argument', introducing his lack of proportion in his antiquarian obsession, and he continually murmurs to himself 'how important, how very important, this discovery is!' (in *DP*, he says only 'how very important this discovery is'). His excitement is seen in *EIM* when he is shown 'grasping' the lantern from the narrator's hand (in *DP* he was merely 'taking' it), and when he 'draws groans of luxurious sensibility' after discovering a bottle.

The moment when the antiquary purloins the statuette is dramatized in *EIM* (none of the following is present in *DP*):

> and at one moment I fancied I saw him slip his hand into his coat pocket.
> 'We must re-bury them all,' say I.
> 'Oh yes,' he answers with integrity. 'I was wiping my hand.'

This both gives the antiquary the opportunity to replace the statue, which he fails to grasp, and establishes the narrator's ethical position, exonerating him of any complicity in the theft. The 'integrity' of the archaeologist's answer is obviously ironic in hindsight and gives the story a clearer moral perspective on his actions than was present in *DP*.

The narrator gives some new details in *EIM* which make the tryst rather more Gothic and macabre. The skeleton, for instance, which they unearth is said to have 'two-and-thirty sound' teeth, and the antiquary 'wipes the perspiration from his forehead with the same handkerchief he had used to mop the skeleton clean'. The latter detail stresses the archaeologist's distracted excitement, as does the narrator's comment that his 'eccentric' friend digs on 'unconcernedly' during the storm: 'he is living two thousand years ago, and despises things of the moment as dreams'.

The subjects of the songs which the narrator imagines being sung by the ancient Britons are slightly augmented in *EIM* (words in square brackets were in *DP*, and italics indicate the additions to *DP*):

> 'on this raised [spot] *floor*, daïs, or [platform] *rostrum*, harps have probably twanged [their wild] *more or less tuneful* notes in celebration of daring, [and] strength, *or cruelty*; of worship, *superstition*, love, birth, [or] *and* death; [though] of simple loving-kindness perhaps never'.

The songs of cruelty and superstition evoke a more pagan society in the earthwork, although the change from 'wild' to 'more or less tuneful' notes suggests also a more advanced and cultured one.

EIM introduces some new information about Mai-Dun which is not in *DP*. We learn that its circumference is exactly 'a measured mile', and that the Romans deserted it only 'on their withdrawal from the island', stressing their continuous occupation. The overlapping ramparts have a cunning construction whose ingenuity is now unappreciated: in *DP*, the reason for this neglect is that such cunning 'is now wasted on prowling winds and the solitary forms of a few wild badgers, rabbits and hares' which now inhabit the ruin. In *EIM*, however, Hardy omitted the prowling winds and added the phrase about the construction being obscured by dilapidation, presumably because the prowling winds never did appreciate the architectural design of the ramparts, then or now.

Other minor changes to *DP* include an addition for *EIM* of ten lines describing the notice prohibiting the removal of material from the earthwork, making it emphatically clear that the archaeologist's removal of the statue is illegal, whereas in *DP* the notice is only mentioned in passing and is said to prohibit digging, not theft. The statue of Mercury in *EIM* is shown to be of the finest quality: 'further inspection reveals the workmanship to be of the highest finish and detail, and, preserved by the limy earth, to be as fresh in every line as on the day it left the hands of its artificer'. The statue is also said to be 'obviously' a figure of Mercury, whereas in *DP* it was only 'apparently' so. Both alterations make it clear that in no sense is the statue the 'debased Roman' which was found among the effects of the late archaeologist and which he had presumably labelled thus to disguise its value.

Finally, the American publication is divided into eleven sections, all but the first one having 'headline' captions to introduce them, such as 'ITS OUTLINES' and 'AS VIEWED BY NIGHT'. These are no doubt editorial, as is probably the reference in *DP*'s title to the two enthusiastic scientists, since there is no indication of the story that such a description could apply to the narrator.

The manuscript and the *English Illustrated Magazine*

The extant MS. of 'A Tryst' is written on fifteen leaves. It is a fair copy prepared for the printers of the *English Illustrated Magazine*, although every leaf has a scattering of revisions. It is entitled 'An Ancient Earthwork' and was preserved by the magazine's editor, Clement Shorter.[4] Hardy prepared the MS. by copying either the original manuscript of the story as it had earlier appeared in the *Detroit Post* or a printed copy of it, and then making revisions to it as he wrote. There are some forty occasions in the MS. when he wrote, or began to write, a word or phrase which had appeared in *DP* before deleting it and writing the new *EIM* reading above it or immediately after it, and there are also about twenty instances where he inserted a new reading after copying *DP*.

The MS. is virtually identical to *EIM*, although there are some 27 substantive differences between the two. These are no doubt mostly authorial and occurred when Hardy altered the proofs of *EIM* which had been set up from the MS. Most are individual words, although there is one insertion in *EIM* which is ten words in length. There are also some fifty differences in accidentals, mainly accounted for by *EIM*'s greater use of commas.

The longest addition to the proofs of *EIM* concerns the uses to which stones from the earthwork were put by local residents, Hardy inserting 'and the corner-stones of this heathen altar may form' the base-course of some ancient village church to create an ironic continuity between ancient and modern forms of worship. Another proof revision is to alter the time of the tryst from an unspecified 'late' (fo. 3) hour to the 'midnight' hour. In the MS., Hardy's narrator says of the warriors who went to battle with the Romans that no 'poet' (fo. 7) or stone has preserved their fame, but he altered 'poet' to 'page' in the proofs, making their oblivion all the greater by stressing that their deeds have no written record of any kind.

Hardy had described in the MS. how columns of infantry must once have entered the earthwork, but now the only columns which enter are the columns of 'mist and rain' (fo. 6). He may have thought this too strained a conceit and changed it in the proofs to columns of 'sheep and oxen', introducing a bathetic contrast to the military splendour of old. At this stage of revision, Hardy took the opportunity to remove an ambiguity from the opening words of the story; in the MS., he had begun by describing how 'At every step forward it rises ~~again~~ higher against the south sky' but in the proofs he added 'one's' after the first word, making it clear that it is the narrator and not 'it' which steps forward. He also added 'British' to his description of the united tribes who may have first planned the earthwork, a change which reinforces Hardy's new view of Mai-Dun's earliest inhabitants, as discussed above. In the MS., Hardy had described how the archaeologist was an 'ancient' (fo. 13) scholar who flourished his tools with the skill of a navvy, but *EIM* substitutes 'venerable' for 'ancient', since the irony which Hardy is expressing concerns the antiquary's learned reputation, and not his age.

Finally, there is a variation between the MS. and *EIM* which may have been introduced by compositorial error. In the MS., Hardy appears to describe the narrator's fancy that he can hear voices from the past as 'these nebulous imaginings' (fo. 7), but *EIM* renders the phrase as 'mere nebulous imaginings', which is what all later editions of the story read. If it originated in error, Hardy either overlooked it in revising proofs or approved it.

1913 Macmillan

'A Tryst' was one of the six stories in *A Changed Man* which had been published in periodicals before 1891, when the International Copyright Law was introduced, and which Hardy said he was 'unhappily obliged to include in my set of books because pirated editions of some, vilely printed, are in circulation in America, & imported into England by the curious'.[5] In preparing 'A Tryst' for its first collected edition in 1913, Hardy took the opportunity to make some forty substantive changes to the story as it had last appeared in *EIM*, twenty years earlier. Nearly all involve individual words, or a short phrase at most, and the longest change concerns a three-line alteration to the postscript, describing the consequences of the tryst many years after.

The narrator's knowledge of Mai-Dun is more definite in *1913*: earlier, he had said in *EIM* that there is, 'no doubt, an entrance of some sort to the fortress; but that must be far off on the other side', but in *1913* he asserts that there is, 'of course, an entrance to the fortress; but that lies far off on the other side' (p. 176). In line with earlier revisions, Hardy makes it clearer that the earliest inhabitants of Mai-Dun were British. The archaeologist in *EIM* had exclaimed that his discovery of the mosaic proved that the earthwork was not a Celtic stronghold exclusively, 'if at all, but a Roman'; in *1913*, however, this phrase reads 'but also a Roman' (p. 183), removing the qualifying suggestion that it may not have been a Celtic stronghold at all. The scale and quality of the archaeologist's finds are made less dramatic in *1913*; for instance, in *EIM* he had come across many 'utensils, weapons', but now he finds only 'a piece of a weapon', and the skeleton, which was previously 'tall and perfect', is now just 'fairly perfect', and we no longer learn that it has 32 'sound' teeth. The statuette in *EIM* had been of 'the highest' quality, but in *1913* it is simply 'good' (p. 184). The Roman presence is made less visible in *1913*: Roman tiles and stone chippings 'tell clearly' in *EIM* that masonry stood on the spot, but in *1913* they merely 'suggest' where the buildings had stood.

The narrator insists in *1913* that they must re-bury '*all*' their discoveries, the new italics increasing his suspicion that the archaeologist has purloined a piece of the treasure and emphasizing his outspoken refusal to be an accomplice to such theft. In *EIM*, the postscript is headed 'FIVE YEARS LATER' and the narrator proceeds to add new information to 'the foregoing pages of my diary'. In *1913*, the heading is removed and there is no suggestion that the story we have just read has been an entry in the narrator's diary; instead, the postscript begins 'It was thus I spoke to myself, and so the adventure ended. But one thing remains to be told, and that is concerned with seven years after' (p. 186). In the earlier version, the archaeologist has recently died five years after the tryst and the narrator writes the postscript at that time, but in *1913* he dies seven years after and the postscript is added on some unspecified later occasion, thereby casting the story backwards in time and showing the tryst in a longer historical perspective, making the tale itself, as it were, a kind of relic which the narrator has unearthed for us.

The bottom of the earthwork in *EIM* is said to be 'dark', but *1913* restores 'dank' (p. 175), which is *DP*'s reading and may also be the MS. reading. Other revisions were perhaps made for stylistic reasons: for instance, the birds in *EIM* are said to fly over the heights with 'careless indifference', but in *1913* Hardy removed the first of the two words, possibly because he thought the phrase was a tautology.

1913 **Harper**

There are six differences between *1913* and *1913H*, half of them substantive but probably editorial or compositorial in origin. *1913H* corrects the misprint in

1913 which says that the castle looms 'out off the shade' (p. 175), an error which is repeated in the Wessex edition of the following year, but it introduces a new one of its own in describing how the archaeologist 'murmurs [to] himself'. *1913H* also talks of 'the' heroic voices of the ancient warriors, a word lacking from the British edition.

1914 Macmillan Wessex edition

The Wessex edition of the story has only three variants, all accidentals, not found in the Macmillan edition of 1913.[6]

Notes

1 Orel, p. 194.
2 See Taylor, pp. 237–8, and *Life*, pp. 263, 537.
3 Millgate, p. 342.
4 See Purdy, p. 154.
5 *Letters*, IV, 300. Hardy made similar comments elsewhere about his wish to avoid pirating: see, e.g., *Letters*, IV, 299, 302, and V, 22.
6 The variant readings are as follows, with the Wessex edition first, followed by *1913*. The pagination is that of the Wessex edition: 'almost,/almost' (p. 171); 'recommence/re-commence' (p. 174); 'wrapt/wrapped' (p. 179).

CHAPTER 32

'What the Shepherd Saw'

'What the Shepherd Saw' was first collected in *A Changed Man and Other Tales* (1913), a volume of a dozen short stories which had been published in newspapers and periodicals between 1881 and 1900 and which Hardy was 'unhappily obliged to include in my set of books because pirated editions of some, vilely printed, are in circulation in America, & imported into England by the curious'.[1] 'What the Shepherd Saw' was one of the six stories in the volume which had first been published before 1891 and therefore did not enjoy the protection of the International Copyright Law.

A fragment of the manuscript of 'What the Shepherd Saw' has survived, as will be described shortly, and the published versions of the story which have textual significance are as follows:

ILN   *Illustrated London News*, Christmas Number (published 5 December) 1881, pp. 19, 22–3.

1913   *A Changed Man and Other Tales* (London: Macmillan, 1913), pp. 187–213. Published at 6s. in an edition of 10,000 copies on 24 October 1913.

1913H   *A Changed Man and Other Tales* (New York: Harper & Brothers, 1913), pp. 185–211.

1914   *A Changed Man and Other Tales* (London: Macmillan, 1914), pp. 185–210. Volume XVIII of the Wessex edition.

The manuscript

The opening three leaves of the manuscript, measuring 6¼" × 8", are located at the Beinecke Rare Book and Manuscript Library of Yale University. The leaves are sewn in a folded sheet of fine paper, on which Hardy has written '"<u>What the Shepherd Saw</u>" A tale written in 1881, & published in English and American Periodicals. Recently included in Collected Works in the volume entitled "A Changed Man". Original MS, being First Rough Draft. (3 pages only – the remainder lost.) Thomas Hardy.' At the head of the first page alongside the title, Hardy has noted in red ink '[First rough Draught] (1881)', and at the end he added '(<u>Caetera desunt</u>)'. This three-page fragment was one of three which Mrs Hardy sent in February 1916 for a Red Cross Sale at Christie's on 26 April 1916.[2] In an unpublished letter to Clement Shorter, wrongly dated by Hardy as 16 December 1912, he says of 'What the Shepherd Saw' that 'I have quite forgotten the story. Though I imagine it to be worth little'.[3]

The surviving fragment of the manuscript is very close to the version of the story first printed in *ILN*, and it abruptly ceases at the foot of the third leaf with

'I have come, Fred, because you entreated me so. What can have been the'. For a first rough draft, it is remarkably free of deletions and alterations. There are only some thirty occasions where the serial does not follow the MS. reading, and these are nearly all individual words or short phrases. The title of the opening section of the story is given as 'The first night', and the serial follows this revised form.

The serial gives a slightly greater definition to the opening's topography. The location of the scene on a spot near the turnpike road from Casterbridge 'before you come to Melchester' is a little more specific than the MS., where the quoted phrase is not present. The serial's first two references to the name of the ruin being the Devil's Door are also absent from the MS. The only substantial alteration for *ILN* is the addition of eight lines in the second paragraph describing how the clump of furze was hollow and the hut was thus completely screened and almost invisible ('with enormous stalks [...] In the rear'). This alteration permits the later substitution of the MS.'s reference to 'the hut & trilithon' (fo. 3) by the serial's 'the trilithon and furze clump that screened the hut'.

The serial and *1913 Macmillan*

The distinctive features of the serial of 1881 are best demonstrated by comparison with the alterations which Hardy made to it when collecting it some thirty years later for its inclusion in *A Changed Man*. When Hardy came to revise it in August 1913, just two months before the publication of the volume, he had, as we have seen, only three pages of the manuscript, and he did not possess even a copy of the periodical publication. Maurice Macmillan had to send him a typed copy of the story made from Clement Shorter's copy of the *Illustrated London News*, and it is this typed copy which Hardy emended.[4] A further link in the transmission of the text is thus introduced, and the relationship between *ILN* and *1913* is further complicated. Certainly in the matter of accidentals in *1913*, all one can say is that Hardy authorially approved them: whether he or the typist of the Shorter copy introduced any changes in accidentals which differentiate *1913* from *ILN* can only be conjecture.

There are quite a few substantive changes to the serial for *1913*. Fred Pentridge, the murdered lover, becomes Fred Ogbourne (the significance of this change will be mentioned shortly), and the young shepherd is Bill Wills in the serial and Bill Mills in *1913*. The earlier version locates the action on the fictional Verncombe Down and the Duke and Duchess live at Verncombe Towers. In *1913*, not only does Hardy change the names but he moves the location northwards to approximate much more closely to the actual sites being portrayed. In the serial, we learn that the hut and trilithon are on 'Verncombe Down, which you cross in its lower levels when following the turnpike-road from Casterbridge eastward, before you come to Melchester' (p. 19). This would seem to indicate that Hardy initially conceived the story to be set in the area of Cranborne Chase, south-west of Salisbury. This also means that Hardy is setting the story just to the north of Wimborne, where he had taken up residence in June 1881, a few months before beginning to write the story in the autumn. The name of Verncombe Down may have been suggested by the town of Verwood, to the north-east of Wimborne. A further indication of the story's serial location is that the name of Pentridge, an actual village on Cranborne Chase, is the serial's surname of the murdered lover. In *1913*, however, Hardy moved the story north to 'Marlbury Downs, which you directly traverse when following the turnpike-road across Mid-Wessex from London, through Aldbrickham, in the direction of Bath and Bristol' (p. 189). Marlbury Downs is the actual Marlborough Downs in Wiltshire, and the Devil's Door, the Druidical trilithon, corresponds to the real Devil's Den in the upper part of Clatford Bottom, two miles west of Marlborough. Ogbourne, the new surname of the lover, is also the name of two villages north of Marlborough. The new name of the mansion is Shakeforest Towers (the real Clatford Hall), a few miles west of Marlborough, and its name was suggested by Savernake Forest, south-east of the town.[5] All of these changes illustrate Hardy's typical tendency at this date to make possible closer identifications between his Wessex and the actual landscape.

The degree of physical contact between Harriet and Fred is much greater and more explicit in *1913* than it was in the serial. In the later version, Harriet complains to Fred that it is unkind of him 'to hold me tight here' (p. 194), whereas in *ILN* she had merely said 'to hold me here'. Similarly, in the serial we are told that 'He still held her hand', but *1913* adds 'and waist' (p. 194). The increased intimacy is not simply a product of the greater explicitness which Hardy felt able to express at this later date, but it is thoroughly justified, and even essential, to motivate the action: the watching Duke is much more likely in *1913* to reach the mistaken conclusion that the meeting between his wife and Fred is 'the assignation of a pair of well-agreed lovers' (p. 195), as a result of which he murders Fred. In the serial he is driven to this merely by the sight of Fred grabbing his wife's hand.

The relationship between Harriet and Fred, as seen in their talk on the Downs, is subtly changed in *1913*, where Hardy creates a greater contrast between Fred, the tragic unrequited lover, and the mildly reproving Duchess. For instance, she calls him 'you silly' (p. 193) for speaking to her in a tragic tone, which was not in the serial, and she refers to him as a 'comrade of my youth' (p. 193), rather than the serial's 'friend of my youth', which makes her seem as if she is trying to suggest that their relationship had been purely platonic (this is before he makes her confess that she had loved him). In contrast, Fred's calling her 'dearest' (p. 193; not in serial) shows him as more intense just as she is made more unmoved. This altered relationship between them in *1913* serves to highlight all the more the Duke's baseless suspicion of his wife and the folly of his murdering her lovelorn swain.

The chronology of the story is different in *1913*. In the serial, the middle-aged Bill when we first see him is 36 or 37 years of age, and the murder took place nineteen years ago. In *1913*, he is 38 or 40, and he witnessed the murder 22 years ago. Perhaps the reason for this revision is that Hardy wanted to increase the sense of time's inexorable revelation of past misdeeds. A more interesting change in the chronology involves the date of Bill's death. In the serial, he reveals the truth about the murder he saw, and then dies within a year or two, before the age of 39. In *1913*, he dies before he reaches 49. Kristin Brady has commented that in 'What the Shepherd Saw' Hardy is presenting 'the familiar Gothic theme – found also in *Caleb Williams* and *The Marble Faun* – that the witness of a murder can somehow share the guilt of the actual criminal', and that Bill's early death is a symptom of this guilt.[6] Brady's comment is made with regard to Bill's revised age of death in his late forties. Hardy is being even more Gothic in the serial, where Bill dies a decade sooner, and perhaps Hardy altered it because he felt that Bill's death within a mere year or two of revealing what he witnessed during the murder points a dubious moral: tell the truth and drop dead.

Two final points concerning the revision of *1913*: firstly, the opening paragraph as we read it today, introducing the genial Justice of the Peace who narrates the story, was not in the serial, and perhaps Hardy introduced it in *1913* because he felt that the vaguely historical subject matter and the presence of a Duchess reminded him of the kind of stories he had written about in *A Group of Noble Dames*, which are narrated by similar figures to the Justice of the Peace. Secondly, there is slightly less dialect in *1913* than in the serial, Hardy removing a 'ye' and two instances of 'hev' and replacing them with standard forms (although he also substitutes an ''ee' for a 'you' in the speech of the old shepherd on p. 190). There is also the usual 'ye / 'ee' substitution which Hardy undertook at this time throughout the Wessex edition of his works.

1913 Harper and *1914* Macmillan Wessex edition

The version of 'What the Shepherd Saw' in Harper's edition of *A Changed Man* (*1913H*) has twelve variants in accidentals from *1913* and one substantive variant, Macmillan's 'the tryst' becoming Harper's 'her tryst' (*1913H*, p. 197).

In the 1914 Wessex edition of *A Changed Man*, there are only five differences from the 1913 Macmillan edition, all of them accidentals.[7]

To summarize the nature of these changes which Hardy made to 'What the Shepherd Saw' over more than thirty years, one can begin by noting that the fragment of the surviving manuscript is very close to the 1881 serial. When Hardy first collected the story in 1913, he changed the location and altered several names. He gave a greater degree of physical contact between Fred and Harriet, and subtly modified their relationship, making him more ardent and her more gently reproving. Finally, the chronology of *1913* is approximately ten years greater in all than it was in the serial.

Notes

1 *Letters,* IV, 300. Hardy makes similar comments about his wish to avoid pirating elsewhere: see, e.g., IV, 299, 302 and V, 22.

2 See *Letters*, I, 145, and Purdy, p. 155.

3 This unpublished letter is also located at Yale. The date is likely to be 16 December 1911, since Hardy elsewhere in the letter asks Shorter about the progress he is making in having his manuscripts bound, because he wants to send one to Edward Clodd, and this was done in March 1912: see *Letters,* IV, 207–8.

4 See *Letters*, IV, 293, and the entry for 5 August 1913 in the Macmillan letterbooks in the British Library.

5 Much of this information regarding Marlbury Downs derives from F.B. Pinion's *A Thomas Hardy Dictionary* (London: Macmillan, 1989). For those interested in Wessex topography, one final alteration that can be noted is that the serial has a reference to 'the Ringdon road'. This may be Ringwood in the New Forest, fifteen miles south of Salisbury, but there is nothing further to help identify it in the story and, as far as I know, it was not used as a placename elsewhere. Ringwood is called Oozewood in 'Master John Horseleigh, Knight', written some dozen years after 'What the Shepherd Saw'.

6 See Brady, p. 165.

7 The following is a complete list of the differences between *1913* and *1914* (the reading in *1914* is given first, and the pagination is that of *1914*): 'exclaimed/exclaimed,' (p. 190); 'days?/days.' (p. 191); 'say;/say,' (p. 191); 'be;/be:' (p. 191); 'shepherd-boy/shepherd boy' (p. 205).

CHAPTER 33

'A Committee-Man of "The Terror"'

'A Committee-Man' was the first new work of fiction which Hardy published after the appearance of *Jude the Obscure* a year earlier, and it was to be the first of five short stories which he wrote after his final novel.

The versions of 'A Committee-Man of "The Terror"' which have textual significance are as follows:

ILN   *Illustrated London News*, Christmas Number (pub. 22 November) 1896, pp. 3–8, with headpiece and two illustrations in the text by H. Burgess.

1913   *A Changed Man and Other Tales* (London: Macmillan, 1913), pp. 215–33. Published at 6*s.* in an edition of 10,000 copies on 24 October 1913. The date which Hardy attached to the story, 1895, is a year in advance of its first publication.

1913H   *A Changed Man and Other Tales* (New York: Harper & Brothers, 1913), pp. 213–30.

1914   *A Changed Man and Other Tales* (London: Macmillan, 1914), pp. 211–28. Volume XVIII of the Wessex edition.

A bound manuscript of 'A Committee-Man' is currently located in the Berg Collection of the New York Public Library. Corrected proof-sheets of the story are in the Huntington Library.

In a letter of 17 December 1895, Hardy promised Clement Shorter, editor of the *Illustrated London News,* that he would write 'A Committee-Man': 'I have not forgotten the short story, & shall have much pleasure in writing it when I have got through the tedious proof-reading for the new edn.' (*Letters*, II, 101). This is a reference to the Osgood, McIlvaine collected edition of his fiction, and Hardy did not complete his work on this until August 1896. A little before then, he wrote to Shorter on 8 July that 'I am straining every nerve to do the story' (II, 126), presumably meaning that he was struggling to finish the collected edition so that he could begin writing. On 25 August he announced to Shorter that he had posted the manuscript of 'A Committee-Man' on the previous day from Stratford-on-Avon (where he and Emma had spent a week at the start of their two-month tour of England and Belgium): 'MS. was sent yesterday. I hope it will do – I had not time to get a type written copy made, so had to send on the original' (II, 129), and he requested duplicate proofs to be sent to Max Gate. From Dover, Hardy wrote again on 3 September to ask Shorter if the Christmas Number of the *Illustrated London News* would also be published in America (it was): 'if not I may as well get the tale into some newspaper there, to retain the Copyright' (II, 129). He ended by identifying the setting of the story as Weymouth, for the benefit of the artist (the illustrations, however, do not feature the town). A week after the story's publication in November 1896, Hardy told Florence Henniker that 'it did not occur to me that my story – or sketch – was a sad one. The marriage wd have resulted in unhappiness for certain, don't you think?' (II, 139).

Sources

On New Year's Day 1897, Hardy told Agnes Grove that 'the little story in the I.L. News had a basis of fact' (II, 142), a point he repeated in a letter to Madeleine Rolland in 1908: 'the real name of the Committee-man I do not know. But he was a real man, according to tradition' (III, 291).[1] The source for the story was first discovered by R.L. Purdy in 1943: it is a letter written by Lady Elizabeth Talbot to her sister in 1797, reporting an incident in London:

> One of the Directory was seen a few days ago in the Strand, and recognized
> by a French lady whose father, mother, and brother he had murdered. She
> fainted away in the street, and before she recovered enough to speak he had
> escaped in the crowd.[2]

Hardy came across the letter in *The Journal of Mary Frampton*, and seems to have made a copy of it: Brady notes that 'there is an excision in the "Facts" notebook at a point between passages that come before and after this source for the story in *The Journal of Mary Frampton* (p. [160]). It is likely, therefore, that Hardy did copy down this letter and later cut it out either to cover his tracks or simply to make use of the note' (p. 216). Gatrell observes that 'an erased line in the notebook just below the excision appears to have read "& before she recovered, he had disappeared". [...] But none of these notes accounts for the narrative potential that Hardy saw in the initial incident. He must at some time have thought to himself: what if the man had not disappeared, but had naturally enough been concerned for a lady fainting away within his sight; what then? And the story is a consequence of this change to the recorded event' (1984, pp. 5–6). In shaping his tale, Hardy placed the events in 1802–3 and moved the scene to Weymouth, permitting the Royal visits and the threatened invasion to serve as a dramatic background.

Hardy also made detailed use of the research which he undertook at the British Museum in 1878-79, nearly twenty years earlier, for *The Trumpet-Major*, a story set in the same time and place as 'A Committee-Man'. Of the following four passages in the story, some of which are lifted almost exactly from the 'Trumpet-Major Notebook', only the first appears to have been quoted before (see Brady, p. 216, and Gatrell, 1984, p. 5):

'A Committee-Man' (serial)	'Trumpet-Major Notebook'
i 'The magistrates acting under the Alien Act have been requested to direct a very scrutinising eye to the academies in our towns and other places, in which French tutors are employed, and to all of that nationality who profess to be teachers in this country. Many of them are known to be inveterate enemies and traitors to the nation among whose people they have found a livelihood and a home.'[3]	The magistrates acting under the alien act would do well to direct a very scrutinizing eye to the academies in the metropolis & its vicinity, in all of which Fch. tutors are employed, many of whom are known to be inveterate enemies to the country which affords them an asylum. (*True Briton*, 18 October 1803, quoted in Taylor, p. 117)
ii [The King's arrival] made it necessary that a strict military vigilance should be exercised to guard the royal residents. Half-a-dozen frigates were every night posted in a line across the bay, and two lines of sentinels, one at the water's edge and another behind the Esplanade, occupied the whole sea-front after eight every night.	At Weyth. the most strict military vigilance is exerted to guard the Royal residents. Not only the frigates & other armed vessels are every night posted in a line across the mouth of the harbour[bay], but two lines of centinels, one at the water's edge & another behind the Esplanade, occupy the whole harbour[bay] after 8 every night. (Taylor, p. 126)
iii the play [...] being no other than Mr Sheridan's comedy of 'The Rivals,' with Mr. S. Kemble as Captain Absolute.	This evening the R[oyal]. F[amily]. are to honour the Theatre with their presence to see the comedy of the Rivals Sir A. Abs. Mr S. Kemble. (Taylor, p. 173)
iv a small muslin shawl crossed over the bosom in the fashion of the time, and tied behind.	October fashions – a round dress of white muslin, long sleeves. A Barcelona handkf. crossed over the bosom & tied behind. (Taylor, p. 132)

Such close reliance on his sources may indicate Hardy's flagging creativity after the arduous revision of the Osgood, McIlvaine edition, and his need for the extended holiday on which he was embarking.

The manuscript

The MS. of 'A Committee-Man' is written on nineteen leaves of ruled paper with many revisions and a short cancellation of six lines which were reinserted on the following leaf. Hardy has deleted some working notes at the head of the first leaf: 'Roy.[1] Fam. at W[eymou].[th] Sept. 1801, 2, 4, 5, &c. Peace of Amiens March 27 '02 Rupture between Fr. & Eng. & arrest of Bsh. travellers: May 12 '03.' Only the years in which the Royal Family visited Weymouth were recorded in the 'Trumpet-Major Notebook' (Taylor, p. 117).

Deleted readings in the MS. show that the Frenchman originally wrote to Mademoiselle V— when he was ill to ask her to act as an interpreter because he cannot make the people with whom he is staying understand what he wants done, in case he dies. This was changed so that he asks Mademoiselle V— herself to perform his wishes, a much greater test of her charity towards a man who was responsible for the execution of her family. The only other deletions of significance are two occasions when Hardy removed 'passion' (fos. 14, 17) as a definition of Mademoiselle V—'s feelings towards the Committee-Man, replacing them with 'emotion' and 'tenderness' respectively.

Serial proofs

The serial first proofs of the *Illustrated London News* consist of thirteen pages, all of which show at least several marginal emendations. There is evidence that Hardy read the proofs for sense, and did not read them against the MS. The proofs are substantively identical to the MS., except in the case of three individual words. The first is an obvious mistake in which 'by' is printed as 'of' in the proofs, and Hardy corrected it in the margin. The other two corrupt readings, however, have had a lasting effect. One is the omission of the word 'here' from a sentence which reads in the MS. as 'I walk here in the sun every day' (fo. 12). The error did not alter the sense and so Hardy did not detect it. The other concerns Mademoiselle V—'s change of heart as she is fleeing from her fiancé in the London coach. In the MS., she asks herself why she should not indulge her tenderness for him, 'since its mortification could do no good' (fo. 17). 'Mortification' was printed in the proofs as 'notification', and Hardy, in an apparent guess at what he had originally written, altered it in the margin to read 'nullification', which has passed into successive editions.

Hardy's alterations to the proofs show him refining the characterization of Mademoiselle V— and the reasons for her attraction to the Committee-Man. For instance, the proofs originally described how she began to be more than merely curious 'about this the only fellow-countryman of hers in the town', but Hardy revised it to read 'about this fellow-countryman of hers', perhaps because he felt that the original wording suggested that she was attracted to him because he was her sole compatriot nearby and she was feeling homesick, which is hardly an appropriate response to the man who has murdered her family. In the next sentence, Hardy added that she could not find it in her 'nervous and sensitive' heart to resist his appeal, making her more vulnerable to him. Another change which makes her attraction seem even more involuntary is that a description of how 'her interest' in him was deeper than she knew is replaced with a reference to 'his influence upon her', so that she becomes a passive object under the Frenchman's spell. Hardy also added later that her tenderness for him 'was founded on awe'. Such changes are necessary to stress that her irrational attraction to her family's murderer is compulsive and is certainly not simply romantic.

There are nine occasions when the serial differs from the amended proofs, and these further changes must have been introduced in the second proofs, or revises. All but two of them are substantive, and the longest is an insertion of twenty words which informs us that 'the King's awkward preference for a part of the coast in such dangerous proximity to France made it necessary that' a strict military vigilance had to be maintained. The other substantive changes at this stage seem to have been stylistic and do not introduce new information, and they involve individual words or a short phrase at most (e.g., 'was' became 'should be', and 'proximity' became 'presence').

The *Illustrated London News* and *1913* Macmillan

In revising the serial for its first collected edition, Hardy made some twenty changes, mostly affecting just a word or two, but there is one significant insertion of nine lines in length. A couple of nights before her intended wedding to the Committee-Man, Mademoiselle V— has a vision of those members of her family whom he had killed:

> That night she saw (as she firmly believed to the end of her life) a divinely sent vision. A procession of her lost relatives – father, brother, uncle, cousin – seemed to cross her chamber between her bed and the window, and when she endeavoured to trace their features she perceived them to be headless, and that she had recognized them by their familiar clothes only. In the morning she could not shake off the effects of this appearance on her nerves. (p. 229)

This certainly serves to motivate better that 'sense of family duty' which is shortly to make her flee, and increases her neurotic sensitivity. Another change in her characterization is seen in the description of her love for the Committee-Man: in the serial, 'she was, by some abnormal instinct, inclining to a tenderness for him that was founded on awe'. Hardy may have felt that this statement was imprecise, because it would not be 'abnormal' for her to love someone of whom she was in awe. It is the awe itself which is abnormal here, and, in any case, awe was certainly not the original basis of her feelings towards her lover, as Hardy's revision in *1913* makes clear: 'she was, by some abnormal *craving*, inclining to a tenderness for him that was founded on *its opposite*' (p. 228; my italics). This better captures the compulsive and addictive quality of her love which has its roots in hatred.

1913 gives a few new details about the Committee-Man. Hardy added the parenthesis describing his lodging as being one '(to which he had removed from the Old Rooms inn for economy)' (p. 224). This both makes his poverty more affecting to Mademoiselle V— and explains why we suddenly find him living over a shop, his removal from the inn not having been previously mentioned. When she is visiting, he obtains from her in *1913* 'a promise to post, in the event of his death, a letter he put in her hand' (p. 225), increasing the sense of his trusting dependency. One other change involves a description of the Committee-Man as 'lonely and dignified' in the serial, which became 'lonely and severe' (p. 228) in *1913*.

In the serial, Mademoiselle V— alights from the coach in which she was fleeing to London and watches it depart, 'starting as she saw' the shapes of the outside passengers, one of whom is the Committee-Man. She thus appears to recognize him at the time, which makes it rather pointless of her to return to Weymouth if she knows he has fled too. In *1913*, this is altered so that an indefinite 'something' in the departing shapes was 'giving her a start, as she afterwards remembered' (p. 231).

1913 Harper

The American collected edition shows nine differences from *1913*. The three which are substantive seem editorial ('the' Mousseaux Cemetery) or compositorial ('county' for 'country').

1914 Macmillan Wessex edition

Hardy did not revise the story for the Wessex edition, and there is only one minor difference between *1913* and *1914*.[4]

Notes

1 Rolland had translated the story into French, working from old proofs which Hardy had lent her in August 1907. Earlier in his letter, Hardy had explained his use of the word 'vengeance' in the story ('this lonely and severe man, who, in her tradition, was vengeance and irreligion personified': *1914*, p. 224): '"Vengeance", strictly, is retributive punishment of an appalling kind, executed in a higher & grander spirit than ordinary revenge. But the word is loosely used to mean violent onslaught of any kind, & I daresay I so used it.' Another French translation of the story was made in 1914 (see *Letters*, V, 33).
2 See Purdy (1943), pp. 554–5. The letter was printed in Mundy, ed. (1885), p. 94.
3 The phrase 'and traitors', not found in the Notebook, was a marginal addition to the serial proofs. The MS. was thus even closer to the Notebook than the serial.
4 *1913* reads 'said, presently', and *1914* omits the comma (p. 218).

CHAPTER 34

'Master John Horseleigh, Knight'

'Master John Horseleigh, Knight' may have been originally conceived as a story in *A Group of Noble Dames*, published two years earlier. Its antiquarian subject matter is typical of much of that volume, and, indeed, its setting in 1539 makes it the earliest one in Hardy's prose. The 'thin-faced gentleman' who narrates the story sounds similar to the members of the Wessex Field and Antiquarian Club, and the only reference to him, a parenthetical one in the opening sentence, resembles the introduction of the narrator in 'The First Countess of Wessex'. Horseleigh's acknowledged wife is called 'dame' on four occasions (and a further one is deleted in the manuscript), while a deleted description of Edith's eyes as 'bright' may have reflected the Miltonic epigraph to *A Group of Noble Dames*: '...Store of Ladies, whose bright eyes / Rain influence.'

It is, however, likely that 'Master John Horseleigh, Knight' was written *after* the original publication of *A Group of Noble Dames* in May 1891. Replying to W.E. Henley's request for material for the *National Observer*, Hardy told him on 21 October 1891 that 'I am pregnant of several Noble Dames (this is an unnatural reversal I know, but my constitution is getting mixed) – I mean I have thought of several more sketches of that sort, but can't touch one yet on account of an incubus of a syndicate story which weighs me down' (VII, 117–18). Hardy at this time was working on *The Pursuit of the Well-Beloved* and therefore asked Henley, 'would you not rather wait till some time (late) next year?' This timescale would accord with Hardy's submission of the story in March 1893 (to a different journal). While 'Master John Horseleigh, Knight' may be one of the 'several Noble Dames' which Hardy mentioned to Henley, the others do not appear to have been written.

The versions of the story which have textual significance are as follows:

ILN | *Illustrated London News*, Summer Number (pub. 12 June) 1893, pp. 5–9, with headpiece and four illustrations by W.B. Wollen.

McClure | As 'Mast^r John Horseleigh, Knyght', *McClure's Magazine*, July 1893, pp. 136–46, with head- and tailpiece and twelve vignette illustrations by Harry C. Edwards. The American serial publication.

1913 | *A Changed Man and Other Tales* (London: Macmillan, 1913), pp. 235–51. Published at 6*s.* in an edition of 10,000 copies on 24 October 1913.

1913H | *A Changed Man and Other Tales* (New York: Harper &

Brothers, 1913), pp. 231–47.

1914 *A Changed Man and Other Tales* (London: Macmillan, 1914), pp. 229–44. Volume XVIII of the Wessex edition.

A manuscript of the story has survived, and will be discussed in detail later. It is currently located in the Harry Ransom Humanities Research Center at the University of Texas at Austin.

The first surviving reference to the story is when Hardy sent it to C.K. Shorter, the editor of the *Illustrated London News* on 28 March 1893:

> I have done the best I could do – & send it herewith. Good measure, I think.
>
> If you don't like the word "bastard" which I have used you are kindly welcome to *dele* it. (*Letters*, II, 6)

(Shorter printed Roger's description of Edith's child as a bastard, while Horseleigh later calls his other children 'bastards'.) Hardy had proofs of the story by 3 May 1893 and sent the published version to Florence Henniker on 30 June 1893: 'I have posted to you today the Summer number of the Illustrated – in case you might like to see the story: but don't read it carefully, as it is of the slightest' (*Letters*, II, 8, 19).

Sources

Hardy found his material for the story in Hutchins's *History of Dorset*, but in the course of writing he seems to have realized that Hutchins's information was incorrect, and he chose to manipulate the historical record to make his tale plausible as fiction, as we shall see in the discussion below of the manuscript and the serial.

Hutchins notes that 'John Horssey, knyght [...] was maryd to Edith Stocker the wyffe late off John Stocker' in December 1539 (I, 50). In transcribing the entry in the opening paragraph of the story, Hardy follows Hutchins almost *verbatim* (Horssey becomes Horseleigh and Po[o]le becomes Havenpool). In the Horsey pedigree which he gives later, Hutchins says that John Horsey married 'Edith, daughter of Richard Phelips, of Monteacute', and in a footnote to this entry Hutchins repeats the information about the recorded marriage to Edith, widow of John Stocker, and comments 'But no notice is taken of this marriage in the pedigree' (IV, 427, 429). There is no date given for the marriage to Edith, daughter of Richard Phelips.

The lengthy description of the Horsey estate is taken in its entirety from Hutchins (IV, 426–7). Hardy says that his description derives from 'a manuscript dated some years later than the events we are regarding'. In fact, the date of the manuscript is given in Hutchins as 1648, more than a century after the events, so Hardy's omission of the date conceals the extent of the anachronism in quoting it.

Kristin Brady suggests that the story may also have been broadly based on a tale which Hardy heard in 1878 about Jane Carlyle's 'witch-neighbour' whose husband turned out to be a married man (see the *Life*, pp. 124–5).

The manuscript and the *Illustrated London News*

The bound manuscript of 'Master John Horseleigh, Knight' is titled 'Sir John Horseleigh, Knight', and is written on fifteen leaves. It would appear to be the printers' copy which Hardy sent to Shorter, although every leaf typically contains some minor revisions.

Changes within the MS. show that originally *both* wives were called Edith throughout the MS. and Hardy initially adapted the Hutchins pedigree for the Horseys/Horseleighs more or less correctly as saying that John Horseleigh was recorded as marrying 'Edith, daughter |& heiress| of S̶i̶r̶ Richard Phelipson of Montislope' (fo. 1). Hardy then deleted the reference to the name Edith here and elsewhere in the MS. One deleted sentence even has Roger musing on the coincidence: 'the same name as t'other, too; I wonder if there's any villainy in that!' (fo. 10). Hardy did not remove the name of the other Edith to avoid the confusion of having both his female characters called by the same name, but to suppress information which would have made redundant the tradition that he invents to account for Horseleigh apparently having two wives. If both women were called Edith, a perceptive reader might have wondered why Edith, the widow of John Stocker whom Horseleigh is said in the Havenpool marriage-register to have married, could not be the same person as Edith, the daughter of Richard Phelipson, whom his family pedigree says he married. Indeed, they were one and the same person.¹ In other words, there is no contradiction in the records as Hardy originally presented them in the MS.: Horseleigh had only one wife, and there would be no need to invent the tradition of bigamy to explain the two references to his marriage. Hardy must have realized this only after completing the story, for the other wife is called Edith on the penultimate page of the manuscript before he deleted all references to her name. The mistaken belief that Horsey had two wives originated in Hutchins, and Hardy seems to have discovered the truth while writing the story. He then altered the historical facts to allow his fictional 'tradition' to make sense. For instance, he invented the description in the Horseleigh pedigree of Edith Phelipson as an heiress, adding it as an interlineation: that description is not in Hutchins, but it serves to create a distinction in the story between a rich wife and a humble one, making it impossible to identify them as the same person.

Hardy apparently made twenty proof revisions to the serial, which would account for the substantive differences between the MS. and the *Illustrated London News*. The MS. reads that Horseleigh, according to the family pedigree, married the daughter of Richard Phelipson 'solely', and adds '(date not given)' (fo. 1). Hutchins does indeed give no date, but he does not say 'solely': Hardy is manufacturing a mystery. The *ILN*, however, removes these four words and replaces them by 'at a date apparently earlier than the above' (an inference for which there is no evidence in Hutchins), making it even more impossible for a reader to consider whether the two women may be the same person, since they now seem to have married Horseleigh at different times. *ILN* also adds the information that this other wife was 'a lady who outlived him' (not in Hutchins), so that we cannot solve the mystery of the two wives by suggesting that Horseleigh may have been widowed and then married again. Hardy's fictional account of the written records seems to lead inevitably to the conclusion that Horseleigh was a bigamist. The MS. sets out to account for 'this silence |concerning the humble Edith|' (fo. 1), but *ILN* makes the story's aim much more sinister: 'how are we to account for these, as it would seem, contemporaneous wives?'

Ten alterations in the MS. show Hardy introducing more archaic language or more dialect: for instance, 'has', 'can' and 'your' became 'hath', 'canst' and 'thy'. 'Must' was changed to 'modden', 'you are' became 'you be', and Hardy began to write 'three' before replacing it with the Dorset 'dree'. At the proof stage, Hardy took the further opportunity to introduce more archaisms and dialect. 'Before' became 'afore', and 'you know' became 'th' 'st know'. Further proof changes include the description of the lagoon which surrounds Oozewood as being a 'fresh-water' one. Edith in *ILN* says that the rumour of her husband being already married is 'fearsome' (MS. 'terrible'). The nursemaid who witnessed the murder says in the MS. that Horseleigh did not die for a long while, 'though he had d received his death wound' (fo. 13); Hardy changed this in the proofs so that she now testifies that 'nobody suspected Sir John had received his death wound'. It is now clear that those present at the murder did not realize Horseleigh would die of the stabbing, and so Edith's order to her brother to 'get himself gone' cannot be interpreted as a plea to escape and save himself, as it could in the MS. One final proof change removes an ambiguity: when Horseleigh's illegitimate son and grandson inherit the title, the MS. says that there was no one 'alive' (fo. 14) to investigate their claims to it. One knows what Hardy meant, but instead of changing the word so that it read 'alive from that time', or some such phrase, he made the very economical revision of 'alive' to 'alert', which would not disturb the surrounding type in the proofs. (In 1913, Hardy had the opportunity to revise without restraint, and he changed 'alert' to 'on the alert'.)

McClure's Magazine

The American version of the story has seven differences from the London publication in the *Illustrated London News* which are no doubt editorial or compositorial in origin and which involve only individual words. The only one of interest is that the British oath 'by God' becomes the milder 'my God' in *McClure's Magazine*.

1913 Macmillan

In preparing the first collected edition of 'Master John Horseleigh, Knight',

Hardy made only a handful of substantive revisions. The longest of these concerns Roger's place of rest when he arrives at Horseleigh's house at dawn to spy on him. In the *Illustrated London News*, he hides in a hole in an elm tree which was 'large enough to allow a man to creep to the hollow interior', where 'he fell asleep upon the stratum of broken touchwood that formed the floor of the hollow'. In *1913*, Roger crept into a heap of hay 'apparently for horses or deer', and here he slept, 'the hay forming a comfortable bed, and quite covering him over'.

Hardy alters the representation of dialect, 'that war' becoming 'that wer'. Edith in the previous versions died 'at no great age', which was altered to 'in middle age' in 1913. The date *'Spring 1893'* was added at the end of the story.

1913 Harper

The American edition of the story in *A Changed Man* has only three substantive differences from Macmillan *1913*, and they all appear to be editorial or compositorial (for example, 'off' for 'of').

1914 Macmillan Wessex edition

The Wessex edition is identical in every respect to Macmillan *1913*.

Note

1 See Pitfield, p. 83.

CHAPTER 35

'The Duke's Reappearance'

'The Duke's Reappearance', as Kristin Brady notes, is Hardy's 'last pure version of a "Wessex tale".'[1] Its subject matter is based on family tradition regarding the Monmouth Rebellion in 1685 and Hardy's maternal ancestors, the Swetmans and the Childses, both of whom are mentioned in the story. Hardy describes the family's involvement in the *Life*:

> Several traditions survived in the family concerning the Rebellion. An indubitably true one was that after the Battle of Sedgemoor two of the Swetman daughters – Grace and Leonarde [spelt 'Leonard' in the story] – were beset in their house by some of the victorious soldiery, and only escaped violation by slipping from the upper rooms down the back stairs into the orchard. It is said that Hardy's great-grandmother could remember them as very old women. Part of the house, now in the possession of the Earl of Ilchester, and divided into two cottages, is still standing with its old Elizabethan windows; but the hall and open oak staircase have disappeared, and also the Ham-Hill stone chimneys. The spot is called "Townsend".
>
> Another tradition, of more doubtful authenticity, is that to which the short story by Hardy called "The Duke's Reappearance" approximates. Certainly a mysterious man did come to Swetman after the battle, but it was generally understood that he was one of Monmouth's defeated officers. (p. 11)

'The Duke's Reappearance' is based largely on the second, more dubious, tradition, and incorporates the first by transferring the sexual threat posed by the victorious loyalist soldiers and attributing it instead to the defeated stranger who attempts to kiss Leonard Swetman in the orchard, ironically the place of sanctuary in the real incident.

Hardy's maternal great-grandparents were John Swetman and Maria Childs. Christopher, the name of the story's protagonist, was a common name in his mother's family, and, indeed, Hardy once remarked that he would prefer to have been called Christopher rather than Thomas.[2] The Swetmans had been 'yeoman landholders' in Melbury Osmond for generations, and Hardy believed that they had been 'ruined in the Monmouth Rebellion'.[3]

Shortly before the story first appeared in the *Saturday Review*, Hardy mentioned it in a letter to Florence Henniker: 'I have a "tradition" in its Christmas supplement – quite short. Something like it occurred in my mother's family, who, from time immemorial down to 100–150 years ago, were yeomen in this county farming their own land – which now belongs to Ld Ilchester' (*Letters*, II, 139; the Swetman land had been absorbed into the Melbury House estates of the Earls of Ilchester, who, Hardy once remarked, had still been 'at plow' when the Swetmans were landowners[4]). Nothing appears to be known about the date of the story's composition, although, as Purdy notes, it seems safe to assume that it was published as soon as possible after it was written.[5]

The versions of 'The Duke's Reappearance' which have textual significance are as follows:

SR   *The Saturday Review*, Christmas Supplement (pub. 14 December), 1896, pp. 14–16.

CB   *The Chap-Book* (Chicago), VI, no. 3 (15 December 1896), 97–107.

1913   *A Changed Man and Other Tales* (London: Macmillan, 1913), pp. 253–64. Published at 6s. in an edition of 10,000 copies on 24 October 1913.

1913H   *A Changed Man and Other Tales* (New York: Harper & Brothers, 1913), pp. 249–60.

1914   *A Changed Man and Other Tales* (London: Macmillan, 1914), pp. 245–56. Volume XVIII of the Wessex edition.

The manuscript and the *Saturday Review*

When Hardy was distributing his manuscripts in 1911, he wrote to Sydney Cockerell on 5 October that 'I have search [*sic*] my cupboard, & discovered one or two unimportant MSS. there – one, a story entitled "The Duke's Reappearance"' (*Letters*, IV, 178). Hardy promised Edward Clodd that he would send him a manuscript on 26 October and later sent him the MS. of 'The Duke's Reappearance' on 24 March 1912. In the accompanying letter, Hardy wrote that

> you must have wondered why the promised Manuscript has not appeared before this time. But the delay has not been mine. Shorter offered to get it bound, which he very kindly has now done (though he ought not to have been let take the trouble), & this was a slow business.
>
> I thought you would be more interested in this particular scrawl than in many, the tale being a tradition in my mother's family, who are mentioned in it under their real names.[6]

The manuscript is currently located in the Harry Ransom Humanities Research Center at the University of Texas at Austin. It consists of eleven leaves of ruled paper, numbered 1–10 by Hardy with a supplementary leaf, numbered 1a. It is a fair copy of the story as it appeared in the *Saturday Review*, although every leaf shows some slight revision. On the first leaf, Hardy has added a footnote to the opening line in red ink: 'Christopher Swetman was one of the author's ancestors on the maternal side.' This note has never been printed as part of the story, and may possibly have been added by Hardy at the time he sent the manuscript to Clodd.

The first two leaves, 1 and 1a, appear to be a revised, and perhaps expanded, version of the opening written after the remainder of the story had been completed. They contain the first three paragraphs and the opening two lines of the fourth. Swetman is given his actual name in these two leaves, whereas in the rest of the manuscript he was originally called Wedman, which Hardy later revised to Swetman by adding the *S* and altering the *d* to *t*. The name thus appears in the manuscript as SWetman, and is so written three times on the final leaf (five occasions when 'Swetman' appears unrevised in leaves 2–10 must have been late additions by Hardy).

Uniquely, the MS. gives the sub-title as 'A tradition of 1685', whereas in the serials it is 'A Tradition' and in the collected editions it is 'A Family Tradition'. Hardy must have altered the MS. reading when revising the serial proofs, one of some twenty changes which he made at this stage and which therefore account for the differences between the MS. and the *Saturday Review*. Most proof revisions involve individual words, but there is one insertion of eleven words, in which Hardy explains that the daughters returned from church 'where the service had been hurried by reason of the excitement'.

Another proof change creates a problem with the story's chronology which Hardy never noticed. In the MS., he wrote that the stranger came to collect the hidden belongings on the Wednesday night, but *SR* and all other editions of the story say it was Tuesday. Hardy possibly made this change because Monmouth was beheaded on Tuesday, 15 July 1685, and so, if the visitor was the *ghost* of Monmouth, it first appeared just a few hours after Monmouth's execution. In the MS., the subsequent chronology can, at a stretch, be accommodated: the visitor comes on Wednesday night, Swetman wakes up on Thursday and says nothing to his daughters, and 'next day', Friday, he sees the lord of the manor, who tells him that Monmouth was beheaded on Tuesday, two (whole) days before. Swetman considers this strange, because his visitor had come to him 'only the night before this present day of Friday' (fo. 10), by which he means the night of Wednesday/Thursday. After the revision of the visit to Tuesday, however, the chronology is unsustainable. The New Wessex edition of the story tries to resolve this problem by silently emending the night of the visit to Thursday, which is consistent with the other times given but lacks the authorial support which both Tuesday and Wednesday have. If my supposition is correct that Hardy wanted the visit to occur on Tuesday to emphasize the coincidence, supernatural or not, of the stranger's arrival on the very day of Monmouth's execution, then it would be preferable for an editor to leave the visit on that day and alter the day of Swetman's meeting with the lord of the manor to, say, Thursday, since its exact timing is of no consequence.

Another proof change seems to increase the evidence that the visitor may be Monmouth's ghost, Hardy adding in *SR* that he seemed to have blood on his neck as well as his face. Two further proof changes, however, serve to remove evidence that the stranger is Monmouth or his ghost. In the MS., he is described as a 'visitant', which seems more supernatural than the 'visitor' which he becomes in *SR*. Also, at one point in the MS., Swetman regrets his part in the 'nobleman's' capture, but Hardy, perhaps realizing that this seems to assert that the visitor was indeed Monmouth, alters it in proofs to make Swetman regret the 'fugitive's' arrest.

A final topographical detail concerns the name of the village where Swetman lives. In the opening sentence of the MS., it was originally called Hintock, and Hardy has inserted 'King's-'. Similarly, the lord of the manor was first said to reside at 'the Court', but Hardy deleted 'the' and inserted 'King's Hintock'. However, neither of the emendations appears in *SR*, which raises the possibility that Hardy made the revisions at a later date. 'King's Hintock' appears in *1913* and in subsequent editions.

The Chap-Book

The simultaneous American publication of the story in 1896 is virtually identical to *SR*. There are some forty differences in accidentals between the two publications, but only two substantive ones which seem authorial in origin. In *SR*, Swetman 'answers' the lord of the manor, who in the next line 'cries' out an exclamation in response. This is also the MS. reading, but the *Chap-Book* puts the two verbs in the past tense, and subsequent collected editions of the story have the American variant. How to account for this? One surmise could be that Hardy altered the proofs of the copy which he was sending to America, and correctly transcribed the revision on to a duplicate copy which he retained and which became the basis of later editions, but omitted to mark the alteration on the proofs which were to form *SR*, so that the English publication follows the MS. with its present tense. If this is what happened, then these minor revisions, involving only a letter or two, would be the very last two of the proof changes which Hardy made to the story. It would seem that his attention simply slipped when the task of proof-reading was nearly complete.

1913 Macmillan

Of the seventeen substantive revisions which Hardy introduced when preparing the first collected edition, the longest occurs in the penultimate paragraph, where we now learn how Swetman dismisses the possibility that his visitor may have been someone other than the Duke: 'that his visitor might have been a friend of the Duke's, whom the Duke had asked to fetch the things in a last request, Swetman would never admit' (p. 264). For the rest of his life, he clung to the belief 'that Monmouth lived' (another new addition). Hardy thus manages to insert a more plausible explanation of the visitor's identity, which he himself believed, while allowing Swetman to retain his more dramatic but doubtful belief.

An addition to the first and final sentences gives the source of the narrator's knowledge about Swetman, and also nominally turns the story into a first-person narrative. *1913* opens with 'According to the kinsman who told me the story', and 'my kinsman' is mentioned again at the end. Another personal detail which Hardy introduced is the expanded reference to the 'one-handed' clock on the stairs, 'that is still preserved in the family' (p. 255). Hardy's narrator, though, does not say that he himself is related to Swetman, permitting Hardy to maintain a narrative distance in this description of his family tradition.

In *1913*, the visitor who returns at night to fetch the hidden possessions is less certainly identified as the same person who sought refuge with Swetman. Where originally Swetman had seen 'the figure of the stranger' in his room, *1913* refers to 'the figure of a man who seemed to be the stranger'. Similarly, the earlier version of the story described the stranger's face as 'unmistakable', but in *1913* it is merely 'quite that of his late guest' (p. 262). The first visitor may have been the Duke, but in the revised version of the story Hardy does not endorse Swetman's belief that it is the same man who returns at night, making it feasible that it is simply a friend who bears a resemblance to him in the dark. Finally, one further revision deserves comment. In the serial versions, the lord's brother is said to have been 'killed in the recent battle' but we do not learn whose side he was fighting on. In *1913*, it is stated that he was 'killed in opposing the recent rising' (p. 262), emphasizing that the lord of the manor has nothing to fear when he tells Swetman later that 'happy is the man who has had nothing to do with this matter!' (p. 263) and reflecting Hardy's belief that his ancestors had suffered because of their involvement in the rebellion while the once impoverished Ilchesters continued to thrive.

1913 Harper

The American edition of the story in *A Changed Man* in 1913 shows only half a dozen differences in accidentals from the Macmillan edition of that year, and there are no substantive differences.

1914 Macmillan Wessex edition

The Wessex edition of the story is identical to the Macmillan edition of 1913.

Notes

1   Brady, p. 188. The story is discussed by Berta Lawrence (1986), 56–8. This has no new information to give about the story and is often incorrect.
2   See Millgate, p. 16.
3   *Letters*, IV, 72.
4   See Millgate, p. 12.
5   See Purdy, p. 156.
6   *Letters*, IV, 207–8. See also IV, 185, 186n, and Taylor, p. 68.

CHAPTER 36

'A Mere Interlude'

'A Mere Interlude' was Hardy's only new work of fiction in the summer of 1885, following the completion of *The Mayor of Casterbridge* in April and the move into Max Gate in June. Much of the story is set in Pen-zephyr (Penzance), and, while there does not appear to be any record of Hardy having visited the town, he clearly was familiar with the place, both at the time of writing the story and later when revising it. This is Hardy's only Cornish setting, either in prose or verse, which is not associated with Emma Hardy, and it takes place further west than any of the other 'Off-Wessex' locations. The story has no direct source, although Brady notes that it may be based on two true reports in the 'Facts' notebook about sudden decisions to marry (p. 172).

The versions of 'A Mere Interlude' which have textual significance are as follows:

BWJ   *Bolton Weekly Journal*, 17 October (p. 2) and 24 October (p. 2) 1885. The division occurred at the end of Section IV, when Baptista marries Heddegan. The story was the second one which Hardy had sold to Tillotson & Son, proprietors of the *Bolton Weekly Journal*, and Purdy notes that it was to be 'widely printed, especially in provincial papers' (p. 154), as well as being pirated in America in Munro's Seaside Library Pocket Edition.[1]

1913   *A Changed Man and Other Tales* (London: Macmillan, 1913), pp. 265–306. Published at 6s. in an edition of 10,000 copies on 24 October 1913.

1913H   *A Changed Man and Other Tales* (New York: Harper & Brothers, 1913), pp. 261–301.

1914   *A Changed Man and Other Tales* (London: Macmillan, 1914), pp. 257–96. Volume XVIII of the Wessex edition.

Bolton Weekly Journal

In the serial, Baptista passes the time in Penzance while waiting for a boat by looking about the town. We learn that the churches soon oppressed her: 'St. Mary's was neither old nor new, St. Paul's was quite new; and she could find no others.' This is topographically accurate: St Mary's was built in 1832 and St Paul's in 1843, and there were no other churches in Penzance. In *1913*, the information about the churches is omitted and replaced with 'She tried the Museum, but came out because it seemed lonely and tedious' (the Museum had been opened in 1839). In the serial, Baptista left the churches and went to 'Barbican-street', another real location in Penzance. In *1913*, she goes instead to 'the town gardens'; she could not have gone there in the serial, because the first municipal gardens in Penzance were not created until the local borough purchased Morrab Gardens in 1889, four years after the story was written. Rather than think of Hardy updating 'A Mere Interlude' when he came to revise it in 1913, it is more likely that this error is simply a historical anachronism. No particular date for the story is mentioned, but, as F.P. Pitfield has shown, it is presumably set in the late 1870s.[2] In its serial version, 'A Mere Interlude' is set in Cornwall, but in its later collected editions Hardy moved the setting to Wessex, which is probably why he removed the real names of the street and churches in what had now become Pen-zephyr. The serial used actual placenames, such as St Mary's, the Scilly Isles, Hugh Town, Truro and Redruth, but these are replaced in *1913* by their Wessex equivalents (St Maria's, the Isles of Lyonesse, Giant's Town, Trufal and Redrutin).[3] The Cornish Duchy became the Western Duchy, and 'the Devonshire village' where Baptista taught became 'the village of Lower Wessex'. However, some actual placenames were retained, such as Mousehole, St Clement's Isle, St Michael's Mount and Falmouth. The only actual change of location which occurred during revision was that, in the serial, Baptista was teaching at a school 'near Exeter', but this became 'near Tor-upon-Sea' (Torquay) in *1913*, apparently the only occasion on which Hardy used the name.

1913 Macmillan

A substantial addition to the serial made the scene of Baptista lying between her two husbands markedly more explicit in *1913*. In the earlier version, the story had simply remarked that she was 'doomed to abide in a hideous situation between the dead husband and the living'. *1913* expands this to read,

> doomed to abide, in a hideous contiguity to the dead husband and the living, and her conjecture did, in fact, bear itself out. That night she lay between the two men she had married—Heddegan on the one hand, and on the other through the partition against which the bed stood, Charles Stow.

The bland 'situation' of the serial is replaced by the graphic picture of Baptista lying in bed between the two men. Another improvement to this scene is that the serial had described Baptista's discovery of her late husband's corpse in the next room as an 'unexpected contingency'. It was no doubt most unexpected indeed, and Hardy deleted the bathetic adjective in *1913*.

The tone of the ending is slightly changed. In the serial, Baptista and Heddegan each confess their secrets, but in *1913* they both talk of the 'tragedy' they have known. There are six occasions when references to 'tragedy' or 'tragedies' are introduced, until the words become drained by repetition, especially when Heddegan trumps Baptista by disclosing his 'four tragedies', who are of course his own children. The ironic deflation of tragedy in *1913* prepares the way for the summary of Baptista's life as a 'tragi-comedy' in the story's final paragraph.

The story's opening sentence, as we now read it, was first introduced in *1913*, giving the source of the story's details as the 'traveller in school-books'. Another addition to *1913* is Baptista's reaction to seeing Heddegan unexpectedly on the boat home: 'Involuntarily she slipped from her left hand the symbol of her wifehood.' *1913* also takes the opportunity to correct an amusing error in the serial, where Baptista had been said to look *up* for Charles Stow. However, she is sitting on a cliff and he is down below in the sea, so *1913* shows her instead looking 'about' for him.

1913 Harper

There are half a dozen substantive differences between *1913* and *1913H*. Some of these appear to be misprints or editorial in origin, but there are three instances of the American edition, like the serial, reading 'ye' where *1913* and *1914* have ''ee'. Perhaps Hardy altered 'ye' to his preferred form in the Macmillan proofs after he had already posted a duplicate copy of them to Harper's.

1914 Macmillan Wessex edition

There are only four substantive differences between *1913* and the Wessex edition, two of which identify the setting as being in Off-Wessex.[4]

Notes

I am indebted to Mr Jonathan Holmes of the Penzance & District Museum & Art Gallery for his generous help in providing information about nineteenth-century Penzance.

1 David Bonnell Green (1960) notes that the story's first American publication was in the *Philadelphia Press* on 18 October and 25 October 1885, before appearing in Munro's Seaside Library.

2 'The "pro-cathedral" at Trufal (Truro) is referred to. Cornwall became a new diocese in 1876 with Truro as its See, when the parish church of St Mary served as a temporary cathedral (i.e. a pro-cathedral) until 1880 when work began on the new cathedral on the same site' (Pitfield, p. 47).

3 All of these placenames were added to the map of Wessex in *1914*. However, 'Lyonesse' was mistakenly given as 'Lyonnesse', which is the spelling in Arthurian legend.

4 The following is a complete list of the differences between *1913* and *1914* not previously discussed (the reading in *1914* is given first, and the pagination is that of *1914*): 'as there understood/as it was there understood' (p. 259); 'Teachers/ Elementary Teachers' (p. 259); 'schoolhouse/school-house' (p. 260); 'begun/began'

(p. 261); 'into Off-Wessex/as far as she could' (p. 261); 'tragedy/tragedy,' (p. 293).

CHAPTER 37

'The Romantic Adventures of a Milkmaid'

'The Romantic Adventures of a Milkmaid' is Hardy's longest short story by far. He appears to have written it in the winter of 1882–83, while living at 'Llanherne' in Wimborne. He wrote to Arthur Locker, the editor of the *Graphic*, on 13 February 1883 that 'the story is nearly finished, & I hope to send it in about a week or ten days. / If it would be any convenience to you I could send the first half a little sooner' (*Letters*, I, 115). As he noted in his diary, he submitted the completed story on 25 February 1883: 'Sent a short hastily written novel to the *Graphic* for Summer Number' (*Life*, pp. 163–4). This short novel, or long story as we would now regard it, was to appear in one of the special issues that the weekly *Graphic* brought out twice a year, one in summer to appeal to the holiday trade, and again at Christmas. These special numbers were substantially longer than the regular weekly issues, and, as Gatrell remarks, 'Hardy showed his professional versatility in meeting happily the demand for a tale of a length somewhere between the usual short story and the novel' (p. 71). 'The Romantic Adventures of a Milkmaid' marks the beginning of Hardy's association with the *Graphic*, a connection that was to last nine years (ending with *Tess*), and in that period his only major novel which was not first published there was *The Woodlanders*.

The versions of the story which have textual significance are as follows:

Graphic	'The Romantic Adventures of a Milkmaid', *Graphic*, Summer Number (pub. 25 June) 1883, pp. 4–25, with four full-page illustrations by C.S. Reinhart.
HW	'The Romantic Adventures of a Milkmaid', *Harper's Weekly*, 23 June–4 August 1883, with three of Reinhart's illustrations. The seven weekly instalments were divided thus: chapters I–III (to 'and rode away'); III–V (to 'she fell asleep'); V–VII (to 'the idea at all'); VII–IX; X–XII; XIII–XV (to 'the next morning'); XV–XVII.
1883	*The Romantic Adventures of a Milkmaid*, Franklin Square Library No. 322 (New York: Harper & Brothers, 1883). Purdy notes that Harper & Brothers sought to protect themselves from an immediate pirating of the story by publishing it in their cheap Franklin Square Library on 29 June 1883, after only one instalment had appeared in *Harper's Weekly*: 'the types for the two printings, save a little resetting at one or two points, are identical' (p. 48). Nevertheless, the story was widely pirated, and was 'more

frequently and cheaply reprinted in America through many years than perhaps any other work of Hardy's' (pp. 48–9). For instance, George Munro published it in his Seaside Library just two weeks after the Franklin Square Library, and Lovell's Library issued a pirated edition in early August.

1913   'The Romantic Adventures of a Milkmaid', *A Changed Man and Other Tales* (London: Macmillan, 1913), pp. 307–413. Published at 6*s*. in an edition of 10,000 copies on 24 October 1913.

1913H   'The Romantic Adventures of a Milkmaid', *A Changed Man and Other Tales* (New York: Harper & Brothers, 1913), pp. 303–406.

1914   'The Romantic Adventures of a Milkmaid', *A Changed Man and Other Tales* (London: Macmillan, 1914), pp. 297–399. Volume XVIII of the Wessex edition.

A bound manuscript of 'The Romantic Adventures' is currently located in the Pierpont Morgan Library, which acquired it in 1912.

Hardy was usually rather dismissive of the story in later years: for instance, he described it to John Lane in 1892 as 'a slight narrative-sketch', adding that 'I did not think it worth reprinting: if I ever do reprint it I shall restore it to its original form, which was not quite as it appeared' (*Letters*, I, 284). Four months later, he expressed the hope that he would soon be able to reprint it, 'correct from the original MS.', because it had previously only ever appeared 'in a modified form' (II, 3). As we shall shortly see, the surviving manuscript does not appear to be the 'original MS.' to which Hardy refers here. (To add to the confusion about the status of the extant MS., Hardy described it as 'the original copy, in my writing' (IV, 199) when he was arranging for its donation to the Pierpont Morgan Library in 1912.) Another assertion by Hardy that the story had been modified is noted by Purdy: 'This story was written only with a view to a fleeting life in a periodical, and having, moreover, been altered from its original shape, was not deemed worth reprinting.'[1] Hardy's final judgement on the story is given in a letter of 1927 to Sir Frederick Macmillan, in which he described it as, 'though readable enough, being but of a slight nature' (VII, 87).[2]

Hardy did not in fact reprint the work until 1913 in *A Changed Man*, whose full title, 'Concluding with "The Romantic Adventures of a Milkmaid"', suggests that he regarded the story as being among the more prominent tales in the volume. Its awkward length appears to have prevented him reprinting it earlier, either in a collection of stories or in a volume of its own: as he reminded Clarence McIlvaine in 1912, they had not included 'The Romantic Adventures' in the Osgood, McIlvaine 'Wessex Novels' collected edition of 1895–96 because 'it would not quite fill a volume' (IV, 199). This difficulty about length had not deterred others from pirating it frequently in America, however, and its continuing popularity in unauthorized editions led Hardy to publish it in *A Changed Man*. As he explained to McIlvaine in 1912, 'owing to the constant inquiries for it here I am intending to include it in the uniform series of novels'

(IV, 199). The numerous unauthorized publications understandably irritated Hardy: he wrote in Clement Shorter's Seaside Library edition that it was 'pirated', as he did in his own copy, and he refused to autograph Rebekah Owen's pirated edition in 1913.[3] The problem of the story's length recurred in 1913, when Tauchnitz approached Hardy with a proposal to reprint the stories in *A Changed Man*, but divided into two books. Hardy suggested that the division occur after 'What the Shepherd Saw', and that '"The Romantic Adventures of a Milkmaid" be placed at the beginning of the second volume, so that this well-known story may give its name to the second volume' (*Letters*, IV, 321), a suggestion which Tauchnitz accepted.

It is impossible to tell whether the *Graphic* exerted any pressure on Hardy to produce a story that they would regard as morally appropriate, as they were later to do with, for instance, some of the Noble Dames. However, a note which Hardy pencilled in the margin of his study-copy of *A Changed Man* in 1927 (now in the Dorset County Museum) indicates his original conception of the story, as he remembered it:

> Note: The foregoing finish of the Milkmaid's adventures by a re-union with her husband was adopted to suit the requirements of the summer number of a periodical in which the story was first printed. But it is well to inform readers that the ending originally sketched was a different one, Margery, instead of returning to Jim, disappearing with the Baron in his yacht at Idmouth after his final proposal to her, & being no more heard of in England.[4]

Since Hardy made this note some 44 years after he wrote the story, it is not surprising that it is factually incorrect: Idmouth was never mentioned in the original version of the tale, but, as we shall see, was introduced only when Hardy moved the location of the story westwards in *1913*. If Hardy did indeed change the plot to satisfy the *Graphic*'s editor, then there is no evidence of it in the extant manuscript, where Margery and the Baron are thoroughly virtuous, so the MS. must therefore, in this light, be a fair copy produced after the desired revision had been made. It seems possible, however, that Hardy's memory in 1927, when he made his note in his study-copy, was being influenced by recollections of his other conflicts with the *Graphic* and that he had not been obliged to alter his original story. A further indication of this is that he made several proof-additions to the serial which show the Baron acting less virtuously: it is hardly plausible that the *Graphic* would have allowed him to introduce such material at this late stage if they had previously required him to remove any hint of impropriety. It may also be significant that Hardy chose not to restore the supposedly 'original' ending when he had the opportunity to revise it in 1913, the year that the story was first collected in *A Changed Man*, although this may simply indicate a reluctance to make a radical revision to a plot that was already established in print.

Alternative endings to the plot can be found in a five-page dramatic scenario of the story which Hardy prepared for T.H. Tilley, probably with a view to him dramatizing it for the Dorchester Hardy Players in the 1920s. This manuscript, together with a revised typescript of it, is now in the Dorset County Museum; it is undated, but a note on the title leaf announces 'this version amplified from April 1908 version'. The surviving scenario, however, dates from after the publication of *A Changed Man*, since Hardy frequently writes 'see book' for further details following stage directions. The first of the two endings reads thus:

> Somebody enters and says the Baron's yacht has just left the Exe – (the Baron is quite well now) – and the news comes that Margery has put to sea with him.
> Jim after a time says, "Perhaps he'll die – and she'll come back after all".

The 'Alternative Scene II' which Hardy gives tells us that 'whilst they are all waiting and wondering she comes, and enters the cottage with Jim. (But this is not so good an ending.)'

Sources

Geoffrey Doel has identified a number of possible origins for various features of the story, ranging from *Cinderella* and *Little Red Riding Hood* to *Paradise Lost.*[5] The most important of the sources which he discusses is a folk ballad called *The Dæmon Lover*, which he summarizes thus:

> *The Dæmon Lover* exists in several different versions, of which the Pepys ballad, although less poetic and dæmonic than the Scottish versions, is closest to Hardy's story. The ballad begins 'There dwelt a fair maid in the West' and is based on the story of a Plymouth woman, betrothed to a sailor, who subsequently marries a carpenter and has children by him. One night a spirit raps on her window, announcing himself as James Harris, her former love, who tempts her to board his ship and go abroad with him. She expresses reluctance to leave her children, but on assurance of his wealth she dresses up in her richest attire (including golden slippers lined with velvet) and sails off with him. The spirit threatens her with hell and the ship is sunk; the carpenter commits suicide. (p. 325)

Hardy switches roles around, so that James Harris, the ballad's sailor, has a similar name to James Hayward, the husband in his story, and some of the attributes of the abducted wife (the Plymouth connection, the deceased sailor-husband) are transferred to Mrs Peach, the widow whom Jim deceives. Similarly, the suicide of the husband in the ballad becomes the Baron's suicide in Hardy's work. Doel's article does not examine the textual history of 'The Romantic Adventures of a Milkmaid', and, if the influence of this ballad on the story is acknowledged, it is also important to stress that Hardy must therefore have sought to strengthen the affinities when he came to collect the story for the first time in 1913, some thirty years after he originally wrote it. For instance, it is only in *1913* that Margery can be seen as a maid who dwelt in the West, for in the earlier versions the story had been set near Casterbridge, and Mrs Peach's link with Plymouth was similarly introduced in 1913 (previously, she vanished to Budmouth at the end of the story).

The manuscript

The MS. of 'The Romantic Adventures of a Milkmaid' is written on 116 leaves of ruled paper, numbered 1–115 by Hardy, with one leaf numbered 14a. Eleven leaves have passages on the verso marked for insertion. Four scattered pages are at least partly in Emma Hardy's hand. The MS. corroborates Hardy's comment that the story was hastily written: although it is the printers' copy for the *Graphic*, there are a number of inconsistencies in the plot, cancelled passages and many unique variant readings which were revised at the proof stage. Originally, the MS. was unparagraphed, as if Hardy were trying to compress as much material as possible on to each page: the only manuscript which shows a comparable density of handwriting is that of *Two on a Tower*, written earlier in 1882, and Gatrell (p. 66) suggests that the cramped leaves are a feature of some unknown kind of copying process which Hardy was using at this time, involving specially manufactured ink and paper (whose cost, presumably, necessitated the economic use of space).

Legible deletions in the MS. reveal Hardy's changing conception of the story as it evolved. Originally, Margery was to have encountered the Baron preparing to commit suicide, taking a revolver and placing 'his finger on the trigger' (fo. 6). This is deleted, and in the serial Margery merely thinks he is very unhappy and sees him slip 'something' into his pocket, the pistol remaining unspecified throughout the story. Another deletion on fo. 9 shows the Baron declaring that it had been his intention to kill himself until she arrived: 'it was desolation with me when you came. I would have perished. The hour had come, but the moment had not. You forbade it – delayed it only, I till now had thought, yet you have that rashness forever hindered.' In the serial, Margery asks what she has saved him from, and the Baron replies evasively, 'That you will never know!' Once again, the serial removes any explicit reference to suicide. Finally, an *undeleted* passage in the MS. states that Margery had 'begged him to spare his own life' (fo. 27): Hardy's failure to remove this vestige of the original plot until the proof stage shows the haste with which he apparently prepared the MS. In the serial, the phrase is replaced by Margery remembering how she had once 'expressed her sorrow for his troubles'.[6]

Although Hardy removed the explicit references to suicide during the opening encounter between Margery and the Baron, he nevertheless took the opportunity at the proof stage to emphasize the Baron's suicidal nature in a later scene. In the MS., the Baron's note to Margery on the eve of her wedding requests her to visit him because he needs her to disperse the 'plaguy glooms' from which he is suffering, and, he adds, 'ǀDisperse them you will,ǀ for you are radiance itself' (fo. 56). There is no hint of any desperate urgency in the note, but Margery postpones her wedding to dash to his side, because she has 'a vague idea of a ǀhighǀ power in the baron, under which the ordinary laws of nature & society had to give way', and her own affairs are as nothing beside 'his simplest whim' (fo. 60). Margery's actions here are not sufficiently motivated and the MS. portrays her as a helpless slave to the Baron's merest foible. When Hardy came to revise the proofs of the serial, he must have realized that this scene needed to be radically altered, not only because of its own inadequacies but because a reader would be left asking how Margery suddenly found the strength of character at the end of the story to resist the Baron's offer to elope with her in his yacht. In the serial, therefore, the fond flattery in the Baron's note about Margery being all radiance is dropped and replaced by the threat that 'If you refuse I will not answer for the consequences.' She no longer responds to his 'high power' and 'simplest whim', but rather

> A conviction that the Baron's life might depend upon her presence – for she had by this time divined the tragical event she had interrupted on the foggy morning – took from her all will to judge and consider calmly. The simple affairs of her and hers seemed nothing beside the possibility of harm to him.

The story's first frank acknowledgement of the Baron's suicidal intentions gives Margery a practical and overwhelming motive to go to him and miss her wedding, so that she no longer appears to be simply mesmerized by his every wish.

Why did Hardy delete the references to suicide and revolvers from the opening scene? It cannot have been at the request of the *Graphic*'s editors, if they were willing to allow him to introduce explicit allusions to suicide in the later scene. Perhaps Hardy wished to prevent the first meeting between Margery and the Baron from becoming too Gothic and sensational, and this desire for reticence is borne out by a later change to the manuscript. When Margery returns home after her visit to the Baron on her wedding day, she originally told her father that she had to leave the house that morning because 'I thought a man's death might have happened by his own hand if I did not go' (fo. 61). This would have been a rather breathtaking declaration for Margery to make, and Hardy removed the scene's potential for melodrama by revising it in the MS. so that her words become unutterable: 'ITo say that she hadl I thought a man's death might have happened by his own hand if I lshel did not go Ito him would never dol.'

The conclusion of the story in the MS. shows the Baron to be wholly virtuous, and he is thoroughly noble and disinterested in reuniting Margery and her husband Jim. The Baron asserts that he has 'always' (fo. 109) had Margery's happiness at heart (Hardy altered this in the *Graphic* proofs to read 'mostly'), and he 'insisted upon her going' (fo. 109) to Jim's house (in the serial he simply 'took her' there). He tells Jim that he will provide 'Iproof of my honourl' (fo. 110), but the serial reads instead 'proof – good and bad'. There is no hint of any *bad* conduct in the MS. because the Baron is entirely scrupulous, and he does not, for instance, take Margery to his yacht and invite her to elope with him (this was another serial proof addition). Instead, in the MS., he picks her up and gives her a pompous sermon on her folly:

> "He IJiml must be a thoroughly good fellow not to have behaved worse than he has done" Ihe continuedl; "& yet you have not had the wisdom to

see that, but have nearly wrecked him & yourself too by your pride. [...] Then go & live quietly with the good husband you possess. Should you not do so, my esteem for you will change to aversion & scorn [...]". (fos. 111–12)

The Baron then takes her directly to Jim's house, kisses her forehead and parts from her forever.

When Margery and Jim are finally reunited, she can tell him in the MS. version that she was justified in obeying the Baron blindly, and Jim agrees. In all later versions, however, because the Baron is a much more ambiguous figure, Margery wonders if 'perhaps' she was *not* justified in obeying him, and Jim can only murmur, 'I don't know.' In the MS., the Baron feels that he has been guilty of only 'the |a slight| thoughtlessness' (fo. 113) in his acquaintance with Margery which he had managed to convert into 'paternal benevolence' (fo. 114), but in the serial he has 'real sorrow' for a 'certain doubtful phase' of their relationship. In the story's penultimate paragraph, Margery in the MS. tells Jim that even now she would have no power to disobey the Baron, but she says it 'with a little laugh' (fo. 114). In later versions, such a lighthearted manner would be misplaced, since she nearly eloped with him, and so her confession is accompanied by 'a mischievous look'.

The manuscript demonstrates how Hardy progressively removed any precise definition of Margery's feelings for the Baron. Originally, he inserted the following lines of conversation between her and the Baron's solicitor when they meet in the street:

> "Now" – & he looked her hard in the face – "shall I guess who has Miss Tucker's heart in his keeping?"
> She blushed painfully, but showed that matters were not quite so bad as the lawyer imagined by saying |firmly| "I respected the baron, & I can't forget him – as a friend. I love neither him nor any one in the way – the exact way – you mean." (fo. 89)

This was deleted in the MS., and Hardy later removed from the serial proofs the comment that 'The lawyer drew not altogether a true inference from her blush'.

Revisions in the MS. show Hardy changing his mind about details of the plot. The story was first set 35 years ago, but this becomes 40 years in the MS. (i.e. the early rather than the late 1840s). Budmouth was originally to have been the location of both the ball which Margery and the Baron attend and Jim's Yeomanry Review, but this was later altered in the serial proofs to Casterbridge. Before going to the ball, Margery and the Baron originally met on two or three more occasions to practise the dance (fo. 18), but a reference on fo. 40 to Margery having 'held meetings with' the Baron is altered in the MS. to '|met|', indicating that Hardy's decision to allow Margery and the Baron to have only one meeting was made relatively late.

Further deletions indicate that Jim was originally planning to take the widow, Mrs Peach, to a ball, and she praises his prowess at the polka (fo. 94). We then learn that Jim has been to a dancing master (fo. 95), and on the next leaf we have the first unaltered reference to the Yeomanry Review which replaces the ball as the site of their romantic tryst. Perhaps Hardy felt that the plot needed a more public location, to which both Margery and the Baron could gain access. This evidence that Hardy changed his mind about the plot within just three pages demonstrates that the extant MS. is not at all a fair copy, but is very close to, if not indeed the actual, first draft of the story.

Another sign of Hardy's haste in preparing the text is that he does not seem to have proof-read the serial against the manuscript, with the result that four apparent compositorial errors went unnoticed, three of which have been repeated in all published versions of the story. The longest involves an omission of seventeen words from the MS.: on the day after their secret wedding, Jim tells Margery that he will call on her father and hear what he has to say about her. The MS. then continues thus on fo. 84 (my italics):

> At any count, I can hear what he's got to
>
> |*coming home, & so find out how he'll*
> say about ye, & *then let him know you be* here, & come out & tell ye on my
>
> *receive ye,* & come back here & tell ye|
> way to my own house.

It would appear that the compositor's eye slipped from the first 'ye, &' to the second almost immediately below it, with the result that all the words in italics were omitted. Another probable error in the proofs which Hardy overlooked concerns Jim's belief that Margery will not be 'hunted into matrimony' until he can provide a suitable home for her. It would seem that the compositor misread the MS.'s 'hurried' (fo. 41) as 'hunted' (unless, of course, this was a deliberate revision by Hardy at the proof stage). A third error occurs in the scene when Jim sees Margery, creeps up to her gate, chalks the Baron's name on it and returns to the place on the other side of the garden where he had 'just' seen Margery. The MS. appears to say that he returns to the spot where he had 'first' (fo. 69) seen her, but all published versions print 'just'. Finally, the error which Hardy did eventually notice and revise was the serials' description of the weir-hatches being 'down' in the meads to drain off the water. The MS. and all collected editions correctly read 'drawn' (fo. 54).

Finally, some miscellaneous observations about the MS.: Hardy began by giving titles to the chapters, the first being called 'An early journey' and the second 'The stranger', but these were then deleted. In chapter II, the postman is said to walk six miles out from 'Yeoborne', a placename which does not appear to have been used by Hardy elsewhere; the serials read 'Anglebury' (Wareham). When the Baron meets Margery in her garden for the first time, a deleted passage shows that he was to have been punctual for his appointment and that he rode out on purpose to see her, but the revision creates suspense by making him 45 minutes late, and he accidentally encounters her on his way home, having distractedly forgotten about the meeting. When they part after the ball, he asks her in the MS. to promise to come to him when he needs her to deliver him from that darkness 'as of Hell' (fo. 33) which sometimes encompasses him. This was altered at the proof stage to read 'as of Death', perhaps because Hardy wished to play down the Baron's demonic or diabolic aspect.

The serials

The story as it appears in the MS. and the serials is located around Casterbridge and the Valley of the Swenn (Hardy's original name for the Frome river). Margery lives at Stickleford (Tincleton, four miles east of Stinsford). The Yeomanry Ball which Margery and the Baron attend is at Casterbridge, which is also the site of the Review. The Ball is hosted by Lord Blakemore (originally 'Blackmore' in the MS.), whose name suggests Blackmoor or Blackmore Vale, north of Casterbridge. The cove where the Baron moors his yacht is not identified by name in the serials, but it has 'miniature Pillars of Hercules' at its mouth, which is recognizably Lulworth Cove. The fork in the highway where Margery's father intercepts Jim and directs him along the wrong road is on Winford Hill (Stinsford Hill) in the serial. Margery's grandmother lives four miles to the west in the serials and four miles to the east in later collected editions. When the story was included in *A Changed Man* in 1913, Hardy moved its setting from South Wessex to Lower Wessex, chiefly around Exonbury and the Valley of the Exe. Since he had first published 'The Romantic Adventures' in 1883, Hardy had of course written *Tess*, another tale of a milkmaid with a rather satanic lover which used the same setting, and he seems to have wanted to avoid any confusion or overlap between two such radically different stories, a comparison which would have been to the detriment of the shorter, slighter work. Simon Gatrell, however, has made a study of the topography and he suggests another possible reason for the change of location: he identifies several inconsistencies in the serial setting, and believes that in 1913, when Hardy came to revise the tale, he must have been 'horrified at the confusion he found in its topography, and rather than undertake the difficult job of re-organising it to represent more accurately some geographical arrangement of houses and natural features, he threw up his hands and moved it off to a part of Wessex uninhabited by other stories' (1987, p. 45). Perhaps it was the double difficulty not only of making the setting internally consistent but also of rendering it compatible with that of *Tess* which prompted Hardy to move the story many miles westward.

The serials (and the MS.) have an epigraph to the story:

> "Where are you going, my pretty maid?"
> "I'm going a milking, Sir," she said.

Later editions omit it, perhaps because the innocence of the nursery rhyme was no longer appropriate for a story that now ended with Margery and the Baron nearly eloping in his yacht.

As we saw earlier, the principal addition at the proof stage of the serials was the Baron's trip to the cove with Margery, where he asks her to sail away with him:

> "Now Margery; in five minutes we can be aboard, and in half an hour we can be steaming away all the world over. Will you come?"

"I cannot," she said simply.

"Why not?"

"Because Jim is not with me, and perhaps it would offend him if he were to hear of it."

Margery's two replies in the serial show her to be virtuously resolute and adamant in refusing the Baron's offer, but in later editions she is much closer to accepting: 'I cannot' becomes 'I cannot decide' (uttered 'in low tones' rather than 'simply'), and then Hardy omitted all but the first word of her touching but rather unrealistic statement of loyalty to Jim (she does, after all, think that he has just eloped with the widow), leaving only the enigmatic 'Because—'. In the serial, Margery has an 'agonised' look on her face (this later became 'bewildered') and she rather melodramatically begs the Baron to deliver her: "'Oh, sir!" she gasped, "I once saved your life – save me now, for pity's sake!"' Later editions omit this plea.

The Baron then takes Margery to Jim's house and they have their final conversation. In the serial, the Baron is said to 'feel his error' keenly and asks her to 'forgive a bad impulse'. Eventually, she replies, "'I forgive you, sir, on one condition. That you send my husband to me."' Their relationship thus ends with a little morality play of vice and virtue, the wicked Baron and the chaste and faithful Margery. In later editions, their relationship is much more complex: the Baron is said to 'feel the awkwardness' of their position keenly, and there is no hint of him having committed an 'error'. He asks her to 'forgive a *lover's* bad impulse' (my italics), the most explicit acknowledgement of his feelings for her in the whole story, and she replies, "'Of course I forgive you, sir, for I felt for a moment as you did. Will you send my husband to me?"' Her forgiveness is unconditional and she admits that she reciprocated his feelings. She also confesses this to Jim some years later, on the news of the Baron's death: in a passage not added until the collected edition of 1913, Margery tells her husband:

'Now that he's dead I'll make a confession, Jim, that I have never made to a soul. If he had pressed me – which he did not – to go with him when I was in the carriage that night beside his yacht, I would have gone. And I was disappointed that he did not press me.'

The Baron's title appears more foreign and exotic in the *Graphic* than in *HW* or the MS., for he is almost consistently called 'Von' Xanten, a proof change which found its way into the collected edition. His conduct towards Margery is seen at the end of the story to be arguably more criticized in the serials than it is in *1913*. The *Graphic* has him feeling real sorrow for a certain 'doubtful' phase of their relationship and for his 'doubtful' sentiments towards her, but these two adjectives were changed in later editions to 'reckless' and 'impassioned', no doubt in part to avoid the repetition of 'doubtful' in the same paragraph (which also contains a reference to 'doubt'). The later readings suggest that the Baron had been moved more by strong emotion than by any dubious morality. *HW* replaces one of the adjectives with 'shady', which is even more critical of him (although this variant might be editorial, to avoid repetition).

Margery seems a more chaste and sentimental character in the serial. She is shy about dancing in front of the Baron, and her feelings for him are said to be 'pure' as well as romantic. She is also less blatant about pretending to be the Baron's widow than she was in later editions: she speaks to Mrs Peach with only the 'slight' air of a Baroness, and she does not 'distinctly' deny the imputation, qualifications which are deleted in *1913*. In the serial, she is 'miserable' at the thought of Jim's secret assignation with Mrs Peach and she cries, but the later, more spirited, Margery is rather 'indignant' about it. At the end of the story, she meekly agrees with the Baron's suggestion in the serial that she ought to be with Jim, but in later editions she stays defiantly silent.

Jim speaks with less of a regional accent in the serials, and it is only in *1913* that he acquires his characteristic pronunciation of 'do', 'too' and 'you', for instance, as 'dew', 'tew' and 'yew'. His new accent reinforces the social distance between him and the Baron, and serves to point the contrast between the two men which Margery experiences, a distinction neatly made in linguistic terms when the Baron follows Jim's use of 'trewly' with a speech beginning 'truly'. While Jim speaks more dialect in the collected edition, Margery speaks less: in the serials, she had said to the Baron when she first met him that she hoped 'you be' not ill, but this later became 'you are', as if she were careful always to speak to him in standard English. (This process of 'refining' her speech may have begun in a serial proof revision to the *Graphic*, where she says to the Baron that she cannot go away with him because 'it would' offend Jim, whereas the presumably earlier reading in *HW* is ''twould'.)

When Jim and the Baron are chasing after each other, they finally meet up in the serials at a hamlet, which had once been a populous village, called Letscombe Cross, on the road to London (Mrs Vera Jesty has suggested that the hamlet could be intended to represent either Pimperne or Tarrant Hinton just north of Blandford Forum: see Gatrell, 1987, p. 44). At a crossroads stands the remains of an old medieval cross which had given its name to the village and which was now 'sadly nibbled by years and weather'. The Baron mounts the steps of the cross and, putting his hand on it, swears that he will disturb Jim and his wife by his presence no more. In later versions, their meeting place is not named and the Baron makes his oath by pressing Jim's hand within his own upon the hilt of a sword, thereby removing any religious associations from his vow.

Harper's Weekly

The American serial has some seventeen substantive variants, which mostly appear to be editorial and involve only individual words. One which may, however, be an oversight by Hardy occurs when the Baron in *HW* says to Margery, on learning that she has come to him on her wedding day, 'How instantly to repair this tremendous blunder that we have made – that's the question.' This is also what the MS. reads, but the *Graphic* prints the first word as 'Now', and it is this reading which is transmitted to the later editions. It is possible that the *Graphic* reading was a misprint which Hardy overlooked and which a Harper editor corrected.

HW omits a whole paragraph (beginning 'We are folk ...') in which the gardener tells his daughter, Harriet, that she must exploit Margery's supposed marriage to the Baron by becoming her companion after his death. It does not appear to have been accidentally omitted, since the first words of the succeeding paragraph are altered to accommodate the deletion ('While this conversation progressed at the gardener's' becoming 'While the gardener was telling his story').

HW and later collected editions quote George Sand's description of *'la jalousie rétrospective'* in the final paragraph, which is rendered in the MS. and the *Graphic* as 'his retrospective jealousy'.

1913 Macmillan

In preparing the story for its first collected edition in 1913, Hardy made revisions in three principal areas: the Baron's suicidal intentions are more explicit, he is made more exotic and foreign, and Margery is shown to be slightly more emotionally involved with him.

In *1913*, there are four references to the Baron's pistol with which he is planning to shoot himself. Margery sees it, but has the tact not to mention it. In the serials, he tells her that she has found him under 'peculiar' conditions, and she has saved him from 'indescribable folly', but in *1913* the planned suicide is more obvious, for he is found under 'ghastly' conditions and she prevents 'an act of madness'. Now that she knows he was preparing to kill himself, she is no longer 'a little puzzled', as she had been in the serials, when he makes her swear silence about what she has seen. Where the serials had told us that 'Margery did not know' what he had been going to do, *1913* explicitly states that 'Margery could guess that he had meditated death at his own hand'.

The Baron twice says 'Gott' for 'God', as he had previously pronounced it, and he refers to 'your' poet Chaucer, stressing that he is not English. Later, he describes the Drum Polka to Margery as a strange dance 'introduced from my country and other parts of the continent', a phrase which had not been in earlier versions. Finally, it is the influence of the Baron's *friends,* and no longer his relatives, which enables him to obtain a special licence from Lambeth Palace for Margery and Jim to marry by his bedside: Hardy must have felt that it would be unlikely for such a foreign figure to have members of his family with influence in the Church of England.

Margery's feelings for the Baron are more fully acknowledged in *1913*. We learn, for instance, that her memory of the dancing lesson may have been distorted by her 'lingering emotions', whereas previously it had been merely 'the lapse of many many years' which might have affected her account. At this point we are told that Margery was not 'at this date' distinctly in love with the stranger, an addition which allows that she was later in love with him. A similar qualification can be seen in the new description of their relationship being 'as yet' innocent at the time of Margery's marriage to Jim.

Margery appears altogether more spirited and robust in *1913* than she had been in the serials. She is described as the most 'agile' of milkmaids rather than the previous 'graceful', and 'her lips became close' at the thought of not going to the ball, where earlier 'her eyes became moist', typical of her rather lachrymose nature as Hardy first conceived her. Her appointment with the Baron 'excited' her, whereas previously the prospect had 'moved [her] deeply'. She is also markedly more assertive towards Jim when telling him what furniture and fittings she hopes to have when she is married, and she ends her list of objects with the remark, new to *1913*, that, 'since you wish to know what I *can* want to quite satisfy me, I assure you I can want those!' She appears more vain in not correcting what is now a clear misunderstanding on the part of Mrs Peach, who addresses Margery as 'dear Baroness' in the belief that she is the Baron's widow. Her more practical self is seen in what are now her final words in the story, when she explains to Jim why the Baron could not move her if he were to return: 'It would be so unfair to baby.'

1913 Harper

There are ten substantive differences between *1913* and *1913*H, all of which appear to be either misprints in the American edition (e.g. 'jutted' for 'jetted', and 'lash' for 'flash') or editorial in origin (e.g. putting dialect into standard English).

1914 Macmillan Wessex edition

There are 53 differences in accidentals between *1913* and *1914*.[7] The only substantive variants occur in the story's opening sentence, in which Margery is said to leave home at half-past four in the morning, rather than half-past five. This revision makes the subsequent chronology more consistent: she walks for a little under an hour to her grandmother's cottage, and on her return she encounters the Baron sitting in the all-the-year-round at six o'clock. Hardy also took the opportunity to add the names of Tivworthy, Silverthorn and Idmouth to the map of Wessex at the end of *A Changed Man* (see *Letters*, IV, 329).

Notes

1 Purdy, p. 49. Purdy does not give a source for this comment, but it may possibly be the note which Hardy wrote on the fly-leaf of Clement Shorter's pirated copy of the story in 1896[?]. See *Letters*, II, 118.
2 This echoes his remark in 1925 that 'it is a story of rather light nature which I do not much value' (*Letters*, VI, 368). For Hardy's opinion that the story was suitable for filming, see *Letters*, VI, 165, 367–70.
3 See *Letters*, II, 118, Rosenbaum (1990), p. 174, and Weber, 1952, p. 168.
4 Quoted in Millgate, p. 283.

5 See Doel (1978), pp. 324–35.

6 Another undeleted reference to the suicide in the MS. occurs at the end of the story, when Jim, Margery's husband, dismissively describes the Baron as the foreigner who rented Mount Lodge for six months 'to shoot himself in' (fo. 106). Hardy must have realized that Jim would not have known about the suicide incident and so he altered the phrase at the proof stage to read 'to make mischief'.

7 The following is a complete list of the other differences between *1913* and *1914* (the reading in *1914* is given first, and the pagination is that of *1914*): 'ground./ground,' (p. 309); 'Baron/baron' (pp. 310, 312); 'calamity':/calamity;'' (p. 315); 'sir/Sir' (p. 318, twice); 'inn/inn,' (p. 321); 'ballroom/ball-room' (p. 323); 'odd!/odd?' (p. 325); 'horses,/horses;' (p. 326); 'bygone/bye-gone' (p. 335); 'lord,/lord;' (p. 337); 'gentleman/gentleman,' (p. 337); 'father/father,' (p. 339); 'old-fashioned/old fashioned' (p. 340); 'feeling,/feeling;' (p. 340); 'home/home,' (p. 341); 'sitting-room,/sitting-room;' (p. 341); 'why,/why' (p. 342, twice); 'side-table/side table' (p. 342); 'unhappiness,/unhappiness' (p. 348); 'feet/feet,' (p. 348); 'locket/locket,' (p. 348); 'case/case,' (p. 351); demi-god,/demi-god' (p. 354); 'door/door,' (p. 354); 'moody,/moody' (p. 355); 'bird,/bird' (p. 355); 'haunt;/haunt:' (p. 355); 'O/Oh,' (p. 357); 'neighbourhood;/neighbourhood,' (p. 357); 'ran the note/(ran the note)' (p. 360; *1913* also has letter in quotation marks); 'murmured;/murmured:' (p. 362); 'O/O,' (p. 365); 'emphatically,/emphatically;' (p. 366); 'betters/betters,' (p. 368); 'farther/further' (p. 368); 'No,/No' (p. 369); 'Ay,/Ay' (p. 370); 'be–/be,' (p. 373); 'Lodge/lodge' (p. 376); 'confidential,/confidential;' (p. 377); 'shipmate!/shipmate,' (p. 379); 'farther/further' (p. 382); 'words–/words' (p. 386); ''lopement/lopement' (p. 387); 'mustachios/moustachios' (p. 389); 'said,/said:' (p. 395); 'sudden/sudden,' (p. 397); 'said,/said:' (p. 399).

Finally, in his Seaside Library Pocket Edition of *The Romantic Adventures of a Milkmaid* (1884), a pirated version of the story which is now in the Dorset County Museum, Hardy deleted 'pulling up at' and substituted in the margin 'going towards' (p. 87). This is a unique variant, because in *1913* the phrase read 'turning and taking the road to [Jim's]'.

Bibliography

Primary works by Thomas Hardy

King, Kathryn R., ed. (1991), *Wessex Tales*, Oxford University Press, Oxford.

Kramer, Dale, ed. (1981), *The Woodlanders*, Clarendon Press, Oxford.

Manford, Alan, ed. (1996), *Life's Little Ironies*, Oxford University Press, Oxford.

Millgate, Michael, ed. (1984), *The Life and Work of Thomas Hardy by Thomas Hardy*, Macmillan, London.

Pinion, F.B., ed. (1977), *Life's Little Ironies [and] A Changed Man*, New Wessex edition, Macmillan, London.

Pinion, F.B. ed. (1977), *Wessex Tales [and] A Group of Noble Dames*, New Wessex edition, Macmillan, London.

'The Merry Wives of Wessex', *Pall Mall Gazette*, 10 July 1891, p. 2.

'Mr. Hardy's Note on the Story', *The Three Wayfarers, The Distracted Preacher* (Programme, Dorchester Debating and Dramatic Society), Dorchester, 15–16 November 1911, p. [4].

'Serial Rights in Stories', *Athenaeum*, 16 May 1903, p. 626.

Secondary works

Archer, William (1901), 'Real Conversations: Conversation II.– With Mr. Thomas Hardy', *Pall Mall Magazine*, vol. 23: 527–37; rpt. in *Real Conversations,* Heinemann, London, pp. 29–50.

Benson, Arthur (1926), *The Diary of Arthur Christopher Benson*, 4th ed., ed. Percy Lubbock, Hutchinson, London.

Brady, Kristin (1982), *The Short Stories of Thomas Hardy: Tales of Past and Present*, Macmillan, London.

Collins, Vere H. (1928), *Talks with Thomas Hardy at Max Gate, 1920–1922*, Duckworth, London.

Doel, Geoffrey (1978), 'The Supernatural Background to "The Romantic Adventures of a Milkmaid" by Thomas Hardy', *Somerset and Dorset Notes & Queries*, vol. 30: 324–35.

Dolman, Frederick (1894), 'An Evening with Thomas Hardy', *Young Man*, vol. 8 (March): 75–9.

Douglas, Sir George B., (1938), *Gleanings in Prose and Verse*, ed. Oliver Hilson, A. Walker, Galashiels.

Ellis, Stewart Marsh (1928), 'Thomas Hardy: Some Personal Recollections', *Fortnightly Review*, vol. 123: 393–406.

Felkin, Elliott (1926), 'Days with Thomas Hardy: From a 1918–1919 Diary', *Encounter*, vol. 18 (April): 27–33.

Flower, Newman (1950), *Just As It Happened*, Cassell, London.

Gatrell, Simon (1984), 'The Early Stages of Hardy's Fiction', in Page, Norman, ed., *Thomas Hardy Annual No. 2*, Macmillan, London, pp. 3–29.

———— (1987), 'Topography in "The Romantic Adventures of a Milkmaid"', *Thomas Hardy Journal*, vol. 3, no. 3: 38–45.

———— (1988), *Hardy the Creator: A Textual Biography*, Clarendon Press, Oxford.

Green, David Bonnell (1960), 'The First Publication of "The Spectre of the Real"', *The Library*, vol. 15: 60–61.

Hardy, Evelyn and Pinion, F.B., ed. (1972), *One Rare Fair Woman: Thomas Hardy's Letters to Florence Henniker, 1893–1922*, Macmillan, London.

Harper, J. Henry (1912), *The House of Harper: A Century of Publishing in Franklin Square*, Harper & Brothers, New York and London.

Hawkins, Desmond (1989), 'Notes and Queries', *Thomas Hardy Journal*, vol. 5, no. 1: 93.

Healey, Frank G. (1992), 'A Further Note on "A Tradition of Eighteen Hundred and Four"', *Thomas Hardy Journal*, vol. 8, no. 3: 84–6.

Hedgcock, Frank A. (1951), 'Reminiscences of Thomas Hardy: I', *National and English Review*, vol. 137 (October): 220–28.

'"Hodge" As I Know Him: A Talk with Mr. Thomas Hardy' (1892), *Pall Mall Gazette*, vol. 54 (2 January): 1–2.

Hutchins, John (1861–73), *The History and Antiquities of the County of Dorset*, 3rd ed., 4 vols., J.B. Nichols, London.

Johnstone, H.F.V. (1971), 'Thomas Hardy and Old Poole', *Thomas Hardy Yearbook*, no. 2, pp. 84–7.

Kay-Robinson, Denys (1972), *Hardy's Wessex Reappraised*, David & Charles, Newton Abbot.

King, Kathryn R. (1988), 'Studies Towards a Critical Edition of Thomas Hardy's *Wessex Tales*', unpublished PhD thesis, Emory University.

———— (1991) See *Wessex Tales* above.

———— (1992), 'Hardy's "A Tradition of Eighteen Hundred and Four" and the Anxiety of Invention', *Thomas Hardy Journal*, vol. 8, no. 2: 20–26.

Lanning, George (1990), 'Hardy and the Hanoverian Hussars', *Thomas Hardy Journal*, vol. 6, no. 1: 69–73.

Lawrence, Berta (1986), 'Thomas Hardy and the Duke of Monmouth', *Thomas Hardy Journal*, vol. 2, no. 3: 56–8.

Lea, Hermann (1966), *Thomas Hardy's Wessex*, Toucan Press, Guernsey.

Lowndes, Marie Adelaide Belloc (1946), *The Merry Wives of Westminster*, Macmillan, London.

Macleod, A. (1968), 'A Textual Study of Thomas Hardy's *A Group of Noble Dames*', unpublished PhD thesis, University of Notre Dame.

Maitland, Frederic William, ed. (1906), *The Life and Letters of Leslie Stephen*, Duckworth, London.

Manford, Alan (1990), '*Life's Little Ironies*: The Manchester Manuscripts',

Bulletin of the John Rylands Library, vol. 72: 89–100.
————— (1996) See *Life's Little Ironies* above.
Millgate, Michael (1982), *Thomas Hardy: A Biography*, Clarendon Press, Oxford.
Morgan, Charles (1943), *The House of Macmillan, 1843–1943*, Macmillan, London.
Mundy, Harriot Georgiana, ed. (1885), *The Journal of Mary Frampton*, Sampson Low, Marston, Searle and Rivington, London.
Orel, Harold (1967), *Thomas Hardy's Personal Writings: Prefaces, Literary Opinions, Reminiscences,* Macmillan, London.
O'Shaughnessy, Arthur (1977), *Music and Moonlight*, Garland, New York.
Page, Norman (1977), *Thomas Hardy*, Routledge & Kegan Paul, London.
————— (1996), 'Introduction', *Life's Little Ironies*, ed. Alan Manford, Oxford University Press, Oxford, pp. xi–xxvii.
Peirce, Walter (1949), 'A Visit to Max Gate', *Colby Library Quarterly*, vol. 2 (November): 190–95.
Pinion, F.B. (1989), *A Thomas Hardy Dictionary*, Macmillan, London.
Pitfield, F.P. (1992), *Hardy's Wessex Locations*, Dorset Publishing Company, Wincanton.
Purdy, R.L. (1943), 'A Source for Hardy's "A Committee-Man of 'The Terror'"', *Modern Language Notes*, vol. 58: 554–5.
————— (1954), *Thomas Hardy: A Bibliographical Study*, Oxford University Press, London.
Purdy, R.L., and Millgate, Michael, ed. (1978–88), *The Collected Letters of Thomas Hardy*, 7 vols., Clarendon Press, Oxford.
Rosenbaum, Barbara (1990), *Index of English Literary Manuscripts*, vol. 4, no. 2, Mansell, London.
Taylor, Richard H., ed. (1978), *The Personal Notebooks of Thomas Hardy*, Macmillan, London.
————— ed. (1985), *Emma Hardy Diaries*, Mid Northumberland Arts Group and Carcanet New Press, Ashington, Northumberland.
Weber, Carl J. (1939), *Rebekah Owen and Thomas Hardy*, Colby College Library, Waterville, Maine.
————— (1952), *Hardy and the Lady from Madison Square*, Colby College Press, Waterville, Maine.
Wharton, Edith (1934), *A Backward Glance*, Appleton-Century, New York.

Index